Employment and Career Motivation in the Arab Gulf States: The Rentier Mentality Revisited

The Gulf Research Center Book Series at Gerlach Press

The GCC in the Global Economy
Ed. by Richard Youngs
ISBN 9783940924018, 2012

Resources Blessed: Diversification and the Gulf Development Model
Ed. by Giacomo Luciani
ISBN 9783940924025, 2012

GCC Financial Markets: The World's New Money Centers
Ed. by Eckart Woertz
ISBN 9783940924032, 2012

National Employment, Migration and Education in the GCC
Ed. by Steffen Hertog
ISBN 9783940924049, 2012

Asia-Gulf Economic Relations in the 21st Century The Local to Global Transformation
Ed. by Tim Niblock with Monica Malik
ISBN 9783940924100, 2013

A New Gulf Security Architecture Prospects and Challenges for an Asian Role
Ed. by Ranjit Gupta, Abubaker Bagader, Talmiz Ahmad and N. Janardhan
ISBN 9783940924360, 2014

Gulf Charities and Islamic Philanthropy in the 'Age of Terror' and Beyond
Ed. by Robert Lacey and Jonathan Benthall
ISBN 9783940924322, 2014

State-Society Relations in the Arab Gulf States
Ed. by Mazhar Al-Zoby and Birol Baskan
ISBN 9783940924384, 2014

Gulf Research Centre Cambridge
Knowledge for All

Political Economy of Energy Reform The Clean Energy-Fossil Fuel Balance in the Gulf
Ed. by Giacomo Luciani and Rabia Ferroukhi
ISBN 9783940924407, 2014

Security Dynamics of East Asia in the Gulf Region
Ed. by Tim Niblock with Yang Guang
ISBN 9783940924483, 2014

Islamic Finance Political Economy, Performance and Risk
Ed. by Mehmet Asutay and Abdullah Turkistani
ISBN 9783940924124, 3 vols set, 2015

Employment and Career Motivation in the Arab Gulf States: The Rentier Mentality Revisited
Ed. by Annika Kropf and Mohamed Ramady
ISBN 9783940924605, 2015

The Changing Energy Landscape in the Gulf: Strategic Implications
Ed. by Gawdat Bahgat
ISBN 9783940924643, 2015

Sustainable Development Challenges in the Arab Sates of the Gulf
Ed. by David Bryde, Yusra Mouzughi and Turki Al Rasheed
ISBN 9783940924629, 2015

The United States and the Gulf: Shifting Pressures, Strategies and Alignments
Ed. by Steven W. Hook and Tim Niblock
ISBN 9783940924667, 2015

Africa and the Gulf Region: Blurred Boundaries and Shifting Ties
Ed. by Rogaia Mustafa Abusharaf and Dale F. Eickelman
ISBN 9783940924704, 2015

Rebuilding Yemen: Political, Economic and Social Challenges
Ed. by Noel Brehony and Saud Al-Sarhan
ISBN 9783940924681, 2015

Employment and Career Motivation in the Arab Gulf States: The Rentier Mentality Revisited

Edited by Annika Kropf and Mohamed A. Ramady

Gerlach Press

First published 2015
by Gerlach Press
Berlin, Germany
www.gerlach-press.de

Cover Design: www.brandnewdesign.de, Hamburg
Printed and bound in Germany by Hubert & Co., Göttingen

British Library Cataloguing in Publication Data.
A catalogue record for this book is available from the British Library.

Bibliographic data available from Deutsche Nationalbibliothek
http://d-nb.info/1068029323

ISBN: 978-3-940924-60-5 (hardcover)
ISBN: 978-3-940924-61-2 (ebook)

Acknowledgements

This book is the outcome of the workshop that was held at the Gulf Research Meeting organized by the Gulf Research Center in Cambridge, UK in August 2014 directed by Mohamed Ramady and Annika Kropf (*Workshop Number 5: Employed, yet Underemployed and Underestimated: Leadership, Ownership and Work Motivation in the Gulf*).

The Editors wish to thank all those who participated in the workshop and especially the Gulf Research Center and its Chairman Dr. Abdulaziz Sager for offering the opportunity to gather so many scholars with diverse interests and expertise who made this publication possible. The workshops would not have been possible without the dedicated guidance and follow up support by the GRC, especially Dr. Christian Koch, Sanya Kapasi and Elsa Courdier

The Editors would also like to express their appreciation to the tireless typesetting and administrative efforts of Mr. Junaid Akhtar.

Annika Kropf
Vienna, Austria

M.A. Ramady
Dhahran, Saudi Arabia

Dedicated to our Families

Contents

Introduction and Overview

All who have meditated on the art of governing mankind have been convinced that the fate of empires depends on the education of youth.

Aristotle

Annika Kropf and Mohamed A. Ramady

The notion of "rentier mentality" has dominated the literature on the Gulf States for almost 40 years now. In 1987, Luciani and Beblawi defined it as a "break in the work-reward causation. Reward – income or wealth – is not related to work and risk bearing, rather to chance or situation." (Beblawi/Luciani 1987: 52)

It is one of those concepts that are often mentioned in a very cursory way. As a "mentality" it seems to belong to the realm of psychology and the political scientist or economist carefully avoids potential blunders of "culturalist" judgments on entire societies. And indeed, rentier mentality has nothing that makes it special to Arab, Middle Eastern or Muslim societies. In the Gulf States in particular, conditions of life before oil used to be very harsh and without hard work, nobody could have survived. It is rather a matter of incentives when people with considerable rentier income are prone to low work motivation. This mechanism is likely to work anywhere in the world.

However, rentier mentality has turned out to be very tenacious in the Gulf States and it persists despite governmental policies to change it. Although the rapidly growing population of the Gulf states should lead to a rising awareness that, in the future, governments will no more be able to provide a living for all citizens, the individual pressure to earn one's own living does not seem to have increased. But is this really so?

While it seems to be a mentality only, rentier mentality has also given rise to and nourished structures and mechanisms in businesses and administration that suited this mentality best. Governments have added their share by their reluctance to abolish privileges for citizens and by even expanding them in times of political instability, as happened following on from the events of the so called Arab Spring in 2011. With rentier income pouring in, especially during the period of relatively high oil prices from 2002-2014, the resulting inefficiencies were affordable and inefficient processes have become deeply ingrained in daily routines of enterprises and administrations. In about the same vein, traditional structures and behaviours that a process of economic development would have changed elsewhere can be sustained longer than in resource-poor countries. This is how collectivism, which is usually thought to give way to more individualism in the course of development and bigger firm sizes, can survive economic development much longer.

Once a mentality has been translated into structures and mechanisms those are even likely to outlive the mentality itself and then pose a hindrance to those who enter the workplace with high motivation and find themselves unable to work as efficiently as they would like to.

What research still considers a "mentality" may thus have become a structural problem that persists even if 90% of the staff is highly motivated to work efficiently and to make a meaningful contribution. However, the mentality may also have become so deeply ingrained in local societies that awareness of it has disappeared and hence, it is neither perceived as extraordinary nor as problematic any more. Already Ibn Khaldun understood well how younger generations who inherited wealth and privileges would come to take them for granted. To him, the nobility of a family originates "in the state of being outside. That is, being outside of leadership and nobility and being in a base, humble station, devoid of prestige". While the "builder of the family's glory knows what it cost him to do the work" (Ibn Khaldun 1969: 105) the qualities of his descendants decline. Eventually, a member of the fourth generation "has lost the qualities that preserved the edifice of its glory. He despises (those qualities). He imagines that the edifice was not built through application and effort. He thinks that it was something due his people from the very beginning by virtue of the mere fact of their descent, and not something that resulted from group (effort) and (individual) qualities." (Ibn Khaldun 1969: 106).

Again this is not a phenomenon that is limited to the Middle East or rentier states but inherited wealth and rentier wealth seem to be a fertile ground for a decline of hard work unless this is precluded by education and policies.

The experience of seeing young Gulf nationals leaving universities highly motivated and becoming increasingly discouraged upon entering the workforce has provided the initial idea for the workshop that has resulted in this publication. This phenomenon, again, is nothing that the Gulf States would not share with most countries in the world. However, compared to many other countries, they still have a safety net to rely on once the discouragement becomes too devastating. The scope of this safety net depends on the country and so does the expectancy to have a secure basic income in the future. For some GCC states, the perspective to live on welfare or an easy public sector job may end much sooner than for others. The question is whether the workforce and in particular the structures it operates in can even respond to those pressures. One may automatically assume that once oil runs out, or more realistically oil revenues decline sharply as happened from the latter half of 2014, efficiency will have to rise and that also the nationals will take private sectors jobs that measure people's efficiency and not their nationality. However, while an individual can change his or her mentality when the economic existence is at stake, individuals may be unable to change structures and this is what happens all over the world in many development countries. There is, hence, a considerable risk that the rentier structures will cause vicious circles of precluding reform that may at some point become poverty traps. There are examples of countries, though small and few such as Nauru, that show that the level of development of a resource rich country is not necessarily maintained by its population once the resource is depleted. It is therefore understandable why the GCC governments pressure so much for localization of the workforce but less easily understandable why these policies have not resulted in the expected success so far.

The question whether rentier mentality has become structural, thus, is very important and several findings of this book point to such a tendency. Rather than tacit assumptions and speculation, this book finally provides empirical results about how Gulf nationals perceive and plan their careers and what drives their professional development. Numerous empirical surveys show that Gulf citizens are highly motivated to "grow" and to achieve something for their workplace. However, other surveys also have shown that they are the least efficient when they work in their own country. This specification of "when working in their own country" may be crucial. It raises again the interesting question about whether rentier mentality is really an inherited state of mind or rather work location and employment specific. Of course, these possibilities are not mutually exclusive. It is possible that a state of mind only comes into effect in a certain setting.

The operationalization of such concepts as "workplace values", "efficiency" or "work motivation" is highly problematic. In many cases, the researcher cannot but ask the employee, student or unemployed directly about these issues. However, people in different cultures may understand these concepts differently and also answer with a different degree of openness to questions regarding their personal motivation. It has, for example, become rather outdated to *admit* that money is a major driver behind work although it certainly is. Or would a student interviewed at his or her university admit that he or she only studied because he or she did not know what else to do before marrying or having kids? And what one person calls efficient could be deemed highly inefficient by others.

These difficulties have to be the lens through which the empirical results in this book have to be interpreted. Nonetheless, the overall conclusion is clear and some results are consistent across many different samples and studies. One of the most striking findings might be that some of the attitudes and expectations they reflect do not deviate that much from what we know from Western countries. This is especially true for women and gender issues. Other results, however, are strikingly different. They point to long-term consequences of the rentier state and hence an institutionalized rentierism that government action needs to address to allow the individual to work more efficiently and with higher motivation. The current youth bulge in the GCC states calls for urgent actions in order to avoid that another generation lingers between unemployment, underemployment, jobs that do not challenge and motivate them and a widespread feeling of the inability to change something for the better.

The GCC governments' policies focus on three realms that are also the focus of this book: the educational system, employment both in the private and public sector, and the fostering of an entrepreneurial culture. A fourth realm crosscuts all these realms but has been less of a focus so far: these are the cultural, religious and psychological roots of work motivation and business ethics.

Overview

The book is structured into four broad focus areas, which are interrelated. The first part of this book, *Career Aspirations of Students*, focuses on both male and female university students and how they view their job perspectives. In a survey with female students at the German University of Technology in Oman, Marike Bontenbal found that young Omani women are keen to find work after graduation from university and even prefer the private sector where they expect to learn more and to be promoted according to their merits. This pledge to learn and to apply their acquired skills in a meaningful way fails to explain why the rate of nationals, and women in particular, is actually so low in the private sector. However, once the students were asked about married life, they prefer the security of a public sector job which seems also what their parents advise them to do. The private sector is seen as an early career phase after which the women are ready to adapt to the role society deems more appropriate for them. The public sector necessarily remains the option of "security" given that the parent generation offers very few role models of private sector careers.

As in many other countries, females in the GCC perform better than their male peers at both schools and universities. In fact, the male youth currently face a reputational problem, being seen more as a problem than an asset in the local societies. Mark Thompson interviewed male students at the Saudi Arabian King Fahd University for Minerals and Petroleum and found that there is a widespread impression of being underestimated. Although the students are well trained and are supposed to become the country's elite in technology and engineering, they are rather pessimistic when it comes to finding a challenging job where they can make a positive difference. Perceived problems are the esteem for age rather than for knowledge and skills and (the lack of) *wasta*, or social networking, but also the fast changing world creates a general feeling of unhappiness.

Students at the Khalifa University are the target sample of Lorraine Charles' survey on how *Emiratisation* is understood and perceived by students in the UAE. Starting from the conclusion that *Emiratisation* has largely failed so far, Charles found evidence for widespread rentier mentality among Emirati citizens that the respective governments have not only constructed but also continue to sustain by maintaining the ruling bargain. Although respondents to her questionnaire widely acknowledge the need for change, they tacitly stick to the entitlements and privileges that this ruling bargain provides them with.

Rather than feeling that they have to be the agents of change, they feel that outside factors such as regional instability or the high numbers of expatriates need to change before.

There is a general tendency of subtle contradictions in the three above mentioned surveys that may point to the existence of underlying misperceptions and a rentier mentality that has become so deeply engrained that it goes unnoticed. While, for example, nationals have rated the willingness to grow and also to learn from expatriates very high, this is sometimes in stark contrast with a very high perception of their own value and the tacit expectation that they should been given priority over foreigners and earn more. A strong pledge that change has to happen is combined with the implicit demand that the current privileges have to be maintained. Problems that are locally made are attributed to outside influences and therefore, also change, it seems, has to come from outside. However, there are also signs of a structuralized rentier mentality that individuals strongly reject but are unable to change, as the survey at KFUPM shows.

The universities that were object of the above mentioned three studies are all elite institutions and the surveys reflect a very high echelon of the local societies. Signs of pessimism in those samples, hence, have to be taken very seriously. The GCC states have imported teachers, professors, expertise and entire universities to increase the quality of their educational systems. However, the problem to provide employment for nationals and to replace expatriates is much more complex. It may be possible to "import" education and knowledge but if it lacks the fertile ground to prove itself, to thrive and to grow, its positive effects on the labour market will fail to appear.

The second part of the book assesses *Surveys of Employee Motivation and Workplace Values* and examines whether assets achieved in the educational system can be translated into more productive and motivated employees largely depends on workplace values and soft-skills.

Pioneering work on workplace values in the Arab world was published by Geert Hofstede in 1980. In general, Hofstede found that workplace values in Arab countries reflect a high degree of power distance as well as high uncertainty avoidance. Both mean that employees may easily find themselves being reduced to the role of mere recipients of orders and avoid any autonomous decisions for fear of losing their jobs. Adel HAMAIZIA replicated Hofstede's model using the two parameters power distance and uncertainty avoidance, applying it to a larger sample that, contrary to Hofstede's model, differentiates between the different Arab countries. Focusing on the UAE and Saudi Arabia, he found that Saudi Arabia has largely kept the high degree of power distance and uncertainty avoidance while the UAE have considerably reduced the degree of power distance and have hence a tendency towards flatter hierarchies. Uncertainty avoidance is particularly high among expatriates who are in a position of extreme insecurity as a loss of their job has much wider consequences for them.

The papers by David JONES and Radhika PUNSHI, Cameron MIRZA and Gauri GUPTA are both based on large surveys that give insight into the talents – strengths and weaknesses – of young Gulf citizens. Both papers highlight the fact that the current youth bulge does not necessarily have to be a burden. It could also be a unique opportunity to replace expatriate labour by a young and highly educated generation of locals. However, the risk of a new paradox of plenty, in this case the paradox of a local labour abundance that nevertheless fails to reduce the reliance on expatriates, is relatively high. PUNSHI, MIRZA and GUPTA point to a lack of important "life-skills" among the young Gulf citizens. These skills are essential and have to be regarded as complementary to the content learnt at school or university. Without curiosity, control, teamwork, autonomy, flexibility or empathy individuals may be unable to apply their knowledge to the benefit of the environment they work in. On many of those crucial abilities, however, the GCC youth score very low although extrinsic as well as intrinsic motivation seems to be high. Nonetheless, most of these abilities can be taught and learnt and could, as the authors recommend, become part of the curricula from an early stage on.

Drawing on a large survey called *Qudurat* (capabilities), JONES provides empirical evidence for the fact that employee engagement and work motivation are relatively low in the region and lowest for the young nationals as compared to young expatriates and also an older generation of locals. Also leadership is rated as rather weak while it seems at the same time that employees have high expectations from their respective leaders. The low work motivation, again, is in stark contrast with the widespread expectation to have a good salary, to be regularly promoted and to reach a position with a high status. While the attitude to be entitled to certain privileges remains high among nationals, JONES discerns signs of an early career crisis as young nationals have to struggle today to reach the normal stages of life such as a home and a family. While these things were rather easy to achieve for their parents, the younger generation faces much more competition and pressure from peers.

These surveys and the resulting datasets can be extremely valuable for the GCC governments to set the right targets and to address problems in a focussed way. Just a "quantitative" increase of the educational system and a rising number of graduates is too general a target to match the demand of the labour market. However, also young nationals can check where they stand and where they need "to grow". While there are programmes that support an increasing number of Gulf nationals studying abroad, many young nationals prefer to stay close to their families. Although they can meanwhile choose from a whole array of excellent international universities that have opened GCC campuses, they often remain without a true international experience that has helped many students all over the world to gain a totally different perspective on their own country and habits. These learning effects are rather unlikely to result from mere contacts with expatriates, especially as long as the two groups live in the same country but with an entirely different status.

The third section of the book addresses *Entrepreneurship as a Solution to the Unemployment Problems.* Faced with an employment conundrum, GCC government have initiated policies and programmes to enhance and foster entrepreneurship. The idea of citizens who create their own jobs and ideally additional jobs for others is naturally a very tempting one and not only in the GCC states. However, the attractiveness of entrepreneurship in the context of a generous welfare state is questionable. The entrepreneurial risk that a truly innovative approach comes with may be perceived as too high in societies with a comfortable safety net. Nonetheless, the entrepreneur does not necessarily have to be the innovative, risk-taking Schumpeterian "exceptional individual" any more. In many cases, the only difference between an employee and an entrepreneur is the fact that the latter is formally self-employed while the work can be the same. From this perspective, Joachim Kolb looked into the entrepreneurship policies and programmes in the UAE. While he finds that there are many and often overlapping programmes in place, the Emirati start-ups are rather short-lived. What is more, many Emiratis keep their public sector job and hence their "safety net" while working on their business. So far, it seems that the most innovative and successful businesses have been established by expatriates.

Analysing small and medium enterprises (SME's) in Qatar, Oman and Bahrain, Jessie Moritz finds that the policies to foster entrepreneurship among nationals have not had the desired results so far. From a qualitative survey, she concludes that many of the perceived obstacles to entrepreneurship have not been overcome by the many programs and subsidies in place. A slow bureaucracy, the lack of skilled and affordable labour or office space as well as a general consumer preference for foreign products are widely perceived as problems. It also seems that the traditional business elites who have always made profit by importing foreign merchandise have little interest in a substitution of the merchandise they import by locally produced goods. And although the governments are aware of the importance of SME's, they continue to undermine their attractiveness by maintaining their rentier policies for example by increasing public sector wages.

SME's are often regarded as the backbone of a country's economy and havens of innovation as large enterprises easily turn to inflexible for true innovation. However, there is a worldwide tendency of entrepreneurship becoming more and more a result of the outsourcing of services that allows companies to be more flexible and to save on social security costs. A former employee may do the same work as he used to do when employed but as a self-employed consultant, he allows a company or government institutions to formally cut back on staff. What is more, in times when a person's status depends a lot on his or her work, entrepreneurship is also often a cover for hidden unemployment. Women frequently opt for low-level entrepreneurship because it allows them to earn a modest income while combining this work with their families. There are indeed several success stories of women in the Gulf who sell their handicraft via social networks without the necessity of large investments.

As Kolb pointed out in the workshop, successful innovation cannot be planned by a government. Although a government can establish stable financial, legal and economic institutions that form a strong framework of rule of law and property rights, many successful entrepreneurs have, to speak again with Ibn Khaldun, originated from "a base, humble station, devoid of prestige". Necessity rather than sponsorship by a government programme was the mother of many a successful multi-national enterprise. Furthermore, there are many cases of entrepreneurs who have actually dropped out of the educational system quite early and have originated from an outsider status such as the proverbial geek who did not care about anything else but a very special field of expertise. Hence, the individual and the importance given to the individual play a huge role. How a society values exceptional young people who sometimes fail to conform to social norms, and whether there are banks or sponsors who believe in young and sometimes rather implausible ideas, is crucial. Young innovators in conservative societies are more likely to be disadvantaged.

The above-mentioned new forms of entrepreneurship deviate from this Schumpeterian, exceptional entrepreneurship but they may, of course, at some point give rise to innovations that become successful because they happen at the right time and are sold and promoted successfully. Successful innovation does not necessarily have to be a high-end technology. However, there are at least two phenomena that render entrepreneurial innovation in the Gulf less likely. Firstly, there is a long history of imported rather than locally conceived technology and innovation. It has become a habit to look at what is coming from outside. Catching up with those technologies often consumes the time that could otherwise be used for genuinely local innovation. Given that foreign companies do not readily share their most recent technologies and want to enlarge their sales markets rather than nourishing competitors, there is a risk that technology importers continuously lag behind.

Secondly, the fact that there is little genuine private sector entrepreneurship in the GCC apart from trade and construction means that there is also a lack of local role models. Few young Gulf citizens have parents who are innovative entrepreneurs. However, mentoring and role models, especially at the first stages of entrepreneurship, are very important.

The final section of the book deals with *Cultural and Religious Roots of Business Ethics and Work Motivation.* While the policies in place and the institutional environment of enterprises are crucial, especially in the start-up phase, the efficiency of companies and their survival after an initial phase depends on the workplace culture and on the efficiency of production, decision making and the implementation of decisions. In his assessment of Saudi manufacturing, Makio YAMADA looks at Japan for comparison because many Asian countries have, like the GCC states, opted for late industrialization with state-involvement and have industrialized quite successfully. It should be added here that, contrary to the GCC states, Asian countries started from a very low GDP level and from a relative labour abundance, hence from an entirely different incentive base. YAMADA finds that many of the values that are today widely considered to be "Asian values" are actually of rather recent origin. Those values consist of the importance of the workers in the production halls as opposed to the importance of the head offices or the management, the preference for bottom-up processes as opposed to top-down processes and the importance and admiration of handicraft in society. What counts is "making things" (*monozukuri*). So far, these principles seem to be the exact opposite of the Saudi values in place, although Islamic work ethics assigns a high value to handicraft and creating things. YAMADA looks into potential reforms of the educational system and the labour market to allow for more of these principles to take root in the process of Saudi industrialisation.

Many of the values that are actually at the core of Saudi society have their roots in history, culture and religion and although many appearances have been "westernized", these old patterns of behaviour are still paramount for the understanding of why so many reforms of the labour market fail. Tanya Cariina Hsu starts from the high expectations of young Saudis. Young Saudis feel that they should have much higher salaries than expatriates as well as large benefits which, in turn, discourage companies from hiring them. Although the people in the Gulf before the oil wealth had to work very hard to survive under the harsh conditions of the region, there are historical and anthropological roots of this behaviour. Hsu explains that, among the Bedouins, manual work was acceptable when it was done for the own family but regarded as "slavish" when done for somebody else. Up to today, tribal affiliation is more important than the actual merits of a person and, as another consequence, *wasta* is still widespread. Likewise, status and image are more important than what is actually done, often resulting in the bragging announcement of huge projects that fail to materialize. Communication traditionally avoids criticism precluding improvements as a result of open discussions of problems. Most of these behavioural patterns have tribal roots and are actually contrary to Islamic principles. There is hence a potential to enhance economic attitudes by focusing more on Islamic than on tribal principles and to thereby foster a genuine Saudi business ethics.

As David Cowan points out in his paper, the GCC have rather emulated Western business ethics than developing their own business ethics. This process has not always gone smoothly, for example when an international company opens a Saudi branch and needs to cope with different standards internationally. However, as Cowan admits right from the beginning, "business ethics" are often just a matter of lip service and to aim for one monolithic business culture would anyway be illusory as it largely depends on how and if individuals translate them into behaviour. Also Cowan sees the importance of Islam in Saudi society as a potential asset as Islam is a religion that blesses trade, hard work and economic activity while demanding at the same time that the economic activity be to the benefit of the entire society. As such, Islamic business ethics could come close to what Western theories of business ethics describe as the stakeholder or even social contract view. However, Cowan sees the potential for such a development as limited – not because a mismatch of Islamic and Western ethics but because economic realism and profit maximization tend to supersede business ethics.

The high power distance, high uncertainty avoidance, reported earlier by Hamaiza, and a high-context communication that avoids criticism form a particularly strong obstacle for young employees to grow. Not only create these features problems when expatriates from countries with flatter hierarchies and low-context, hence more blunt and outspoken communication have to cope with these structures. Also young nationals who are familiar with these structures are often denied the feedback and constructive criticism that is essential for them to improve and to grow. Rather than learning by mistakes, they often work with the fear of making a mistake and are likely to follow instructions very closely rather than to take responsibility for a project. What is more, the strong hierarchy and top down rather than bottom up processes easily leave employees with a perceived lack of power that is very discouraging in the long run. Hence, the motivation to learn and to grow at their workplace, that was reported by so many Gulf nationals in the studies in part one and two, will probably continue to be frustrated by workplace realities.

Outlook

In reviewing the above contributions, a common thread that runs through all the papers is the unstated assumption that the rentier mentality and social pact will continue unchallenged due to high revenue flows to the Gulf countries. This premise is now under strain due to sharply reduced forecasted oil revenue flows arising from a 60 percent fall in oil prices since the latter half of 2014 and which, according to EIA estimates, will reduce the GCC countries' oil revenues by between $150-200 billion a year. So far, oil prices plummeted from around $100 a barrel to $49 a barrel. While there is some debate on how long and sustained such a fall in oil prices will last, it is clear that, with a few exceptions such as Saudi Arabia, Qatar and Kuwait, who hold large financial reserves, the pattern of government expenditure, public sector job creation and subsidy payments will have to be reconsidered. This will undoubtedly put the social rentier pact under strain, as governments turn to the private sector to act as the "engine of growth" and primary focus for national job creation. Even countries with large financial surpluses like Saudi Arabia, with reputed reserves of around $790 billion, recognize that maintaining 2014 expenditure levels of $300 billion a year, as well as a forecast erosion of its oil exports due to rising domestic energy demand, is not a sustainable option.

The Gulf States have opted, to one degree or another, on 'localization' policies with the aim to replace foreign labour with nationals. Some countries have aggressively pursued this 'localization' effort, with Saudi Arabia introducing its so-called '*Nitaqat*' or points based system, through which it measures private sector localization compliance according to whether companies are in the 'green' – compliant – yellow, or non-compliant red zones. Despite some success, the '*Nitaqat*' system has not been as effective as hoped, with exceptions being made for companies that employ low-skilled and menial jobs which nationals shun, especially in the important construction sector. Other Gulf countries have adopted policies that encourage entrepreneurship to foster a positive climate for the growth of the SME sector, most notably Oman and Bahrain, as these two countries are the most diversified economies of the Gulf States.

The treatment of foreign workers is marked by a love-hate relationship that also the papers reveal. Partly, they are considered a threat to the employment of the locals or to the countries security and partly, their necessity and their hard work and loyalty are recognized.

It is crucial to retain skilled expatriates and to ensure they willingly pass on their skills to locals without being threatened with arbitrary localisation policies and this is something that all GCC states have to address under increasing international pressure. The ongoing campaign to ensure that Qatar changes some of its labour policies, especially the *Kafeel* or sponsorship system, holding labourers to bondage to local companies, illustrates the external pressure the Gulf countries are coming under to reform their labour policies .While there has been some discussion on unifying GCC labour policies, this has not yet materialised and in early January 2015, the Gulf states abandoned plans to a unified contract for domestic workers. This in turn added more pressure on Qatar to revamp its own labour polices and the hope now is that such GCC individual country reforms might be later adopted by other member states.

To ensure that international best practices are applied in the domestic economies, some steps are being taken to foster a more competitive private sector and the application of international work standards, especially for those companies who participate in contracts with national oil companies who are deemed 'Centres of Excellence'. This applies to 'local content', which involves, not only the application of modern processes and standards, but also the quantity and quality of local labour being used in these projects. The overall aim is to widen and deepen local contractors' skills base through 'learning by doing', and thus making the private sector more competitive and attractive to motivated national graduates as their jobs of first choice. Amongst some of the larger GCC economies, there are plans being studied to establish knowledge based business clusters, with Saudi Arabia planning a car industry hub utilising local aluminium and other cheap petrochemical products to manufacture a new generation of SUV's for worldwide exports. Under such circumstances, there is definitely a possibility that the Japanese *Monozukiri* production and self-improvement Japanese method might take root and change current work habits.

The accession of all the GCC states to the World Trade Organization (WTO) has brought with it both opportunities and challenges to the Gulf private sector, especially for national companies involved in international trade, who have now to compete on a more 'level playing field' with foreign competitors without reliance on state subsidies. A new breed of local professional management has evolved that understands the necessity for continuous self-improvement, R&D and best business practice, and the high rewards that can accrue for such entrepreneurship compared with more secure, but less intrinsically rewarding public sector jobs. Again the aim is to attract talented Gulf youth into the private sector. In several of the Gulf countries, centres of applied research and excellence are being established, such as science parks in Qatar, Saudi Arabia and the UAE as well as so called *Techno Valleys*. These are modelled on the USA's silicon valleys to attract local start-up venture capital companies in association with international companies or by themselves.

The GCC public sector has also recognized that there is a limit to how many new jobs can be created to cope with national job entrants, and have begun exploring methods in assessing new civil servant job applicants as well as measuring civil servant productivity.

The first involves applying some civil service aptitude examination tests to ensure that the most competent are attracted into the public civil service, and to thereby reduce the element of '*Wasta*' or use of social networking connections to obtain jobs. A second policy involves the introduction of "*E-Government*" which requires a higher level of technical skills. The fact that *e-government* reduces the effectiveness of *wasta* and makes the success or failure of government transactions immediately felt by the general population will shed more light on the real aptitude of public sector employees. In an age of heavy use of social media within the Gulf, with Saudi Arabia in particular being one of the highest users of social media in the world, the effects of 'failure' are quickly publicized. It is no coincidence that the new Saudi King, Salman bin Abdulaziz, is reputed to have around 1.5 million twitter followers, and even the late King Abdullah bin Abdulaziz was said to have encouraged citizens to send him their grievances on social media.

The widespread use of social media has also been a major catalyst for official Gulf-wide anti-corruption campaigns and the establishment of anti-corruption bodies who are mandated to investigate all ministries and public officials. Some have agreed that such government measures were driven by the so-called 'Arab Spring' events, with its core demand for youth job creation and combating of official corruption and lack of accountability. Despite some hesitant starts, the anti-corruption campaigns have had a noticeable effect, in so far Gulf youth now believe that a semblance of accountability is in place. This, in turn, gives some hope for those with a more entrepreneurial spirit, to start their own businesses without fear of corruption and patronage, something that came out from the research done in this book. These Gulf anti-corruption campaigns draw heavily on Islamic ethics, and appeal to a higher set of moral and religious duties and social business obligations.

The issue of women's effective participation in the labour force is another area where some progress has been made, albeit not at the same pace in terms of scope and opportunities for all the Gulf countries. While major advances have been made in countries such as Bahrain, Qatar, Oman and Kuwait, women's work participation has been the slowest to rise in Saudi Arabia due to deep-rooted and tribal based customs and traditions. It will be interesting to see if the reforms introduced by the late King Abdullah of Saudi Arabia on women's rights will continue at the same pace under the new Saudi leadership. However, even in Saudi Arabia, the use of ITC technology has enabled Saudi females and entrepreneurs to enter the labour force by working from home, or in segregated environments, especially in customer support call centres. Gradually new professions are being opened up for Saudi females, in the legal and even engineering professions, besides some impressive advances in the financial sector where some Saudi women hold senior finance executives roles. This is illustrated by the head of the largest Saudi and Arab bank – the National Commercial's Bank- NBC Capital- being a female.

The above changes take time to bear fruit. However, a combination of rising social expectations, diminished revenue outlook over the next few years, and the need to transform and diversify the Gulf economies away from oil, has brought about a greater degree of pragmatism on the choices faced by both the rulers and the ruled, and the realisation that the current rentier 'social contract' is not sustainable.

In the final analysis, the Gulf states do not have to look far back in their history to recall that, in the pre-oil boom era, the local population exhibited all the traits required for hard work, resilience, craftsmanship and entrepreneurship, whether it was in pearl diving, agriculture or handicrafts. The thousands of young Gulf nationals currently on international academic scholarships in far flung countries – with Saudi Arabia alone boasting of around 200,000 male and female students on the King Abdullah Scholarship program - is a sign that these Gulf nationals will hopefully apply a different set of acquired hard and soft skills on their return. This again, is not new to the Gulf, as in the pre- oil boom period the scions of leading Gulf merchant families often spent years learning their trade in Bombay and other parts of Asia, to acquire best business practice (often Anglo-Indian) and establish acquaintances to help them build up their home operations. There was no "social contract" then, and today the most successful family businesses of the Gulf are those that learned to pass on to their younger generation the virtues of hard work, entrepreneurship and risk taking, as well as dealing with many different cultures and business practices. If young Gulf citizens need to turn to role models that espouse all that is best in their cultures and traditions, they do not have to look far.

1

Meeting Career Expectations? The Perception of Female Students towards Employment in Oman's Segmented Labor Market

Marike Bontenbal

Introduction

Gendered labor participation in the Arab world has been widely studied but little is known about the Gulf region, in particular Oman. The rentier nature of the economy and the subsequent distribution of oil wealth have had profound implications on the participation of citizens in the work force, particularly women. Despite government efforts to replace expatriate labor by nationals and even though changing norms in society as well as political leadership are increasingly in favor of women that work, female labor participation (FLP) in Oman has been below desired standards. This is particularly striking in the private sector: while almost 35% of the public sector jobs are taken up by Omani females, they fill only 2.7% of private sector positions. In other words: one in every 37 jobs in the private sector in Oman is taken up by Omani women (MoMP, 2012).

This strong preference for public sector employment is embedded in the context of oil rents and welfare policies, where government jobs are characterised as ubiquitously available, well paid, secure and socially acceptable (Forstenlechner & Rutledge, 2010; Hertog, 2012; Al Waqfi & Forstenlechner, 2012).

Low satisfaction with work conditions, low pay and a mismatch between qualifications of graduates and job requirements have often been mentioned as reasons undermining private sector employment among nationals. However these issues have largely remained understudied in Oman. While the qualifications of graduates improve, most private sector jobs require low skills and education, resulting in a mismatch between academic-oriented higher education and vocational jobs. Although understudied, it is widely acknowledged that the current low-status nature of the majority of private sector jobs does not meet the career expectations and preferences of recent graduates with higher education degrees. In an earlier study by the author about career expectations of Omani tourism & hospitality students

(Bontenbal & Aziz, 2013), it was found that high and unrealistic career expectations among students pose a threat to future job satisfaction.

Understanding career expectations, perceptions and preferences of students is an important step in the discourse on human capital development in the Arab Gulf, and in the challenge to better understand the relationship between education and labor market trends in Oman. The challenges of matching education and employment in the country appear to be more deeply manifested for females. Women currently enjoy a very strong profile in the public sector segment and young female graduates are generally better educated than males. However, due to various constraints that this Chapter will discuss, the employment challenges for women are intensified.

This Chapter addresses the perception of Omani female near-graduates towards work in general and private sector employment in particular and discusses the importance of work according to female near-graduates, perceived chances of finding employment, career preferences, and perceptions of public vs. private sector jobs - against the background of the specific Oman rentier economy characteristics and current labor market challenges. Empirical research was carried out by means of qualitative methods – focus groups and semi-structured in-depth interviews among female soon-to-be graduates from a private university in Oman. The study builds on earlier work by the author addressing labor nationalization in Oman and career perceptions among nationals (Bontenbal & Aziz, 2013; Zerovec & Bontenbal, 2011).

Women and Employment in Oman's Rentier Economy

In Oman the exports of oil and gas currently account for more than 50% of the country's GDP, and 80% of state revenues. The socio-economic position of citizens in oil rentiers is generally not derived from labor participation, rather it is strongly linked to how citizens are able to position themselves vis-à-vis the distribution of oil wealth.

Various mechanisms have been put into place to facilitate the distribution of oil wealth, turning Arab Gulf states into welfare states that provide citizens free or subsidized access to a range of services. In addition, governments have provided employment to their citizens in the ever expanding public sector, described by Forstenlechner & Rutledge (2010) as the 'key component' of this benefits package available to citizens. Traditionally Gulf States' citizens have been absorbed by the public sector, the preferred type of citizen employment, with more attractive working conditions, benefits packages, shorter working hours and better social security.

After the discovery of oil and in absence of a skilled national workforce, Gulf countries imported labor on a large scale and currently the region proportionally has the largest share of migrant workers in the world. In Oman currently about 44% of the population is expatriate (NCSI, 2014), however this segment accounts for 79% of the total labor force.

The dynamics of rentierism, oil wealth distribution through social benefits and government jobs, and the heavy reliance on imported labor in oil, construction and service sectors have greatly affected the structure and segmentation of Arab Gulf's labor markets. The dimensions of segmentation include national versus expatriate labor, public versus private sector employment and male versus female labor participation. Moreover, they are strongly interrelated: government jobs have been considered appropriate for nationals to accept, including women, being well-remunerated and secure. The private sector, never designed to absorb nationals, is predominantly filled by migrant labor where women are underrepresented.

This section presents Oman's labor market in 2012 according to gender, nationality and sector. Private sector data derive from the Ministry of Manpower (MoMP)'s Annual Statistical Yearbook (2012), reflecting on the year 2011. Public sector data are drawn from the National Centre for Statistics and Information (NCSI)'s statistical yearbook of 2012.

In 2011, the total labor force of the country comprised of 1,433,605 persons. Roughly 21% of the total labor force were Omani nationals, whereas the large majority (79%) were expatriates. Most of the labor force is allocated to the private sector (90%). Women comprised 15% of the total labor force in 2011, representing 11% of the private sector labor force against 46% of the public sector labor force (Figure 1).

Figure 1 **Segmentation of Oman's Labor Market according to Nationality, Gender and Sector, 2011**

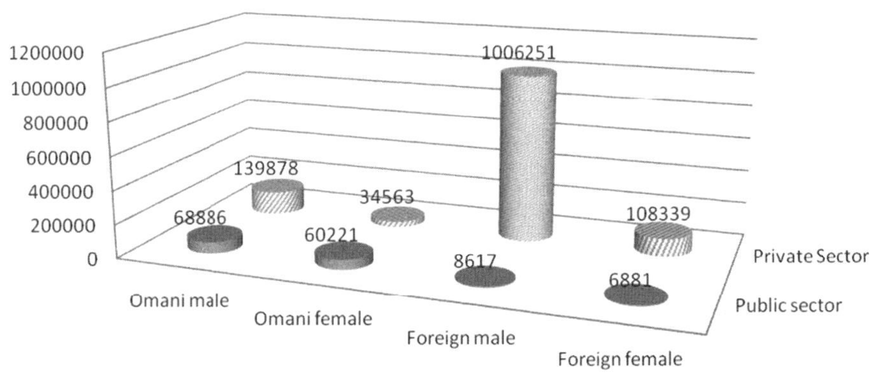

Source: MoMP, 2012; NCSI, 2012

Expatriates are almost uniformly employed in the private sector (99%). On the other hand, the public sector has traditionally been reserved for employing Omani nationals, and in 2011 only 11% of the jobs were taken by expatriates. Only in recent years, when the public sector became saturated and could no longer absorb the ever growing number of national job seekers, have the number of nationals employed in the private sector increased. Whereas in 2003 the number of Omani citizens employed in the private sector almost equalled the number in the public sector (74,816 versus 79,099), in 2011 there are more nationals working in the private sector (174,441) than in the public sector (129,107).

Oman's labor market has grown explosively since 2003. The total labor force increased from roughly half a million in 2003 to 1.4 million in 2011 (Figure 2). Between 2003 and 2011, the segment that has responded primarily to the expansion of the labor market has been the private sector expatriates, with a growth of 174%. The number of Omani nationals in the private sector has increased with 133% during that time. The main growth of the labor market has taken place in the private sector.

Figure 2 **Growth of Oman's Labor Market, total and according to Sector and Nationality, 2003-2011**

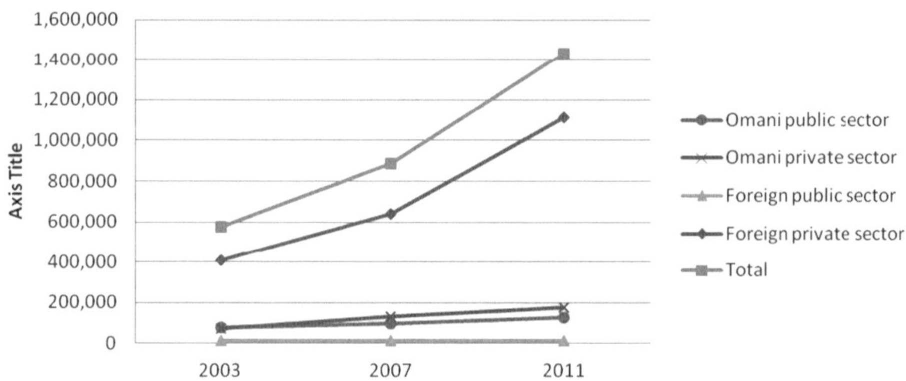

Source: MoMP, 2012; NCSI, 2012

There is general agreement that Gulf labor markets are characterized as unproductive, migrant-dominant, and inefficient. A range of policies have been introduced in Oman to tackle these rentier-based challenges, relating to human capital development on the one hand, including education and preparing new entrants for the labor market, and labor market restructuring on the other hand, through e.g. nationalisation policies. This section will discuss these policies and related actions for Oman in more detail.

Labor Market Restructuring: Omanisation Efforts

The challenges of increasing unemployment in the Gulf's rentier economies have been well described and relate to high levels of fertility, a growing youth bulge, and saturation of the public sector (e.g. Shah, 2008; Forstenlechner & Rutledge, 2010; Assaad & Roudhi-Fahimi, 2007).

Gulf countries therefore have started implementing policies to nationalise their labor force, e.g. through quota-based systems to increase the number of nationals in the private sector and various incentives for companies to hire them (Maloney, 1998; Harry, 2007; Ruppert, 1999; Randeree, 2009).

In the late 1980s, a policy of 'Omanisation' was introduced which was part of a wider agenda of diversification and privatization of the economy as spelled out in the Vision 2020, the national development plan created in the 1990s. The Omanisation policy aims to increase the participation of Omani nationals in the labor force, to maximize the use of national human resources and to enhance the return of investments of the rapidly expanding educational attainment of Omani nationals in the last two decades. In the public sector, 89% of the jobs were filled by Omani nationals in 2012. In the private sector however, this percentage was much lower at 13.5% (MoMP, 2012). The growth of the private sector in recent years has hardly benefited the Omani segment of the labor market, as the majority of employment growth was covered by the expansion of the expatriate labor force, leaving the overall Omanisation rate across all sectors of the economy at 21% in 2012 (MoMP, 2012).

Human Capital Development: Higher Education

Many studies have described the 'knowledge gap' that has emerged in the rent-based Gulf Cooperation Council (GCC) states (Abouammoh, 2012; Muysken & Noor, 2006; Brandenburg, 2013; UNDP, 2003). There is common understanding that the formation of human capital falls behind the region's current economic growth rate and levels of wealth. As oil rents defined economic output, labor was never a prominent 'factor of production', requiring few investments in human capital development through education. Nowadays in Oman education is considered essential for human capital development and consequently, a more productive labor force. A general push for universal education was instigated and primary education now has approximate participation rates for both genders of 96% for years 1-6, 83% for years 9-7 and 78% for years 10-12 (MoE, 2012).

In more recent years, higher education has become more accessible and the rate of participation in higher education has exploded. In the academic year 2012-2013, 26 private universities and colleges were registered to offer Diploma and Bachelor degree programs. Together with the public Sultan Qaboos university, public Colleges of Applied Sciences and a number of public vocational schools, the total number of students in higher education in Oman reached almost 90,000 in 2010 (HEAC, 2011). The amount of scholarships has grown explosively during recent years and almost doubled from 14,753 in 2009 to 27,998 in the year 2011 (HEAC, 2012).

Persistent Challenges of Employability

While human capital development is in full swing thanks to a massive growth in higher education, this does not yet seem to translate well into enhanced labor productivity of nationals. There are several reasons that explain this phenomenon.

Firstly, national human resources development is serious challenged by the mismatch between education and labor market. The current offer of higher education is leaning towards higher diploma and bachelor degrees: while roughly 69% of higher education students follow academic education, only 31% follow vocational training (HEAC, 2011). However, private sector jobs in Oman are dominated by low skill and low pay occupations: Currently almost half of the Omani nationals working in the private sector did not complete secondary school, and only a minority of 13% have completed tertiary education. Those holding bachelor degrees newly entering the labor market in the private sector are only 5% of the total new entrants. Furthermore, roughly two-thirds of Omani employees fall in the two lowest salary levels (MoMP, 2012). As a result, the academic education profile of new graduates does not match the dominant low skill-low pay nature of private sector employment, making it difficult for young graduates leaving Oman's universities and colleges to find a proper connection to the private sector job market.

Secondly, the rentier state seems to have left an obstinate culture of work and work ethic with the national population that only public sector employment is suitable to take up, while private sector jobs should be left to the expatriate labor force. It has been mentioned that many nationals wait for a public sector job and decline private sector employment, even if that means they remain unemployed for a longer duration of time (Al Waqfi & Forstenlechner, 2012).

Thirdly, Omani nationals have to compete for private sector jobs with expatriate labor that is usually higher qualified, more flexible, experienced and skilled. Various studies of higher education in the Gulf (see e.g. Karoly, 2010) have demonstrated the poor performance and poor quality of education in the Gulf compared to other countries.

Fourthly, while it is not only difficult to attract Omani nationals to the private sector, it is also very difficult to retain them, and job turnover is high in the private sector. One-third of Omanis left their job in the private sector in 2012 (36% or 62,482). Of the terminated jobs, 69% of employees left due to resignation (MoMP, 2012).

Traditionally, women's participation in the labor force has been low in the Arab region. Roudi-Fahimi and Moghadam (2003) note that only 20% of women aged 15 and older in MENA countries are formally employed, the lowest level of any world region. Within the MENA region, women of the Arab Gulf states are least likely to be economically active. Moreover, the large majority of women in the region outside agriculture are college-educated and are employed by the government sector.

During the last decades, however, female labor participation (FLP) in the Gulf countries has increased. Between 1980 and 2008, it approximately doubled in Bahrain, Kuwait, Qatar and Saudi Arabia and almost tripled in the UAE. Oman is the exception as the change between 1980 and 2008 is more modest (World Bank, 2008), a trend explained by persistent high fertility rates that undermine FLP according to Salehi-Isfahani (2011).

According to MoMP (2012), a total of 94,784 Omani women are working, comprising 6.6% of the total labor force in 2011. The figure of FLP becomes more meaningful when compared against the entire female population of working age. According to NCSI, total national labor participation, measured as the number of Omani nationals employed in public and private sector as share of the total population of working age (15-64) years was estimated at 24% in 2012. The rate was 15% for females and 33% for males. In comparison, the rate of FLP worldwide is estimated at 51% (NCSI, 2013).

The gender gap in national public sector employment has been sharply reduced over the past years, with women now representing 47% of the national employment in the public sector in 2011 (against 34% in 2003). In the private sector the gender gap among Omani citizens is however still significant with 80% of jobs filled by men.

Based on the rapid growth in female educational attainment in the last two decades in the region, especially at the university level, a faster pace of FLP would be expected (Al Shamsi, 2008; Roudi-Fahimi & Moghadam, 2003). In Oman, in recent years, females comprised almost 50% of enrolments at all levels of education (MNE, 2009). However, judging by their small share in the total labor force, a large majority of them did not seem to enter the job market.

The rise of female education has been tremendous. As with many countries in the Gulf, today there are no more gender differences in terms of primary and secondary education enrolment (Karoly, 2010). Also in higher education, the gender ratio is balanced: in the academic year 2010-2011, 50,4% of enrolled students were female versus 49,6% male (HEAC, 2011). The share of scholarships distributed to females increased from 44% in 2009 to 55% in 2011 (HEAC, 2012). Girls tend to study more at private institutions (58% of the enrolled students), whereas males dominate at the public Technical Colleges (63%).

Many studies have described the strong discrepancy in educational performance between males and females in the Gulf (Rutledge et al, 2011; Gallant & Pounder, 2008; Zovighian, 2012; Karoly, 2010). Although there are no figures at hand as regards gendered higher education performance in Oman, the data from secondary school performance demonstrate a striking difference. Whereas in 2011 more than 50% of the boys failed the general secondary school exam, only 15% of their female counterparts failed. Also girls score significantly higher on the exam (HEAC, 2012). Karoly (2010) found a similar pattern of better performance among girls in Dubai, Kuwait, and Qatar. Furthermore, the ratio of graduates from Higher Education Institutions leans positively to females: whereas in the academic year 2007-08, 48% of the new entrants were female, females accounted for 59% of the graduates four years later in the academic year 2009-2010 (HEAC, 2011). Hence, females tend to have a higher chance of completing higher education than males.

Deepening Challenges for Women

The changing landscape of higher education has made higher education more ubiquitously available. This has drastically altered the opportunities for girls to become educated and enter a career. Girls have especially benefited from the growth of higher education, in particular through the emergence of private colleges and universities.

However, in the discussion on the role of education in the labor market and human capital development, many of the employment challenges appear to be more deeply manifested for females. First of all, it was discussed above that females in particular study at private universities, obtaining bachelor degrees, whereas males dominate in technical and vocational colleges. Especially bachelor degrees do not fit the profile of the majority of jobs in the private sector. Furthermore, girls tend to choose careers in health, education and management and commerce (HEAC, 2012), however these sectors have already achieved fairly high Omanisation rates (such as teaching and banking). Also the public sector, main absorber of Omani females, has become saturated. Despite their better performance and higher graduation rates, these trends lead to a gender imbalance in employability, as the trends in the job market run against females' educational attainment profile. For the case of Saudi Arabia, Karoly (2010) observed a similar paradox where the higher educated women are, the lower their employment rates.

Methodology

This Chapter addresses the perception of Omani female near-graduates towards work in general and private sector employment in particular and discusses the importance of work according to female near-graduates, perceived chances of finding employment, career preferences, and perceptions of public vs. private sector jobs.

Twenty-three female students in their final year of three BSc programs at the German University of Technology (GUtech) in Muscat were asked about their preferences and perceptions of future employment and their expectations with regard to career development and work attitude by means of a questionnaire for each respondent and focus group interviews. The questionnaire was filled by the respondents prior to the focus group interview, with a return of 22 questionnaires, in order to obtain detailed information on respondents' backgrounds and individual opinions and preferences. It contained detailed questions on current and future job search strategies, career preferences and expectations, value of work and their perceptions towards public vs private sector employment. The questionnaire also served as an introduction and teaser to the focus group interview, by introducing the main subjects of discussion and preparing participants to develop their opinions on these subjects. Given the small sample size, descriptive data analysis was performed.

The three focus groups consisted of 6-9 participants (with a total of 23 participants) and the sessions commenced after the participants had completed the questionnaire. The group interviews were recorded and transcribed and covered subjects including chances of getting a job, the role of work in life, important aspects of a future job, job search strategies, public vs. private sector employment, the position of women on the work floor and combining family and work obligations. The students were enrolled in BSc programs Computer Science (7), Sustainable Tourism and Regional Development (8) and Urban Planning and Architectural Design (8). All participants were expected to graduate 2-4 months after the interviews took place (in March and May 2014). The respondents were Omani female, aged between 21 and 24 years old. Four respondents were married but none had children. Those that were not married lived with their parents and siblings. Married respondents lived with their husbands, sometimes with their parents or parents in law. More than half of the respondents (13) consider themselves to be from Muscat governorate. Five respondents were from Dakhiliyah region, four from other regions of Oman.

Findings

The survey responses and group interviews reveal that in general female near-graduates are very career-minded and consider it very important to find employment. While seven students planned to continue their education upon graduation, all other participants are keen to find a job after they finish their studies. None of the near-graduates preferred to stay at home upon graduation, whereas one person expressed interest to start up a business. A few students explained they explored both avenues of continuing education and job search, to see what would come up first.

One first main reason to work is the feeling of being rewarded with a job after spending a number of years at university. As one respondent put it: *"I think that the job [...] is the [reward] of studying. What's the benefit of all of this [education] if I don't find a job?"*. Others had similar comments: *"[After all these years of study], I think I deserve to work!"* and *"I definitely didn't waste five years [at university] in order to stay at home"*.

Survey responses confirmed that the main reason for respondents to work was 'to make good use of my education' (mentioned 19 times, or 86%). The second reason was 'to earn money for myself' (15 respondents, 68%) followed by personal development and fulfilment (11 respondents, 50%). A second set of reasons, that were mentioned between six and three times included 'to do something interesting during the day', 'to contribute to the household/family income' and to 'meet and socialize with people'.

In the interviews, the importance of earning an income was stressed, in order to *"be independent"* and *"to take care of oneself"*. As one respondent stated: *"[Money] is very important. I don't want to count on my father's salary only. I also want to work to provide things for myself."* Respondents also explained that rising living expenses have increased the need to earn an income: *"I think now life is very expensive, it's very important to have a salary"*.

While earning money for oneself was more important than earning money to contribute to the household income, some respondents mentioned they value the idea to contribute: *"I want to earn money for myself and be independent, but I would also love to help my dad handle the expenses"*. Some respondents mentioned they felt some pressure from their families who expect them to work after having been educated and to pay back: *"I think nowadays life is much more expensive. And I think five years ago our parents would give us everything and now it's time for us to stand on ourselves and pay it back. And show what we are worth"*.

To further assess the meaning of work in the respondents' lives, a set of Likert statements was introduced in order to probe different aspects of the construct "value of work".

Figure 3 presents the findings and reveals that respondents consider work to be of strong importance in their lives and that they identify with working: Twenty respondents strongly agreed and two agreed with the statement "I see myself as a working woman". The majority of near-graduates also strongly agreed that it is important to earn an income, to be recognised for their knowledge and skills, and that they are determined to have a career. The Likert findings confirm the results that the desire to earn an own income is considered more important than earning an income to contribute to the family or household income. Also, the majority of respondents said they would be bored if they didn't have any work or study obligations.

The data thus reveal that female students want to work, identify with themselves as working women, and consider work to be important. At the same time they are concerned about finding a job and worry about unemployment. This section considers their preparedness to transition to the labor market, the respondents' perceptions of their chances to find employment, and their job search strategies.

Figure 3 **The Value of Work according to Female Near-Graduates (N=22)**

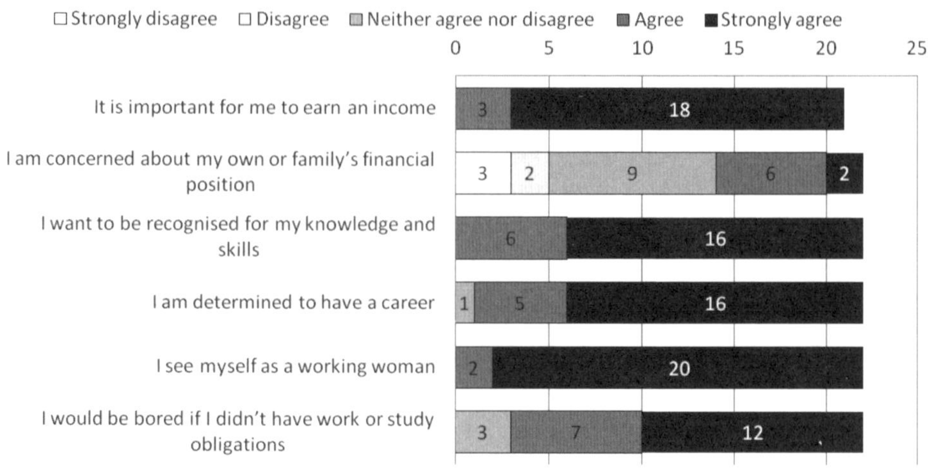

Preparedness to Enter the Labor Market

Many students commented they do not feel prepared to enter the job market. They perceive a strong need for more work experience in order to increase their chances to find employment. *"Theoretically we are prepared, but practically not. We need to be trained still more, once we get trained then we can apply for [suitable] jobs"*. One student mentioned that nowadays two years of work experience is the bare minimum in order to obtain a starter's jobs.

Students are aware of the need for training, and internships were a much appreciated part of their curriculum. Twenty of the 22 respondents had obtained some work experience, the large majority by means of internships. These internships, many of them a compulsory and credited part of the curriculum, ranged between one and five months, with an average of 2.2 months. Most students had had one or two work experiences, with in total just over three months' work experience on average by the time they graduate.

Students were asked in the survey if they had already applied for jobs or internships and if they had not been successful, what were the main reasons for this. The most frequently mentioned reason was the lack of the right connections *('wasta'),* indicated by 55% of the respondents (12). Eight students (36%) felt a key reason was a lack of work experience, while 18% (4 students) thought the main reason was that their qualifications were not good enough. Other reasons mentioned were the lack of work skills (3) and age (1). Having 'wasta' was also mentioned most frequently as the single most important thing that would affect their chances of getting a job after graduation (36%), followed by having the right skills (27%) and the right qualifications (18%). Also in the group interviews, in addition to work experience, the importance of *'wasta'* as a critical precondition to finding a job came up frequently: *"Unfortunately this is how it still works. Connections really help."*

Perceived Chances of Finding Employment

In general, near-graduates were concerned about the likeliness to find employment that fits their skills and qualifications. Students perceive their efforts of finding a proper job as "difficult", "depressing", "we are lost", "the chances are zero". The negative perception partly derives from stories they hear from other job seekers. One respondent mentioned: *"We have seen people that graduated last year [...] most of them had good grades but whenever they applied they never got a reply from most of the companies. When they go and apply and the company tells them 'yes, you will get accepted just give us another week' and then there is no reply".*

Students from the BSc programs 'Sustainable Tourism and Regional Development' and 'Urban Planning and Architectural Design' (UPAD) were worried about finding suitable jobs relating to their field of study. The UPAD students commented that their peers from earlier years were *"all still at home"*, being unemployed: *"half of them are still at home. Some of them started their own business with a totally different thing, some of them are still waiting for a job. It's only few of them that got a job [...] but some of them are only CAD drawers or something, the easiest thing you can do [in our field]".*

Students in Computer Science (CS) were slightly more positive about their chances to find a job, although in general they did not think it would be easy. Similar to the UPAD students, they commented that many of the CS students who graduated last year, still have not found a position.

Job Search Strategies

What kind of strategies do near-graduates employ to search for a job? None of the respondents said they would do nothing to increase their chances to find a job. The most common strategy is to build work experience by doing further internships and traineeships. Second came the option to improve qualifications by continuing education. Another common job seeking strategy is to send open applications (CVs) to preferred companies. Using their network and connections was also mentioned as a strategy, but although respondents mentioned *'wasta'* was the key aspects of being successful in finding a job, it was not mentioned as the main job seeking strategy. Searching for job vacancies in social and general media was not a common strategy, one reason is that students mentioned that there are almost no jobs advertised that way (Figure 4).

Some students commented that companies do not hire efficiently to reach relevant candidates, and that many positions are vacant but that they are not advertised so job seekers do not learn about these opportunities. In the focus group interviews, the picture was drawn that many job search strategies are not very promising, and that taking a pro-active approach to finding a job often does not yield any result. One participant explained: *"One of my graduated friends she told me that she printed like fifty copies of her CV and she put it in her car and she was like 'whenever I pass by a company where I might find a job I just go there and leave my CV' and until now she didn't get a job."*

Figure 4 **Job Search Strategies of Female Near-Graduates (N=22)**

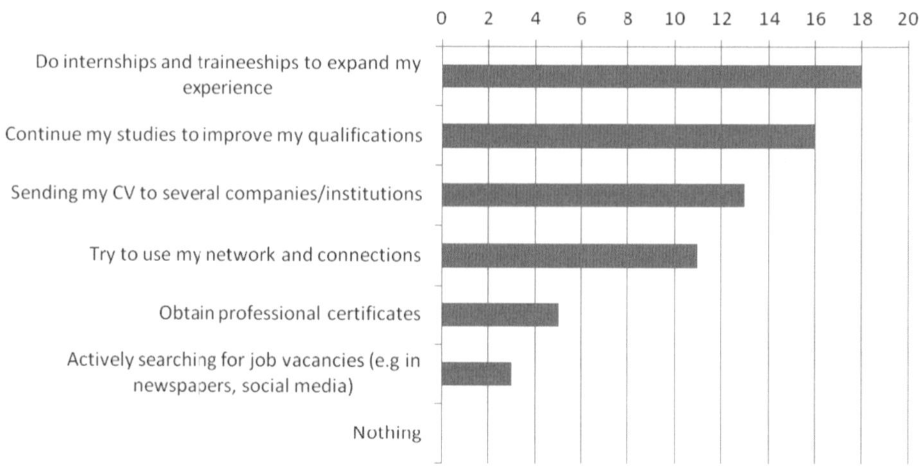

In the interviews, the strategy to start in lower positions that require less than a Bachelor's degree was also discussed. Some students saw this as a promising start: *"Starting will not be that difficult. And if you know that you have to start low, then it will be easier to accept"*. Other students however commented that starting in a position with lower required qualifications would limit their opportunities to develop and get up to the level of their qualifications. Also, these jobs do not appeal much: *"I would rather stay at home than working at a bad job, I'm an engineer and [don't want to be] sitting at a counter to check attendance."*

In order to be hired for a job, either in the public or in the private sector, candidates in Oman need to be registered as job seekers at the Public Authority of Manpower Register

(PAMR), also known as the job seekers office. Job vacancies in companies and government sections are then communicated to the PAMR, who will select candidates from their data base to apply for these jobs. Some students are left with a feeling of powerlessness as a result of this system. "*You always have to wait for a job. If you want to have a government job, you need to register at the job seekers office and wait*". For private sector jobs, the system is similar, although some companies advertise job vacancies in the media, and students also send open applications and CVs to their preferred employers. Students can only register as a job seeker at the PAMR after they have completed their studies, hence there are limited opportunities to apply for jobs whilst still studying.

Job Conditions

Contrary to the mainstream literature on female labor preferences in the Arab Gulf, the majority of the near-graduates in our study prefer to work in the private sector: 12 or 55% of the respondents preferred a private sector job, while 4 or 18% indicated the desire to work in the public sector. Six respondents (27%) did not have a clear sector preference.

Figure 5 presents the reservation wages (the acceptable minimum monthly salary according to respondents) comparing public and private sector. The findings demonstrate that the reservation wage is lower for public sector jobs, where most respondents indicated 700 or 900 OMR as a minimum acceptable monthly salary level. For private sector jobs, the dominant acceptable salaries are the same, however a number of respondents have much higher reservation wages for private sector jobs, ranging from 1,200 to 2,000 OMR per month. On average, the reservation wage for public sector job is 804 OMR while for a private sector position it is 941 OMR.

Figure 5 **Monthly Reservation Wages for Public and Private Sector Jobs (in OMR) (N=22)**

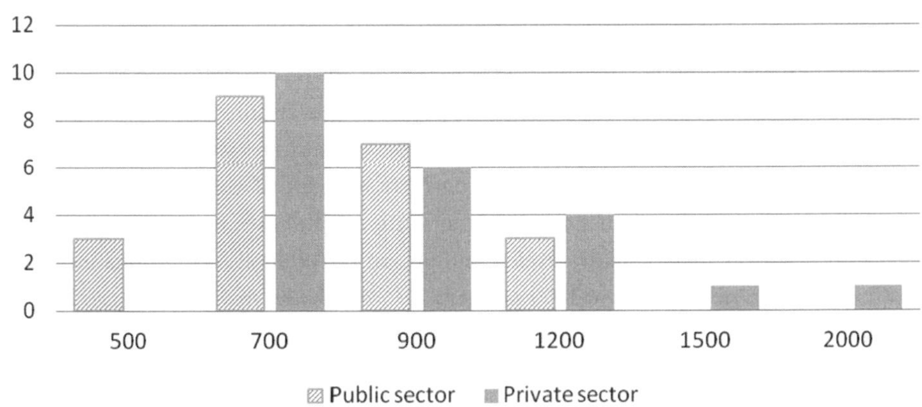

Finance and business is the most preferred employment sector for the near-graduates, followed by construction, transport & communication, tourism, and education.

All respondents except one indicated they wanted to work full time (defined as more than four hours a day). Most respondents wanted to work 5-6 hours (10 students) or 7-8 hours (9 students) per day. Three students wanted to work 3-4 hours per day, while no one indicated the desire to work 1-2 hours or more than 8 hours per day.

Important Aspects of a Job

The two most important aspects of a future job were "an interesting and enjoyable job" and "a good working atmosphere and colleagues that I can get along with". In other words, the main values ascribed to a future job do not relate to salary or benefits, but to the daily experience of the job and the comfortable interaction on the work floor (Figure 6). Third and fourth come the opportunities for promotion and career advancement; and a job that is respected. Salary came in fifth, followed by the possibility to combine work with family responsibilities. Job security, bonus and fringe benefits and the location of the job close to home were not considered important aspects of a future job by the students.

Figure 6 **Important Aspects of a Future Job (N=22)**

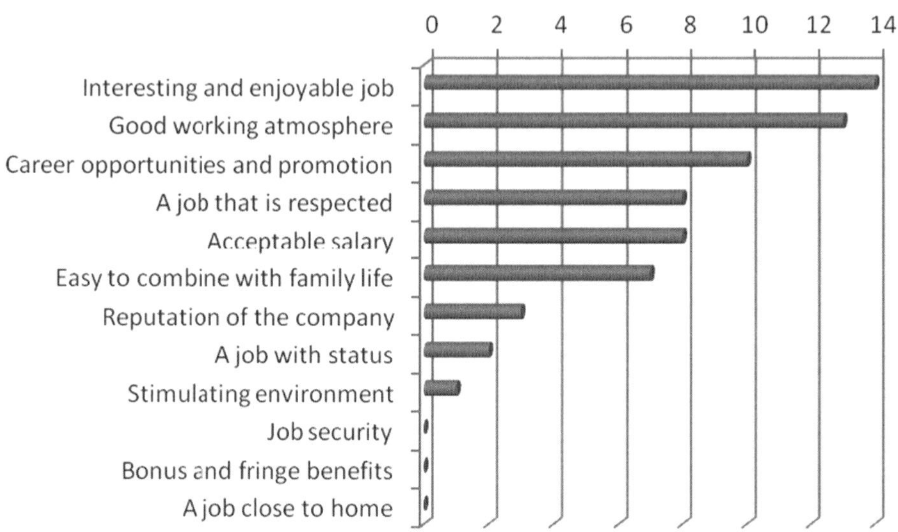

In the focus group interviews, the work environment stuck out as the single most important aspect of a job. In the three groups it was the single most mentioned feature that makes or breaks a job. Related to the concept of work environment were aspects of *"being comfortable around your colleagues"*, *"having a good relationship with your manager"*, *"enjoying to be at*

work". Students furthermore ascribed various values to a positive work environment, such as "*not competitive*", "*comfortable*", "*friendly*", "*a learning environment where one can learn from each other*", and "*motivating*". One participant explained: "*I think the most important is the atmosphere. If you get [a] good salary but the environment is not good, you won't be satisfied there. That's why I think the environment is really important.*"

This section discusses the perception of public versus private sector employment, which in the context of rentier economies tend to have very different characteristics and values ascribed to them. At the same time, the findings presented go beyond the mere comparison of these sectors and their work conditions, but also take into account patriarchal values and issues of female employment, reputation, and combining work and care responsibilities, as these issues are intrinsically connected to the public-private sector dichotomy.

Comparing the Government and the Private Sector as an Employer

Contrary to the literature and current statistics on FLP in the region that stress a strong tendency for women to work in the public sector, which is highly preferred over private sector jobs due to various reasons as discussed in Section 2, the female near-graduates in this study take a positive attitude to private sector employment. At the same time, they ascribe a number of negative values to government jobs. Government jobs are perceived to be slow, bureaucratic, repetitive, not challenging, unproductive and above all, hold very few opportunities for career development and promotion. Respondents considered private sector jobs on the other hand to be more exciting, more rewarding, and with more opportunities for learning and exposure. As one respondent reflected: "*I think the government sector is not as challenging as the private sector [...] to move on and better your career that's not possible. That's important to me because I really want to build something out of what I did for four years [of study]. I don't think I can do that in the government sector.*" Box 1 spells out in more detail the opinion of various interview respondents as to why they prefer to find a job in the private sector and avoid the public sector. Also, Figure 7 demonstrates that nearly all respondents either strongly agree or agree with the statements 'there are good opportunities for promotion and career advancement in the private sector', and 'private sector offers a more stimulating and exciting work environment than the public sector'.

The general opinion was furthermore that in order to be promoted and advance one's career, it is *wasta* that matters in the public sector, while in the private sector it is based on performance. One respondent explained: "*It takes a long time in the public sector to get promoted. Actually it is not only about time, but more about wasta. My mother, she is working for forty years now and she is not getting any higher. The opportunities are given to someone else with less experience but more wasta.*" Many students disliked the idea of career development being related to *wasta* and connections and not to performance merits, and for some it was a reason to avoid working in the public sector.

While it has often been mentioned that mixed environments and working with expatriates are considered obstacles for women in the Arab Gulf region to be taking up private sector employment, it was the opposite view for the female near-graduates of this study. Instead, they felt that mingling with expatriates and working in a mixed (multi-gender, multi-culture) environment would hold important advantages relating to opportunities of learning and knowledge and skills transfer: *"I prefer working in the private sector because [...] it has people from different nationalities. That will help. Because they have a lot of experience. So you will also get more experience."*

Box 1 Female Near-Graduates Perceptions of Public versus Private Sector Employment

- *"In government you stick with a specific job and tasks, just doing one thing for the rest of your life. You just follow orders. But you don't learn."*
- *"A government job? I can't imagine doing that!"*
- *"In the private sector there is more experience. You can apply what you have studied all these years but in the government sector you will only apply very slowly and it will take time."*
- *"When I imagine government sector I only think of people sitting at their desk drinking coffee, reading the newspaper. I think it's a waste of the years [of study]."*
- *"Even people like my mum, she worked for 35 years and she is still in the same position."*
- *"I think that is why we want to work in the private sector because the private sector there is more chance to work and develop yourself than the government. In the government you stay at the same level, your salary will increase every year but your knowledge, you will not develop it."*
- *"In private sector they recognize you for your skills and knowledge. They pay attention. And they train you."*
- *"I'd choose the private sector because I think you get more exposure. You get to see more things."*

Various work conditions were compared between the public and private sector, such as salary levels, working hours and the work environment. Salaries were perceived to be better in the government sector, especially given a recently introduced steep increase of minimum salaries for government jobs. A Bachelor graduate now has an entry salary of 900 OMR, which the students considered to be *"...actually good. It's really good. In private sector you won't get this when you start."* Still, the large majority of respondents felt they could earn a good salary in the private sector as well (Figure 7). Furthermore, the working hours in the private sector were perceived to be very long and unattractive, which a number of students experienced during their internship placements: *"I hate these private sector long hours – they are too long. You go back home and you are dead. You don't have time for your family, you don't have time to go out, you just feel you want to stay home. This for me is a very negative thing".*

Figure 7 **Perceptions of Work Conditions in Public vs. Private Sector (N=22)**

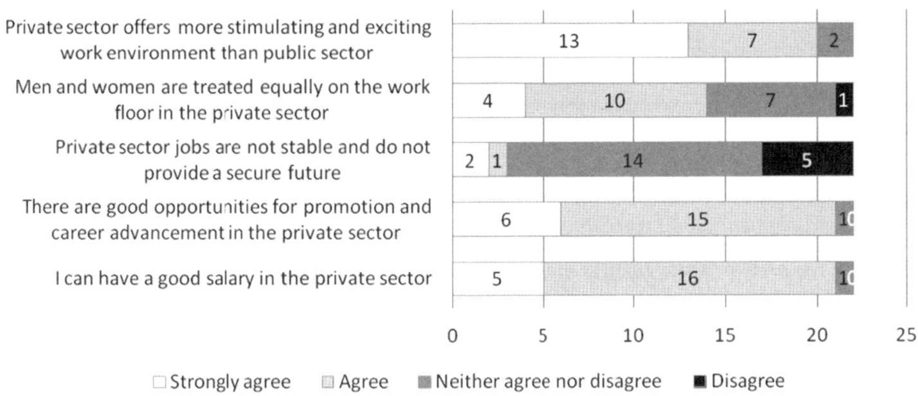

Patriarchal Values and Female Reputation

The comparison between public and private sector employment is not only about working hours, salary levels, job security, or promotion and *wasta*, but also take into account patriarchal values and issues of reputation and respect – important aspects in the societies of the Arab Gulf. It is generally agreed that the government sector holds the important advantage for women that it is perceived as a respectable place to work, that does not compromise the reputation of women.

Is reputation of the employer of importance to female near-graduates? Yes, it matters, for various reasons. Some mentioned it is important to work at a 'good' company for career reasons, as it would enhance their CV and increase their options for a next job with a good reference. Others mentioned that the reputation matters in order to have a 'respectful' job. As one respondent described it: *"It's important that it is a respectful place. About where do we work, do we need to go to a construction site, and how do they respect women".* Another student mentioned a respectful job is about *"...how they deal with each other and if they respect each other, especially women."* However, private sector jobs are not considered disrespectful *per se*, as the majority of students disagreed or strongly disagreed with the statement 'private sector jobs are not respected' (Figure 8).

Families play an important role in the choice of study and work, as I have described elsewhere (Bontenbal & Aziz, 2013), and parents' perceptions still reflect the dominant patriarchal values in society. How do the respondents' families see their career ambitions? All students confirmed that their families are in support of them taking up employment. However, parents generally lean strongly to a public sector job preference for their daughters. Cultural constraints and working hours were mentioned as the main reasons: *"Parents they prefer the government sector for their daughter because of cultural issues." "And because of the working hours, especially because of the working hours"*. Survey findings reveal that only a minority of respondents agree with the statement that their parents would be proud of them working in the private sector, and roughly half of the students think that the view from society in general ("others") is that women should aim to find a government job (Figure 8). There is, hence, a discrepancy in perceptions and preferences of future employment between the female students and their families. This could potentially affect the eventual choice of career for near-graduates.

In addition to sector preference, a number of jobs are not considered appropriate for females. Examples mentioned include jobs in remote places (offshore, desert), work that requires shifts, sales work, work in hotels, hospitality and airline cabin crew, and work in the banking sector. The main reason stated for these constraints was *"...the reputation. Because we are women"*. One student illustrated this with her father's perception of working at a bank: *"For my father it's like working in a bank, there are issues. Because you are dealing with men. That is the image that he has of a bank, that it is crowded and that people go in and out."* One student added that it is important for her parents that she would not be the only female employee on the work floor, and at least have a few other female colleagues: *"I did my internship in the company of a friend of my father. He told my father, it is better to work for me in the morning because then a female colleague would be there. But in the evening it would be all men. This is important."*

Figure 8 **Patriarchal Values and the Reputation of Private Sector Employment**

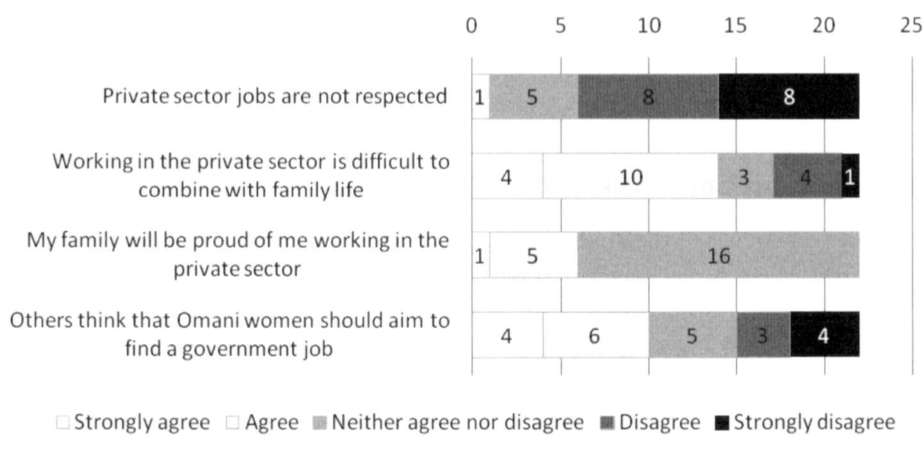

Shifting Preferences for a Married Life with Children

The findings reveal that female near-graduates are in favor of private sector jobs. However, when a new set of variables was introduced into the discussion, the perceptions changed considerably. These variables were marriage and children. The general view was that while a private sector job was the preferred choice after graduation due to the potential for learning, career development, and a dynamic work environment, this preference would change into a government job once married life with children started. One respondent explained: *"For now, I think we should start in the private sector, to get the experience, because we don't have any responsibilities, we have time. Maybe in a few years we can then work in government"*. Another participant added: *"Also when you get older if you get married you will have more responsibilities and also you want more time to spend with the family"*. Someone else said: *"I know a lot of women after their first child they changed to government sector"*. Various reasons were given why a government job would be easier to combine with family life and child care: shorter working hours, better benefits during maternity leave and breastfeeding, longer holidays, and a generous retirement scheme. However the shorter working hours were considered the main advantage. The survey findings confirm these interview observations: only five students (23%) strongly disagreed or disagreed with the statement 'working in the private sector is difficult to combine with family life' (Figure 8).

Some participants even mentioned that having a private sector job as a woman could potentially hold back future marriage proposals, as men would see their future married and family life being compromised with a wife who works long, and at time irregular, hours: *"For the working hours it would be difficult for us when you get married and have kids. That is the culture and the environment here in Oman. [Men] would prefer getting married with a woman who works in public sector, thinking about the future.* Another student added: *"It is really uncomfortable for the husband to see his wife go out at 8 pm to work which is not really good. Although he trusts her but still ideas come into mind."* These examples reflect that even though women's perception of private sector work seems to be changing radically, they are aware of the patriarchal values that continue to dominate the general society view and that could negatively affect the approval from their families, and even their position as a marriage candidate.

Discussion and Conclusions

The rentier economies of the Arab Gulf region are characterised by a highly segmented labor market where strong gender and nationality patterns define the public and private sector labor force. Omani women are underrepresented in the labor force and have traditionally been employed in the public sector, both for cultural and work conditions reasons, whereas their presence in the private sector is minimal. Despite Omanisation policies, the high growth rate of Oman's private sector of the last decade has been mainly facilitated by the male expatriate segment. Thanks to government efforts to boost human capital development, higher education has become widely available to young Omanis and the number of graduates has exploded in recent years. However, persistent employability challenges remain that undermine citizen participation in the private sector. These challenges seem to be intensified for female graduates. Social and cultural constraints, a career preference among women towards professions in which Omanisation has already been fulfilled to a large extent (such as teaching and nursing), and the deepened mismatch between educational attainment (girls perform better than boys and obtain higher degrees on average) and the low quality nature of private sector jobs intensify the employability challenge.

Understanding career perceptions and preferences of students is an important step in the discourse on human capital development in the Arab Gulf, and in the challenge to better understand the weak relationship between education and labor market trends in Oman.

The findings reveal that despite traditional patriarchal values and a general understanding of a compromised work ethic and rentier mentality among nationals, the female respondents of this study find work of great importance and are work-minded. The role of education appears significant in this respect, as it puts value to work through a desired return of investment in education. Rising costs of living and the wish to be independent were other important reasons to work. The students however did not think their chances of finding suitable employment would be high, and mentioned having '*wasta*' and more work experience as key preconditions to find a job. Students noted weaknesses in labor market mechanisms to match candidates to jobs, such as the job seekers administration system and companies' hiring and job advertising practices. A job that is interesting and a good working atmosphere are more important aspects of a job than salary, status and job security.

Contrary to general rhetoric and previous studies, the female students of this study prefer working in the private sector over a government job. Public sector is perceived to be slow, unproductive with few opportunities for development, and considered a waste of their educational investment. Private sector jobs on the other hand are considered more challenging and rewarding, with better options for career development.

However at the same time, patriarchal values and issues of female reputation continue to exercise influence on the career choice of female near-graduates. While a private sector job holds more career advantages for themselves, they are aware of the need to protect their reputation and that they need to maneuver within the context of family preferences and society values. A number of jobs are not deemed suitable for women. From society's viewpoint, a government job is still highly preferred. A shift was observed in work preferences when marriage and children come up, and a private sector job was perceived to be difficult to combine with family responsibilities. Government jobs remain the preferred career choice of married women with children.

The findings suggest that the constraints for Omani female near-graduates towards employment are the weak connection between education and labor market in the short run (lack of experience, lack of suitable jobs, lack of effective hiring mechanisms) even though the private sector is considered attractive now. In the long run, the constraints derive from persistent patriarchal values - the dominant belief that women are better off in the government sector, especially when married with children, embedded in a rentier-based welfare society context in which public sector employment continue to have more advantageous work conditions.

2

Self-Motivation, Career Aspirations and Work Responsibilities: The Perspective of Saudi Male Undergraduates at King Fahd University of Petroleum and Minerals

Mark C. Thompson

Introduction

In March 2011 as the ramifications of the Arab Spring on socio-political and economic issues became apparent, it was reported by the Saudi-British Relations Information Service (SaudiBrit, 2011) that "In general, employers say that young Saudi male graduates have an overdeveloped sense of their own value in the marketplace and an underdeveloped commitment to hard work". This statement supports the argument that unemployment in Saudi Arabia is a "behavioural problem" as young Saudi men are unwilling to accept job offers particularly in the blue-collar and manual work sectors whether public or private (Al Anazi, 2011: 15). This oft repeated idea assumes that self-motivation and career aspirations in Saudi Arabia, as related to personal fulfilment through study and / or work, do not constitute an important factor for any young Saudi man. In addition, this type of sweeping generalization dismisses an entire constituency of well-educated individuals many of whom desire to play a constructive role in the development of the Kingdom. Furthermore, in the case of many male undergraduates at King Fahd University of Petroleum and Minerals (KFUPM), these young Saudis not only expect to assume significant work responsibilities upon entering the workforce, but in fact, also want to do so; they consider that their university studies have prepared them for this eventuality. However, even though many KFUPM undergraduates would like to assume leadership responsibilities they are often disappointed, and more dangerously, demoralized. Unfortunately, as these undergraduates undergo the transition from education to employment they sometimes find themselves underused and / or overlooked once in a full-time position.

Regrettably, this situation often mirrors the societal environment, one where young male Saudis are caught between two opposing attitudes. On the one hand, they are either ignored or marginalized, and on the other, young unmarried men are deemed to be irresponsible and in consequence, blamed for social ills. Usually referred in Arabic as *shabab*, this term is often understood in a negative sense; Dresch and Piscatori note that in contemporary usage it often refers to "wild young men misbehaving" (2013: 249). Not surprisingly, many youth-related problems stem from the fact that, rightly or wrongly, many young male Saudis feel neglected; hence, there is a sense of not being able to participate constructively either in the workplace or in society.[i] Indeed, Prince Alwaleed bin Talal noted that for overall Saudi governmental reform to be effective, the younger generation needs to be included, especially as youth "has become increasingly intertwined with its counterparts in other parts of the world" (2011: 1).

Overview, Methodology and Rationale

This Chapter discusses whether KFUPM undergraduates think that their university education is aligned, or misaligned, with the labour market and whether their career expectations are matched with those of employers. It also considers career aspirations related to work responsibilities, leadership and an individual's willingness to compromise in the search for gainful employment. In discussing these issues, this paper hopes to highlight not only undergraduate career aspirations, but also their overall concerns regarding the important transition from education to employment.

This Chapter is based on primary research including questionnaires, interviews, class discussion, classroom observation and student reports conducted with approximately 210 undergraduate students taking a new "Globalization" course piloted and taught by the author at KFUPM during the academic year 2013–2014. The paper utilizes primarily a qualitative approach based on open-ended questions, either oral or written, that allowed the students to express their views at length. Some of the questions animating this paper are as follows:

- To what extent do you think your university education matches your career expectations and those of potential employers?
- What are your career aspirations? Where do you see yourself in five years' time? Do you feel this is realistic? To what extent do you think your qualifications and experience will match your actual work responsibilities?
- If you cannot find a job that matches your qualifications, to what extent are you willing to compromise and take a job you do not really want? Would you do any job? What would / wouldn't you do?
- To what extent do you feel that you will graduate as a well-rounded individual? After you enter the workplace, to what extent do you feel that you will be able to operate effectively in a globalized world?

- In your opinion, can you find personal fulfilment and happiness through study and / or work? Why / why not?
- To what extent are you self-motivated and / or ambitious? Do you want to be a leader? In your opinion, are you challenged at KFUPM? Is being challenged beneficial to you? Do you expect to be challenged the workplace?
- In general, do you think you are taken seriously (for example, by the university / society)? To what extent do you feel that you are listened to and your opinion taken into consideration?
- In your opinion, do you think that young Saudi men are marginalized by society? Why / why not? Is it easy being a young Saudi man?

Responses to these questions facilitated the identification of major themes and trends that are discussed throughout the paper. In addition, a quantitative method in the form of a brief online survey with 109 respondents was also conducted in order to support some of the identified trends.[ii] Relevant findings from this survey are presented in tables throughout the text.

Contemporary Saudi societal issues remain an under-researched area particularly by non-Saudi academics, in part due to lack of access to Saudi societal constituencies and in part due to a limited understanding and / or knowledge of contemporary Saudi society. Although previously I have examined youth-related issues on a broader scale (Thompson, 2012) this paper has a much narrower focus as it necessarily draws heavily on the attitudes and experience of KFUPM students, the majority either in their junior or senior year. It recognizes that this elite sample of KFUPM students does not represent Saudi youth in its entirety. However, KFUPM students come from all regions of Saudi Arabia as well as from a wide variety of family backgrounds, therefore, it is hoped that this will allow an interesting and distinct group of Saudi voices to be heard with regards to the topic. In the final analysis, the future of Saudi Arabia is their future and consequently, their opinions should be heard.

Background

In 2014 the influence of rapid societal transformation on Saudi socio-politics appeared to be driven by a potent combination of three youth-related issues: demographics, increased education and expanding social media usage. However, as a delegate at the 2014 Jeddah Economic Forum (JEF) on "Growth through Youth" (19–20 March) what was striking was the lack of input from youth itself. Whilst there were many interesting and relevant presentations related to employment, job creation schemes and entrepreneurship, only one session (Youth Discussion with King Abdulaziz Center for National Dialogue) included presentations from two youth participants (both male). This absence of a "youth voice" at an official forum dedicated to youth issues and in a country where approximately forty-five per cent of the population is less than twenty-four years of age appeared to constitute a glaring omission (CIA, 2014). Indeed, Saudi demographics are central to understanding some of the most pressing societal issues facing the Saudi government in the immediate future. Issues such as unemployment and / or underemployment, as well as the contentious issue of affordable housing pose significant difficulties for the government as it attempts to find a solution to its demographic problem or so-called "youth bulge".

Another concern for the government is that young Saudis are now connected to the world in ways that would have been unthinkable five years ago. They are also more knowledgeable about life in general and, as Murphy (2011) notes, more outspoken as the Internet offers them a degree of protection through its anonymity. Since 2010 there has been a huge increase in online participation on social networks and instant-messaging applications such as Whatsapp, Facebook and Twitter, which is "more popular in Saudi Arabia than in the US or China taking into account the different levels of population" (Cockburn: 2014). For example, the 2010 Twitter usage increased by 440 per cent in the Kingdom in comparison to a ninety-five per cent increase worldwide (Atwood: 2011). A 2013 study found that Twitter's penetration growth rate increased by 3,000 per cent from 2011 to 2012 with the majority of users aged 18–34 (Muhammad, 2013). Kinninmont (2013: 5) argues that Twitter is part of "a wider distribution of power over information away from governments and towards individuals" especially youth. Even when it is not used for political purposes, it is impacting on state-society and inter-generational relations. Before the advent of the Internet in the Kingdom, as Cockburn points out (2014), popular views, dissenting or approving, were seldom heard and although control over opinion remains tight, it is not total. Furthermore, whilst some commentators note that nowadays young Saudis have almost unlimited access to Western information sources, it is contact with other Arab peers, in particular in neighboring Gulf States, that is often more significant. For example, a young man in Riyadh is now fully aware of the opportunities, and distractions such as cinema, enjoyed by his peers in Kuwait or Abu Dhabi. All of which leads young Saudis to wonder why they cannot enjoy the same opportunities at home.

Underlying these developments is a growing generational divide and the crucial fact that those in elite positions are often several generations older than the majority of the population:

> Blogger Saeed Al Wahabi has this really interesting post about the generational divide in Saudi Arabia between the leadership and the population. Al Wahabi did some simple math to calculate the average age for officials in different parts of the government, and these are some of his findings: the average age of ministers is sixty-five; the average age of governors is sixty-one; and the average age of Shura Council members is sixty-one. Similar

> numbers are found when we try to see the ages in the Supreme Judicial Council, the Supreme Ulama Council, and even members of King Abdulaziz Center for National Dialogue (KACND). Now compare the aforementioned numbers with these two numbers: seventy per cent of the population is under thirty, and average age of Saudi citizens is nineteen years old (Al Omran, 2011).

In consequence, many senior government officials and media commentators have been compelled to turn their attention to youth related issues and the alarming realization that failure to address youth aspirations could threaten the Kingdom's stability and future. Indeed, Ramady (2013b) points out that states with a large "youth bulge" can "experience a high level of political violence and civil strife" if exacerbated by a lack of meaningful employment opportunities. Ulrichsen also highlights the urgency of addressing unemployment in a region where youth constitutes such a high proportion of the population (2012: 283) and Jones and Punshi (2014: 19) point out that "our collective choices and actions" will be determined whether the Gulf Cooperation Council (GCC) states "can reap this demographic dividend or decelerate towards a demographic disaster".

The Correlation Between University and the Working Environment

King Fahd University of Petroleum and Minerals

In order to provide context to this paper it is necessary to look briefly at KFUPM and its student profile.

As one of the premier universities in the Middle East, KFUPM's stated vision is to be a preeminent institution known for its globally competitive graduates, cutting edge research, and leadership in energy discoveries with teaching and research as its two core functions. Apart from Islamic studies and Arabic literature, English is the language of instruction—although this is a controversial issue as some argue that the students could do just as well, if not better, by studying in Arabic. In addition, the university recognizes that for its graduates to be globally competitive this requires that its students acquire a high degree of knowledge in their related disciplines in addition to acquiring effective leadership, strategic and critical thinking skills in addition to an ethical life/work approach. Underpinning the vision and mission are KFUPM's values which are guided by Islamic principles that form the foundation upon which KFUPM builds its reputation and success, i.e., integrity, fairness, transparency, passion, inclusiveness, care, discipline and creativity.

KFUPM students are selected on merit regardless of background whether family, tribe, region or sect. Due to this policy students come from every part of the Kingdom and this necessitates living on campus in student dormitories. For Saudi Arabia, this is unusual in terms of students being separated from their families at eighteen years of age. However, what is significant is the space and freedom this allows. Specifically, it gives many students the chance to develop as individuals and form friendships outside of their normal constituency often as a member of a student club and / or through participation in extracurricular activities. There are even examples of Sunni students deliberately choosing a Shia roommate and vice-versa. Meanwhile, many of the students' peers outside the university spend a great deal of their free time driving female relatives to shopping malls and other appointments. For a twenty something young man this is "seriously uncool".

KFUPM and its departments tailor their curricula and programmes to the needs of the marketplace and as Makenzie Smith (2008: 18–19) notes Saudi Aramco's work with KFUPM is a well-established example of cooperation involving collaborative research, teaching, professional training and technology commercialization between the two institutions. In KFUPM engineering this is often related to the Saudi oil and petrochemical industries and for this reason there are more relevant sub-disciplines and / or specific modules in these areas. Indeed, Niblock and Malik (2007: 165; 209) contend that KFUPM engineering graduates are considered to be as good as those of anywhere in the world and that the university is "consistently complimented". In this respect, KFUPM aims to avoid a familiar problem often seen in the GCC states whereby "churning out of graduates with the 'wrong' skills has contributed to high levels of unemployment" (Sultan et al, 2011: 35).

University Studies

In general, KFUPM students believe that their university education is related to their future careers as well as the requirements of prospective employers both in and outside Saudi Arabia. The academic programmes at KFUPM are considered to be well-designed so that the graduate serves the industry's needs by becoming a leader in his field. Moreover, there is recognition that the university produces qualified candidates for a variety of jobs; hence, for many students their education appears to correlate to career expectations. In fact, many students are confident that KFUPM prepares them to become effective employees; ones that can operate at a "world class level and are capable of working in any part of the world".

***Table 1* Are you confident about your working future?**

	No. of respondents	Percentage
Yes, very confident	37	34
Quite confident	46	42
50/50	18	17
Not confident	7	6
Not sure / have not thought about it	1	1

The university not only prepares relevant materials and projects for engineering courses that match employer requirements, but in addition, most professors provide students with examples of actual engineering situations in the field in order to better explain detailed concepts. On the whole, students are satisfied with their major courses.

Table 2 **Do you find your major interesting?**

	No. of respondents	Percentage
Yes, all the time	32	29
Most of the time	58	53
Sometimes	17	16
Not very often	1	1
Never	0	0
I would prefer to study another major	1	1

Thus, many students feel confident that their KFUPM courses and modules are chosen carefully so as to provide skills needed in the workplace in order for the graduate to be competitive. Indeed, the specialized nature of KFUPM education, in particular in the engineering fields, appeared to be underscored by the September 2014 annual report of the Saudi Council of Engineers (SCE) that revealed that Saudis only make up 6 percent of the total number of engineers registered in the country. The SCE report cites 9,122 Saudis registered with it, while there are 135,035 expatriates on its books (Arab News, 2014). In fact, students frequently point out that "they are in demand" as major Saudi companies as well as recruitment officers from multinational corporations seek to recruit KFUPM graduates because they have the necessary work-related skills.

Many undergraduates maintain that the university not only provides knowledge, it also teaches students effective time/project-management skills that are linked closely to notions of self-accountability and self-responsibility. In addition to their majors, as part of their overall university education, students are required to take two social-science courses that are provided by the Department of General Studies (DGS). The stated aim of DGS is to expand and enrich the educational experience of KFUPM engineering, science, and industrial management majors through a social science curriculum. The educational goal of this curriculum is for students to gain substantive knowledge in these fields of study, and in the process to develop their critical thinking and communication skills as well as cultivating their creative abilities. Indeed, KFUPM understands that it is important for its students to understand human behavior and the socio-political, socio-cultural, and historical processes that impact individuals and societies. Not only is it important from the perspective of the university, in fact, many students show a marked thirst for knowledge in these areas.

However, in spite of the acclaimed success of these academic programmes and methods, there are other students who find that studying too much "generalized knowledge" means that some aspects of certain subjects are not particularly useful when more detailed scientific analysis is often required. Certainly, university education enables students to develop their critical-thinking skills in particular related to their majors. Nevertheless, students complain that rote-learning is commonplace—"inserting information into a student's memory"—regardless of whether there is a practical application that can be measured successfully. Students also criticize what Alnassar and Dow categorize as "large group teaching", or traditional lectures, as entailing "one-way communication, focusing on imparting knowledge" which can be "dull, boring and repetitive" (Alnassar and Dow, 2013: 53). In addition, there is concern that a traditional teaching approach that treats students as "receivers of knowledge rather than constructors of knowledge" (Wyn, 2011: 46) might not reflect the realities of future employment, in particular as students are concerned about the rapidly changing nature of the contemporary working environment.

Depending on the specific discipline, individuals often have different perceptions of their university education. In the earlier part of their university experience some students believed that approximately eighty per cent of their course material and instruction would match employer requirements. However, after discussion with KFUPM graduates in the workplace, these individuals lowered their expectations in line with their working colleagues because it was realized that the working environment differs from university studies so the correlation between the two was lowered to approximately forty-five per cent.[iii] In addition, a number of students believe that in the Saudi working environment they will only be able to apply knowledge from specific courses as there are a limited number of these that are directly relevant to the requirements of many Saudi companies. For example, a software engineering student estimates this to be around forty per cent although he also points out that many of the practical applications he has studied might prove more relevant to the working environment outside the Kingdom. Thus, better prospects overseas may provide opportunities to utilize approximately eighty per cent of his gained knowledge and expertise. Another problem for some students is that Saudi Arabia does not have an industry that matches their majors. One individual states that his career aspirations are unclear, because the Kingdom is not one of the pioneers in his field of Aerospace Engineering. Therefore, there is a limit to what he can achieve domestically, at least for the time-being. Of course, he recognizes that he will be qualified to work abroad in the aerospace industry for companies such as Boeing or Airbus where his qualifications will "almost completely match the job", but if he remains in Saudi Arabia the match "will be much less of course".

Whilst many students agree that they study the fundamentals of their respective subjects, some maintain it is the responsibility of the employer and / or KFUPM work experience programme (Coop) to provide more specific courses in order for the student to be able to perform specific assignments. In fact, the aim of the Coop programme is to provide students with the following work-related skills and opportunities:

- Training and hand-on experience for students before graduation;
- Enhance group work, communication skills, and job-related skills;
- Expose students to the industry and business in the region;
- Bridge the gap between engineering science and industry.

Therefore, students hope that they will have the chance to consolidate their university knowledge through practical work-related tasks.

Summer and Coop Training

High academic standards and rigorous application undoubtedly prepare the individual for work-related challenges ahead, enabling him to assume any sort of responsibility and work to the very best of his ability. Nonetheless, amongst some students there appears to be a perception that their university education matches their career expectations only at a basic level. For this reason, undergraduates appreciate the valuable opportunity provided by the summer and Coop training programmes as these allow students to experience real life working situations. These programmes are a compulsory part of the undergraduate degree (although students can choose between the two programmes) and each student must successfully complete summer training or a Coop placement in order to graduate. Indeed, many senior students stress that although they have not experienced full-time employment their Coop work experience provided invaluable insights into important future career related issues.

Nevertheless, summer and / or Coop training frequently highlight a division between studies and work leading many students to argue that a great deal of their university instruction is theoretical in nature, representing "perfect scenarios", and not always related to the real world —or the actuality in the workplace. Furthermore, whether true or not, it is believed that many professors lack "practical experience" and therefore, concentrate on the theoretical; hence, there is a belief that the skills not taught at university must be acquired in the work place. Moreover, the university may teach a subject in a general way, but Coop training highlights the fact that the market actually requires more specialized skills. Unfortunately, other students note that although they study a specific type of engineering at university, during Coop the individual is usually employed as "simply an engineer" and not because of his specific area of specialization—a situation they find demoralizing.

Another problem arises when students attend interviews and notice a disparity between their studies and employer requirements with some individuals stating that they do not see a resemblance to what they have been studying at university. Indeed, job applicants remark that first impressions about most of the opportunities that they apply for are frequently "mislabelled" as most of the work responsibilities, when explained, are mundane and not at all challenging. Nevertheless, students point out that in the workplace the problems they are likely to face will be far more complicated, thus necessitating greater knowledge than they acquire from their university studies. In sum, although education at KFUPM within the students' respective disciplines is recognized as being amongst the best in the Middle East, there is concern that qualifications and career expectations will not match employer expectations due to lack of real "hands on" experience.

Career Aspirations

Students often say they expect to become "normal engineers" or would like to work in "corporate finance" with very little idea of what their future responsibilities might entail although they hope to find an "enjoyable job" that allows them to take care of their families. According to this group, finding employment with a large, well-known company and / or working as part of a team in an important one such as Saudi Basic Industries Corporation (SABIC) would be suitable particularly if they can contribute to the growth of the company. Thus, it would appear that individual students make a distinction between finding a job and creating a career path.

Table 3 **After graduating are you looking for a job or a career?**

	No. of respondents	Percentage
Job	46	42
Career	43	39
Not sure	10	9
It does not matter	3	3
Start own company	6	6

However, some are more ambitious and wish to become high achievers or "someone who could be an inspiration to youth such as Steve Jobs". A few would like to establish their own companies although admit they are not sure how feasible this might be.

Leadership

Some individuals express a strong desire to assume leadership positions although recognize the necessity of gaining experience and working their way up the ladder: "As for work responsibilities, I think all graduates need at least several months until they are ready to fulfill their work responsibilities".

Table 4 **Are you ambitious?**

	No. of respondents	Percentage
Extremely. I want to be a leader and successful	52	48
Yes, I want to do well in my career	45	41
Not much, but I take my work seriously	7	6
No, not at all	3	3

Following a period of "five working years" it is assumed that the graduate will be sufficiently experienced to begin undertaking a serious leadership role and in a strong position to achieve his goals. Furthermore, it is hoped that after five years graduates will be qualified to handle work responsibilities effectively, but in terms of actual, practical experience there is recognition that this will be learnt on a year-to-year basis.

In addition, these fledgling careers will not only constitute a challenging path on the way to becoming a team leader, but will also involve team-work and most significantly the opportunity to be creative. This is seen as a realistic goal (depending on the correlation between qualification and company); however, many students also emphasize that their aspirations not only involve attaining a leadership position, but also making an effective and productive contribution to the overall development of the Kingdom.

Table 5 **Is it important to contribute to national development?**

	No. of respondents	Percentage
Of course. That is the reason we are at KFUPM	38	35
It is my responsibility to contribute	34	31
Yes, and my family and friends expect this	16	15
I want to, but it is not possible	7	6
I do not know / care	5	5
I have never thought about this	8	8

Being Willing to Compromise

The third finding from the ASDA'A Burson-Marsteller Arab Youth Survey (2014) shows that:

> With youth unemployment an issue across much of the globe including the Arab world it comes as little surprise that survey respondents cite the spectre of unemployment as their second most pressing concern. Across the region, half (49 per cent) are concerned about the issue, demonstrating a steady increase over the last four years, up from 44 per cent in 2013 and 2012 and 42 per cent in 2011, broadly in line with rising unemployment rates. Though still high at 39 per cent, youth in the Gulf are less concerned than their counterparts in the rest of the Arab world, with oil-rich governments providing some reassurance.

Many individuals assert that for a KFUPM graduate it will not be a problem to find work because they are proficient in English. In addition, KFUPM graduates state they have priority over graduates from other Saudi universities when it comes to employment opportunities. Nevertheless, although KFUPM graduates maintain that it is far easier for them to find employment than their peers from other Saudi universities, many students are under no illusions that the "dream job" may not materialize. Indeed, Ramady points to the problem of "structural unemployment amongst educated citizens" which is acute given the Saudi age structure and numbers of graduates trying to enter the job market (2010: 382).

Table 6 **Do you think you will find work in your major?**

	No. of respondents	Percentage
100% (definitely)	24	22
80% (most likely)	49	45
50% (possible)	24	22
25% (unlikely)	9	8
Do not know / not sure	2	2

In fact, many individuals comprehend that after graduating a first position might not be a perfect fit and the spectre of unemployment may force some graduates to compromise. Furthermore, a certain amount of perseverance may be required in order to locate a position that exactly matches the candidate's qualifications. This might require accepting employment outside the candidate's field until he has the opportunity, or luck, to find a more suitable position. Another solution is to work in a closely related field such as an aerospace graduate taking a position as a mechanical engineer. Therefore, compromise might be necessary before eventually locating a position related to the graduate's major. This might mean accepting a job that an individual does not really want to do; however, it is also recognized that these "unwanted" opportunities facilitate self-awareness as well as adding a great deal to the personal learning curve in terms of the knowledge a person gains regarding what he knows he wants to do and more importantly, what he does not want to do. However, compromise would not be an acceptable option for some students who say they are only willing to work in their respective disciplines and would be most unlikely to accept a job that is of little interest or far-removed from their field of expertise.

Comprise might also entail relocating to another part of Saudi Arabia or even a period overseas. However, young Saudi men are often unwilling, or find it extremely difficult, to relocate to find a job, as Bosbait and Wilson note because "there is a marked preference for Saudis to work close to home" reflected in strong kinship ties and obligations (2005: 542). Even if a young man wants to move away, it is often very difficult due to pressure from family and relatives to remain nearby. In fact, some undergraduates are persuaded to get married and produce children whilst still studying. Others much prefer to remain "at home" and if forced to move away for employment/Coop opportunities consider the situation "disappointing", but they still believe that they can remain self-motivated although say that the quality of their work output might be affected detrimentally.

Salary

Increased urbanization and the housing shortage coupled with the rising cost of living have made life in the Kingdom difficult for some constituencies. Although some students would accept a position in a different field from their area of specialization, as well as being willing to take a lower than expected salary, they still point out that a good salary is a major factor in taking a job. Furthermore, the offer of a reasonable salary is an attractive proposition regardless of the actual nature of the work as long as the work environment is safe. On the other hand, if an individual has a job that he does not like because he cannot find one that matches his qualifications then he might be working to earn money, but his heart will be telling him to search for a position suited to his qualifications. One student summarizes this situation:

> In the unfortunate event that I do not find the job of my dreams, I would be willing to compromise and take a job I did not really like, but at the same time keep on exerting an effort to find better opportunities. I hope never to sell my soul to the devil to earn a living.

Unfortunately, and all too often, career aspirations are often tempered by a strong dose of reality: "Actually, I do not expect much, but at least expect to be well-paid".

Other Alternatives

Another option is to continue with academic study and this is believed to be practical due to the standard of KFUPM undergraduate qualifications. For this reason, individuals sometimes consider the option of continuing their studies overseas, possibly on the King Abdullah Scholarship Program, as they see this as "more than realistic" and one of the best options.

Coop training is also understood to be beneficial as additional industry experience can prove invaluable in graduate studies. In addition, going into business could also act as a springboard for further academic study.

Although the Saudi government has a strong policy to encourage entrepreneurship and the setting up of new businesses, particularly those associated with the knowledge economy (Al Ohali and Burdon 2013: 164), KFUPM students believe that one way to increase the numbers of Saudis entering the workforce and simultaneously enhance job satisfaction is more emphasis and encouragement from the government in setting up entrepreneurship schemes.[iv] However, they note that there are many barriers to the development of entrepreneurship in particular technology start-ups. A 2014 student "Globalization" project cites market entry regulations, shortage of funds and lack of market experience as three of the principal problems facing young entrepreneurs. In addition, the complexity of laws and regulations and not knowing "who to talk to" pose real challenges to young people with innovative ideas.

Other Concerns

Many students look to the future with varying degrees of apprehension. They point out that questions related to career aspirations are "extremely hypothetical" even though most of them believe they are mature enough to have a well-defined plan. The more optimistic note that "it may take time", but eventually they hope to find a suitable job. On the other hand, the pessimistic say it may be necessary to take any kind of employment as long as it is legal.

One of the students' main concerns is *wasta*. As Yamani notes, "the practice of *wasta*, economic benefits through family connections, is widely criticized by young Saudis" (2011: 120). Indeed, the perennial problem of *wasta* is of great concern to those who believe they do not have any and / or sufficient *wasta* to get promoted. Some students state that they "know" that after five working years they will be in the same position due to a lack of *wasta*. If you are lucky enough to have enough *wasta* they argue "then you will be fine and get your annual upgrade", but if you are unlucky you will remain in the same position forever.

A final problem, as some astute students note, is that KFUPM is an all-male campus. Hence, everyone including students, faculty, secretaries, cooks, and cleaners is male and increasingly enforced gender segregation in society is at odds with the contemporary working environment. As one senior student comments:

> I have friends who found themselves working with Saudi women and it was very difficult for them at first. I had a Coop interview with Zain and to my great embarrassment was interviewed by two Saudi women. I simply did not expect it and coming from Riyadh I am not used to this.

In short, unpreparedness for real life could have consequences for male graduates in dealing with others, particularly increasing numbers of working Saudi women, once they enter the workforce. Furthermore, as Ridge (2014: 121) notes, young Saudi men are faced with increasingly strong competition in the labour market from better qualified female nationals (as well as expatriates). Thus, these students have identified an important issue that is largely ignored as they prepare for the transition from education to employment.

Personal Fulfillment, Challenges and Self-Motivation

The idea that study and / or work can bring happiness and a sense of personal achievement clearly resonates with many students; one student even quotes Bertrand Russell "Even the dullest work is to most people less painful than idleness". If someone is passionate about his/her discipline/ job then real happiness can be achieved. In fact, some argue that there is absolutely no doubt that study/work is an essential ingredient for happiness in any person's life as it lends a sense of purpose and at the very least helps to maintain a routine as well as some sense of order even when other things in life go astray.

Table 7 **How important is work for you?**

	No. of respondents	Percentage
Very important	66	61
Quite important	41	38
Not important	0	0
Only the salary is important	2	2

However, this notion is balanced with the view that happiness cannot be found through study/work alone because an individual needs self-awareness that doing something positive and constructive is an indispensable requirement to achieve self-fulfillment. Likewise, some students maintain that everyone can find a way to create his/her own supportive environment. The key point is to be positive and think positively as this habit will be reflected in "personal psychology", thereby providing the necessary drive to perform well and tackle new challenges.

Indeed, studying at KFUPM triggers fulfilment because the university system, rules and courses are considered "professional". Undergraduates are taught to be responsible for their own learning and overall university conduct, i.e. they are made to feel accountable for their actions and this in turn influences the student to be professional in his conduct. However, according to some students, whilst it is not possible to live without study/work, at the same

Table 8 **Do you enjoy studying?**

	No. of respondents	Percentage
Very much	13	12
Usually	25	23
Sometimes	31	28
Never	0	0
It depends on the subject	25	23
It depends on the instructor	11	10
I prefer self-study rather than classes	4	4

time it does not necessarily bring happiness as certain conditions need to be met for this to be realized; for example, being allowed to study a preferred major as well as receiving proper support and motivation within the university environment. Study/work is not always associated with happiness, according to some individuals, as passing examinations and / or completing projects produces a sense of relief rather than happiness; relief that the student is on track to graduate. Furthermore, if attending seminars is only about grades and doing university community service only about "showing off" then for some this does not constitute happiness and / or a feeling of community. Certainly, some individuals believe that they are unhappy because there is too much work to be done at KFUPM compared to other (Saudi) universities. Others who have participated in the KFUPM exchange programme point to their positive social experiences at US universities such as Georgia Tech as a reason for frustration. They highlight the concept of "entertainment and learning together" citing the different kinds of activities, students club and events that are available to students in the US; ones which they feel are absent at KFUPM.

At this point in their lives some students feel that they will be happier after they graduate and are able to start work, but acknowledge that feelings of unhappiness might also be linked to not knowing which career is going to suit the individual. Thus, study/work related unhappiness could be closely related to a lack of concrete "life plans" made early on in life. There is also awareness amongst some, particularly senior students, that they are in fact better suited to the working environment than the university; they see themselves as "an employee rather than a student" because they believe they are more productive when working. They point to the variety of tasks and personal relationships with managers, other employees, subordinates and customers as frequently being more satisfying and real. Nevertheless, these individuals concede that it would be difficult to find happiness in an unsuitable position, but adjusting goals and expectations as well as establishing a rapport with colleagues could help to foster happiness and personal fulfilment even in a less than perfect job.

Being Challenged and Self-Motivation

The study environment at KFUPM is seen as challenging, but it is understood that this benefits the student as it prepares him for the real world with all its accompanying tests and stresses. Challenges at university improve the work ethic as well as assisting an individual in coping with future work responsibilities as without these challenges the ambitious individual will neither be able to fulfil his career/life goals nor assume a leadership role. Therefore, KFUPM challenges are seen as beneficial precisely because students expect far more difficult challenges in the workplace. In fact, students recognize that as new employees they will face new problems which cannot be solved by manuals or books; in other words they will have to think and come up with solutions. However, some believe that the competitive university environment helps to bring the best in them and these students would like to experience a similar working environment providing that it is not "unhealthily over-competitive". For example, they would not enjoy working for a company where an employee is always "on edge" because he has to deliver on a daily basis or else lose his job. Hence, being challenged is frequently beneficial, according to some students, because it motivates the individual, but they point out, at other times it can also demoralize.

Students contend that university grading system is designed to be challenging as it makes the individual work hard in order to be better than his classmates. Furthermore, because the university environment is perceived as being stressful students often realize that the stress needs to be managed effectively. Moreover, this "way of challenging students" has a profound impact on the student's personality by establishing an "understanding of competition" that will benefit him later in his career. It can also instil high levels of self-belief and leadership. On the other hand, some individuals reject this approach, stating that they are not ambitious at all and do not want to be leaders. It is their opinion that the challenge at KFUPM is to "show how strong you are" and even though they acknowledge that they will confront multiple work-related challenges they believe that the working environment will be easier than that of the university. According to this group, it is important to be realistic about personal ambition and to set reasonable limits based on self-awareness as related to personal qualifications and skills. They also ask whether it is necessary to be a leader as some individuals prefer a subordinate role. Although they realize that they are challenged at KFUPM, and some agree this is personally beneficial, they are skeptical that they will face the same challenges at work "especially here in Saudi Arabia".

Self-Determination Theory (SDT) makes a basic distinction between two types of motivation: intrinsic and extrinsic motivation (Ryan and Deci, 2000: 55). Whether intrinsic, the student does something because it is interesting and enjoyable, or extrinsic, the student does something because it leads to a separable outcome, many undergraduates believe self-motivation is an important factor on the road to success and being challenged is beneficial because it motivates the student to try and excel. However, being self-motivated can be difficult and it is argued that many students only complete tasks because they are instructed to do so rather than for intrinsic reasons. Even individuals, who consider themselves fairly ambitious and motivated, in comparison to their KFUPM peers, do not necessarily want to become leaders if being a leader is fraught with compromise and undue responsibility. Others remark that they consider themselves motivated and ambitious with leadership aspirations, but only if they can be guaranteed a position within their field of specialization and not be forced into either a "boring assignment" or even worse "routine bureaucratic tasks".

To conclude, there is a perception that being challenged at university is beneficial and can even be enjoyable. However, many students understand from talking to working friends that what follows graduation can be a disappointment, in particular if the individual is not challenged in the workplace. This often leads to demoralization, for example, the experience of this recent graduate: "This represents me: take an emerald and keep it in the dark place where it cannot shine and nobody can see it so nobody benefits from it".

Being Taken Seriously and Marginalization

Is it easy being a young Saudi man? As in any society, the answer depends on an individual's circumstances whether at university, in the workplace or at home. Whilst some students contend that by and large it is easy being a Saudi man the majority point to a variety of problems that impact negatively on all aspects of life. Certainly, the prestige attached to KFUPM means that students' opinions are considered (to a degree) so many students believe that their position is unique in Saudi Arabia because they are taken seriously by the university—as demonstrated by constructive meetings with the university rector and senior officials. Furthermore, on 24 February 2014 Eastern Province governor Prince Saud bin Nayef visited KFUPM to listen to student concerns. When the author asked students who were present at a question and answer session with Prince Saud whether his predecessor (Prince Mohammed bin Fahd) ever did the same thing, the unanimous answer was "never". In fact, Prince Saud's visit appears to indicate a changing attitude towards societal issues amongst third generation princes. However, others strongly disagree and do not believe that the university considers their views seriously, although some concede that this might depend on the student's discipline. Hence, whilst some students feel that university instructors listen to them, as well as family and friends, in wider Saudi society recognition is considered to be "negligible"—unless the topic is related to religion, customs and / or traditions. Nonetheless, others speculate that "not being listened to" might be because young men simply do not know how to deliver important messages to those in positions of authority. In contrast, and frustratingly, a young Saudi can get his/her message across to a global audience through social media networks.

A frequent complaint is "Nobody wants to hear from us or is willing to help us achieve our goals". This problem is exacerbated by the lack of activities or events for young Saudi males, as most of these are "family only". Nevertheless, self-believe is seen as necessary in order to make others "believe in you" as the individual needs to see himself as part of the community, with responsibilities to that community and society. However, if the decision-makers deem that young people are in no position to participate in the socio-political process, then young Saudis will neither feel that they are being listened to nor taken seriously. In sum, from the perspectives of these young men, the problem appears to be that an individual might be taken seriously by the university, but not by the authorities and / or society.

Marginalization

Marginalization by society is understood to be problematic although to what degree is contested; for example, some students claim that young men are as equally marginalized as young women. However, many students accept that being male in Saudi is an advantage as the gap between men and women is significant, but they still argue that marginalization of young men by society in terms of trust remains a problem, in particular with regards to "appropriate behavior". This explains the reason for not allowing young men into shopping malls as the worst is expected of them so "even after the king gave his word" security guards routinely block young men from entering. The situation is exacerbated by the dearth of public entertainment with young men complaining that there are no cinemas, funfairs or similar parks where they are allowed entry.

Marginalization can also vary depending on location so even though Saudi constituencies are controlled by their societal / tribal norms "more than religion" a great deal depends on the region. Hence, on the west and east coast men and women enjoy greater freedom than in the centre (Najd) or in the far north and south. Societal and religious norms are also often blamed for the marginalization of young people of both genders and some point to a "misunderstanding" of Islam, particularly as anything "new" is considered *haram* (forbidden). One student argues that whatever the location or norms if an individual is accepted by his/her constituency then it is possible to live as a human being, but when rejection occurs then the individual will be treated as "a nobody".

The most politically aware students, and levels of political awareness amongst many students are extremely high, claim that all Saudis are marginalized by the government regardless of background because the government is "frightened of allowing more socio-political space and freedom" as this will weaken its hold over the state. Murphy notes that "Today's twenty something Saudis are not the first to criticize their leaders", but "their enhanced awareness of a multiplicity of views on any given subject has made them feel more entitled to question authority"—Murphy attributes this to cyberspace (Murphy, 2013: 19–20). Furthermore, the government refuses to address contentious socio-political issues as it does not wish to be in conflict with the religious establishment, thereby threatening the stability of the system. In fact, young Saudis worry that the situation could become worse because most of the population is young and this will exacerbate problematic societal issues. In addition, other societies take into consideration the opinions of their young people, but in the Kingdom this is not happening because the decision-makers, including government officials and the media "are not open-minded". Another problem is that "all ambivalences" in Saudi society come from the fact that in general, society does not take its responsibilities seriously and accepts the situation that only a few decision-makers determine the future of the country.

Finally, one individual says the sad part is that most young men and women are not aware they are being marginalized even though society thinks these young people are "needy" due to their aspirations and ambitions. This assumption is incorrect as many young people only demand what is best for them and their society "especially as youth is the future".

Conclusion

Many students consider that KFUPM's reputation, both domestically and internationally, is a distinct advantage in assisting them to find gainful employment especially in comparison to graduates from other Saudi universities. Indeed, many students state that the university prepares them "in the best possible way" to enter the workplace and although self-evaluation is difficult due to lack of experience, many students feel that after graduating they will be ready to go out into the "real world" and utilize their knowledge, skills and abilities. In addition, the KFUPM environment shapes a student's world outlook because interaction with people from an array of different cultures, and with extremely different values, helps to broaden minds. For many, KFUPM is seen to provide a challenging environment that helps produce educated young men who can enter the workforce and most importantly, feel confident to contribute to the Kingdom's development and growth. In consequence, the university assists the student to operate in a globalized world.

Nevertheless, there is a high recognition that all aspects of Saudi life are undergoing rapid transformation as a result of the impact of globalization. As Yamani points out "globalization is expanding the space for Saudi youth" creating a highly complex challenge for the government" (2011: 122), but also causing many students to feel varying degrees of anxiety about entering the workplace. In fact, many are concerned about operating effectively in today's competitive world as they are also acutely aware that life in the Kingdom is changing rapidly and the consequences this will have for their working lives. Some of the more astute students point to several potential problems. For example, the ability to operate effectively might be it dependent on the organization. If the graduate is lucky, he will be employed by one with high standards that provides its employees with the necessary orientation and training. Indeed, some argue that work efficiency depends more on the work environment and the nature of the job than on the graduate (however willing) as some companies do not give the employee the chance to be effective. Indeed, it has already been noted that graduates who find themselves in a well-paid job, but with little of consequence to do become seriously demoralized.

There is also the problem of being valued as an individual. This paper argues that many young Saudi men believe their opinions and views are of no consequence to those in positions of authority. Clearly, this constitutes a serious oversight, in particular when these opinions are relevant, insightful and carry weight. Research undertaken for this study illustrates that KFUPM undergraduates want to be taken seriously; they want their opinions heard and they want the chance to participate constructively. In short, it is evident that many KFUPM students do not simply want jobs; they want rewarding careers that contribute to individual, corporate and / or national development.

In conclusion, Saudi Arabia's greatest resource is not oil; rather it is the Kingdom's educated and ambitious young people many of whom are more than willing to participate in the decision-making process. Certainly, young people and the Kingdom face many challenges, but these can also be viewed as opportunities. According to these KFUPM students, it is the role of youth to expand the economy, to innovate and think creatively in order to help build their country. It is to be hoped that they have the opportunity to do so.

Notes

i Multiple KFUPM student sources, 2013–14.

ii Questionnaire 109 respondents: 49% senior students; 38% junior students; 13% sophomore students.

iii Students in other disciplines cite different figures, for example: 70% Industrial System Engineering; 40% Industrial Engineering; 20–40% Aerospace Engineering.

iv KFUPM has its own Entrepreneurship Institute. See, KFUPM Entrepreneurship Institute - An Introduction: http://www.youtube.com/watch?v=cxsCFQ7dAIM. Two thirds (67 per cent) of young Arabs believe people of this generation are more likely to start a business than in previous generations, as access to higher education improves the skills of youth, and governments and banks provide much-needed funding to help set up private companies. The split is similar across the Arab world with 66 per cent agreeing with the statement in the Gulf and 66 per cent in non-GCC countries (ASDA'A Burson-Marsteller 2014).

3

The Perception of Young Emiratis on *Emiratisation*

Lorraine A. Charles

Introduction

The transformations which have occurred in the UAE since the discovery of oil have been unmatched by any other modern state. The formation of the federation in 1971 orchestrated by Sheikh Zayed bin Sultan al Nayhan, the UAE's founder and first ruler, as well as the discovery of oil, brought about the necessity to quickly evolve into a modern state, with modern institutions and bureaucracies. Like the other Arab Gulf states, during the UAE's early developmental stage, rapid transformation resulted in a mismatch between the human resource capital and the financial resources of the state. This rapid development was facilitated by the importation of large "armies of expatriate workers, foreign advisors, and entire industries under the auspices of import- substitution industrialization" (Kamrava, 2012). This resulted in "islands of efficiency" - as coined by Hertog in his description of Saudi Arabia – within large inefficient systems (Hertog, 2010), particularly affecting the public sector. Yet, the economic development that has occurred in the UAE has been unprecedented. Due to a local population that has become increasingly educated[i], and a dramatic increase in population, the employment demands have become crucial. Between 2000 and 2012, the UAE's population increased from 3 million to over 9 million (World Bank, 2014), with Emiratis currently making up approximately 12% of the UAE's population. While this increase is mostly due to the growth of expatriate labour, the numbers of UAE nationals, particularly those with tertiary qualifications, entering the job market is increasing every year.

Since the 1970s, Emiratis have been predominantly employed in the public sector. Previous research has documented that the preference for private sector employment is due to several factors. First, the labour market environment of the public sector is skewed in favour of UAE nationals, with salary and benefits disproportionate, not only to the skills and education of the employee, but also to the job. In general, UAE nationals are deemed by employers in the private sector to have lower skills and competencies, as well as poorer work ethics in comparison to expatriates (Al-Waqfi & Forstenlechner, 2010), yet are usually paid higher salaries. Furthermore, working hours in the public sector are also comparatively shorter than in the private sector -the private sector has a 48-hour workweek, in comparison to a 40-hour week in the public sector. Second, cultural norms are also thought to play a part in preference for public sector employment among UAE nationals. It is seen as prestigious to secure a job in the public sector, with employment in the private sector seen as unsuitable for UAE nationals. This, as will be discussed below, is a result of the influence of occupation on social status for UAE nationals. Another influencing factor is the mismatch between local graduates and the employment expectations of the private sector. Recently, employers have expressed concern that recent university graduates lack the skills required for the labour market. UAE universities are graduating students who lack skills, such as teamwork and analytical thought, which are necessary for today's labour market. In other words, the skills possessed by many UAE graduates are "not compatible with what is needed for professional work in the private sector" (Al-Waqfi & Forstenlechner, 2014: 171), an issue that further hinders private sector participation. As suggested above, many UAE nationals view private sector employment as unsuitable, mostly due to the structural issues discussed above, and also the fact that it is predominantly staffed by expatriate workers. Therefore, working for the government is deemed the only suitable type of employment for UAE nationals. Yet despite this preference for public sector employment, government jobs are not being created at a rate sufficient to accommodate the demand from UAE jobseekers. Currently private sector employees are overwhelmingly non-national, with Emiratis comprising less than 1 per cent (Sabry, 2013), accounting for about 22,000 of the four-million private-sector workforce (Salama, 2013). This translates to only 10% of working aged UAE nationals employed in the private sector (UAE Labour Force Survey, 2014). The public sector cannot accommodate the new job market entrants. The unemployment rate amongst Emiratis is 14% (Sabry & Zaman, 2013), and is even higher for the young nationals and particularly females, where unemployment is 25%, comprising 80% of all unemployed nationals (Swan, 2013). The rate of unemployment amongst nationals remains high despite the UAE's economic prosperity and the ability of the economy to create new jobs. Between 1995 and 2005, the economy created an average of 116,000 jobs annually. Notably, the majority of these (89%) were created by the private sector, which contributed 103,000 jobs annually (Rahahleh, 2012). As the public sector jobs are scarce, there is a great need for UAE nationals to work in the private sector.

The Emiratisation policy pursued by the UAE government, introduced in the early 1990s, has received much publicity. Despite investment in the policy and various initiatives the government has implemented to promote private sector employment, most UAE nationals still prefer public sector. This reluctance on the part of UAE nationals to work in the private sector has thus resulted in renewed efforts on the part of the government to promote its nationalization policies. While there has been no formalized method to implement Emiratisation, the UAE government has established various initiatives (National Human Resources Development and Employment Authority, Emirates National Development Program and Abu Dhabi Tawteen Council) with the mission of promoting this policy and encouraging private sector employment among Emiratis. These bodies not only support UAE nationals in their search for jobs, but also provide training in order to bridge "the gap between the educational outputs and labour market requirements" thereby providing "the public and private sectors with qualified skilled national employees" (Abu Dhabi Tawteen Council, 2014). Initiatives such as these have had limited success as demonstrated from the low proportion of nationals in the private sector. In 2012, a new initiative, Absher, was established, again with the purpose of increasing the numbers of Emirati nationals employed in the private sector. This initiative differed from previous attempts as it targeted students currently in tertiary education. Along with campaigns at national universities where the benefits of private sector employment were highlighted, it provided training for new graduates with guaranteed private sector jobs upon completion of the period. This focus on university students as the target of the current Emiratisation initiative is the motivation for this research.

Previous research has been conducted to examine the Emiratisation process from a business and human relations perspective, with analysis providing details of the flaws of the programme and detailing reasons why private sector employment is unpopular amongst UAE nationals. There has also been analysis of the policy decision of the state in relation to nationalization policies. Past research has also focused on employers, both national and non-national, gauging their perception of Emiratisation, as well as the rationale for their recruitment policies. While there has been a study investigating the perceptions of young UAE nationals, it examined the factors that determined their career choice and perceptions of this decision. However, there has been no research examining the extent to which young nationals understand the policy of Emiratisation, and linking these perceptions to the UAE's 'ruling bargain' through an examination of the rentier state theory, but more specifically the rentier mentality. This research aims to fill this gap in the literature. An understanding of how young nationals perceive Emiratisation could provide insight into why the policy has had limited success and could highlight further measures which need to be taken to address the issue of Emiratis engaging in private sector employment. This study will initially examine the characteristics of the policy. Next, the premise for this investigation will be discussed using a constructivist perspective of the rentier state theory as the theoretical framework, and connecting this to the UAE's ruling bargain. The results of the investigation will then be discussed and an examination and the implications of the findings will be analysed. This research concludes with an assessment of the current strength of the ruling bargain and its relevance to the perceptions of this group of young Emiratis, as well as policy recommendations that may contribute to greater success of Emiratisation.

The Essence of Emiratisation

While many definitions have emerged for Emiratisation, most commonly it is defined as an interventionist policy on the part of the UAE government aimed at reducing reliance on expatriates and encouraging Emirati workers into the private sector, whilst addressing the social issues arising from this shift in the labour market. Thus, it is a means by which the UAE government tackles the unemployment of Emiratis and the demographic imbalance. In most research, Emiratisation is solely defined in terms of labour market reforms. However, Forstenlechner et al. (2012) describes Emiratisation beyond job creation for UAE nationals. Essentially, Emiratisation has been described as having three main elements – labour market reforms, economic diversification and education reforms (Forstenlechner et al., 2012). It is this definition of Emiratisation, encompassing the elements of labour market restructuring, economic diversification and education reforms that will be utilized in this research, and which may be most useful in assessing the challenges to the success of the policy.

The first element of Emiratisation encompasses the implementation of labour market reforms such as quotas for private sector organizations, restricting certain visa categories for expatriates and the allocation of certain jobs for nationals only[ii]. In effect, the quota system mandates that in the private sector a specified proportion of jobs be set-aside for UAE nationals. The banking sector has perhaps been the most successful industry in terms of achieving Emiratisation quotas. Currently, approximately 32% of all bank employees are Emirati, accounting for 53% of the 22,000 UAE nationals employed in the private sector (Al Ghurair, 2013). However, despite levels of Emiratisation attained by the banking industry, labour market reforms have had limited success. The structural impediments to these reforms have been discussed above, and suffice to say, as will also be seen from the following discussion, without the other two elements of the policy (education reform and economic diversification), nationalization of the workforce would continue to be a challenge.

The second tenant of Emiratisation is diversification of the economy away from dependence on the hydrocarbon sector. Gulf states have been described as largely allocative (Luciani, 1990), meaning that the functioning of the state is disconnected from the local economy. Despite the fact that the non-oil GDP currently accounts for two thirds of its economy (UAE Interact, 2013a) and that growth of the non-oil sector is at higher rate than the hydrocarbon sector (Emirates 24/7, 2013), approximately 80% of the government's total revenues still originate from the export of fossil fuels (Schiliro, 2013). This means that the hydrocarbon industry remains the driving force of the UAE's economy, and therefore economic diversification is vital. For the UAE, diversification entails a shift from one sector (hydrocarbon sector) to another, and generally from a primary to secondary and tertiary sectors. In effect, the UAE government aims to "drive toward economic diversification, as this is the nation's surest path to sustainable development in a future that is less reliant on oil. This means expanding new strategic sectors to channel our energies into industries and services where we can build a long-term competitive advantage" (UAE 2021 Vision, 2010:17). Moreover, economic diversification means that new jobs would be created, thereby serving the purpose of labour market restructuring and supporting the Emiratisation policy.

The third element of Emiratisation is education reform as a means to match labour market requirements. A report by the World Bank stated that the GCC education system had failed to provide students with skills relevant to the labour market (World Bank, 1999). In 2007, Abu Dhabi embarked on an overhaul of the entire education system and, as the UAE is striving to create a knowledge-based economy with workers equipped to meet the demands of the labour market, it has thus invested heavily in education. In fact, in 2010 the education sector (schools and higher education) received the highest share of federal funds (22.5%), amounting to approximately $9.8 billion (UAE Interact, 2009). However, this financial investment in education has yet to benefit the labour market. While it is recognized that change in education systems occur slowly and it may take a generation for genuine gains to be realized, research has nevertheless shown that the existing education reforms and the investment "has not succeeded in bringing about sufficient improvements in the quality of the public education system to satisfy the demands of the knowledge economy" (Farah, 2012:4) and as Forstenlechner and Rutledge concluded "the mismatch between the needs of the private sector and the skills of most graduates at both the secondary and tertiary levels is considered to be one of the principal obstacles to both economic development and diversification" (Forstenlechner & Rutledge, 2012: 41). Thus, if Emiratisation is to succeed, the importance of three elements – labour market reforms, economic diversification and education – needs to be realized and measures taken to ensure that each is prioritized.

The UAE is currently at a crucial point of development. It has a rapidly increasing population (3% annually) and a high national unemployment rate (approximately 14%). Yet there are hundreds of thousands of jobs created annually (mostly in the private sector) unavailable to many nationals due to a lack of skills. This has resulted in increased pressure to provide employment to nationals and to restructure the labour market. Therefore, in order to overcome these challenges, the structural barriers to the employment of nationals need to be addressed. The rapid economic development in the UAE has created jobs in industries such as the energy and petro-chemical, travel and tourism, trade and construction, yet many young nationals lack the required skills to fill these roles. Hence education reform, particularly an emphasis on vocational training, a fledgling element of the UAE's education system, has become crucial to address the skills gap. Therefore economic diversification, although significantly benefiting economic growth, has not alleviated employment demands among UAE nationals, as they are unprepared for the jobs that have been created. Thus, the concept of Emiratisation viewed only as labour market restructuring needs to be reconsidered to also include the elements of economic diversification and education reforms.

Re-Examination of the Rentier Mentality from an Alternative Perspective

The rentier state theory (RST), initially described by Beblawi and Luciani (1990), is the most commonly used framework to analyse state-society relations and governance in resource-rich states that generate most of their income from external rents. While the RST has been generally accepted as the preeminent theory in the analysis of political behaviour of oil producing Gulf States and Iran, many challenges have emerged due to some of its apparent failings. Although the RST seemed to describe, for example, the lack of democracy in Saudi Arabia and the UAE, it has failed to explain such phenomena as the presence of a parliament in Kuwait and the existence of trade unions in Bahrain and Oman. Moreover, it has not adapted to fit the economic shifts that have occurred more recently in Dubai, Bahrain, Qatar and Abu Dhabi. Therefore, with the changing nature of the influence of oil on some of these traditionally hydrocarbon-dependent states, RST has also evolved as an analytical framework to better describe the current nature of the Gulf States. While Ross (2001) outlined three effects of rents, which acted to prevent democracy in oil states, others (Hertog, 2010; Valeri, 2009) have accepted the core tenants of RST as a component of theories to explain state function and behaviour, as opposed to a comprehensive paradigm for the entire political structure. Theories of 'late rentierism' have emerged to attempt to better address the changes that have taken place in the Gulf States in the early 21st century, the influence of globalization, the new economic initiatives upon which the states have embarked, as well as demographic and employment issues (Grey, 2011). According to Grey, this model describes a state that is "more responsive, globalised and strategic in its thinking" (Grey, 2011: 24). These characteristics illustrate late rentierism, and provide an analysis of a state whose action can be examined beyond external rents. States have matured with the ruling elite more responsive to social changes for reform, with entrepreneurship being encouraged, and with economic diversification becoming central to economic development. In fact, states have begun to plan for future generations, as the establishment of Sovereign Wealth Funds attests.

The premise of this research will be based on a constructivist perspective of the RST. In order to examine the RST paradigm from this perspective, consideration is given to what Beblawi (1990) described as a rentier mentality. The caricature of a citizen of a rentier society as "a member of a special group, who though he does not partake in economic production receives nevertheless a share in the produce and at times a handsome share" is often used to describe the citizens of the GCC. Beblawi continues, "the distinguishing feature of the rentier, thus, resides in the lack or absence of a productive outlook in his behaviour" (Beblawi, 1990: 86). This implies a disruption of the work-reward relationship, where reward is not related to work or risk bearing, but to chance or situation (1990: 88). In the case of the UAE, nationals are influenced by this lack of productive outlook. This nature has a profound effect on the nationalization policy of the UAE. Thus, this project will argue that the notion of the rentier mentality is one that is socially constructed and greatly influenced by the 'ruling bargain[iii].'

Examination of the rentier state theory, as postulated by Beblawi (1990) can be divided into three core tenets. First, rent situations dominate the economy, although not completely. This characterisation applies to the UAE as, although the non-oil GDP exceeds that from oil, 80% of the country's revenues still originate from the hydrocarbon sector. Moreover, rentier economies rely on external rent in order to sustain the economy without the necessity of a strong productive domestic sector. While the UAE's economic diversification efforts have, to some extent, produced domestic industry and reduced complete dependence on the revenues from fossil fuels, it has yet to overcome structural problems and become completely independent from external rents. Second, only few are engaged in the generation of this rent (wealth), with the vast majority engaged in the utilization or distribution of the wealth. In the case of the UAE, the lack of general entrepreneurship and innovation, as well as the prevalence of public sector employment among UAE nationals, means that the majority of the population is unable to contribute directly to wealth creation. This, in turn, can potentially have a negative effect on Emiratisation, as with the majority of national population unable – because of inadequate education and skills, or unwilling, due to the 'rentier' nature of the individual – to become engaged in productive work, nationalization efforts may be in vein. Third, the government is the principal recipient of the external rent in the economy and plays the central role in its distribution to the population (Beblawi, 1990: 87-8). This arrangement is particularly significant in the UAE and is central to the ruling bargain. The distribution of external rents by the UAE government – in the form of public sector jobs with high salaries and low expectations, subsidies and privileges which originate from being a UAE national – all come in exchange for loyalty to the state. While it can be argued that this arrangement has recently come under scrutiny with the advent of the 'Arab Spring', the basic structures remain largely in place. In fact, the UAE government, as a way to avoid general discontent within its population, has increased incentives to reinforce loyalty to the ruling elite and state. There have been increases in public sector salaries – 100% increases in some cases – one off payments to all citizens and creation of new jobs within the already-saturated public sector.

The RST, including its newer versions, can be criticized for considering only the economic perspective of state behaviour – including the power structures – of the GCC states and, to an extent, overlooking non-economic aspects such as the effect of the ruling bargain on rentier mentality. A constructivist perspective may provide better answers. The UAE government encourages a system where the population benefits from the rents accrued, so that there is no call for greater decision-making ability and more political freedom. Yet, they now desire citizens to become productively employed and contribute to the diversification of the economy through, among other things, employment in the private sector. However, the government continues to encourage reliance on the state through subsidies, comfortable public sector jobs, and more recently quasi-private sector employment, as well as guaranteeing the well being of citizens. Nevertheless, the rulers are encouraging entrepreneurship whilst discouraging over-reliance on the state. A constructivist perspective of the rentier state theory may provide an alternative perspective on this contradiction.

Constructivism allows the analysis though examination of perceptions, ideas and, by extension, culture. Whether culture shapes the socially constructed notion of perceptions and ideas of a given society, or whether culture is shaped from these, is debatable. This concept of the influence of culture and ideas and its effect on national and the international system is constructivism's contribution to International Relations. Essentially, it offers a potential "approach for uncovering those features of domestic society, culture, and politics that should matter to state identity and state action" (Hopf, 1998: 914). It can offer a framework for thinking about the nature of social interaction without "providing substantive explanations or predictions of political behaviour until coupled with a more specific understanding of who the relevant actors are, what they want, and what the content of social structures might be" (Finnemore & Sikkink 2001: 393). Thus, state actions are shaped by state identity and, by extension, the socially constructed notion of societal culture. As Finnemore and Sikkink assert, while constructivists agree that "state identities are constructed within the social environment of international and domestic politics", they disagree on the definitions of identity and the weight of international versus domestic environments that actually shape these state identities (2001:399). It should be noted, however, that Checkel (2004) warns against ignoring the international environment, promoting an exploration of the interactions between domestic and international systems instead. This implies that an understanding of how things (culture, society, state) are constructed is an essential element in explaining how states behave and what causes political outcomes. Constructivism understands that actors are shaped by the social environment in which they exist. This notion can be adapted to the RST and used to examine how and why rentier states have been shaped the way they have, and what the consequences of their actions have been. Thus, this analysis can give an alternate view of the behaviour of the state and answer some questions that the RST, taken in isolation, struggles with. An examination of rentier nature of the states, and more specifically the UAE, through a constructivist lens gives an alternative perspective on their behaviour, taking into account the influence of social interests. It allows for analysis of the reason for the behaviour, rather than only a predictor, while also considering perceptions in analysis of state behaviour. Therefore, by viewing the RST through a constructivist paradigm, this project can explore how and why perceptions and the ruling bargain, argued to be socially constructed, can affect Emiratisation.

Methodology

Students from Khalifa University (KU) in Abu Dhabi were selected as the sample group in this research. Khalifa University students represent an interesting case study of UAE university students for many reasons. First, it is the only co-educational tertiary government institution in the UAE. The fact that many parents choose to send their children to study in such an environment may indicate that the families may be relatively open minded (this is particularly relevant to the female students) than those that opt for single-sexed tertiary educational institutions. Furthermore, the entry requirements for KU are higher than other government universities (federal and Abu Dhabi government). Students are required to attain an IELTS 6 for full entry into undergraduate programs (as opposed to IELTS 5 at the Higher Colleges of Technology and Zayed University) and a minimum grade in math at high school and to pass in the university math entry exam. This implies that the students at KU have often been top of their classes in high school. Moreover, as an engineering university, KU students have the potential for employment in both private and public sector jobs. Therefore, their perception of Emiratisation is of great interest, as they are prime targets for such an initiative. Although students in all years and nationalities were surveyed, the results were analysed and categorized according to nationality, only taking into account data for UAE nationals.

Surveys: An online survey was addressed to all students at Khalifa University. It comprised of 20 questions based around the research questions, as well as demographic questions so that categorization was possible. Initially 30 students were questioned to gauge the appropriateness of the questions. Next, questions were compiled and placed online via Survey Monkey and piloted with 5 students chosen by the researcher, to assess the accessibility of the language and the tone. Upon completion the students were asked whether they had understood the questions (language and tone) and if they felt any were too difficult to answer or confusing. The updated online survey was emailed to all students from the Khalifa University Office of Research Support. This call was sent out twice, at two-week intervals. With permission from university management, the researcher also spoke directly to students in two humanities classes to encourage participation in the survey. At the end of the survey period, 140 responses were obtained, representing approximately 13% of the student body, with 120 (86.3%) of the respondents being UAE nationals.

Follow-up focus group study: This part of the research questioned students in more detail about issues surrounding Emiratisation and the ruling bargain (the term was not directly mentioned in the interviews but discussions surrounded issues related to its existence and influence). In total, 23 students (10 females and 13 males) from all academic years were interviewed in 7 groups of between 2 and 5 students. There were 2 female groups, with 5 students in each group, and 5 male groups with between 2 and 4 students in each. The groups were initially arranged to contain between 4 and 5 students, but due to scheduling, the groups had to be changed to accommodate the students. The focus groups were recorded and lasted between 40 and 60 minutes. The interviews were semi-structured to allow students to engage in discussion and further explore issues around their perception of Emiratisation and how this may affect them as they embark on employment. The research was first introduced, thereby allowing students to understand the background to the study.

The students were encouraged to engage in discussion about the issues, with little prompting from the researcher. In the second part of the interview, the students were presented with a list of options and asked which they perceived to be the biggest problem facing Emirati workers and why. They were again allowed to engage in further discussion.

Results and Analysis

This research hypothesizes that there is a lack of understanding of the policy of Emiratisation and that the ruling bargain is a significant contributor to the perceptions of these young UAE nationals. As discussed above, analysis of the perceptions of this group of young Emiratis is conducted through the lens of a constructivist view of the RST, but more specifically, the rentier nature of the citizen of a rentier state. Moreover, the ruling bargain is assumed to result from the rentier structure of the political system. This paper argues that these characteristics (rentier nature and effect of the ruling bargain) are socially constructed, as they are not inevitable, but the product of social forces. These social forces, it can be argued, are due to the origins of the society, for example, the tribal origins. While it would be myopic to argue that the current phenomenon – skewed work-reward relationship, perceptions of deserving privilege, the effects of the ruling bargain – are completely due to the history of the peoples and societies described using the RST, it could be argued that these are socially constructed. Thus, the behaviour of the state, as described through the paradigm of the RST, is affected by social interests of the society. A constructivist perspective of the rentier nature, therefore, assumes that perceptions, actions and beliefs exist due to the social function. This perspective will be taken into account throughout the analysis.

There is a general lack of understanding of Emiratisation.

The survey confirmed the general lack of understanding of the meaning of the policy of Emiratisation among young nationals. Less than half (45%) could identify the policy as embodying the three tenants of employment, education and economic diversification, while 30% deemed it solely as for employment of Emiratis. Broken down according to the emirate of origin, approximately half of those respondents from Abu Dhabi, Sharjah and the Northern Emirates (Ajman, Fujairah, Ras al-Khaimah, and Umm al-Quwain) were able to identify the policy as embodying the three elements, while only 25% of those respondents from Dubai were able to do so. Interestingly, approximately half of respondents from Dubai believed the policy's main objective was job-creation for nationals. This could be explained by the fact that Dubai already has a relatively diversified economy and residents of Dubai may not perceive their wealth to completely originate from income from the export of fossil fuels. Moreover, in Dubai, education reform has not been as aggressive as in Abu Dhabi, and therefore the link between education and employment may not be as reinforced to Dubai residents as for those in Abu Dhabi. The focus groups reiterated this lack of understanding of the meaning and scope of the policy. There was very little consensus among those interviewed about the meaning of the policy. One interviewee perceived Emiratisation to mean a "*minimum percentage of workers (in a company) who are local in order to get visas for non-locals*," while another believed that it was "*a way for locals to get jobs easier.*" While some correctly assumed that the policy was aimed to encourage locals into employment in the private sector, there was confusion over the intended target by others. The majority believed that the focus was both sectors, commenting that "*Emiratisation is (a way) to increase the numbers of locals in (the) private and public sector and reduce the number of non-locals*," and was "*aimed at all sectors to reduce expats*" giving "*advantage to Emirati people in all work places – public and private sector*". Furthermore, there was some understanding that the policy extended beyond employment. When asked about what the policy of Emiratisation entailed, one interviewee stated that it was the "*empowering (of) the economy of the UAE by (the) Emirati workforce,*" while another recognized that Emiratisation was part of the UAE's 2021 vision because '*the economy will depend more on the Emirati work force.*" This confusion about the meaning of the Emiratisation policy was evident throughout all of the focus group interviews. These conflicting opinions on which sector the policy targeted – a strong consensus that public sector was the intended benefactor – was justified by the belief that the public sector was more crucial to the country's domestic security, the "*public sector controls how the country is ruled and I don't want non-Emiratis to work in the public sector…the country should be ruled by Emiratis*". There was also the belief that because the public sector is financed directly from the UAE's income, it should be reserved for citizens, "*the public sector gets the money from the funds of the country, so the government would want to spend the funds of the country on the people, rather than give it to someone else…the government would rather have foreigners making their own money by investing rather than giving them the funds of the country.*" This sense that it was the government's responsibility to look after the citizens, and in return they would aid in the development of the country was evident throughout the research. This highlights the strength of the ruling bargain in the UAE (discussed below), where the welfare of the citizens, through guaranteed public sector employment, is the responsibility of the rulers. Interestingly, there was a belief that the public sector provided greater economic benefit to the country. The "*public sector impacts the country more, so the private sectors consists mostly of business and we don't need business to develop the country…we need more like oil.*" Not only does this show the misperceptions among this group of young Emiratis about Emiratisation, but a lack of awareness about the UAE's leaders desire for economic diversification. These misconceptions highlighted not only the lack of information disseminated to young people about Emiratisation, but also the belief that as citizens, they deserved to benefit from the resources of the state, thus reinforcing the strength of the ruling bargain and corresponding with the rentier nature. It can be argued that this acceptance of the relationship between state (rulers) and citizens has been constructed by social interests, and as constructivism contends, this understanding is an essential element in explaining the behaviour of the individual.

While respondents understood the need for Emiratisation, only a minority (8% of respondents) understood the scale of the issue facing the UAE – that only 10% of working-age Emiratis were employed in the public sector, and comprised 1% of this workforce. Approximately two thirds of respondents thought that 30% to 50% of Emiratis were employed in the private sector. This lack of awareness of the scale of the issue could stem from the education system, where inquiry- based learning is not practiced, thus students do not seek information about their environment, often resulting in a lack awareness of domestic (and international) issues, even ones which directly impact them. Furthermore, the majority of respondents (approximately 50%) believed that the main motivation for the implementation of the policy was to tackle the unemployment rate among Emiratis, while 17% felt that the policy was primarily aimed at addressing the demographic imbalance by reducing the number of foreign workers in the UAE. A further 18% believed that the policy's primary aim was to guarantee loyalty and commitment of UAE citizens to the government. Although the importance of employment of Emiratis and the demographic imbalance was recognized as the main motivation for the policy by the majority, the fact that a significant minority believed that the aim of the policy was the assurance of loyalty of citizens, again highlights the strength of the ruling bargain. When questioned about their perception of the ultimate goal of the policy, 32% of respondents believed that the government's aim was the employment of all Emiratis, while a further 31% felt that economic factors were core to the implementation of the policy. Additionally, 30% of respondents believed that security factors prevailed as the primary reason for Emiratisation, with 20% and 10% respectively believing that reducing the influence of foreign workers and foreign countries were significant factors in the implementation of the policy. When questioned about what they perceived would be the outcome if the policy were unsuccessful, the greatest concern was for the domestic security of the UAE. Half perceived that a failure of the policy might result in greater foreign influence in the UAE with expatriates gaining political power. The perceived fear of the threat presented by expatriate workers has long been a security concern for the rulers of the GCC, UAE included (Janardhan, 2009: Cooke, 2014). This fear, to some extent, has hastened the efforts of nationalization. This perception that expatriates were a threat to the UAE was evident throughout the research.

Despite efforts to encourage private sector employment, three quarters of respondents had preference for the public sector upon graduation. In fact, the focus groups revealed that the students had the perception that the Emiratisation policy, and thus private sector employment, was mostly aimed at Emiratis with lower education levels, "*those with lower education will benefit from Emiratisation because they have no work. In our case, the government needs local engineers so we will work for the public sector.*" As future engineers who are well educated and qualified, the students believed that they were necessary for the development of the country and thus, a public sector job was where they could best contribute. Therein lies a contradiction in education, "while the right sort of education will equip individuals with the skills needed for the private sector, obtaining more qualifications (especially tertiary-level ones) tends to increase salary expectations and does little per se, in the regional context, to change a given national's sectoral preferences" (Forstenlechner & Rutledge, 2010: 41). In other words, students whose education and skills equip them for private sector employment still have a preference for public sector employment despite the initiatives encouraging the former, in essence contradicting the process of Emiratisation. Furthermore, although the majority (75%) surveyed indicated a preference for public sector employment, there was a significant minority, 25%, who would initially seek private sector employment upon graduation. When examined according to Emirate of origin, over 85% of respondents from Abu Dhabi and Sharjah had preference for public sector employment, while proportions were lower among respondents from Dubai and the Northern Emirates. In both these emirates, approximately 35% of respondents had preference for private sector employment upon graduation. This may indicate a shift in perception about employment among these young Emiratis and a growing interest in private sector employment. This also reveals a difference in the perception of private sector employment between the different emirates. Dubai and the Northern Emirates, with less income from the export of oil, might arguably have been less affected by a rentier mentality. Moreover in Dubai, private enterprise is well established, with a long history of trade and the presence of foreign companies well accepted in the society, resulting in perhaps less of a stigma among UAE nationals to work in the private sector compared with Abu Dhabi. Of particular interest is the almost 60% that said that they would be happy to look to private sector employment if no public sector job were available, whilst 30% would continue with further studies. Interestingly, the proportion of those respondents from Dubai and Sharjah who would opt for further studies was greater than that from Abu Dhabi and the Northern Emirates; approximately 40% of those from the former would opt to continue their studies as compared with approximately 25% from the latter. There was also a difference between genders when questioned about alternatives to public sector employment; 64% of males would opt for the private sector compared with 53% of females, while 21% of males and 40% of females would opt for further studies instead of public sector employment. Yet another interesting finding was the proportion of respondents who would choose to open their own business as an alternative to public sector employment. Overall, 6% of respondents would choose this option. Yet, the numbers vary significantly depending on the emirate of origin of the respondent. No respondents from the Northern Emirates expressed a desire to start a business, while 4% and 7% respectively from Sharjah and Abu Dhabi expressed this desire. In contrast, 14% of respondents from Dubai expressed the desire to be entrepreneurs. This does not come as a surprise given the nature of Dubai compared to the other emirates. Its focus on economic development through financial services, industry and trade, coupled with its relatively lazier-fair economic system creates an environment which is perhaps more suitable for entrepreneurship than the other emirates and thus the relatively high proportion of respondents who would opt to start businesses may be a reflection of this. Furthermore, the focus groups revealed that those who preferred private sector employment believed that that as ambitious young professionals, this sector had more to offer. "*I think if I am ambitious and seeking opportunities, I will get it more in the private sector. I will be shining more, not only locally in the UAE, but internationally,*" was the response from a female student from Dubai. However, the private sector was perceived to be less accessible than the public sector, as the interviewees thought that without experience, it would be difficult to secure a job, "*most private companies ask for people who have experience, so most graduates go to the public sector.*" When questioned about the changes necessary to make the private sector more appealing, as expected, the overwhelming majority agreed that the salary and benefits needed to be changed to be equivalent to what they would earn in the public sector. However, there was also a concern that training and professional development were lacking in the private sector, "*we prefer to work for the government because they will educate us.*" This stemmed from the belief that the UAE government cares about the citizens and sought their interests, while the private sector was primarily financially motivated, "*the government has more training and development for the locals because they care about us, the private (sector) cares about the money.*" This belief that the government would provide, educate and care for them is encompassed in the ruling bargain. The government has projected itself as the benefactor, and in return the beneficiaries are unquestionably loyal. Yet another reason why private sector employment was less attractive was the belief that jobs in this sector were insecure. The interviewees cited the effect of the 2008 financial crisis in Dubai where many people had lost their jobs, thus justifying their preference for public sector employment as job security, "*the private sector has a risk.... they might close,*" "*government jobs are more stable.*" The notion that jobs in the private sector are less secure than government jobs is commonly held, not only in the UAE, but also in other parts of the GCC. The above discussion alludes to a lack of understanding about Emiratisation among the students. This perception – the notion that as nationals they are entitled to public sector employment – is part of the ruling bargain, and is one mechanism for rent distribution. An examination of the RST through a constructivist perspective highlights that the rentier nature is one that exists due to the social function. In other words, this relationship has been constructed to accommodate the function that the rulers are politically autonomous to the ruled and the rents are provided in exchange for this autonomy.

The 'ruling bargain' as it stands in the UAE contributes significantly to the perception that young Emiratis hold about Emiratisation.

The effect of the 'ruling bargain' and the 'rentier nature' of the individual on Emiratisation, the theoretical framework on which this research is based, are investigated through the lens of constructivism, where perceptions are thought not to be inevitable, but the result of social forces. One distinct effect of the ruling bargain, and hence rentier nature, is the responsibility of the state for the welfare of the individual. This was evident in the discussions about the understanding of Emiratisation. This perception was also evident when directly questioned about where the responsibility for job creation lay, where an overwhelming majority (73%) believed the onus was on the government. When further examined according to the emirate of origin and gender, interesting insights are observed. A greater proportion of respondents from Sharjah and the Northern Emirates compared with those from Abu Dhabi and Dubai believed that the responsibility for job creation lay with the state – approximately 90% for the former two emirates compared with approximately 60% for the latter. The difference in perception according to gender is also distinct. 79% of females compared with 65% of males believed that the government was responsible for creating employment. The disparities observed according to the emirate of origin can perhaps be attributed to the differences in development and sophistication of the economy and society among the various emirates in the UAE. Abu Dhabi and Dubai are both relatively wealthy and, although differing in the main sources of income, have a well-developed economy with a wide range of employment options available. The Northern Emirates (including Sharjah in this group), in contrast, have more limited employment opportunities and lesser-developed economies. The differences in gender perceptions can be attributed to the nature of the UAE society, where males play a paternalistic role and in general take responsibility for females. Generally, this sense of responsibility for the family is transferred to the male heads of families. Thus, for females, this responsibility is perhaps shifted toward the state for matters beyond the family. This shifting of responsibility from the individual to the state reaffirms the unique relationship that exists in rentier states with a firmly established ruling bargain, which as has been argued, is socially constructed. This dependence on the state was also reasserted by the preference of majority of the respondents (76%) for public employment, because of the assumption that the public sector provides sufficient remuneration with low expectations from the employee. The belief commonly held was that government jobs – with high salaries, shorter working days and long holidays – were guaranteed for UAE nationals. In fact, some went so far as to describe the work-reward relationship that is used as a caricature of Emiratis, "*Emiratis think they can sit and sleep at home and still get a high salary.*" This stereotypical perception of the work-reward relationship was also highlighted in the discussion:

> Respondent AM002: *Even if the job description says that they would get 20 000Dhs (£3500), they would apply and ask for more than this. That is kind of the big problem.... there is always the issue of wanting extra incentives.*
>
> Researcher: *Do you think locals have the perception that they deserve more money than non-locals?*
>
> Respondent AM003: *Sadly, yes. Even though we are locals, sadly yes... for some reason many locals actually think that... they are better than non-locals and deserve a higher salary.*

The sentiment that the low employment expectations in the public sector made it favourable to the private sector was reiterated in many of the focus groups, and was summed up by one of the interviewees. "*Emiratis don't like to struggle, especially men.*" This skewed work-reward relationship is the core of the rentier nature described through the RST and has persisted due to the ruling bargain. It could be argued that this social construction is favourable to the rulers, as UAE nationals who fit within the paradigm of this skewed work-reward relationship, would tend to submit political participation in exchange for a comfortable existence.

Respondents were also questioned about the challenges facing Emirati workers. Overwhelmingly, in both the survey and focus groups, 'wasta'[iv] emerged as the most serious problem, with 78% of surveyed respondents agreeing that it was either a significant or very serious problem. There was little difference in perception among the various emirates about the significance of this issue. In Dubai and Abu Dhabi, approximately three quarters of respondents reported wasta to be a significant or very serious problem, while in Sharjah and the other Northern Emirates, this proportion was slightly higher at approximately 83%. There was little distinction in the difference of perception between the genders, with 75% of males and 80% of females believing wasta to be a significant or very serious problem. In the focus group interviews, there was also agreement that wasta was problematic. The mistrust of locals in positions of responsibility was attributed to the prevalence of wasta.

> Respondent AM003: *Wasta is the main problem for everything; because of wasta, who knows if the Emirati doctor actually studied or got his job because of wasta. Because of the period where many locals got their jobs because of wasta, this left the impression that many locals can't do their job. The common stereotype of locals is that we are stupid.*

Furthermore, wasta was thought to be responsible for the poor performance of many nationals, as it places people in positions for which they are unqualified. This reflects the research on the effect of wasta on workplace performance. It was found that when unqualified candidates obtain jobs solely on the basis of influence or connections, it creates an environment that feeds frustration among qualified and well skilled individuals (Mohammad & Hamdy, 2008).

> Respondent FM001: *Wasta kills the performance and productivity.*
>
> Respondent FM002: *Wasta gives jobs not based on merit and puts the wrong people in the wrong place.*
>
> Respondent FM003: *(It) kills productivity of those more qualified for the job as it gives advantages (on things rather) than on merit.*

Moreover, respondents believed that wasta was not only responsible for underperformance of the individual, but would also obstruct the economic growth of the UAE, and thus have a negative effect on Emiratisation. Economic growth can be considered to be "spurred by a social system that prizes fairness and effectiveness – fairness being societally determined; effectiveness governed by the market" (Cunningham & Sarayrah, 1994: 39), thus in contradiction to the perceived benefits of wasta.

> Respondent BF001: *Wasta is the biggest problem. It hinders the development of the country. Unskilled people who get higher positions.*
>
> Researcher: *Do you think this happens a lot?*
>
> Respondent BF001: *Yes.*
>
> Respondent BF002: *It will discourage Emiratis from working hard and is detrimental to Emiratisation.*

The dependence on 'wasta' highlights the propensity for the transference of responsibility away from the individual (this responsibility is transferred either toward the state or another individual). This shifting of responsibility is encouraged by the state, claiming obligation for the wellbeing of the citizen, in return gaining absolute loyalty, thus reinforcing the ruling bargain and fitting within the paradigm of the RST.

The converse perception of wasta was also evident during the interviews. This is also recognized in research. While it is obvious that wasta has the negative effect of "entrenching the haves and excluding the have-nots" serving as an "affirmative action for the advantaged", it also has a positive side – that of humanizing bureaucracy (Cunningham & Sarayrah, 1993). While it was recognized that wasta gave an unfair advantage to some Emiratis to the detriment of the individual, the UAE's development and Emiratisation, it was accepted that the recipient of the benefits gained from wasta often overlooked these negative effects, "*if you have wasta you think it's OK, if you don't you think it's unfair.*" The interviewees recognized that wasta was part of Emirati culture, ingrained in its society and not always destructive.

> Respondent HM001: "*we all benefit from wasta; in my grandfather's time if he wanted something he would ask the sheikh…not all wasta is harmful.*"

It was also acknowledged that wasta could be an illegal practice, but in the UAE it was perceived that it was practiced within the constraints of the law.

> Respondent CM001: *Wasta is not a problem. It is a good thing. Here in the UAE, wasta happens in a good way, not bad like in Saudi Arabia.*
>
> Researcher: *Explain why it's good here.*
>
> Respondent CM002: *Our wasta in the UAE is not above the law; our wasta is just to make something running in its procedure but faster. For example, you want to*

apply for a house…people who put the form, sign the form on this waiting list, nobody will take this form…so wasta making this form….finish faster.

Researcher: *So you think wasta is a good thing?*

Respondent CM002: *Only in the UAE perspective, not other perspectives…*

The practice of wasta can be traced back to the tribal origins of the UAE and has continued to play a major role in all aspects of society. To some extent, it is sanctioned within the institutions of the state and encompassed as part of the ruling bargain. Historically, the practice of wasta involved conference with the rulers creating a sense of equality between rulers and the ruled. This sense of equality was expressed in one of the focus groups.

Respondent CM002: *All the people (are) the same…even Respondent CM001* (referring to the other interviewee*), he is (a) Sheikh… you read his name…but my money is same as his…even he having more because his father doing work, it's not because he is Sheikh he is taking money…his father (is an) engineer and he working and he becoming like this…we are in the same level…all…some small difference between people…I have a Range Rover…our sheikh has a Range Rover also…some normal people have Rolls Royce, and the Sheikh has a Rolls Royce…and this is not different. We believe they have more money than us, but we are not feeling we are poor. In this country…we are not feeling we are poor.*

This is sense of equality and familiarity with the leaders is an important aspect of the ruling bargain. This, combined with the acceptance of the practice of wasta in UAE society, reinforces the social contract and fits within the RST model. Moreover, 'wasta' is a socially constructed phenomenon and can be argued to exist as a by-product of social interests. In this case, the social interests lay in the maintenance of the status quo – the rulers bearing the responsibility for guiding and supervising society, while the ruled forgo any political participation in return for a share in the rents.

It can be argued that perceptions are socially constructed, and these are a result of the environment, which in turn is influenced by the nature of the political and social structure of the state. Therefore, the perceptions of this group of young Emiratis are a direct result of the political and social structure, which has been formed as a result of the functioning of this society and thus socially constructed. The characteristics of the young Emiratis observed throughout the research fit within the paradigm of the rentier nature described in the RST. The perceptions of Emiratisation observed in this research reinforce the continuing relevance of this theory to describe the UAE. Most significant was the impact of the ruling bargain on the perceptions of this group. The belief that the state is responsible for their welfare, that they would be cared and provided for by their rulers, in exchange for service and loyalty to the state – characteristics of the UAE's ruling bargain – was strongly evident, thus supporting its influence in the perceptions of Emiratisation.

Conclusions and Recommendations

The desire of the state for nationalization of the workforce is an ambitions aim. Whilst the young Emiratis who were questioned as part of this research believed in the virtues of the policy, the majority were unwilling to partake in its goals. On one hand, they trusted the state's decisions and its policies and were overall very loyal and grateful for all the benefits bestowed upon them. Yet, they seemed adverse to the main intention of the Emiratisation policy – private sector employment. They held the perception that only in public sector jobs would they be looked after and that this was their entitlement as citizens; the essence of the ruling bargain, which this research argues is socially constructed and is a result of the political and social structure of the UAE. Moreover, the paradigm of the rentier mentality was evident, reinforcing the continued relevance of the RST, although viewed through a constructivist perspective to understand the behaviour of the individual and the state.

In order for the UAE to accomplish its aims of Emiratisation, several measures can be taken. Recommendations can be classified according to the three elements – labour market reforms, education and economic diversification – that are important for Emiratisation. Moreover, the recommendations made would also contribute to changing the perceptions of young people about Emiratisation and encourage more alignment between the desire of the rulers and citizens.

A. Labour Market Reforms

1. Genuine engagement between the state and the private sector to devise strategies to recruit and retain UAE nationals.
2. Abolish the quota system for the private sector and introduce a more appropriate measure of Emiratisation that focuses on issues such as professional development and career progression.
3. Clear and transparent human resource policies, in both the public and private sector.
4. Implement job-sharing systems and/or flexible working hours.
5. Implement professional development (PD) and training with qualifications and skills gained through PD recognized and used in performance management for the purpose of promotion.

B. Education Reforms

1. Align the skills required for employment with education via the implementation of the National Qualifications Framework.
2. Implement vocational education in addition to the academic stream.

3. Encourage critical thinking and questioning in the curriculum by introducing more humanities in the K-12 system.
4. Develop entrepreneurship and innovation as subjects in the education curriculum.
5. Focus on soft skills in the education curriculum.

C. Economic Diversification

1. Encourage entrepreneurship in the form of SME's.
2. Reform of the bankruptcy law.
3. Abu Dhabi and the Northern Emirates need to adopt a more open economic model, similar to Dubai.
4. Continue investment in Sovereign Wealth Funds.

The UAE urgently needs to continue its nationalization policies. Along with the above recommendations, if the UAE is to be successful in its efforts for Emiratisation, the ruling bargain needs to be renegotiated. The incentives that the population is provided due to the very nature that they are citizens needs to be reconsidered if the government's aim for a population who are productive is to be realized. However, the recent instability in the region, including the recent Islamist threat, has made the government less willing to renege on the benefits the state has traditionally provided. However, reliance on the state and belief that as, UAE nationals, they should be provided for, act in direct contradiction to Emiratisation. There needs to be a shift in behaviour and perceptions among UAE nationals for this policy to be successful. The goals of the government to diversify the economy and provide suitable jobs for all citizens are indeed noble, yet without a change in perception, success is unlikely. However, the government of the UAE, and other governments in the region, are facing a dilemma. Renegotiation of the ruling bargain, relinquishing dependence on the state for livelihood, is required if the state is to achieve its aims of Emiratisation. However, this could cause resentment among the population, a situation that could be dangerous, given the current political climate in the region. Therefore, although the UAE government has clearly defined goals, a renegotiation of the ruling bargain in order to achieve these goals may need to be postponed.

Notes

i The enrolment in further education of UAE nationals has increased from 1582 in 1980 to 121626 in 2012 (UNESCO, 2014).

ii The implementation National Qualification Framework, due to be launched later this year, has identified a list of professions that are reserved for Emiratis only.

iii The existence the 'ruling bargain' in the UAE is thought to be due to the rentier structure of the system. In essence, it is said to define patterns of state–labour and society relations and has established expectations and obligations that have proved deeply resilient (Yousef, 2004: 6). It defines the relationship between the rulers and the ruled, defining and limiting the rights and duties of each. In exchange for the distribution rents, which provide prosperity and an economically satisfying life, the rulers expect almost complete autonomy from the society and full control of politics. Thus, the UAE rulers assure citizens generous social security programs, which include strict workforce regulations, the guarantee of state employment with relatively high wages and generous benefits, as well as investment in projects for the development of infrastructure, education, industry and culture in exchange for unquestioning loyalty and the political autonomy of the ruing elite.

iv Wasta is a form of nepotism that is embedded in Middle Eastern societies, including in the UAE. It implies that social connections are used to obtain benefits that would otherwise not be obtained (Mohammad & Hamdy, 2008). Wasta is practiced openly in the Middle East (including the UAE) without any apparent sense of remorse, guilt or shame (Barnett et al, 2013).

4

Cross-National Heterogeneity of Hofstede's 'Arab Countries'

Adel Hamaizia

Introduction

This study will investigate heterogeneity across two countries within Hofstede's (1980) 'Arab countries' regional cluster, that were included in his seminal work concerning national culture and workplace values. Hofstede's (1980) study remains the most commonly used tool for cross-national analysis, consequently a replication of his methodology, including the duplication of his survey and the usage of his formulae to score two of his cultural dimensions, will guide this study.

Firstly, the paper will define national culture and will introduce and highlight strengths and weaknesses of Hofstede's (1980) research, with a particular focus on its shortcomings and limitations. This will include Arab specific limitations, and will be followed by a review of literature concerning traditional and more contemporary influencers on workplace values and national culture in the region.

The study will then display the research aims and objectives and the proposed methodology. This will illustrate the proposed tests that will enable cross-national analysis between the Kingdom of Saudi Arabia (KSA) and the United Arab Emirates (UAE) with reference to the 'power distance' and 'uncertainty avoidance' dimensions of national culture. The results will also be compared with Hofstede's (1980) original 'Arab countries' cluster.

The results of the tests will be analyzed and discussed in order to seek explanations for heterogeneity, or alternatively homogeneity across these countries, including within-country differences concerning national and non-national workers and those working in public and private sectors in KSA and UAE. The study will conclude with reemphasis and summary of key findings, with limitations of the study being highlighted and avenues for further research proposed.

Literature Review

Defining Culture

Scholars have defined the notion of culture as having numerous and variously inclusive definitions (Kroeber and Kluckhohn, 1952; Mulholland, 1991; Bock, 1999; Vinken *et al.*, 2004). However, Hofstede's (2001) definition will be employed for the purpose of this study, as it is the most recognized by management scholars (Mead and Andrews, 2009). His definition outlines culture as "the collective programming of the mind that distinguishes the members of one group or category of people from another" (Hofstede, 2001, p. 9).

Hofstede's (1980) Framework: Timeless or Archaic

Hofstede's (1980) model published in his book, *Culture's Consequences*, was based on research that "compared work-related values across employers in branches and affiliates of IBM" (Mead and Andrews, 2009, p.35) in over 50 countries and three regions including 'East Africa', 'West Africa' and 'Arab countries'. It is his focus on the 'Arab countries' that will be paramount to this paper. Survey responses from over 116, 000 employees were gathered between 1968 and 1972. The model takes a quantitative approach, whilst the values are expressed through behaviour and "may not be consciously articulated" (ibid).

Hofstede (1980) developed indices that provided four universal dimensions/values which enable comparisons to be made across national cultures (See Table 1), subsequently ranking 'nations' through their scores (see Appendix 1). One further dimension was later added to the framework, namely Confucian Dynamism. The dimensions are positively highlighted for tapping into embedded cultural values, allowing for noteworthy comparative analysis across cultures and perhaps, most importantly, the framework's parsimony, clarity and resonance with managers (Koen, 2005; Kirkman, Lowe and Gibson, 2006; Mead and Andrews, 2009; Minkov and Hofstede, 2011). Conversely, the framework has been denounced for "reducing culture to an overly simplistic four or five dimension conceptualization" (Kirkman, Lowe and Gibson, 2006, p. 286).

The study has garnered the greatest attention in its field, and is the largest cross-cultural research conducted hitherto. It has received the most notice from business scholars due to its substantial empirical support and high research quality (Sivakumar and Nakata, 2001; Fougere and Moulettes, 2006). Smith (2002) describes the framework's profound influence on cross-cultural studies, while Trompenaars (1993) credits Hofstede with "opening management's eyes to the importance of the [cross cultural management] subject" (Kirkman, Lowe and Gibson, 2006, p. 285).

The model's plaudits reinforce the use of Hofstede's framework over alternative comparative models (Kluckhohn and Strotdbeck, 1961; Hall, 1976; Laurent, 1983; Trompenaars, 1993; Schwartz, 1994; House et al. 2004). Although the model remains

Table 1 Culture Dimension Definitions

Dimension	Definition	
Power Distance (PDI)	The extent to which the less powerful members of organizations and institutions accept and expect that power is distributed unequally. The basic problem involved is the degree of human inequality that underlies the functioning of each particular society.	
	High Power Distance	**Low Power Distance**
	◆ Austria	◆ Malaysia
	◆ Denmark	◆ Slovakia
	◆ Israel	◆ Philippines
	◆ Ireland	◆ Russia
	◆ New Zealand	◆ Mexico
Uncertainty Avoidance (UAI)	The extent to which a culture programs its members to feel either uncomfortable or comfortable in unstructured situations. Unstructured situations are novel, unknown, surprising, different from usual. The basic problem involved is the degree to which a society tries to control the uncontrollable.	
	High Uncertainty Avoidance	**Low Uncertainty Avoidance**
	◆ Denmark	◆ Belgium
	◆ Jamaica	◆ El Salvador
	◆ Singapore	◆ Greece
	◆ China	◆ Guatemala
	◆ Sweden	◆ Portugal
Individualism versus Collectivism (IDV)	The degree to which individuals are supposed to look after themselves or remain integrated into groups, usually around the family. Positioning itself between these poles is a very basic problem all societies face.	
	Individualism	**Collectivism**
	◆ USA	◆ Guatemala
	◆ Australia	◆ Ecuador
	◆ UK	◆ Indonesia
	◆ Canada	◆ Pakistan
	◆ Hungary	◆ China
Masculinity versus Femininity (MAS)	The distribution of emotional roles between the genders, which is another fundamental problem for any society to which a range of solutions are found; it opposes "tough" masculine to "tender" feminine societies.	
	Masculinity	**Femininity**
	◆ Slovakia	◆ Norway
	◆ Japan	◆ Netherlands
	◆ Hungary	◆ Sweden
	◆ Austria	◆ Costa Rica
	◆ Venezuela	◆ Chile
Long-term Orientation versus Short-term Orientation (LTO)	The extent to which a culture programs its members to accept delayed gratification of their material, social, and emotional needs.	
	Long-term Orientation	**Short-term Orientation**
	◆ China	◆ West Africa
	◆ Hong Kong	◆ UK
	◆ Japan	◆ USA
	◆ Taiwan	◆ Canada
	◆ South Korea	◆ Philippines

Source: Adapted from Hofstede, 2001

synonymous with cross-national analysis, it is said to be both undervalued and overused, and has faced a number of criticisms ranging from obsolescence to methodological flaws (Williamson, 2002; Peterson, 2003).

Due to the evolving nature of culture, criticism of Hofstede's model has included accusations of obsolescence regarding the 1980 findings (Shenkar, 2001; McSweeney, 2002; Smith, Peterson and Schwartz, 2002; Nakata, 2009). Meanwhile, Hofstede suggests that recent replications do not show any loss of validity, stating that his dimensions "are assumed to have centuries-old roots" (Hofstede, 2002, p. 2; Siew et al., 2007, p. 168).

This criticism may be comprehensible with relative shifts amongst nations occurring over the years, with the argument put forward that "only if on a dimension one country leapfrogs over another will the validity of the original scores be reduced" (Hofstede, 2001, p. 36).

Furthermore, it is important to account for the phenomenon that is globalisation, which drives the free movement of peoples and has been the force behind the fusion of cultures, with many citing a quasi-convergence in some excessively globalised locations (Movius, 2010). Multiculturalism "is a level of analysis, which Hofstede, Trompenaars etc. have not considered in their work at all" (Jacob, 2005, p.524). Sivakumar and Nakata (2001) similarly criticize Hofstede for ignoring within-country cultural heterogeneity.

Using nations for the study of cultures has been frowned upon in relation to the overlooking of subcultures (Smith, 2002; Kwek, 2003). Adler (1997) condemns Hofstede's failure to mitigate parochialism and ethnocentrism whereas Mead and Andrews (2009) criticise Hofstede's 'nation state' as a component of analysis, which is said to compel synthetic limitations on the concept of a cultural group. This criticism is accepted, whereas it is conceded that "they [nation states] are usually the only kind of units available for comparison and better than nothing" (Hofstede, 2002, p. 2).

Mead and Andrews (2009) commend Hofstede's model in controlling its informant population over such a large spectrum of cultures, with survey respondents coming from a single company (IBM). According to Smith, Dugan and Trompenaars (1996) some strong MNC corporate cultures may override or conflict with national culture more than others, however, Hofstede (1994; 2009) explains that local values are always likely to be dominant.

Further factors to consider concerning survey respondents, include the claim of a response bias, arising from the fact that "some of the questionnaires were completed within groups and not individually" (McSweeney, 2002, p.103). This could result in the conceptual outcomes of groupthink, conformity and social desirability where 'appropriate' and not 'genuine' responses may be given. The majority of the respondents also worked in sales, marketing and administrative roles within IBM, thus provoking a further biased methodological factor to take into consideration (Koen, 2005; Fougere and Moulettes, 2006; Hofstede, 2011[i]).

Hofstede's IBM exertion is best summed up by an anthropologist stating that "Hofstede's work is used and admired at a very high level of generalisation... there is perhaps no other contemporary framework in the general field of culture and business that is so general, so broad, so alluring, and so inviting to argument and fruitful disagreement" (Chapman, 1997, pp. 18-19).

This distinguishes the model as a pioneer of broader thought when comparing cultures (quantitatively) at a high level of generalisability, and suitable for rudimentary insight, whilst referring to the dimensions for in-depth or serious managerial decisions, likely to be beyond the model.

Hofstede's 'Arab Countries': Pertinent or Extraneous

Hofstede's (1980) 'Arab countries' region cluster generated 141 responses (79 in 1969 and 62 in 1972) from a range of countries including Egypt, Iraq, Kuwait, Lebanon, Libya, Saudi Arabia and the United Arab Emirates (Hofstede, 1997; 2001).[ii] The relatively low numbers of respondents were limited by the number of employees working at IBM in the region at the time. Further to the earlier mentioned broad-spectrum weaknesses and shortcomings cited in reference to Hofstede's (1980) model, a particular issue not yet highlighted and pertaining to the Arab world (alongside the East and West African countries), is the clustering and amalgamation of these nations into a single region and cultural indicator.

Hofstede (2001; 2011) concedes the grouping of the 'Middle East region' as a problem, albeit, as a problem that could not be helped or circumvented. Following the surveys received in 1969 and 1972 in the 'Arab countries', when an extension to his country list was proposed, "it turned out that IBM had not only inadvertently wiped the tape with the raw survey data, it had destroyed the data printouts as well. The only data printouts that were saved pertained to the total region" (Hofstede, 2001, p.52).[iii] In an interview, Professor Geert Hofstede (2011) regretted the blunder and even before, he acknowledged that "now the region is culturally less homogenous than would be desirable" (Hofstede, 2001, p. 52).

Demographics across the 'Arab countries' vary greatly (See Table 2), exhibiting diverse economic and population characteristics. Three of the seven countries studied by Hofstede, which made up the amalgamated responses that formed the 'Arab countries' were from the GCC, a sub-region displaying unique population characteristics owing to a large (and in some countries a majority) expatriate population.

The UAE, for example, formed as a state in 1971. Hofstede's survey responses were collected in this 'region' in both 1969 and 1972, therefore prior to and after the UAE's formation as a nation state. As previously displayed, the UAE's population has increased exponentially between 1970 and today, while imported labor (migrant workers) has resulted in a lopsided labor market and a resulting 'local' minority (Davidson, 2008). UAE nationals account for less than 20% of the country's population, with South Asian

Table 2 **Demographics of selected Arab countries**

Country	Population (1970)	Population (2010)	GDP Per Capita (2010)
Egypt	33,574,026	81,121,077	$2,698
Saudi Arabia	6,109,051	27,448,086	$15,836
UAE	249,369	7,511,690	$39,625
Qatar	113,262	1,758,793	$61,532

Source: OS-Connect, 2001, World Bank, 2010

migrants accounting for more than 50%, and other Arabs, Africans and Europeans making up most of the remaining inhabitants (State.gov, 2011). Contrary to the proverbial salad bowl that is the UAE, Egypt's inhabitants are predominantly 'Egyptian', thereby highlighting the extreme ends of the spectrum when comparing Arab characteristics of the populace, and the peril in assuming homogeneity in the region (Schwedler and Gerner, 2008).

The Arabs

The aforementioned demographic heterogeneity displays just some of the disparities when quantifying and understanding the Arab countries (Pearce and Osmond, 1999).

Thus far, there remains a dearth of literature on business and management related issues in the Arab and Middle Eastern world, when compared to other regions (Hunt and At-Twaijri, 1996; Robertson, Al-Khatib, Al-Habib and Lanoue, 2001). Moreover, much of the literature concerning business culture and workplace values that is provided for the region take an orientalist, Anglo-etic (at times ethnocentric) approach, opposed to an emic stance that may help to contextualise and deepen thought further in this area. This emic research scarcity can be attributed to both American educational (management) hegemony of sorts and Arab management thought in its infancy (Fukuyama, 1989; Al-Aiban and Pearce, 1993; Ali, 1995; Neal and Finlay, 2008). Much of the literature that has concerned the region has often referred to "Arabs", the "Arab world" or the "Middle Eastern countries" unified bodes despite a multiplicity of differences (Hourani, 1991; Nehme, 2003; Noland and Pack, 2007; Al-Omari, 2009, Ronen and Shenkar 1985).

These groupings can provide a cultural panacea for the predicament of understanding variance amongst the Arab countries (Kantor, Roberts and Salter, 1995; Robertson et al., 2001). Research suggests that the clustering of these Arab nations into a single unit as inappropriate (Hickson and Pugh, 1995).

This suggests that the Arab world is at least in some respects fragmented, separated and may equate to a cultural salad bowl, against a converged melting pot idealised by scholars including Hofstede (1980).

To avoid a myopic focus on culture alone and to further comprehend differentials across Arab countries, allusion to influencers that assist with understanding both the paradoxical mosaic and harmonized nature of the Arab countries' cultures (and workplace values), will follow. These influencing features include Tribalism and Family, Islam, Colonialism, and Labor Markets. The study will focus on the Kingdom of Saudi Arabia (KSA) and the United Arab Emirates (UAE), though references to the region at large will also be made.

Tribal and Family Influence

Tribal and family influence and their characteristics are fundamental in understanding the structure and composition of many of the Arab countries (Ali, 1993). Khoury and Kostiner (1990) state that there are no current examples of a 'pure' tribal society in the region.

Literature has often fallen short of highlighting that tribes can exist in different ecological systems, and that some may be nomadic (now very few), many sedentarised, and moreover, that they display different ethnic origins. Further, tribal segments including clans may coalesce independently into tribes, displaying both Bedouin (or tribal) fusion and fission (Gellner, 1990). Inter-tribal marriages are an example of this fusion in both UAE and KSA; such as the House of Saud meta-tribe (Mohammed, 2003).

Tribal and merchant classes (bourgeoisie) have had great influence on the values and norms present in today's Arab workplace. These include intense loyalty, *shura* (consultative decision-making/consultation) and a strong trading acumen (trade being the *raison d'etre* in the pre-oil periods of many Arab countries). More negative associated characteristics include authoritarian structures and *Wasta* (nepotism) (Sharabi, 1988; Ali, 1989; 1993; Al-Yahya, 2009).

Leaders and managers in power are often responsible for distributing power, wealth (rents), and even positions at the workplace with the public and private sector often blurred and overlapping.(Cunningham and Sarayrah, 1993; Partick, 2009; Wenlin, 2011).

Informal institutions and interpersonal relationships are paramount to the values and norms expected at the Arab workplace and undoubtedly reflect national cultures. Tribal behaviour and values have prevailed in society, often co-mingling with new state institutions and bureaucratic procedures (Khoury and Kostiner, 1990; Herb, 1999).

Islamic Influence on National Culture, Society and the Workplace

Whilst there are numerous religions present in the Arab world, most countries display a majority Muslim (Sunni) population (Blanchard, 2006). According to Donno and Russett (2004) Islamic ideas are responsible for shaping attitudes and behaviours.

Arab professionals are described as being far from homogeneous in their orientations, though many display central values that reflect Islamic and tribal traditions (Maududi,

1967; Ali, 1990; Bjerke and Al-Meer, 1993). The goals of Islam are not principally materialistic, and not, therefore, in line with the capitalist Friedman doctrine (Rice, 1999; Tripp, 2006). Islam is understood to have an impact on the cultural dimensions of Hofstede's (1980) Arab countries, as well as influencing implicit leadership characteristics (Hofstede, 1983).

Management styles and organizational philosophy in the Arab countries are geared towards a consultative approach *inter alia*. Arab professionals are said to prefer consultative styles and are uncomfortable with delegation (Ali, 1995). "The concept of consultation, a counterpoise of autocratic rule, has a special value in the Islamic tribal societies as it is strongly recommended by the Koran and emphasized by Bedouin traditions" (Kabasakal and Dastmalchian, 2001, p.486)." The Quran states that: "This reward will be for those... who conduct their affairs with consultation among themselves" (42:38). In spite of the favored *shura*, autocratic values and approaches are commonplace, with a pseudo-consultative style often supplanting a pure consultative one (Ali, 1993; Hammoud, 2011). The Orwellian notion of 'doublethink' characterizes contradictory beliefs among many Arabs that portray Islamic ideals that are breached in practice (Ali, 1993).

Further Islamic ideals include meritocracy, fairness and justice (*Qist and Adl*), which are contravened in some quarters by means of *wasta*. This *wasta* is considered endemic and a norm in much of the region, though devout Muslims see favouritism as deviant and dishonest (Cunningham and Sarayrah, 1993; Rice, 1999; Sarayrah, 2004).

Also at the Arab workplace, and in society at large, Muslims have been characterized for an established tendency towards the concept of fatalism. The omnipresent expression of 'insha' Allah' which can be translated as 'Allah (God) willing', is a depiction of this notion. Allah is regularly referred to when explaining uncertainties in life and at times for reposition decision-making (Welsh and Raven, 2006; Pistrui and Fahed-Sreih, 2010).

Differences across the Arab countries pertaining to Islamic connection to the state vary with levels of secularity (Nevo, 1998; Donno and Russett, 2004). The UAE for example was previously dominated by religious rather than national identity, though this changed post state-formation. A more liberal and tolerant nature is now present, following mass migration to the UAE, whilst maintaining a somewhat nationalist stance (Al-Sayegh, 1998; Foster, 2004).

Conversely, neighboring Saudi Arabia remains synonymous with autocracy, conservativeness and the mobilizing of Islam ("*Wahabbism*") to protect it. Gender segregation in social and work settings alongside a restricted freedom of press and speech are a personification of this conservativeness and authoritarianism (Yamani, 2000). Despite Islam being the overriding identity in KSA, a national identity has been sought after by the regime. The concept of nation state and a common identity alongside

Islam are said to have enhanced the Saudi regime's legitimacy (Piscatori, 1981; Yamani, 2000).

The aforementioned 'nation state' and pre-state conditions across the Arab world are also influencers on national culture and workplace values and will be discussed in the following section.

Arab Countries: Colonial Influence, the Nation State and Citizenship

The Arab countries also display heterogeneity with reference to their respective pasts, encompassing a variety of regional influences, colonialism (not all were colonized) and exhibiting differing initial conditions post state-formation.

In North Africa for example, when looking towards the Algerian war for independence from the French (1954-1962), "there is every indication that it has shaped the Algerian mindset in a way that is extremely different from say Tunisia on the one side and Morocco on the other" (Al Omari, 2009, p.81).

Elsewhere in the Arab world, British hegemony in the Gulf region remains ever-present despite its slow decline between 1930 and 1970 with most of the respected Sheikdoms having negotiated independence from their colonial master (Owen, 1992; Rugh, 2007; Hanieh, 2011). Italian, Portuguese, Dutch and Ottoman (Turkish) colonial influences are also a component of history in some Arab countries. This suggests that the 'Arab' mindset, values and the initial conditions that the new Arab nation states inherited, varied significantly, whilst the concept of nation state is a novelty in the region (Khoury and Kostner, 1990; Issawi, 2010). The western creation of the 'nation' by way of imposed borders in the Arab region (for example the Sykes-Picot or Asia Minor agreement of 1916) weakens the concept of Arab state-formation (Owen, 1992; Heard-Bey, 2005).

The nation as a unit of analysis, therefore, is questionable. (Pearce and Osmond, 1999; Al-Yahya, 2009). As aforementioned, Hofstede (2002) suggests that the nation state as a unit of analysis, unlike that of his 'Arab countries' cluster, remains the best option, not accounting for factors including within-country heterogeneity *inter alia.*

Citizenship and state theory posit that citizenship supplant all other patterns of authority, and that "no other authority structure in society – be it based on the family, religious, leadership, or tribal organization - can legitimately demand loyalty from one of its members in a way that contradicts his or her obligations toward the state" (Butenschon, 2000, p. 13). For example, this would suggest that GCC nationals' tribal and religious linkages would be superseded by the state, which is not the case. In Weberian terms, traditional foundations of authority have weakened, though they persist, whereas rational-legal authority structures are present but not strong. The coexistence of contradictory authority structures misrepresents legitimacy in much of the Arab region. "Arabs are still socialized into accepting traditional rationales for obedience based on kinship, religion, dynastic despotism and feudalism. Yet at the same time, they are influenced by Western ideologies which justify authority on altogether different grounds like 'the will of the people'" (ibid).

The varying past experiences that the Arab region has encountered, and their remnants, juxtaposed with the differing conditions, including the economic environment (e.g. resource-rich or resource-poor) have clearly influenced the shaping of the workplace values and national culture of Arab countries. The next section will focus on labor markets and other more topical features in the region.

Arab Labor Markets and Recent Events

Homogeneity and heterogeneity across the Arab countries also apply to labor markets and other economic and more topical factors that concern the workplace, which are important to understanding the influence and discourse surrounding national culture. Nations within the region can be classified into various groups including rentier and non-rentier, labor-scarce or labor-abundant and resource-rich or resource-poor. Within borders, labor markets across the region remain highly segmented at several levels including between male and female, between formal and informal sectors, between public and private sectors, and in particular reference to the GCC, between nationals and non-nationals. The latter of the two segment lines display an obstinate division, characterized through public sector jobs that are synonymous with prestige, better pay, lesser hours and numerous additional benefits *inter alia*; acting as the preferred destination, and often reserved, for nationals in the GCC (Beblawi, 1990; Kapiszewski, 2001; Maleek and Awadallah, 2011). More unimpressive characteristics of the public sector from both a workplace and productivity perspective include being oversized, inefficient, heavily bureaucratic, wasta-oriented, autocratic and organized along traditional power structures (Said, 2001; Davidson, 2008; 2009; Baldwin-Edwards, 2011).

Moreover, a developed and robust private sector in the Arab region remains absent; with larger, successful 'private' companies often questioned on how 'private' they really are, due to ambiguous ownership and boardroom directors from the public sector (and/or government) in overlapping roles (Davidson, 2008; 2009; Maleek and Awadallah, 2011). The private sector, usually more dynamic than in the public sphere, is often associated with long hours, stress and high labor turnover yet more meritocratic and rewarding in nature (if not financially). In the GCC, approximately 70% of the labor force (and almost all of the private sector in most of the member countries) are non-national or 'migrant workers' of whom are often described as being permanently in a state of impermanence (Ali, 2010; Maleek and Awadallah, 2011). This may refer to the temporary status given to non-nationals (who cannot become GCC nationals)[iv] by means of renewable visas (*time periods vary*), despite many having spent their lives growing up and working in these countries (Shah, 2004; 2009).

As previously mentioned, migrant workers are often large minorities and even majorities (in UAE, Qatar, Bahrain, Kuwait) in the GCC, consequently, they are viewed as a perceived threat (see Figure 1 for KSA and UAE national-expat populations). This has subsequently led to government led-policies to protect 'national' workers through nationalisation of workers' initiatives e.g. Emiratisation, Saudisation and the like, which aim to reduce the migrant population and provide further jobs for the populace that boast 'national' status (Girgis, 2002; Harry, 2007; Neal, 2010; Forstenlechner et al., 2011; Baldwin-Edwards, 2011).

Figure 1 **Citizenship Status in KSA and UAE**

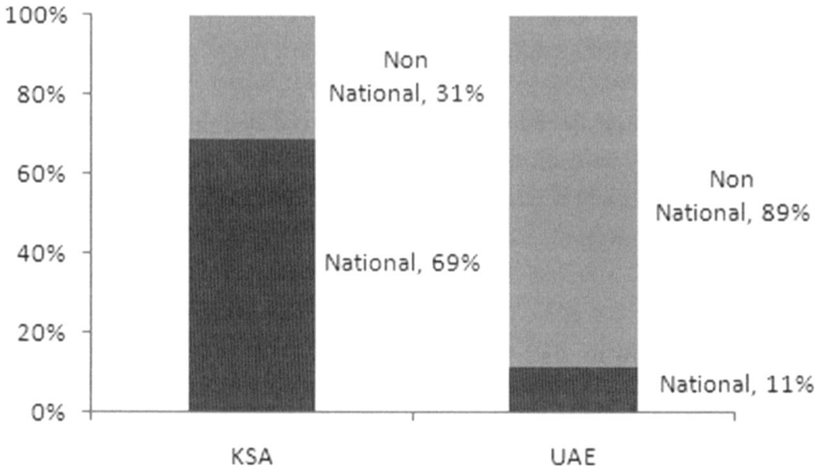

Source: Emirates 24/7, 2010; Sambridge, 2010

In addition to the lopsided labor markets present in some quarters, low female labor force participation and mass unemployment are also major features of the Arab labor market (World Bank, 2004; Schwedler and Gerner, 2008). Endemic unemployment and other economic ailments, together with political aspirations and the need for basic freedoms and human rights, were at the heart of the recent Arab uprisings that grabbed worldwide attention.

This dissatisfaction has been partly appeased through economic measures in other countries not as prominent during the uprisings, including Saudi Arabia and Algeria, with the former's monarch, King Abdullah, announcing a $126 billion investment program in early 2011 directed at social areas including housing, employment creation, wage increases (public sector) and unemployment benefits (Darbouche and Fattouh, 2011; Dessi, 2011).

Other topical features of the GCC are the negative social and cultural implications of a multicultural migrant presence on 'local' or 'national' identity. The Asianisation of the workforce is said to worry authorities in the GCC, however, the omnipresent western education systems, civilisation, culture and consumption patterns are strangely overlooked (Kaspiszewski, 2006).

The contemporary features of the 'Arab' workplace are undoubtedly heterogeneous in nature, despite some commonalities, with topics varying among the countries (rentier, non-rentier and so forth) across the region, and are likely to influence national culture and workplace values in different ways.

The various histories, facets and characteristics across the Arab countries display many similar influences; meanwhile it is the various differences that management practitioners and scholars must also be aware of. Discovering these disparities in national culture, that are displayed through workplace values at nation-level, can enable this deeper understanding of this complex region.

Research Aim and Objectives

Overall Aim

This paper aims at determining and further developing knowledge on the cross-national heterogeneity of Hofstede's (1980) cultural dimensions in the 'Arab Countries', through a comparison of Power Distance and Uncertainty Avoidance index scores across Saudi Arabia and the United Arab Emirates.

Research Objectives

RO1. Investigate and compare the index scores among the two countries subject to study.

RO2. Identify whether the index scores differ between nationals and non-nationals.Identify whether the index scores differ between private and public sectors.

Research Questions

RQ1. Is there a difference between the index scores of Saudi Arabia and the United Arab Emirates?

RQ2. Is there a difference in the dimension scores of Saudi Arabia and the United Arab Emirates when comparing nationals with non-nationals?

RQ3. Is there a difference between the index scores of Saudi Arabia and the United Arab Emirates when comparing private and public sectors?

Methodology

Research Framework

The current research aimed to test for heterogeneity in PDI and UAI scores between two specific Arab countries (KSA and UAE) originally in Hofstede's 'Arab countries cluster', by conducting a Hofstedean micro-replication (based on Hofstede's original survey). Comparison against Hofstede's original 'Arab countries' scores were also made. Consequently it was necessary to establish the extent to which respondents from both countries accept and expect inequality in power, and their attitudes to dealing with uncertainty through a comparison of two independent samples (Hofstede, 2001). Further analyses were carried out in an effort to discover score disparities across samples and whether there are any moderating factors that are related to the strength of the indices.

Country Selection

This current study aimed to examine whether the index scores vary across KSA and UAE. According to Hofstede (2001) at least two countries must be used, as comparisons are being made across cultures (See Table 3 for country selection rationale).

Table 3 **Country Selection Rationale**

Original Inclusion	KSA and UAE are two of seven nations within Hofstede's original 'Arab countries' cluster
Demographic Disparity	Demographic differences amongst the populace in both KSA and UAE with reference to the national/expatriate ratio vary significantly
Tribal Influence	Both KSA and UAE share tribal influences and geographic proximity, therefore it is reasonable to assume that should scores display significant difference, other Arab countries further afield from each other may display even greater difference
Professional Network	The author's professional network in both countries was a catalyst for this decision due to the likelihood of a higher survey response rate

Dimension Selection

The power distance and uncertainty avoidance dimensions were selected primarily on the grounds that they "tend to be strongly intercorrelated and difficult to separate" (Hofstede, 2001, p.465). They are also the most sensitive dimensions and therefore most likely to show differences if they exist (Hofstede, 2001).

Respondent Selection

In contrast to Hofstede's original work, which solely focused on IBM respondents (in sales, marketing and administrative positions) in the technology industry, a wide spectrum of companies and industries have been selected in an effort to eliminate any moderating influence from an industry and/or organizational culture. Entities in both the public and private sectors including multinational corporations (MNCs), family businesses and small to medium enterprises (SMEs) were targeted in order to achieve a more representative sample.

Sampling Process

Target Population

A clear requirement from the onset was that the study is focused on professionals that work in both the KSA and UAE, irrespective of citizenship status, as workplace values are central to this study and are a reflection of national culture (Pearce and Osmond, 1999; Hofstede, 2001). Consequently, both nationals and non-nationals were targeted, with non-nationals making up the majority of the UAE population and a significant proportion of the Saudi population. As aforementioned, targeting entities in both the public and private sectors allowed for a more lucid sample.

Although this study employed convenience sampling methods (see next section), some clear provisions were made in reference to the target population (See Table 4), including the element, sample unit, extent and time feature of the population definition (Malhotra and Birks, 2003).

Table 4 **Target Population**

Element:	Male and female, aged 18-55+ Private and public sector workers Management and non-management positions Nationals and non-nationals
Sampling Unit:	Professional employees in SMEs, MNCs, family businesses and Government entities
Sampling Frame:	Pre-owned list of professional employees
Extent:	KSA; Riyadh, Jeddah, Dammam, Dhahran UAE; Abu Dhabi, Dubai
Time:	August through to October, 2011

Sampling Technique

Best practice research for quantitative studies recommends probability sampling, as it entails arbitrary respondent selection and is therefore free of human judgement and bias (Kent, 2007). Nevertheless, due to time and budget constraints of the present study, a non-probability techniques were employed. A combination of convenience and snowball sampling was used to achieve suitable responses from the respective countries. Moreover, it was chosen as the main sampling technique as it is the fastest and least expensive to implement (Kent, 2007).

Following initial responses, snowball sampling was employed to collect responses from the participants' colleagues, as they were likely to have the required characteristics of the target population (Malhotra and Birks, 2003).

Sample Size

Hofstede (2001) suggests a sample size of between 20-50 respondents per country sample as a guideline, however, the minimum parameters of good research practice lie within 100-150 respondents (Malhotra and Birks, 2003). Therefore a total sample size of 300 respondents (circa 150 per country) was targeted, as the current study aims to analyse only two countries rather than the entire Arab region.

Analytical Approach

In order to satisfy the research aim and objectives, the data was entered into the SPSS statistical program for the purpose of analysis. Various types of analysis were conducted in order to establish whether the data is normal and to determine the dimensions of the sample. These included descriptive statistics such as descriptives, frequencies, and explore (Field, 2005).

Reliability analysis is usually required to assess the reliability of scales used within research, however, Hofstede (2001, p. 463-464) argues "the reliability of the instrument can simply not be tested in the textbook way and has to be taken for granted based on the literature."

This is because reliability analysis can only be conducted across countries where the number of countries within a study numbers 10 or more, which was not the case in this current research.

Measurement

Due to this study being a replication of Hofstede's (1980) cultural dimensions (Power Distance and Uncertainty Avoidance), the same questions and formulae will be used in this study (survey). The respective formulae for the power distance and uncertainty avoidance dimensions are as follows:

Power Distance:	**Uncertainty Avoidance:**
135 - 25 x (mean score employees afraid)	300 - 30 x (mean score rule orientation)
+ (percentage perceived manager 1+2)	- (percentage intending to stay less than 5 years)
- (percentage preferred manager 3)	- 40 x (mean stress score)

The power distance samples are likely to be smaller than those for the uncertainty avoidance, as managers were not included in these indices (as per formula guidelines). This is due to the fact that "all three questions were answered by the subordinates rather than the superiors - that is, by the least powerful partners in the relationship, who are better judges of power distance than their more powerful superiors" (Hofstede, 2001, p. 87). (See Appendix 3 for questionnaire and individual questions.)

Data Collection

An online survey approach was adopted to thwart any previously mentioned response bias with respect to phenomena including groupthink, conformity and social desirability (Malhotra and Birks, 2003).

All data was collected using the online survey so that data gathered followed a strict, standardised collection process and ensured that variation in results was due to the cultural dimensions and not disparate means of data collection (Romaniuk, 2008). Also, an incentive was used to amplify the response rate and enhance the quality of data, as respondents are prone to respond more carefully in these circumstances (Kent, 2007).

Preliminary Data Analysis

Preliminary Tests

The online survey resulted in a total of 451 valid responses (214 in the KSA and 237 in the UAE), which surpassed both Hofstede's (2001) recommendation, the number of respondents in his 'Arab countries' cluster, and good research practice (Malhotra and Birks, 2003). Some variables required recoding and computing before the proposed tests were conducted (Pallant, 2007).

Descriptive statistics were used to assess whether there were outliers in any of the variables, which proved to be non-existent and hence no cases required removal. All variables were also tested for normality (see Appendix 4).

Sample Comparability

The comparability of the two country samples was explored with respect to the age, citizenship status and sector variables (for other variables including industry, employment level, religion and gender see Appendices 5-8). The comparison of the age group variable indicated that samples display significant similarities (see Figure 2), which is most likely a result of the large youth population present in the KSA and UAE alongside the fact that much of the author's network are also predominantly in the under 35 group of whom 75% of KSA respondents and 69% of UAE respondents belong.

Figure 2 **Age Group Comparison**

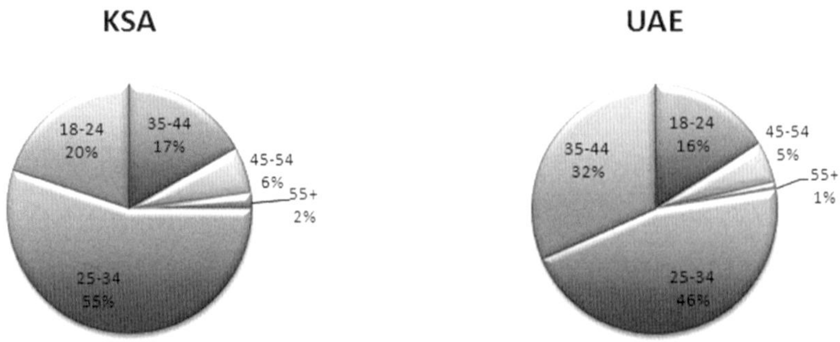

Comparison of the citizenship status variable displayed significant differences in national to non-national in the two countries (see Figure 3). This asymmetry is expected as these lopsided figures somewhat resemble the real population of KSA (31% non-national) and UAE with its minority 'local' population (89% non-national) (Sambidge 2010; Emirates 24/7, 2010) (See Figure 1).

Figure 3 **Citizenship Status Comparisons**

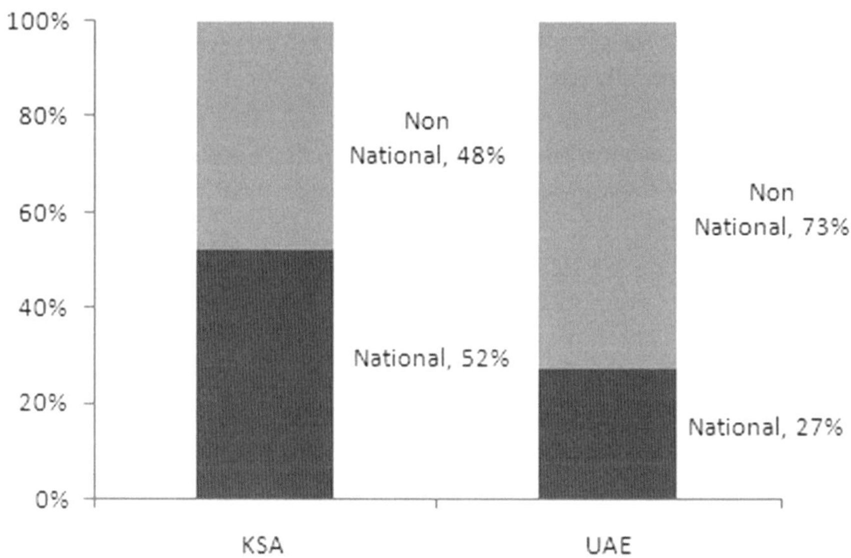

The comparison of the sector variable displays similar samples from the two countries (see Figure 4). In relation to the previous citizenship variable, most nationals work in the public sector, a fundamental aspect of aforementioned labor market segmentation in the GCC region (Emirates 24/7, 2011).

Figure 4 **Sector Comparison**

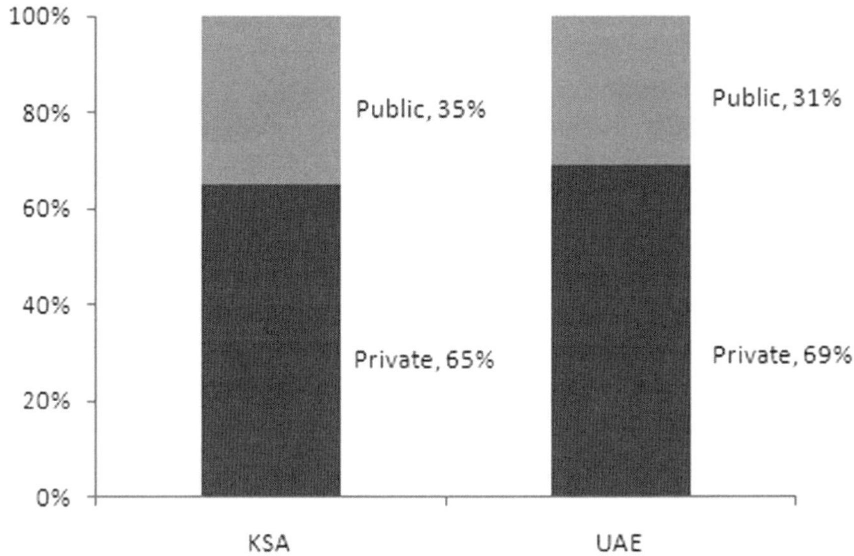

The response breakdown (all respondents) for questions on Hofstede's (1980) power distance dimension for the KSA and UAE are as follows (see Figures 5-7):

Figure 5 **PDI: Non managerial employees' perception that employees are afraid to disagree with their managers**

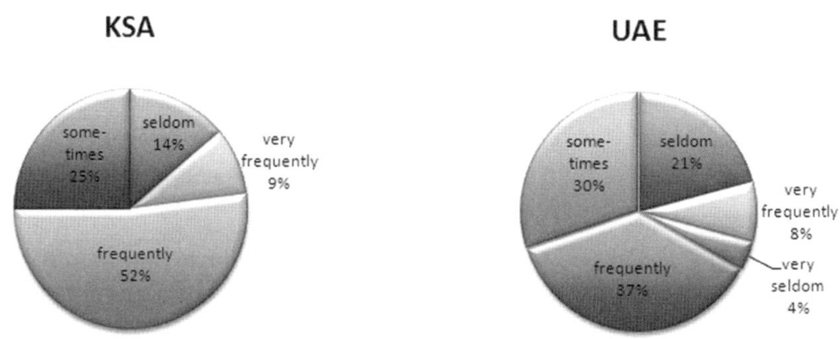

Figure 6 **PDI 2: Subordinates' preference for anything but a consultative (manager 3) style of decision making in their boss; that is, for an autocratic (manager 1), a persuasive/paternalistic (manager 2), or a democratic style (manager 4)**

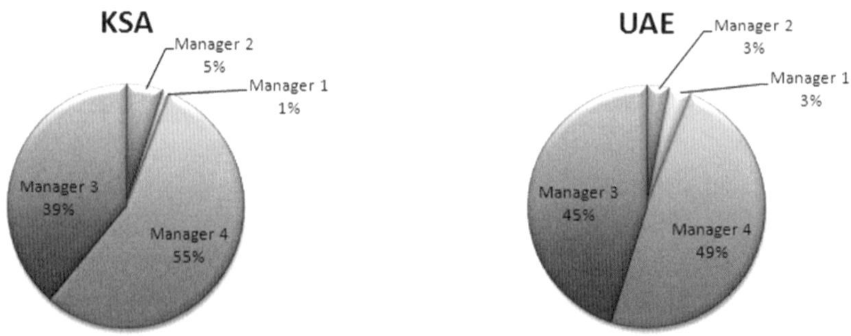

Figure 7 **PDI 3: Subordinates' perception that their boss tends to make decisions in an autocratic (manager 1) or persuasive/paternalistic (manager 2) way**

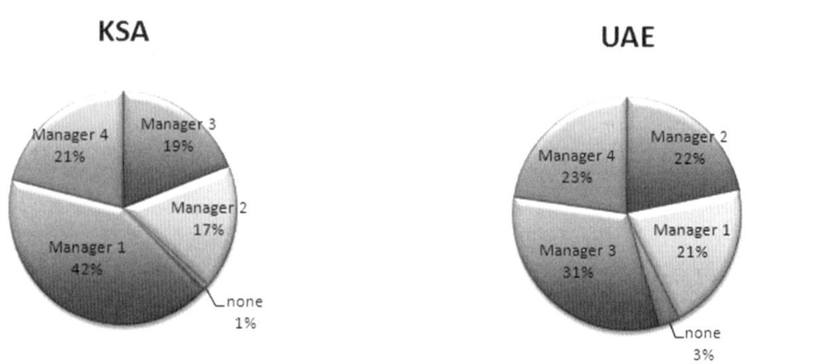

The response breakdown (all respondents) for questions on Hofstede's (1980) uncertainty avoidance dimension for the KSA and UAE are as follows (see Figures 8-10):

The samples for each question display both variances and similarities that were formulated into power distance and uncertainty avoidance indices using Hofstede's (1980) aforementioned formulae and are discussed further in the following section and chapter.

Figure 8 **UAI 1: Company rules should not be broken - even when the employee thinks it is in the company's best interest**

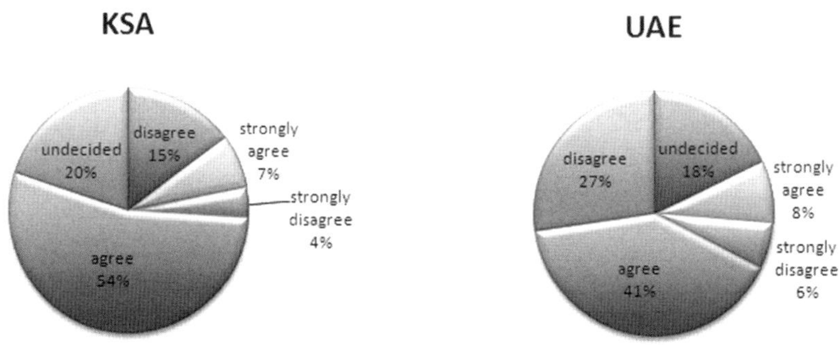

Figure 9 **UAI 2: How often do you feel nervous or tense at work?**

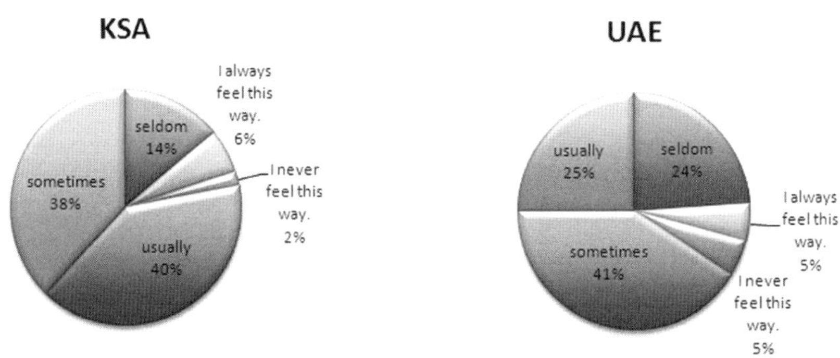

Figure 10 **UAI 3: Employees' statement that they intend to continue with the company for a period of:**

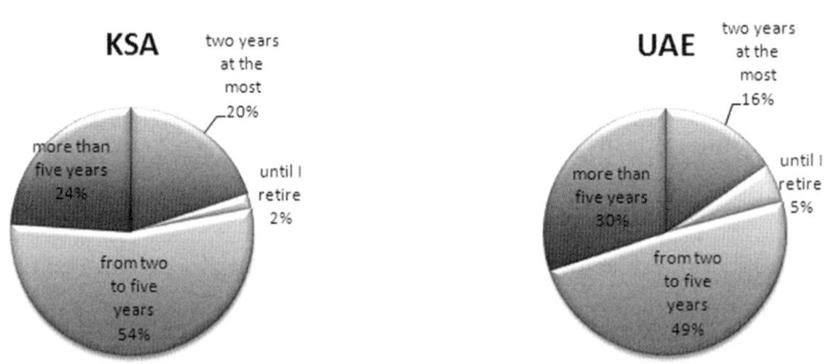

Results and Discussion

Introduction to Results

Taking into consideration the cross-national nature of the following comparisons (each respondent being from either KSA or the UAE), independent samples t-tests must be conducted (Field, 2005). The aim of these tests is to determine whether (i) there is heterogeneity between country scores within Hofstede's (1980) original 'Arab countries' cluster (KSA and UAE); (ii) to ascertain if there is any significant variance among national and non-national scores within the respective countries and (iii) to discover if there is any significant difference in the scores across private and public sector employees.

It is important to note that RQ2 and RQ3 exhibit far less cases than RQ1, which is due to the fact that sub-samples are being analysed. In some instances the number of cases falls below 30, which is the minimum required (dictated by good research practice) in order to make reasonable inferences on the whole population (Malhotra and Birks, 2003).

Further, in order to complement the Hofstedean replication, informal interviews were conducted with key individuals so that both academic insights and on-the-ground realities would enable a deeper understanding of Arab workplace values and cultures (see Appendix 9 for a list of interviewees).

Research Question One

Since the two samples are independent of one another, Levene's Test for Equality of Variances is carried out to assess the respective variances of the two samples (unequal for PDI and equal for UAI). The t-test for Equality of Means is then conducted for both PDI and UAI. The significance values are below 0.05 (5% alpha value) and therefore indicate that both KSA and UAE samples are significantly different on both indices. The difference in mean values is 8.279 and 20.343 for PDI and UAI respectively (see Table 5 and 6), which indicates that KSA respondents (all nationalities) display a greater willingness to accept differences in power and are less capable of dealing with uncertainty than their UAE counterparts (all nationalities).

Table 5 **RQI Group Statistics**

Variable	Dataset	N	Mean	Std. Deviation	Std. Error Mean
PDI	Saudi	131	80.73	17.105	1.495
	UAE	108	72.45	23.494	2.261
UAI	Saudi	214	115.01	56.091	3.834
	UAE	237	94.67	57.956	3.765

Table 6 RQI Independent Sample Test

	Levene's Test for Equality of Variances		t-test for Equality of Means	
Variable	Variance	Sig.	Sig. (2-tailed)	Mean Difference
PDI	Equal variances assumed	0.00	0.002	8.279
	Equal variances not assumed		**0.003**	8.279
UAI	Equal variances assumed	0.296	**0.00**	20.343
	Equal variances not assumed		0.00	20.343

Power Distance

Evidence suggests that KSA is more conservative than the UAE, characterized by the larger influence of Islam and tribalism, hence explaining the slightly higher power distance score. This is strengthened by the higher proportion of Muslims and Saudi nationals among the KSA population when compared to neighboring UAE. In comparison to Hofstede's (1980) Arab countries score on power distance (80), KSA is almost identical (81), thus showing that the recent sample from KSA bears great resemblance to the decades old study. Conversely, the UAE's score (72) shows a lower power distance than both Hofstede's and KSA scores (see Figure 11).

Figure 11 Country Dimension Scores

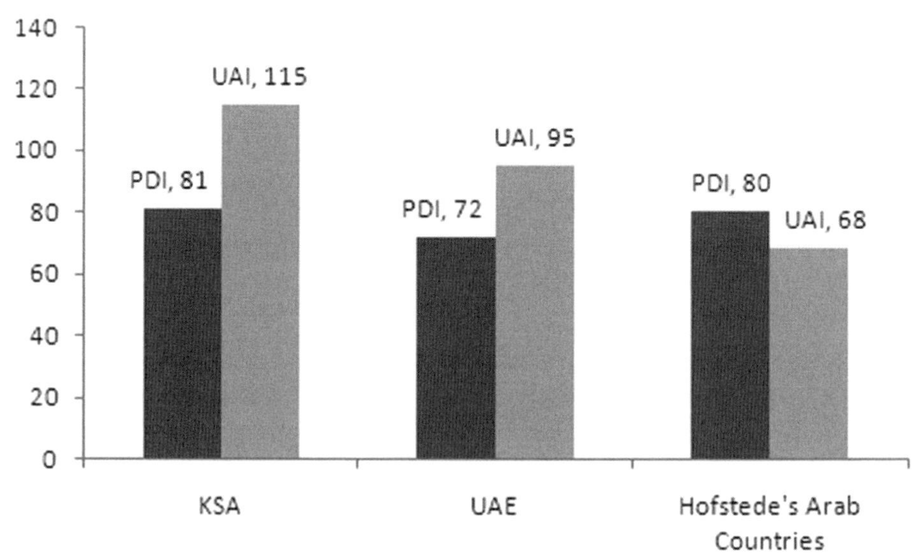

In contrast to the greater Islamic influence in KSA, the UAE exhibits a more liberal and tolerant environment, influenced by a large presence of Western organizations across a spectrum of industries that import western management styles (DeNicola, 2005; Telegraph, 2010).

It is also important to understand the exponential oil-led changes and developments that have taken place, more so in the UAE than KSA, since Hofstede's survey collection in 1969 and 1972 (Davidson, 2008; 2009). These changes have surely influenced workplace values.

In relation to two core components of power distance, the 'preferred' and 'perceived' manager, the vast majority of KSA respondents (non-management) prefer consultative (39%) or democratic (54%) management styles, whereas the largest single proportion of actual managers are viewed as autocratic (41%). UAE respondents similarly prefer consultative (45%) and democratic (49%) styles, whilst in reality the 'perceived'-'preferred' equilibrium point in the UAE is not as far off as KSA, with UAE managers perceived and characterized as consultative (32%) and democratic (23%) (see Figures 6 and 7).

Chbani (2012) who has worked in both KSA and UAE private sectors' explains that "management styles in both Saudi and UAE are traditional in nature and though they may seem *shura* and group-oriented, they are pretty autocratic and top-down… UAE still remains more Western and Anglo-Saxon in its approach due to the number of expats".

These comments are aligned with the aforementioned pseudo-consultative management style in Arab countries, described by Ali (1995), thereby displaying similarities in these countries, despite some noteworthy differences.

The neo-patrimonial structures which reflect Weber's traditional authority, with some rational-legal features seem to persevere, as does the Anglo-hegemony in education and increasingly western popular culture in the GCC countries (Wenlin, 2011). Al Awar (2012) describes Islam and informal ties as "not as influential on the whole as western philosophies at work, with many Islamic practices no more than a gimmick at the workplace…though many local companies avoid interest [in banking] and dealing with alcohol."

Interviewee B (2012), a hotel maid (degree-holder) in Riyadh, KSA, describes Islamic and tribal influences on workplace values as "very important and very influential" in the kingdom. Literature suggests that "compared to citizens of the UAE, the Saudis are a much more religious people" (DeNicola, 2005, p.73). Interviewee B (2012) also explained that at her company, "western business practices are implemented but are usually ineffective and not carried out properly".

Both countries clearly display traditional and autocratic, societies and workplaces, whilst the might of these attributes is clearly stronger in KSA, thus displaying a small but significant difference pertaining to the power distance dimension.

Uncertainty Avoidance

The uncertainty avoidance scores displayed a larger disparity than the power distance dimension across KSA and UAE (see Figure 11). The difference between Hofstede's original UAI score (68), the KSA (115) and UAE (95) was particularly large. The perceptive nature of this dimension may play some part in explaining this, with power distance more constant, whereas the UAI is more sensitive and vulnerable to externalities and the macro-environment (Hofstede, 2001).

Factors surrounding the UAI included respondents' views on rule breaking for company interests, stress at work and their intention or expectation to continue with/leave their current employers. In the KSA 61% of respondents strongly agreed/agreed that rules should not be broken, even if it was in their company's interests versus 48% in the UAE (see Figure 8). This displays somewhat of an authoritarian structure in both countries, though KSA illustrate a more unremitting composition (Lindsey, 1991; Nehme, 2003).

On the subject of feeling stressed (feeling nervous or tense) at work, 46% of KSA respondents always, or usually, feel that way compared to 30% in UAE (see Figure 9). Similarly associated to this is the respondents' intention to stay with their company, with 74% of employees in KSA and 65% in the UAE expecting to remain with their employer for less than 5 years (see Figure 10).

Results show that both countries display high scores on stress and proposed employee loyalty/turnover, with KSA the more suppressive of the two. Some reasons for this may pertain to the omnipresent segregation amongst men and women in KSA (including a ban on women driving), religiosity at work, and the greater restrictions on freedom and expression which may also compound the feelings and mindset of the populace (Ali, 1995; Galani, 2010). Moreover, and in reference to both KSA and UAE, the aforementioned nationalisation (of workers) policies, visa issues and restricted workers' rights are large contributors to stress, dependency (see Kafala system later) and uncertainty also reflects the attitudes and values of non-nationals (who are a large share of the population) in both countries (Shah, 2009; Ali, 2010; Baldwin-Edwards, 2011).

Neal (2012) explains that blue-collar workers in the GCC (predominantly Asian expatriates) are often "stuck and understandably stressed" with dependants back home relying on their remittances. Conversely, Al Awar (2012) states "nationalisation and layoffs following the financial crises are a cause of stress for non-nationals…but in UAE due to the 90/10 situation emiratisation is inevitable and completely understandable." This stress is also taking its toll on employee health in the region, with chronic fatigue a common problem *inter alia* (Asger, 2011).

Furthermore, another factor pertaining to the high UAI scores is that respondents completed surveys during 2011 amidst political and civil unrest/uprisings in the Arab world.

This is likely to have impacted this cultural dimension score as many of the respondents in both KSA and UAE were nationals of countries including Egypt, Yemen, Syria, Tunisia and Palestine; countries displaying major unrest, strife and turmoil (see Appendix 10) (Fattahova, 2011). Interviewee A (2012) who is a senior employee at a UAE government organization in the energy sector, highlights the three most important factors influencing stress and uncertainty in recent times as the emiratization policy, the impact of the 'Arab Spring', and the global financial crisis. This displays both macro- and micro-environmental aspects influencing UAI at the workplace.

The PDI and UAI scores display similarities in nature, but differences are significant enough to distinguish the neighboring countries from one another. Vom Bruck (2012) states, from an anthropological perspective, that "similarities do not outweigh differences [in the Arab region]".

These comments on face value, complement literature mentioned earlier regarding the peril in assuming homogeneity across Arab countries, despite many commonalities that have been discussed (Schwedler and Gerner, 2008; Owen, 2012). This gives sound reason to take the nation state (at the least) as the unit of analysis when trying to understand the Arab region (Khoury and Kostner, 1990; Hofstede, 2002).

Research Question Two

The Levene's Test for Equality of Variances was carried out to assess the respective variances of the two samples (equal for both PDI and UAI), as the two samples are independent of one another. The t-test for Equality of Means is then conducted, the significance values for both PDI and UAI are below 0.05 (5% alpha value) and therefore indicate that both samples are significantly different on both indices. The difference in KSA mean values is -0.058 and -11.072 between national and non-nationals for PDI and UAI respectively (see Tables 7 and 8), which indicates that KSA nationals and non-nationals display almost identical willingness to accept differences in power (original Hofstede score almost the same at 80). In contrast, non-nationals in KSA are less capable of dealing with uncertainty than KSA nationals.

Table 7 **RQ2 Group Statistics (KSA)**

Variable	Citizenship Status	N	Mean	Std. Deviation	Std. Error Mean
PDI	National	53	80.70	18.266	2.509
	Non-national	78	80.76	16.391	1.856
UAI	National	112	109.73	60.571	5.723
	Non-national	102	120.80	50.381	4.988

Table 8 **RQ2 Independent Samples Test (KSA)**

	Levene's Test for Equality of Variances		t-test for Equality of Means	
Variable	Variance	Sig.	Sig. (2-tailed)	Mean Difference
PDI	Equal variances assumed	0.395	**0.985**	-0.058
	Equal variances not assumed		0.985	-0.058
UAI	Equal variances assumed	0.103	**0.150**	-11.072
	Equal variances not assumed		0.146	-11.072

Similar to the KSA test (Table 8) The Levene's Test for Equality of Variances shows both PDI and UAI to be equal, with the difference in UAE mean values being 2.184 and -24.416 amongst national and non-nationals for PDI and UAI respectively (see Tables 9 and 10). This indicates that UAE nationals marginally display a greater willingness to accept differences in power than their non-national co-residents. In contrast, non-nationals in UAE are considerably less capable of dealing with uncertainty than their UAE national counterparts.

Table 9 **RQ2 Group Statistics (UAE)**

Variable	Citizenship Status	N	Mean	Std. Deviation	Std. Error Mean
PDI	National	17	74.29	26.967	6.540
	Non-national	91	72.11	22.939	2.405
UAI	National	64	76.84	56.103	7.013
	Non-national	173	101.26	57.392	4.363

Power Distance

Evidence suggests that KSA is, as previously mentioned, a conservative and hierarchical society, thus resulting in a unified high power distance score for both nationals (81) and non-nationals (81) in the country (Khoury and Kostiner, 1990; Lindsey, 1991; Interviewee B, 2012).

Table 10 **RQ2 Independent Samples Test (UAE)**

	Levene's Test for Equality of Variances		t-test for Equality of Means	
Variable	Variance	Sig.	Sig. (2-tailed)	Mean Difference
PDI	Equal variances assumed	0.570	**0.727**	2.184
	Equal variances not assumed		0.757	2.184
UAI	Equal variances assumed	0.406	**0.00**	-24.416
	Equal variances not assumed		0.00	-24.416

UAE power distance scores for both nationals (74) and non-nationals (72) are also very similar, and are both significantly lower compared to KSA, and also Hofstede's (1980) original PDI score (80) (see Figure 12).

Figure 12 **Country Dimension Scores - Citizenship Status**

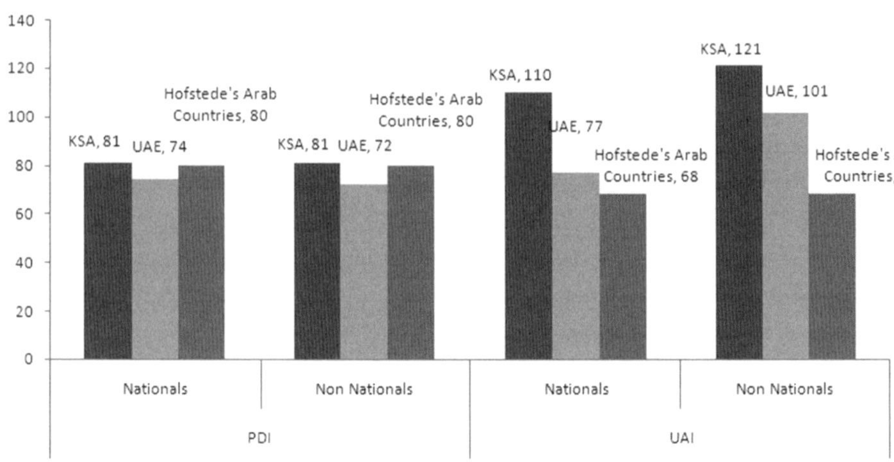

The similarity across both national and non-national scores within their respected countries displays some homogeneity among those living within the borders of KSA and UAE, irrespective of nationality.

The PDI scores across the countries, when compared to Hofstede's original score, have less than a 10 point difference between them, further highlighting the constant nature of power distance and the relevance that Hofstede's PDI scores have to these 'Arab countries'. Chbani (2012) states that "Saudis and Emirati nationals are quite authoritarian in their management approaches and this is likely to rub off on their non-national subordinates and colleagues." This contextualizes the closeness of the PDI scores in the countries.

Uncertainty Avoidance

Uncertainty avoidance scores for non-nationals in KSA (121) and UAE (101) are higher compared to KSA nationals (110) and UAE nationals (77) (see Figure 12). This may be, in part, due to the previously discussed visa renewal situation (with a component of the score formula deriving from plans to stay with a given company) and the Kafala[v] (sponsorship) system (Girgis, 2002; Shah, 2004). Further, the ongoing Emiratization and Saudization initiatives which seek to replace non-nationals with nationals, compound the uncertainty surrounding non-national employment (mainly in the public sector and white collar employment) (Davidson, 2008; 2009).

Higher wages for nationals alongside non-pecuniary benefits may also assist in generating additional security for nationals and consequently reduce uncertainty. (Kaspisewski, 2001; 2006; Baldwin-Edwards, 2011). Al Awar (2012) describes the higher wages, given as a result of labor market segmentation to UAE nationals, as "owed to us…we are the income tax". In line with literature (Kaspisewski, 2001; Fasano and Uqbal, 2003; World Bank, 2004, Kaspisewski, 2006), nationals are explained as having "a weight off their shoulders with respect to their financial security" (Interviewee A, 2012). This is contrary to the situation that many expatriates, particularly blue-collar workers find themselves in. Some watchdogs have described financial and working conditions among these strata as nothing short of modern day slavery in the GCC (Migrant-rights.org, 2012b). These factors will undoubtedly exacerbate stress and ambiguity facing this group.[vi]

In spite of this, it is both national and non-national UAI scores that are markedly high compared to Hofstede's original score (68). As previously emphasized, the vague and stressful political situations in the region may have acutely affected behaviors and feelings at the workplace and beyond (Interviewee A, 2012; Barada, 2012).

In reference to the 'UAE' culture, Al Awar (2012) explains that "naturally it is the culture of the 90% [expatriates] that dominates the UAE as the overall culture and reflects these workplace values the best, however heritage of nationals must be maintained".

This suggests that the multiplicity of nationalities meet to create one 'UAE' culture, though power-holders and decision-makers (who are almost always nationals) are likely to influence greatly. These power-holders and traditional structures remain strongest in KSA (Herb, 1999; Interviewee B, 2012).

Research Question Three

The two samples being analyzed are independent in nature and therefore it is necessary to carry out The Levene's Test for Equality of Means to gauge the respective variances of the two samples (unequal for both PDI and UAI). The significance values in the t-test for Equality of Means for both PDI and UAI are below 0.05 (5% alpha value) and therefore indicate that both KSA and UAE sample scores are significantly different. The difference in KSA mean values is 7.111 and 25.017 across the public and private sector for PDI and UAI respectively (see Tables 11 and 12), which indicates that those working in KSA's public sector display less willingness to accept differences in power than those working in the private sector. Further, respondents from the KSA public sector are more capable of dealing with uncertainty than respondents from the KSA private sector.

Table 11 **RQ3 Group Statistics (KSA)**

Variable	Sector	N	Mean	Std. Deviation	Std. Error Mean
PDI	Private	93	82.80	15.539	1.611
	Public	38	75.68	19.768	3.207
UAI	Private	139	123.78	50.234	4.261
	Public	75	98.76	62.755	7.246

Table 12 **RQ3 Independent Samples Test (KSA)**

	Levene's Test for Equality of Variances		t-test for Equality of Means	
Variable	Variance	Sig.	Sig. (2-tailed)	Mean Difference
PDI	Equal variances assumed	0.006	0.03	7.111
	Equal variances not assumed		**0.052**	7.111
UAI	Equal variances assumed	0.012	0.00	25.017
	Equal variances not assumed		**0.00**	25.017

The Levene's Test for Equality of Means for the UAE shows PDI to be unequal and UAI to be equal. The difference in UAE mean values being -5.997 and 19.295 across the public and private sector with reference to PDI and UAI respectively (see Tables 13 and 14). This signifies that those in the UAE public sector marginally display a greater willingness to accept differences in power than their private sector counterparts. In contrast, UAE private sector workers are considerably less capable of dealing with uncertainty than those working in the public sector.

Table 13 RQ3 Group Statistics (UAE)

Variable	Sector	N	Mean	Std. Deviation	Std. Error Mean
PDI	Private	85	71.18	24.794	2.689
	Public	23	77.17	17.544	3.658
UAI	Private	164	100.61	58.993	4.607
	Public	73	81.32	53.571	6.27

Table 14 RQ3 Independent Samples Test (UAE)

	Levene's Test for Equality of Variances		t-test for Equality of Means	
Variable	Variance	Sig.	Sig. (2-tailed)	Mean Difference
PDI	Equal variances assumed	0.035	0.280	-5.997
	Equal variances not assumed		**0.193**	-5.997
UAI	Equal variances assumed	0.252	**0.018**	19.295
	Equal variances not assumed		0.014	19.295

According to Ali (1986) those working in the public and private spheres hold divergent workplace values, with the public sector synonymous with a Marxist and bureaucratic approach. Bozeman (1987) suggests that the public sector/government entities represent their society's espoused values to a greater extent than private businesses. This suggests that survey respondents from the public sector reflect their nation's advocated culture, which is often aligned with the political structure (Al-Rasheed, 2003; Rugh, 2007).

Power Distance

The private sector in KSA, which is more diverse with regards to nationalities in comparison to the public sector, uncharacteristically displays higher power distance (83) than in the public sector (76) (see Figure 13). This could be a result of the types of organizations that respondents may be working for, with some 'local' family businesses likely to exhibit a top-down patriarchal environment, thus supplanting the bureaucratic and hierarchical nature in the public sector (Booz and Co, 2011; Interviewee A, 2012).

Respondents from the UAE public sector display a higher power distance score (77) than in the private (71) (see Figure 13). This is likely to be a result of the higher share of nationals working in the public sector 'safe haven', as they are more influenced by Islamic and tribal factors including the neo-patrimonial structures reflected by society and the political sphere.

The scores in both countries are significantly close to Hofstede's (1980) original PD score (80) with the UAE and KSA public sectors, respectively, a mere 3 and 4 points above and below the score.

Figure 13 **Country Dimension Scores - Sector**

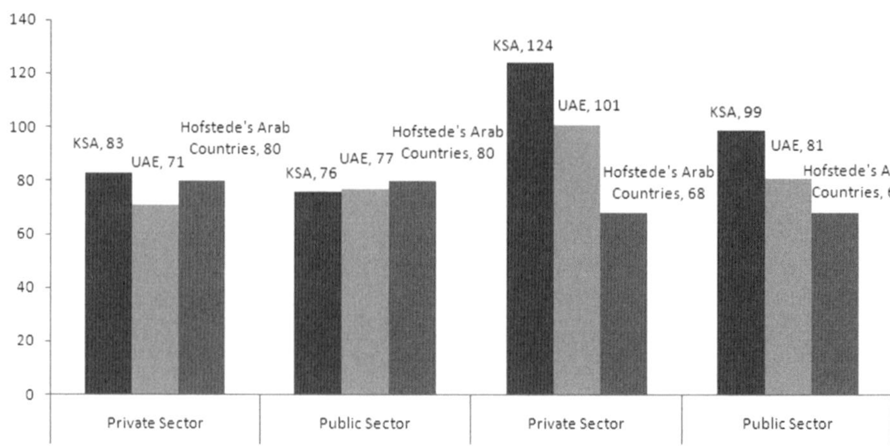

Interviewee A (2012) explains that the GCC public sectors exhibit very traditional power structures and that "the government entities usually operate in monopoly markets with a lesser focus on efficiency and therefore hierarchies tend to be considerably larger compared to MNCs and the private sector".

Uncertainty Avoidance

Uncertainty avoidance scores for KSA (124) and UAE (101) private sector workers show significant disparity when compared to employees in the public sector in both KSA (99) and UAE (81). This difference may arise from the fact that non-national workers make up most of the private sector, with nationals preferring and queuing for the more rewarding and secure public sector (see Figure 13). In addition to the visa and Kafala policies, the nationalisation initiatives which seek to replace non-nationals with nationals are the most relevant to the public sector, thus compounding the uncertainty surrounding non-national labor turnover, pressures and stress (World Bank, 2004; Kaspiszewski, 2006). The KSA and UAE scores in both sectors are substantially higher than Hofstede's (1980) 'Arab countries' scores (68) with many of the reasons referred to influencing the large variance.

The public sector is also often, one of the first economic recipients of rent distribution (gained from hydrocarbon revenues) alongside the nationals of the GCC countries, by means of subsidies, handouts and the like (Maleek and Awadallah, 2011; Darbouche and Fattouh, 2011). This reinforces the financial strength and security that is associated with the bloated public sectors in the KSA, UAE and throughout the region. Companies in the private sector do not have these luxuries, as average salaries have decreased following the financial crises, consequently adding to the anxiety that many private sector (predominantly expatriate) workers encounter (Barada, 2012; Chbani, 2012).

Despite this, Barada (2012) describes the public sector as "rigid and bad for one's career [referring to graduates]... the private is more meritocratic and encourages ideas". Furthermore, *Wasta*, a prevailing feature of society, may be used to circumvent and remedy uncertainties, though it is usually nationals in KSA and UAE that have the higher level of *Wasta* connections to realize their wants and needs (Chbani, 2012). This phenomenon, though often referred to as social capital, is stigmatised and notoriously used with regards to gaining public sector jobs and other rent-seeking activities (Cunningham and Sarayrah, 1993; El Sayed and Harrigan, 2009).

Power distance scores in the KSA and UAE public and private sectors, exhibit high scores similar to Hofstede's original score. This emphasizes the assertion that the dimension is particularly steady and permeates within a nation's borders (Hofstede, 2001). In contrast, the UAI scores in the countries' sectors show wider variations and even larger disparity when compared to Hofstede's Arab UAI scores.

Various historical, micro- and macro-factors affect both PDI and UAI dimensions, while the latter is most sensitive to such influencing factors. These influences shape the complexity of a far from homogeneous region (see Figure 14 for cultural triangle highlighting cultural complexity in the Arab region).

Limitations and Further Research

Limitations of this study include the usage of a slightly biased sample that was not totally random. This is a result of the convenience and snowball sampling techniques used, although this could not be helped. Furthermore, the inclusion of a missing survey question asking for employees' education level may have assisted further analyses pertaining to workplace values and survey respondents' educational attainment.

Figure 14 **Increasing complexity of National Culture and Workplace Values: Arab Region**

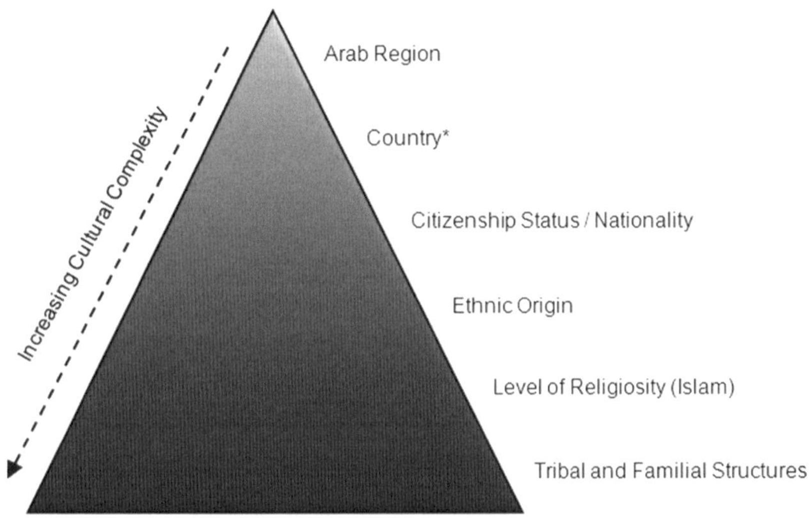

*This includes colonial history or influence (now a largely Western influence in most Arab countries), government type, demographics, economic structure (e.g. rentier).

The time constraints and the scope concerning this research only allowed for two neighboring 'Arab countries' (and two cultural dimensions) to be studied, instead of being more regionally representative.

Further avenues for research may include expanding the Hofstedean replication to other Arab countries and across all of the cultural dimensions. The potential development of an additional cultural dimension specifically relevant to Arab countries may also assist in understanding Arab-centric workplace values and Arab national cultures further. This may include a dimension pertaining to tribal, Islamic and western (including colonial legacy) influencers. Hofstede developed a Chinese-oriented dimension that was added to the original four dimensions, namely Confucian Dynamism.

Conclusion

Evidence suggests that there is significant heterogeneity across Arab countries as displayed through the Hofstedean replication that formulated power distance and uncertainty dimensions scores for KSA and UAE in this study. This confirms the need for literature and management practitioners to prevent from viewing the region as a cluster when trying to understand national culture and workplace values.

Tribal, Islamic, colonial and more contemporary influencers on national culture in the Arab countries illustrate both commonalities and differences. KSA and UAE as neighboring countries, both display similarities in traditional structures in the face of a rational-legal appearance, with KSA, the more traditional, autocratic and conservative of the two nations. The lopsided labor markets and broad diversity that are present in both countries make research more complex, though essential.

Furthermore, the culture and heritage of any 'indigenous' population is important, however, the large share of expatriates, particularly in GCC countries, makes it necessary to include them when considering national culture. Therefore, it is important to dismiss citizenship status, and instead include those actually present at the workplace for a more rigorous understanding when conducting business and management research.

Public and private sector workers display divergent beliefs and values, with the former said to present society and the nation, the greatest. In reference to KSA and UAE, family businesses may also help present 'society', though it will be the wider private sector that FDI suitors and international companies are likely to be most interested in.

Power distance scores in both countries remain relatively constant when compared to Hofstede's original PDI scores, and still high, across the whole population, among nationals and non-nationals and between both the public and private sector. This supports the timeless research conducted by Hofstede, in reference to power distance and two of his 'Arab countries'. Nevertheless slight differences establish the need for the disassembling of this cluster into nation states as the unit of analysis, at the very least.

Uncertainty avoidance scores, despite their great sensitivity, strengthen this need with even larger differences between KSA and UAE, and displaying large disparity when compared to Hofstede's original scores.

The disparate and often ambiguous political and economic environments *inter alia* across the region, compounds this incongruence surrounding features of uncertainty.

Cross-national research, often produced and monopolised by scholars in the western hemisphere, must take a new approach to this region and apply the philosophical message behind the following French expression; *Vérité en deça des Pyrénées, erreur au-delà*[vii]- Blaise Pascal, 1623-62 (Hofstede, 2001).

Appendices

Appendix 1. Hofstede's Country Dimension Scores

Hofsted's Dimensions	Power Distance	Uncertainty Avoidance	Individualism	Masculinity	Long-term Orientation
World Average	**50**	**45**	**43**	**55**	**64**
Arab Countries	**80**	**68**	**38**	**53**	-
Argentina	49	86	46	56	-
Austria	11	70	55	79	-
Belgium	65	94	75	54	-
Brazil	69	76	38	49	65
Canada	39	48	80	52	23
Chile	63	86	23	28	-
China	-	-	-	-	118
Colombia	67	80	13	64	-
Costa Rica	35	86	15	21	-
Denmark	18	23	74	16	-
East Africa	64	52	27	41	-
Equador	78	67	8	63	-
Finland	33	59	63	26	-
France	68	86	71	43	-
Germany	35	65	67	66	31
Great Britain	35	35	89	66	25
Greece	60	112	35	57	-
Guatemala	95	101	6	37	-
Hong Kong	68	29	25	57	96
India	77	40	48	56	61
Indonesia	78	48	14	46	-
Iran	58	59	41	43	-
Ireland	28	35	70	68	-
Israel	13	81	54	47	-
Italy	50	75	76	70	-
Jamaica	45	13	39	68	-
Japan	54	92	46	95	80

Malaysia	104	36	26	50	-
Mexico	81	82	30	69	-
New Zealand	22	49	79	58	30
Norway	31	50	69	8	-
Pakistan	55	70	14	50	-
Panama	95	86	11	44	-
Peru	64	87	16	42	-
Philippines	94	44	32	64	19
Poland	-	-	-	-	32
Portugal	63	104	27	31	-
Salvador	66	94	19	40	-
Singapore	74	8	20	48	48
South Africa	49	49	65	63	-
South Korea	60	85	18	39	75
Spain	57	86	51	42	-
Sweden	31	29	71	5	33
Switzerland	34	58	68	70	-
Taiwan	58	69	17	45	87
Thailand	64	64	20	34	56
Turkey	66	85	37	45	-
Uruguay	61	100	36	38	-
USA	40	46	91	62	29
Venezuela	81	76	12	73	-
West Africa	77	54	20	46	16
Yugoslavia	76	88	27	21	-

Source: Hofstede 2001

Appendix 2. Arab Contextualization of Hofstede's Cultural Dimensions

Power Distance	The Arab world scores high on this dimension (score of 80) which means that people accept a hierarchical order in which everybody has a place and which needs no further justification. Hierarchy in an organization is seen as reflecting inherent inequalities, centralization is popular, subordinates expect to be told what to do and the ideal boss is a benevolent autocrat.
Uncertainty Avoidance	The Arab culture scores 68 on this dimension and thus has a high preference for avoiding uncertainty. Countries exhibiting high uncertainty avoidance maintain rigid codes of belief and behaviour and are intolerant of unorthodox behaviour and ideas. In these cultures there is an emotional need for rules (even if the rules never seem to work) time is money, people have an inner urge to be busy and work hard, precision and punctuality are the norm, innovation may be resisted, security is an important element in individual motivation.
Individualism	The Arab culture, with a score of 38 is considered a collectivistic society. This is manifest in a collectivist culture is paramount, and over-rides most other societal rules and regulations. The society fosters strong relationships where everyone takes responsibility for fellow members of their group. In collectivist societies offence leads to shame and loss of face, employer/employee relationships are perceived in moral terms (like a family link), hiring and promotion decisions take account of the employee's in-group, management is the management of groups.
Masculinity	The Arab world scores 52 on this dimension and is thus a masculine society. In masculine countries people "live in order to work", managers are expected to be decisive and assertive, the emphasis is on equity, competition and performance and conflicts are resolved by fighting them out.
Long-term Orientation	No scores available for the Arab World on this dimension.

Source: Hofstede, 2012

Appendix 3. Online Survey Questionnaire

Power Distance

1. How frequently, in your experience, does the following problem occur:

	Very Frequently	Frequently	Sometimes	Seldom	Very Seldom
Employees being afraid to express disagreement with their managers	1	2	3	4	5

2. The descriptions below apply to four different types of managers. First, please read through these descriptions:

Manager 1: Usually makes his/her decisions promptly and communicates them to his/her subordinates clearly and firmly. Expects them to carry out the decisions loyally and without raising difficulties.

Manager 2: Usually makes his/her decisions promptly, but, before going ahead, tries to explain them fully to his/her subordinates. Gives them the reasons for the decisions and answers whatever questions they may have.

Manager 3: Usually consults with his/her subordinates before he/she reaches his/her decisions. Listens to their advice, considers it, and then announces his/her decision. He/she then expects all to work loyally to implement it whether or not it is in accordance with the advice they gave.

Manager 4: Usually calls a meeting of his/her subordinates when there is an important decision to be made. Puts the problem before the group and invites discussion. Accepts the majority viewpoint as the decision.

Now for the above types of manager, please mark the one which you would prefer to work under:

Manager 1
Manager 2
Manager 3
Manager 4

3. And, to which one of the above four types of managers would you say your own manager most closely corresponds:

Manager 1
Manager 2

Manager 3
Manager 4
He/she does not correspond closely to any of them

Uncertainty Avoidance

4. We are interested in whether the personal opinions of employees differ from country to country. The statement below is not about the company as such, but rather about general issues in industry. Please indicate the extent to which you personally agree or disagree with the following statement.

   Remember: We want your own opinion (even though it may be different from that of others in your country).

	Strongly Disagree	Disagree	Undecided	Agree	Strongly Agree
Company rules should not be broken - even when the employee thinks it is in the company's best interests	1	2	3	4	5

5. How often do you feel nervous or tense at work:

   I always feel this way
   Usually
   Sometimes
   Seldom
   I never feel this way

6. How long do you think you will continue working for this company:

   Two years at the most
   From two to five years
   More than five years (but I probably will leave before I retire)
   Until I retire

Demographic Data

7. Which sector do you work in:

   Private
   Public

8. Which industry do you work in:

   Energy
   Manufacturing
   Finance / Banking
   Consultancy / Brokerage / Legal
   Real Estate / Construction / Infrastructure
   Tourism / Hospitality
   Sport / Leisure
   Pharmaceuticals / Health
   Aviation
   Trade / Logistics
   IT / Telecommunications
   Retail
   Other

9. Which best describes your employment level:

   Senior Management
   Mid-Management
   Non-Management

10. Which gender are you:

    Male
    Female

11. How old are you:

    18-24
    25-34
    35-44
    45-54
    55+

12. Are you a UAE national:

    (If yes, please ignore the next question)
    Yes
    No

13. Which nationality are you: (Optional)

    [A full list of nationality options was presented here]

14. What are your religious beliefs:(Optional)

    Muslim
    Christian
    Hindu
    Sikh
    Agnostic
    Other

15. What is your email address:

    Please state: ____________________________________

Appendix 4. Data Normality

Normality was assessed through skewness and kurtosis values, together with normal Q-Q plots and histograms. All variables exhibit a normal distribution with both the skewness and kurtosis statistics between -1 to +1 and -4 to +4 respectively (Pallant, 2007), except for PDI 2 (see below).

Table 4. Descriptive Statistics

	N Statistic	Mean Statistic	Std. Deviation Statistic	Skewness Statistic	Kurtosis Statistic
PDI 2 (KSA)	214	3.46	0.661	**-1.139**	1.351
PDI 2 (UAE)	237	3.41	0.687	**-1.292**	2.370

Appendix 5. Industry Breakdown

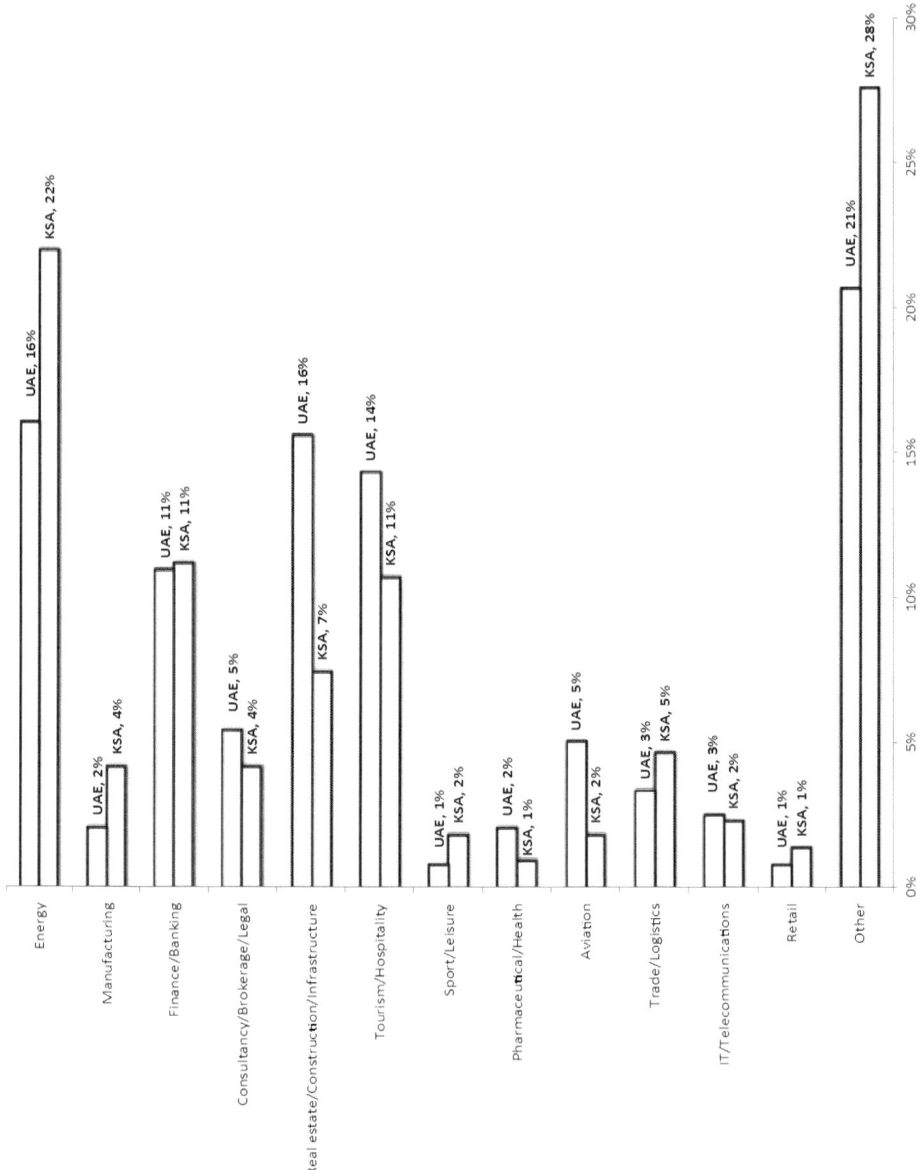

Appendix 6. Employment Level Breakdown

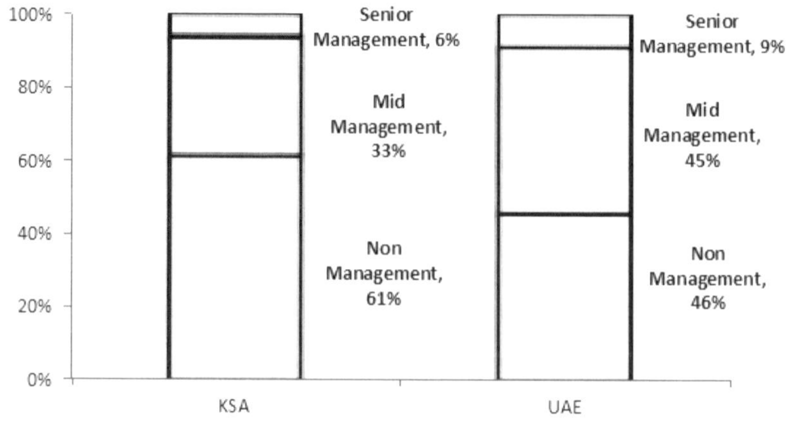

Appendix 7. Religion Breakdown

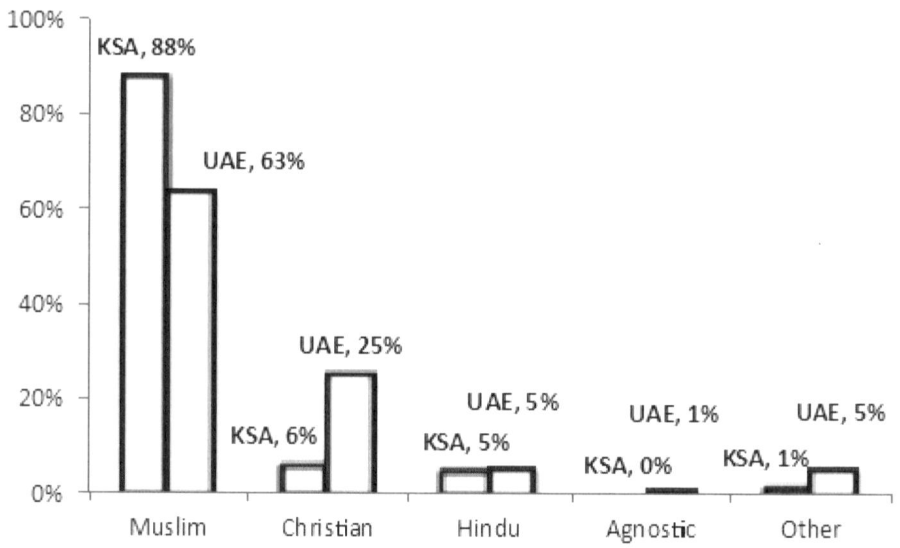

Appendix 8. Gender Breakdown

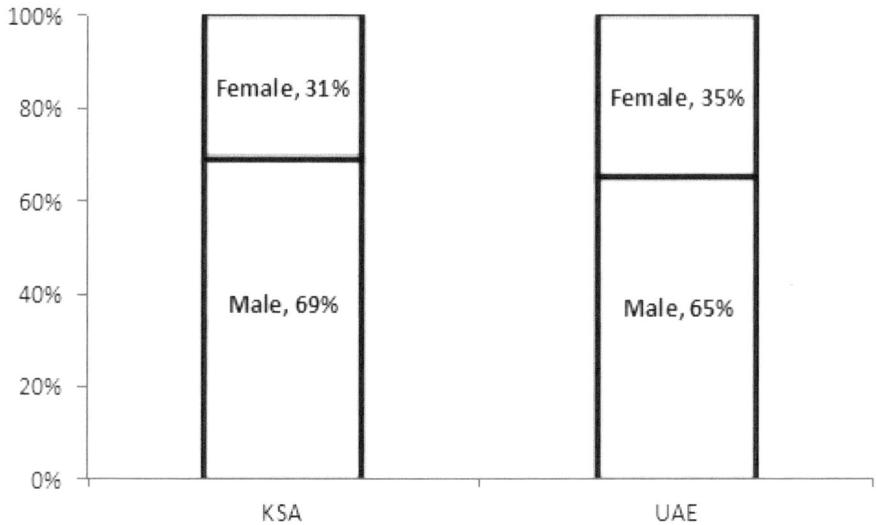

Appendix 9. Interview Participants

Name and Position	Company/Institution	Country Experience	Sector
Professor Geert Hofstede Social Pscyhologist	N/A	N/A	N/A
Professor Roger Owen Professor (Middle East History)	Harvard University	N/A	N/A
Dr Mark Neal Senior Lecture (Business and Management, MENA)	SOAS, University of London	UAE and Oman	N/A
Dr Gabriele vom Bruck Senior Lecture (Social Anthropology, Middle East)	SOAS, University of London	N/A	N/A
Ahmed Barada Operations Executive	Ali and Sons Company LLC	UAE	Private Sector

Masood Al Awar Cheif Executive Officer	Tasweek Real Estate	UAE and Middle East	Private and Public sector
Nabil Chbani Corporate Credit Head	Saudi American Bank	UAE and KSA	Private sector
Anonymous Participants			
Interviewee A Senior Employee	Government Organisation	UAE	Private and Public sector
Interviewee A Hotel Maid	Hospitality industry	KSA	Private sector

Appendix 10. Respondents from Countries Displaying Unrest

Respondent Country	N
Egypt	22
Yeman	12
Syria	11
Iraq	5
Palestine	5
Tunisia	4
Total	**59**

* These numbers do not account for dual nationality e.g. a British Egyptian

Notes

i Email correspondence from Professor Geert Hofstede on the 25th November 2011 conceding the potential response bias arising from specific roles/departments.

ii See Appendix 2 for Arab contextualisation of Hofstede's cultural dimensions.

iii Hofstede's (1980) IBM surveys were translated into Arabic for the 'Arab countries' region, thus South Asian and other non-Arab workers (non-nationals) are unlikely to have been accounted for in the study.

iv The exception to gaining national status in GCC countries occurs almost only when female non-nationals marry male GCC nationals (Nazir and Tomppert, 2005; Ismail, 2011).

v The sponsoring system that often involves the withholding of a migrant workers' passport/documents is known as 'Kafala', is a custom practice in the GCC in order to help regulate the employment and residency of migrant workers. Salaries, accommodation, meals and the mobility to leave jobs and even return home are often at the mercy of the GCC national 'employer' (migrant-rights.org, 2012a).

vi The author worked in the labor-intensive real estate industry in the UAE for a period of two years and witnessed manual laborers' poor working conditions and learned of their small salaries.

vii Translation: There are truths on this side of the Pyrenees that are falsehoods on the other. (Pensées in Hofstede, 2001).

5

Key Drivers for Employee Engagement and Productivity of GCC Nationals and Expatriates: A Longitudinal Study 2010-2012

David Jones

Introduction: The Paradox of Plenty

Creating more positive and productive employment opportunities for the local population of the GCC states is the most important HR priority for the decades ahead. However, the region languishes towards the bottom of international benchmarks in terms of engagement, employee well-being and labor productivity. Taking into account the ongoing shift in demographics, positive indications of economic growth and the experience of the region in the wake of the 'Arab Awakening', organizations today are facing a unique employment environment. The broad – based demographic pyramids forming across the region - a significant youth bulge, along with troubling levels of youth unemployment and incidents of socio-political strife are fuelling a surge in formal and informal regulatory amendments to accelerate the participation of local talent in the labor market. There are also increasing efforts towards educational reform. However, from a long term growth perspective and with visible skill gaps persisting, labor markets continue to depend on foreign workers to take on both white collar and blue collar jobs which the local talent supply is currently unable or unwilling to perform. Thomas Piketty (2013) predicts the continued relative diminishing of the global value of labor compared to capital across twenty – first labor markets. However, at this point in the GCC, real wages are high and increasing on average, both for GCC nationals and some categories of expatriates. Rather than the price of labor, it is the value of labor which is the primary lacunae in the regions labor markets. Pride in your efforts, the honour of work, the focus on personal contribution remains deficient.

This paper sheds light on the fascinating dilemma faced by the region with regards to its economic and social future. There is a limited window of opportunity to harness the region's demographic potential. "At a broad level, the Middle East & North Africa (MENA) region, and more specifically the Gulf Co-operation Council (GCC) countries, need to provide more plentiful, positive and productive employment opportunities to absorb its expected demographic surplus in the decades ahead. This is a crucial juncture in the making of the region. The choices made today will determine the fate of these nations for many years to come. This is essentially the 'Paradox of Plenty'. The GCC is endowed not only with the world's largest proven energy reserves but also a young, growing and educated workforce that can enhance its future growth trajectory. The key question is how this enormous potential may be unlocked and channeled in the right direction. Failure to do so will squander one of the greatest demographic dividends in recent times. This is in sharp contrast to other parts of the world, which either do not have the financial endowments or are facing a steady decline in their population, or both, as a means to steer their economies forward" (Jones & Punshi, 2013).

It is critical for policy makers, business leaders, HR professionals and individuals to understand the underlying expectations and aspirations, attitudes and behaviors and workplace orientation of employees, and how this may vary or be similar across various demographic constituencies which form the region's highly segmented labor markets, men and women, young and old, and national and foreign workers in particular.

At the most fundamental level, a pertinent question remains: What truly drives and motivates talent in the region? How to unlock this paradox of plenty?

The Talent Landscape in the Middle East: A Macro Perspective

The phenomenal growth experienced over the past few decades has led to an unyielding belief that anything is possible within the GCC. It is a place where ambition meets opportunity (Jones & Punshi, 2013). Broadly, at a national level, policymakers are concerned with transforming the productivity of the local population into the future engine of economic growth, diversification and stability, supporting job creation. Employers are impacted by the factors influencing supply, demand and the cost of talent. Finally, individuals living and working in the region are concerned with personal standards of living, where they live, how they get to work, where their kids go to school, etc. All of these aspects are in some way dependent on the structure of the labor market.

Without doubt, the single-largest dominating factor moving forward is the unprecedented local demographic growth forecast for the region. According to the World Bank (2014) 'the dynamics of demography in the Arab Region have created some of the most intense pressures on labor markets observed anywhere in the post-World War II period.' At a time when most

Figure 1 **Key Characteristics of the GCC Labor Markets**

Source: From Unlocking the Paradox of Plenty, Jones & Punshi (2013)

other populations in the world are in decline, the Arab world's population is expected to double by 2050 (UNDP, 2010). A significant majority of the population is of working age, as a result of high fertility rates in the region. This 'youth bulge' has resulted in the most rapid growth of young people as a proportion of the region's population in recorded human history. The increasing youth bulge is also complemented by rapid growth in the representation of women in the local workforce. Though coming from a lower base compared to global standards, more women are not only entering the formal labor market, but also participating for longer periods of time.

Another key feature is the highly segmented nature of the labor markets. The early exploitation of fossil fuel discoveries and the lack of capacity within nascent labor markets resulted in a massive inflow of foreign workers into the GCC. The monetary strength provided by the energy endowments over the subsequent decades allowed the reliance on expatriate workers to continue. This is especially pronounced for the vast majority of jobs providing physical and service labor, along with a high proportion of more specialized technical and managerial roles. Remarkably, even today, of the world's twenty countries with the highest proportion of international migration, approximately half are in the Arab world (Mirkin, 2010), with Qatar and UAE leading.

Further, the public sector continues to dominate employment of national talent, with the private sector significantly lagging behind as the employer of choice for nationals. It is estimated that 72.3% of all public sector jobs in GCC are held by its citizens (Al Masah Capital, 2011). As a result of the historically lower national population base, an oversaturated public sector and the decades of reliance on imported labor, there are deeply entrenched views about employment among the local population. Participation rates especially in the private sector among nationals are startlingly low. As an example in the UAE, a report released the National Bureau of Statistics (The National, 2012) reported that only 19,874 Emiratis worked in the private sector at the start of 2012, only around 0.5% of the sector's total workforce of nearly 3.89 million.

In sum, against a spectacular canvas of economic growth and an unprecedented population surge, the GCC is transforming.

Brief Introduction to Employee Engagement

Employee engagement matters. Decades of research in the areas of employee motivation, engagement and productivity have proven that organizations which achieve higher levels of engagement demonstrate better business results, organizational performance and increased level of customer service. This creates longer term value for stakeholders. In sum, engaged employees are more driven and willing to exert discretionary effort towards supporting the success of their organizations. "Achieving higher levels of employee engagement in the Middle East matters significantly. It is critical that human capital development further accelerates economic growth" (Aon Hewitt, 2011).

The primary aim of the *Qudurat* (meaning "capabilities" in Arabic) study was to understand the distinct triggers for engagement and productivity across the GCC and broader Arab World. Though there are varying definitions of employee engagement, for the purpose of this study, an engaged employee was defined as one who is committed, emotionally and intellectually, to their work. The engagement model used measures whether employees speak positively about the organization to others (say), have an intense desire to be part of the organization (stay) and are willing to exert discretionary effort (strive) to contribute to its overall success.

Qudurat Research Overview

(The *Qudurat* research was funded by Aon Hewitt and the author retains academic publishing rights.)

Qudurat was conceptualized and designed as an exploratory, 'hypothesis-forming' research study. This was largely due to the considerable lack of previous, quality research in the GCC on the theme of employee engagement and also to minimize any researcher bias while designing the study. One of the aims of the study was to understand whether the 'rentier state theory' translated more specifically into rent-seeking behavior within the region's labor markets.

The *Qudurat* study was launched in 2010 with a sample size of 4599 respondents in the GCC from over 40+ private and public sector organizations. In 2012, over 100+ organizations participated in the study with a total sample size of 15,865, including all the 6 GCC countries and Egypt. Representing the voice of approximately 20,500 employees completing a self-report questionnaire from 150+ organizations across UAE, Oman, Qatar, Bahrain, Kuwait, Saudi Arabia and Egypt, the *Qudurat* research provides compelling and often counter-intuitive insights into the region's talent landscape, with data captured in 2010 and 2012. To date, the study constitutes the largest workplace study conducted within the Gulf region, unmatched in scope and scale in terms of the data driven insights into workplace behavior. The insights offered by the resulting analysis also lead to powerfully practical recommendations and implications for the future of work in the region.

Research Design

The research design was based on an extensive review of literature, including labor market economics, human resources, organizational behavior and positive psychology. It also relied heavily on the practical experience and expertise of the research team conducting the study.

The approach throughout the study was to have an appreciative and positive understanding of the unique strengths and aspirations of talent in the GCC.

Employee engagement was the primary outcome variable measured by 6 questions, 2 each for the following 3 constructs:

Say: speak positively about the organization to co-workers, potential employees and customers;

Stay: have an intense sense of belonging and desire to be a part of the organization; and

Strive: are motivated and exert effort towards success in their job and for the organization.

The *other outcome variables* were spread across 5 broad dimensions and 32 overall 'drivers', as depicted in the table below.

Table 1 Qudurat Research Design: Outcome Variables

Self	Work	Others	Work Environment	Identity
1. Grit 2. Flow 3. Goal Setting 4. Optimism 5. Pro - activity 6. Resilience 7. Self Efficacy 8. Zest 9. Responsibility and Skill	10. Accomplishment & Meaning 11. Pride in Work 12. Work Preparedness 13. Pay and Growth 14. Preference for Hierarchy 15. Job Orientation 16. Career Orientation 17. Calling Orientation 18. Mobility	19. Positive Relationships 20. Level of Support from Manager 21. Confidence in Leadership 22. Level of Trust 23. Tolerance to Diversity	24. Learning & Development 25. Level of Support from Organization 26. Structure & Communication 27. Fairness at Work	28. Identity Alignment 29. Work Identity 30. Family Identity 31. Religious Identity 32. National Identity

1. *Self:* This dimension focuses on understanding the personal attributes and psychological strengths of employees at the workplace. Research in this area clearly relates personal strengths and attributes to better performance, higher levels of work commitment, job satisfaction, better health, etc. Aspects such as grit, flow, goal setting, optimism, pro-activity, resilience, self-efficacy, zest, perceptions towards own responsibility and skill expectations were assessed.
2. *Work:* This dimension focuses on understanding employee attitudes and preferences towards work. It probes into how people primarily approach their work, their work preparedness, mobility, sense of pride and meaning, growth and pay expectations and so on.
3. *Others:* This dimension focuses on the impact of the relationships with peers, Managers and leaders on an employee's work life. It also probes on aspects such as acceptance to multiple facets of diversity, such as age, seniority and nationality.
4. *Work Environment:* This dimension seeks to understand the current work environment and the impact of various opportunities available for the employee. The dimension also looks at aspects such as learning and development, communication preferences and organizational support.
5. *Identity:* This dimension seeks to understand how various socio-cultural aspects of the employee impact the world of work, including family, work, religion and national identity.

Salient features of the survey questionnaire:

- The online survey questionnaire included a total of 91 questions, including 12 demographic questions.
- Since the data was collected 100% online, the coverage was largely limited to white-collar workers, and did not include a significant proportion of blue-collared workers.
- The survey questionnaire was designed in such a way that most 'drivers' were measured by two questions or more.
- The initial questionnaire was validated by a select team of advisors who provided their feedback on the socio-cultural relevance and considerations.
- To ensure ease of completion, most of the questions were either forced choice, drop-down options or on a 6-point scale (e.g. ranging from strongly agree to strongly disagree).

Data collection process:

- The survey was administered to a cross-section of employees from participating organizations from UAE, Bahrain, Qatar, Saudi Arabia, Kuwait and Oman across the public and private sectors in 2010 and 2012. Egypt was included in the 2012 study.
- The survey was administered online in both English and Arabic and the average time taken to complete the survey was 15-20 minutes.
- To ensure complete accuracy of translation, the survey was translated into Arabic and then independently reverse translated into English.
- There were no financial implications or costs associated for any organization or partner to participate in the study.
- As an incentive, each organization participating in the research received a complimentary copy of their own results report compared to the overall country norm group.
- The online survey was hosted on an independent survey platform to protect the confidentiality of individual respondent data. All measures were taken to protect individual confidentiality and no organization, partner or third party had access to any employee-wise data. All data reported was for groups of over 10 individuals.

Results and Interpretation

The *Qudurat* data is ground-breaking, both in terms of its scale and scope, as the single largest endeavor to understand the workplace motivators and orientations of the GCC workforce. The findings from the study could inform the on-going labor market reform and steps taken by governments and policy-makers across the region to achieve their economic vision and goals to diversify into 'knowledge-based' economies. Further, in addition to measuring levels of employee engagement, *Qudurat* also sheds light on critical workplace indicators such as confidence in leadership, tolerance to diversity, attrition risk, and employee performance. It explores the inter-relationships of each of the research drivers with these positive workplace indicators.

Section 1: A Comparative Analysis of Employee Engagement

Findings from the *Qudurat* study reveal that the GCC has some of the lowest levels of reported employee engagement in the world, second only to Africa. The results are 10% lower than the global 2012 average. This is an alarming finding, considering the very nature of the labor markets in the GCC, constituting expatriate workers and nationals. First, one would assume that most expatriates, at least the white-collared workers (whom were the target sample for this research), have made a positive choice to work in the region and would demonstrate higher levels of engagement. Further, national talent, a relatively smaller part of the local labor market, have experienced a privileged position within the GCC, including pervasive positive discrimination in the workplace. They have been witness to the tremendous economic growth and development of their nations and could be expected to report much higher levels of work motivation.

A further cause for concern is that the average level of engagement in the GCC has decreased by almost 4.5% since 2010.

Table 2 **Global and Regional Engagement Levels (2010 to 2012)**

Year	2010	2012
Global	58%	60%
Asia Pacific	59%	58%
Europe	53%	57%
Africa	58%	48%
Latin America	73%	74%
North America	64%	63%
GCC	54%	49.5%

One of the most distressing trends is that GCC national talent report significanly lower levels of employee engagement, compared to their expatriate counter-parts. This is true, without exception, in every GCC country from Oman to Saudi Arabia. Further, engagement levels have declined considerably for GCC nationals to 43.7% in 2012, compared to 51% in 2010. On the other hand, engagement levels for expatriates have remained consistent at 56.1% in 2012 and 57% in 2010. The widening gap in the levels of employee engagement needs to be urgently addressed by policy-makers, organizational leaders and HR professionals, particularly as the region seeks to successfully continue the transition towards 'knowledge-based economies' during the rest of the century ahead.

In a comparative analysis of each of the GCC nations, Saudi nationals were the least engaged at 40.6%, followed by Emiratis at 41.6%. Omanis, Bahrainis and Kuwaitis displayed moderate engagement levels and the Qataris were the highest at 51%. On the other hand, expatriates are most engaged in Bahrain and Kuwait, followed by UAE and Qatar, with lower engagement levels being reported in Saudi Arabia and Oman.

From a gender perspective, the trends are also interesting. Females report higher levels of engagement than men in Qatar and Oman, while there is much more to be desired towards engaging the female workforce in Saudi Arabia & Egypt. In all other countries, males report higher levels of engagement than females.

Table 3 **Regional Engagement Levels (2012)**

	Overall	Nationals (N)	Expats (E)	Males	Females
GCC	49.55%	43.67%	56.14%*	50.38%	47.04%*
UAE	49.40%	41.60%	56.8%*	52.40%	44.7%*
KSA	46.90%	40.60%	51.3%*	47.1%*	39.0%
Qatar	53.30%	51.00%	56.40%	52.40%	55.7%*
Bahrain	48.40%	44.8%	63.60%	50.00%	45.8%*
Oman	48.40%	47.6%*	51.10%	47.10%	51.9%
Kuwait	61.90%	43.90%	63.7%*	62.10%	61.10%
Egypt	44.80%	44.7%*	50.00%	45.7%*	37.90%

**Denotes statistical significance at a confidence interval of 95%*

It is important to highlight some critical considertions regarding the timing of the *Qudurat* research. The first wave of data was collected in 2010 in the pre-Arab Spring era. The 2012 data was collected in the midst of / just after the Arab Spring. Since 2011, most GCC countries have taken steps towards reforming their labor markets and providing greater opportunities and benefits for their local population. As an example, Saudi Arabia has introduced a series of far-reaching reforms in the past few years. Most recently, the Saudi government introduced the *Nitaqat* program (DLA Piper, 2012). Of all the initiatives undertaken by the Kingdom, *Nitaqat* stands out as one of the most innovative and radical

(Jones & Punshi, 2012). *Nitaqat* is an approach to reduce the number of sponsorship visas (or *iqamas*) granted to expatriates seeking work in the private sector, thereby increasing employment of Saudi nationals in the private sector. Another program introduced in Saudi Arabia is the *Hafiz* income support program for job-seekers. *Hafiz* has approximately 1.3 million registered on the program (Gulf Business, 2012), and more than 80% of the beneficaries of the program are female (IMF, 2013). Based on a series of reforms led by the Ministry of Labor and the HRDF, and the subsequent efforts of employers, there was a massive 84% surge in Saudi women working in private sector from 2012 to 2013 (Arabian Business, 2014). It is to be seen whether an increase in labor force participation of female nationals, especially in the private sector, will lead to higher levels of employee engagement in the future.

The *Qudurat* findings underline the fact that the GCC faces extraordinary challenges with regards to motivating its young population. There is an on-going and disquieting trend of dismally low levels of engagement amongst the younger generation of national talent. The 2010 *Qudurat* study had highlighted a significant concern amongst the engagement levels amongst the 25-34 age cohort of GCC nationals at 45%. This group still has the lowest average engagement in 2012 at 40.1%. However, unfortunately, there is also a significant decline in engagement levels for nationals under the age of 25 at 47.7% (compared to 64% in 2010) and 43.4% for the 35 to 44 age group (reported at 49% in 2010).

Figure 2 **Comparative Analysis of Changes in Engagement Levels between 2010 and 2012**

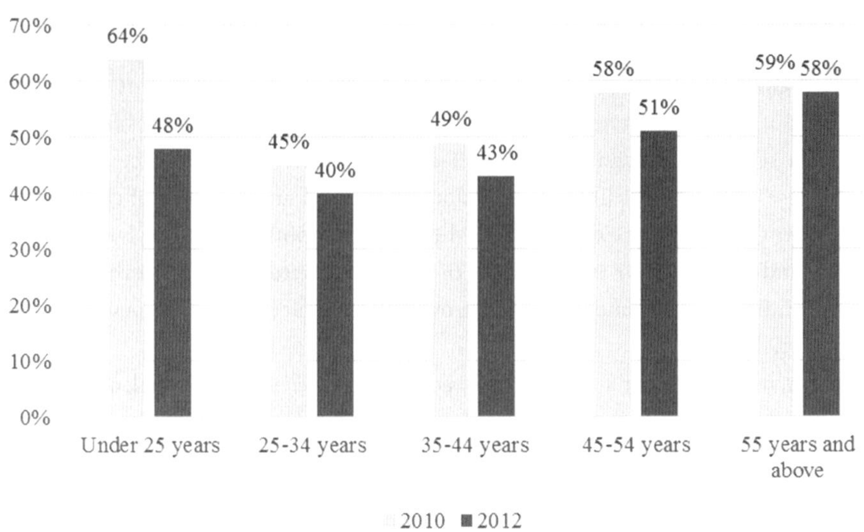

Hence, according to Jones & Punshi (2013), the region is experiencing the onset of an 'early–mid career' crisis in the Arab world, seen almost a decade earlier than most other parts of the world, where a more typical mid-career crisis in the forties would prevail. The strikingly low levels of youth engagement significantly impacts performance, productivity, well-being and long-term health at all levels – individual and organizational across the GCC labor markets.

This is supported by a recent report by WEF (2012), which states that "young people (in the Middle East) are seeking to achieve the transition to adulthood, competing with a large cohort of peers to secure places in preferred educational fields and gain employment in scarce positions in the formal sectors of the economy. They are also trying to successfully reach other important milestones in the transition to adulthood, such as marriage, child - rearing and household formation. Over the past two decades, efforts to achieve these normative milestones have been increasingly met with growing frustration and failure, as evidenced most clearly by the poor outcomes in the region's labor markets.

On further deliberation, one of the root causes associated with the 'early–mid career' crisis is in some regards counter-intuitive as reported by younger nationals. It may be attributed to an overemphasis on formal, structured development. From the time of education into early employment, local talent are exposed to a didactic, traditional and hierarchical approach to learning and development, led primarily by classroom-based instruction. As they transition from education to the world of work, most nationals would go through a 'national development' program in their early twenties, ranging anywhere from between six months up to five years, often on an accelerated leadership career track to take them rapidly towards a '*mudhir*' (manager) or management position by the end of their traineeship. Soon after, most nationals are then placed into jobs within the organization. In many cases, these jobs are unrelated to their educational backgrounds. Some are placed in people management roles having to manage expatriates from different cultures and higher levels of work experience. They display lower levels of workplace resilience (ability to deal with setbacks), confidence and self-efficacy (belief in the impact of your own actions). These foundational life skills are not emphasised at all as part of the education or employment training provided. Indeed, the highly supportive and passive educational experience and introduction to the world of work may actually be exacerbating, rather than ameliorating, this phenomenon of growing workplace disengagement and "early mid-career crisis".

Further, national talent also experience additional accelerated personal, economic and social responsibilities. On average, starting families earlier whilst retaining the responsibility of looking after the older generations, as well as establishing higher average levels of personal debt, most often during the same period. This leads to increased levels of stress and a lack of preparedness to cope with career and general life challenges.

Table 4 Engagement Levels by Age (2012)

	Under 25 years			25-34 years			35-44 years			45-54 years			55 years & above		
	Overall	Nationals (N)	Expats (E)	Overall	Nationals (N)	Expats (E)	Overall	Nationals (N)	Expats (E)	Overall	Nationals (N)	Expats (E)	Overall	Nationals (N)	Expats (E)
GCC	47.80%	47.72%	48.21%	44.55%	40.14%	50.7%*	50.40%	43.44%	56.2%*	59.20%	50.89%	64.7%*	63.88%	57.84%	66.0%*
UAE	47.10%	45.81%	53.85%	44.10%	38.74%	51.4%*	50.40%	41.19%	56.3%*	63.70%	54.37%	67.5%*	63.70%	58.62%	64.7%*
KSA	43.30%	43.53%	42.7%*	44.20%	37.64%	49.2%*	47.50%	42.13%	50.1%*	57.40%	56.06%	57.7%*	61.20%	45.00%	63.4%*
Qatar	54.70%	55.8%*	N/A	47.30%	49.3%*	43.09%	52.10%	48.70%	55.48%	61.80%	48.89%	67.3%*	69.20%	73.33%	68.25%
Bahrain	48.10%	48.7%*	N/A	42.90%	41.30%*	60.00%	48.40%	43.4%*	62.43%	53.70%	49.7%*	65.15%	62.90%	56.9%*	70.45%
Oman	87.50%	85.71%	N/A	39.00%	37.5%*	50.00%	50.00%	47.6%*	58.33%	48.00%	53.85%	41.67%	53.30%	N/A	45.45%
Kuwait	63.90%	N/A	66.7%*	53.10%	35.48%	55.3%*	64.20%	N/A	64.1%*	71.30%	33.33%	74.8%*	69.40%	N/A	70.3%*
Egypt	44.20%	44.23%	N/A	43.30%	43.1%*	N/A	45.20%	45.1%*	N/A	45.80%	46.43%	N/A	61.10%	61.11%	N/A

**Denotes statistical significance at a confidence interval of 95%*

Another frequently cited reason has to do with the mismatch in expectations, feeling of entitlement and lack of incentives for self-development. Along with a lack of work readiness and life skills, unfortunately, the education system (including career guidance support, as well as influence of family and peers and the overall structure of the regional labor markets) fail to provide effective support in terms of setting realistic expectations about the world of work. With an heightened sense of entitlement, national talent often enter the workplace with a different sense of expectations, which can be far removed from reality in terms of what the saturated public sector or a commercial employer can offer.

Dealing with this crisis requires the adoption of a sustainable approach towards education, learning and development, versus an over-reliance on didactive classroom-based instruction, as is currently the case. On-going career guidance, coaching and a focus on fostering employability skills and character education would be essential in overcoming the early–mid career crisis. Further, early stage internship, traineeship and apprentice programs would help showcase the world of work at an earlier stage, and youth could have an opportunity to form more realistic expectations of the workplace when they graduate.

Table 5 **Engagement Levels by Education (2012)**

	Primary	Secondary	Vocational or Technical Diploma	Bachelor's Degree	Master's Degree	PhD	Other
GCC	58.6%	50.2%*	46.9%*	50.6%*	47.5%*	34.2%	55.4%*
UAE	63.60%	54.50%	50.30%	49.60%	45.20%	34.40%	50.00%
KSA	66.70%	45.60%	41.40%	48.50%	47.80%	NA	50.80%
Qatar	NA	50.30%	45.80%	57.40%	47.10%	NA	54.50%
Bahrain	NA	51.70%	49.20%	48.40%	45.30%	25.00%	61.00%
Oman	NA	68.00%	37.00%	47.90%	57.60%	NA	NA
Kuwait	NA	64.90%	57.30%	63.30%	58.70%	NA	81.80%
Egypt	55.30%	45.70%	42.50%	45.40%	39.60%	NA	NA

**Denotes statistical significance at a confidence interval of 95%*

An atypical feature of the GCC labor market has been the over-saturated public sector. It has been the primary source of employment and according to estimates by The Middle East Policy Council, 72.3% of all public sector jobs in GCC are held by its citizens (Al Masah Capital, 2011). The ratio of nationals in public sector jobs is high in Saudi Arabia (91.3%), Bahrain (90.8%), Oman (80.5%) and Kuwait (74.6%).

A report by Booz & Co (2010) states that "the region's ability to depend on oil revenues has resulted in the creation of a welfare system in which the government is the largest employer of nationals". There are widespread stereotypes about the attractiveness of public sector jobs for local talent based on a number of favorable conditions including higher pay, shorter working hours, job security and other associated benefits. Recent increases in public sector pay and benefits are a retrograde step in the move to try and reduce the reliance on public sector employment and the private sector more attractive to young GCC nationals, regardless of whether young GCC nationals are attractive potential recruits for private sector employers.

Therefore, it could be expected that national talent in the public sector would have reasonably higher levels of employee engagement. However, the *Qudurat* data proves the opposite. The overall level of engagement of employees in the public sector, and of GCC nationals in particular, is significantly lower that of those employed in the private sector, with averages of 39.3% and 52.9% respectively. This distinction is even more pronounced in countries such as the UAE, where there is a 25% difference in engagement levels with government (at 29.9%) and private sector employment (at 54.9%).

Table 6 **Engagement Levels within the Public, Semi-Government & Private Sectors (2012)**

	Overall	Nationals (N)	Expats (E)	Males	Females	Under 25	25-34	35-44	45-54	55+
GCC Public	39.3%	36.6%*	52.6%	39.7%	38.9%*	43.5%	34.0%	39.7%	47.0%	55.0%
GCC Private	52.9%	44.8%	56.9%*	52.9%*	52.8%	46.8%	48.7%*	54.9%	64.0%	66.9%
GCC Semi-Govt	52.4%	50.7%*	55.3%	52.0%	53.8%*	51.9%*	46.3%	52.1%*	62.5%*	66.5%*

**Denotes statistical significance at a confidence interval of 95%*

With a majority of national employment stemming from the public sector, there are notable consequences of such chronically low levels of engagement within this sector. Despite extremely preferential working conditions, job security and on-going emphasis on higher wage differences and benefits as compared to private sector organizations, the public sector is failing to capture the motivation and discretionary effort of a vast majority of its employees. No significant differences were reported by gender. However, the younger age cohorts, the 25-34 and 35-44 age groups are reporting the lowest engagement levels in the public sector across the GCC. Therefore, there is a growing sense of dissatisfaction amongst the younger generation employed by these more traditionally hierarchical and bureaucratic governmental organizations. Hence, even though the private sector across the GCC is arguably less developed than elsewhere in terms of total employment, it seems to be doing a better job in motivating its workforce, including national talent.

These reported levels of lower engagement in the public sector overturn the general belief that significantly higher wages, longer holidays, better working hours, etc. would necessarily lead to higher levels of engagement. In fact, it is observed that other aspects, such as career growth, learning & development, and effective managerial and leadership support have a much more significant impact on work motivation, that wages or benefits per se. This is reminiscent of the classic Herzberg two-factor theory of workplace motivation from the 1960's, where aspects such as pay or working conditions may be considered hygiene factors, rather than work motivators.

However, there is one area where the public sector clearly outshines the private sector. The *Qudurat* study found that nationals report a greater sense of pride and status by being associated with the government sector, and a keen sense of positive contribution to the community and country. 86.7% of GCC nationals working in the public sector believe their work is making their country or community a better place, as compared to only 66.6% of nationals in the private sector.

Finally, while looking at comparative trends in employee engagement, some interesting themes arose by industry classification. On average, the Manufacturing sector had the highest levels of engagement (doesn't include blue collar workers), followed closely by the Energy sector. Banking and Service sectors seem to report the lowest scores at 43.5% and 46.4% respectively.

Table 7 **Engagement Levels by Industry (2012)**

	Overall	Nationals (N)	Expats (E)	Males	Females
Energy	59.81%	58.01%*	70.08%	58.27%	64.71%*
BFSI	43.58%	43.09%*	49.06%	42.53%	45.66%*
Manufacturing	61.45%	63.50%	60.17%*	61.36%*	62.05%
Services	46.45%	40.51%*	56.25%	46.01%	48.09%*
Conglomerates	51.30%	44.70%	55%*	51.4%*	51.20%

**Denotes statistical significance at a confidence interval of 95%*

It may be worth discussing the difference in the levels of engagement between the Banking & Energy sector, due to their historic focus on nationalization. Broadly speaking, outside of the public sector, efforts to increase the percentage of nationals have been most prolonged and most prominent within these two sectors, with most GCC states having significantly high levels of quotas for nationals. As an example, it is estimated that Omanis now represent close to 85 or 90% of the workforce in key sectors such as Energy and Banking (Ministry of Manpower, 2011). Over time, Energy companies and Financial institutions have achieved much success towards their nationalization targets and usually have well defined and well executed talent strategies with regards to attracting, developing and retaining local talent, including but not limited to fairly competitive pay and benefits packages. Thus, it is somewhat surprising to observe such a striking difference in engagement levels between both these industry groups. A possible explanation for the lower levels of engagement within Banking & Financial services was that the industry was still recovering from the global financial crisis when this data was collected in 2012. This may have led to a sense of insecurity and lack of motivation. Alternatively, energy companies are often joint ventures between foreign and national companies, and their workforces have remained thus balanced for some considerable time. Banking on the other hand, has typically been a priority for quota-driven hiring of nationals, and this could be leading to a looming sense of 'tokenism' as an unintended consequence of anachronistic, quota-driven approaches towards nationalization over time.

Section 2: Work Preparedness

One of the dominant discourses worldwide has been on the relevance of education to employment. According to a global study (McKinsey, 2012), less than half of the students (45%) and employers (42%) believe that the education system has prepared them for the workplace. Ironically, 72% of educational providers believe that the students are adequately prepared for the workplace. However, students report that the relevance of their education to the job market is insufficient. Fewer than half of the students are confident that they would study the same subject, if they were given a choice again. Furthermore, most students need to wait six to twelve months to find employment and more than half are unable to do so in their chosen area of study (McKinsey, 2012).

These same global trends are being witnessed in GCC as well, and arguably, the situation may be even more alarming. Only 29% of GCC employers feel that education prepares students with necessary technical skills and only 19% agree that it prepares young people with the right attitude for work (EY, 2014).

One of the key aspects measured in the *Qudurat* research was on work preparedness. On average, only 69.3% of GCC nationals, compared to 85.7% of expatriates believe that their educational background has adequately prepared them for their jobs.

Surprisingly, the youngest nationals, those under 25 years reported the lowest scores at 62.5%. With the lowest scores amongst the youngest nationals, this clearly points to a current gap in terms of the education systems in the region, arguably seeming to be obsolete or irrelevant, hence, leading to a sense of dissatisfaction amongst its most immediate products once they arrive in the workplace. Interestingly, there is a significant difference between nationals who were educated locally versus those who studied abroad. 66.6% of those with local education are reporting a lack of preparedness as compared to 78% who have had international educational opportunities. This clearly indicates that there is more to be desired from reforming the local education systems with schools and institutions of higher education. From a comparative country perspective, the lowest scores were reported by Saudi and Qatari nationals at 65.8% and 69% respectively.

Interestingly, females reported lower levels of work preparedness compared to their male counterparts. Education is also driving change and increasing the complexity of workplace gender relations within the Gulf. The *Qudurat* findings may be viewed in the light of more recent research (Ridge, 2014) which highlights the growing gender divide in education, highlighting that GCC national boys are consistently disadvantaged and underperforming within the region's educational institutions. Ridge highlights that whilst girls are generally outperforming boys in all subjects globally, apart from the STEM subjects, in the GCC they outperform boys in all subjects. One of the main reasons for this is the importance of role-modeling with the region's public school systems. Whilst typically, GCC national girls are educated almost exclusively by GCC national women, their male counterparts are almost exclusively educated by expatriate men. It is argued that the lower social status of expatriates, the precarious employment contracts of foreign teachers and their long-term commitment to their pupils in particular are instrumental in determining the pronounced differential educational outcomes of men and women across the region. The lack of respect afforded to the educators of boys limits the scope of positive role-modeling in male education compared to that of females and this has a direct impact on educational and life outcomes more generally. Though these claims of the reverse gender divide may seem to be in slight contrast to the findings of *Qudurat* (where females feel less prepared for work than males), this could be explained by the fact that though women have better educational outcomes, i.e. perform better academically, they still need support with the job ready skills in order to the fully cognizant of the world of work.

To sum up, building character strengths and skills in young people have long been considered essential for social, personal, and vocational success. Employability skills may constitute aspects such as having the functional skills required for the job (business English, IT etc.), but also other aspects such as communication, team-work, work ethics, problem solving, decision making and the like. Arguably, having a positive attitude and mindset, and possessing key characteristics are the single-most important determinants of achieving success in life and work outcomes, such as academic performance, productivity at work and even in aspects such as being able to find a job. These characteristics include key aspects suchas the ability to deal with setbacks (resilience), set long-term goals (grit), being empathetic and working with others (social intelligence) and achieving a sense of meaning and contribution that is beyond one's own immediate zone of concern (pro-social purpose).

Table 8 Education & Work Preparedness by Country, Sector & Industry (2012) (% who believe that their educational background adequately prepared them for their jobs)

	Overall	Nationals (N)	Expats (E)	Males	Females	Under 25	25-34	35-44	45-54	55 above
GCC	78.0 %	69.3 %	85.7%*	80.4 %	71.0%*	65.3 %	74.4 %	81.7 %	86.9%*	89.1%*
UAE	74.9 %	66.2 %	80.0%*	78.8%	67.9%*	58.0%	70.6%*	80.2%	86.2%	89.9%
KSA	75.1 %	64.2 %	83.0%*	75.4%*	62.2%	66.9%*	73.3%*	75.7%	87.2%*	88.6%
Qatar	80.0 %	69.0 %	89.5%*	84.1%	68.4%	65.2%	74.5%	85.7%*	86.3%*	90.9%
Bahrain	74.1 %	70.1%*	91.4 %	77.6%	68.4%*	58.8%	68.3%	77.4%*	84.3%*	84.8%*
Oman	77.6 %	75.9%*	83.0 %	77.9%	76.9%	81.3%	70.7%	75.9%	96.0%	86.7%
Kuwait	81.0 %	62.1 %	82.9%*	82.4%	75.8%	75.0%	75.4%	81.4%	88.1%*	90.3%*
Egypt	70.0 %	70.0%*	71.4 %	69.8%*	71.6%	67.3%*	67.8%*	70.6%*	76.8%	87.0%
GCC Public	76.1 %	69.7%*	92.8 %	81.2 %	68.1%*	60.5 %	69.6%*	81.5%*	84.7%*	89.3%*
GCC Private	79.1 %	67.4 %	84.0%*	80.1%*	74.9 %	66.9%*	77.4%*	81.5%*	87.6 %	89.5 %
GCC Semi-Govt	77.4 %	70.6%*	87.2 %	80.3 %	69.7%*	65.2%*	72.1 %	82.1%*	88.0%*	88.4%*
Energy	74.1 %	71.1%*	91.3 %	76.2 %	67.6%*	62.2%*	68.2 %	78.5 %	89.3 %	93.7%*
BFSI	79.2 %	70.2%*	85.0 %	82.3%	72.9%*	67.9%*	76.8%*	85.1%*	82.5%*	88.1%
Manufacturing	80.5 %	71.8 %	85.9%*	81.2%*	75.9%	70.1%	77.3%*	79%*	90.8%*	90.3%*
Services	75.4 %	69.2%*	85.6 %	76.5%	71.5%*	66.2%*	71.1%	78.3%*	86.5%*	83.3%*
Conglomerates	77.6 %	67.5 %	83.2%*	78.2%*	73.6%	67.1%*	76.1%*	78.5%	86.5%	90.7%*

**Denotes statistical significance at a confidence interval of 95%*

The emphasis by employers on the urgent need to develop employability skills has been re-iterated in the recent MENA Labor Market Confidence Index released by The Talent Enterprise (2014), reflecting the views of over 1250 organizational and HR leaders. The study reported that building employability skills for entry-level graduates and working closely with educational providers was one of the top three priorities, in addition to nationalisation and recruitment. In another study by PwC (2014) surveying CEO's, 70% of CEO's believed that the largest threat to their businesses is the availability of key skills. This trumped all other aspects of the economy and business such as regulatory support, financial growth, bribery and cybercrime.

A promising finding from the study is that students who gained vocational education seemed to report similar levels of work readiness as compared to those with more traditional, academic degrees, at 72.2% and 78.9% respectively.

Table 9 Education & Work Preparedness by Qualification (2012) (% who believe that their educational background adequately prepared them for their jobs)

	Primary	Secondary	Vocational or Technical Diploma	Bachelor's Degree	Master's Degree	PhD	Other
GCC	76.7 %	64.9%*	72.2%*	78.9%*	89.4%*	93.3%*	75.6%*
UAE	72.7 %	65.6 %	72.4 %	79.4 %	89.3%*	96.9%*	77.3%*
KSA	80.0 %	67.1%*	66.9%*	80.2%*	90.0 %	NA	65.6 %
Qatar	78.9 %	67.8%*	77.3 %	82.6 %	94.2 %	90.0 %	63.6 %
Bahrain	NA	56.3 %	72%*	72.7 %	85.9%*	92.9%*	87.8%*
Oman	NA	56.0 %	74.1%*	78.1 %	93.9 %	NA	NA
Kuwait	NA	57.9 %	79.6%*	80%*	91.4%*	NA	72.7 %
Egypt	68.4%*	63.0 %	59.9%*	72.7%*	79.2%*	NA	58.9%*
GCC Public	84.2 %	62.3 %	75.6%*	75.0 %	85.9%*	95.9%*	82.4 %
GCC Private	72.7%*	66.3%*	71.9 %	80.4%*	90.1 %	87.5 %	75.4%*
GCC Semi-Govt	80.0 %	64.3%*	70.0%*	80.5%*	92.6%*	93.8 %	71.1 %
Energy	NA	61.6 %	69.8 %	76.2 %	88.1 %	NA	73.3 %
BFSI	NA	68.4 %	63.4 %	74.8 %	87.9%*	NA	67.7 %
Manufacturing	NA	52.5 %	78.3%*	81.4%*	89%*	NA	69.5%*
Services	71.7%*	63.8 %	67.7%*	78.7%*	91.6 %	NA	64.3 %
Conglomerates	73.8%*	67.9%*	70.3 %	80.3%*	90.6 %	NA	78.5 %

**Denotes statistical significance at a confidence interval of 95%*

In the recent past, there is growing consent amongst policy makers and employers on the relevance of technical and vocational training to supplement graduate education. Access to quality technical and vocational training can enhance employment opportunities for national talent especially in the private sector. Further, educational and training programs can be developed to match the skills needed in the private sector. Vocational training can hence be a critical part of ensuring that educational outcomes match private-sector demands. In the recent past, Saudi Arabia has witnessed the establishment of several vocational training centers in partnership with private companies and foreign institutions. The Technical and Vocational Training Corporation (TVTC) in Saudi Arabia offers vocational and technical training in Saudi Arabia, and covers both public and private sectors. Enrollment in these programs has tripled over the past decade to currently around 250,000. Finally, in additional to increasing the focus on vocational education, there is a need to professionalise skilled and semi-skilled work and afford it the status it receives elsewhere as an honourable craft (Jones & Punshi, 2014).

Section 3: Learning & Development

The MENA Labor Market Confidence Index (The Talent Enterprise, 2014) reported that approximately one-fourth of organizations have increased their learning & development budgets in the past 12 months, clearly signifying that a focus on talent development continues to be a priority for public and private sector employers. 64.3% of employees feel like they are actively learning and developing their skills and capabilities, and interestingly, there are no significant differences amongst nationals and expats, and males and females. The results also seem quite consistent amongst the GCC nations and Egypt. The main point of differentiation seems to be the views of private and public sector employees, with the former reporting significantly higher levels of satisfaction with learning & development.

In the future, the impact of learning can be further enhanced by harnessing engaging e-learning, social learning platforms and gamified development opportunities to spread the knowledge required for the workplace of the future amongst young people, who are amongst the most connected and technophile anywhere in the world.

On the other hand, coaching and mentoring seems to be grossly under-utilised as an effective development tool and the benefits of building a comprehensive process always outweigh the time and effort to create the framework. In the region, only 37.9% of employees believe that they have received adequate coaching or mentoring in the past 6 months. Though the private sector seems to be relatively better off at 41.7% compared to the public sector at 30%, employers and individuals can greatly benefit from increased capacity for mentorship and support. Moreover, creating a supportive coaching environment provides an opportunity to create a positive role for, and positive role models of, expatriates in the workforce.

Table 10: Satisfaction with Learning & Development (2012) (% who believe that they are actively learning and developing their skills and capabilities)

	Overall	Nationals (N)	Expats (E)	Males	Females	Under 25	25-34	35-44	45-54	55 above
GCC	64.3 %	62.7 %	66.1%*	65.1 %	62.1%*	66.4 %	60.8 %	65.0 %	69.6%*	73.1%*
UAE	66.0 %	63.6 %	68.2%*	67.3 %	63.8%*	70.7 %	64%*	64.5%*	71.5 %	72.6 %
KSA	62.8 %	62.2 %	63.3%*	62.9%*	59.8 %	65.6%*	59.2%*	65.1 %	69.0 %	73.3 %
Qatar	64.6 %	62.9 %	66.4%*	65.8 %	62.1%*	64.0 %	61.8 %	65.3 %	68.2 %	75.5 %
Bahrain	63.5 %	62.9%*	66.2 %	65.6 %	60.3%*	63.4 %	58.0 %	64.1%*	70.6%*	72.6%*
Oman	58.3 %	57.9%*	59.6 %	60.0 %	53.8 %	87.5 %	50.0 %	68.5 %	52.0 %	46.7 %
Kuwait	68.1 %	56.1 %	69.3%*	69.2 %	64.3 %	72.2 %	65.2 %	68.1%*	67.8%*	77.8%*
Egypt	62.5 %	62.5%*	71.4 %	63.3%*	56.8 %	66.7%*	61.3%*	60.9%*	66.2 %	70.4 %
GCC Public	58.3 %	57.68%*	61.2 %	59.0 %	57.39%*	68.1 %	53.2 %	58.0 %	63.96%*	72.51%*
GCC Private	65.7 %	63.5 %	66.72%*	65.7%*	65.5 %	65.69%*	62.38%*	67.7 %	70.9 %	73.5 %
GCC Semi-Govt	66.7 %	67.22%*	66.0 %	67.4 %	65.05%*	66.8 %	64.3 %	66.2 %	72.1 %	73.1 %
Energy	65.8 %	65.5%*	67.7 %	67.4 %	60.8 %	63.6%*	59.1 %	68.8 %	76.7 %	79.4%*
BFSI	65.3 %	65.2%*	65.4 %	66.5 %	63.2%*	71.3 %	62%*	68.9%*	66.2%*	75.0 %
Manufacturing	72.0 %	74.8 %	70.2%*	72.3%*	69.7 %	66.7 %	73.4%*	69.8%*	74.2%*	71.8%*
Services	64.8 %	62.3%*	69.0 %	64.4 %	66.6%*	66.5 %	61.2 %	65.2%*	70.6%*	72.4 %
Conglomerates	63.6 %	62.3 %	64.3%*	63.7%*	62.5 %	65.5%*	60.7%*	64.2 %	68.1 %	73.8 %

**Denotes statistical significance at a confidence interval of 95%*

Table 11 Satisfaction with Coaching & Mentoring (2012) (% who believe that they have received adequate coaching & mentoring in the past 6 months)

	Overall	Nationals (N)	Expats (E)	Males	Females	Under 25	25-34	35-44	45-54	55 above
GCC	37.9 %	37.9 %	37.9%*	37.6 %	38.7%*	50.8 %	38.5 %	34.6 %	34.4 %	34.1 %
UAE	40.5 %	41.0 %	40%*	40.3 %	40.8%*	50.4 %	41%*	37.6%*	40.6 %	38.0 %
KSA	40.2 %	41.5 %	39.3%*	40.2%*	39.0 %	50.2%*	40%*	35.3 %	39.0 %	37.0 %
Qatar	39.6 %	43.0 %	35.8 %	37.9 %	43.2%*	52.8 %	38.8 %	39.2%*	32.8 %	36.2 %
Bahrain	32.0 %	31.9%*	32.4 %	30.3 %	34.6%*	48.1 %	34.2 %	27.7 %	27.3%*	27.4 %
Oman	29.7 %	29.7%*	29.8 %	29.3 %	30.8 %	75.0 %	19.5 %	27.8 %	32.0 %	40.0 %
Kuwait	35.7 %	36.4 %	35.6%*	35.4 %	36.9 %	58.3 %	35.1 %	33.8 %	35.7%*	31.9%*
Egypt	33.1 %	33.1%*	28.6 %	32.6%*	36.8 %	46.2 %	33.4 %	27.8 %	31.7 %	37.0 %
GCC Public	30.0 %	29.92%*	30.3 %	27.7 %	32.65%*	49.2 %	31.0 %	25.8 %	25.6 %	28.1 %
GCC Private	41.7 %	44.5 %	40.31%*	41.62%*	42.0 %	50.4 %	41.8 %	38.8 %	41.4 %	37.1 %
GCC Semi-Govt	38.1 %	40.59%*	34.5 %	36.2 %	43.24%*	52.2 %	38.9 %	35.31%*	32.2 %	34.5 %
Energy	42.4 %	43.2%*	37.8 %	40.6 %	48%*	54.5%*	43.0 %	38.0 %	35.9 %	36.5 %
BFSI	36.6 %	34.9%*	40.6 %	35.4 %	38.8%*	54.0 %	37.2%*	31.7 %	33.1 %	42.9 %
Manufacturing	36.3 %	38.3 %	35%*	36%*	37.9 %	42.5 %	37.4%*	33.8%*	37.3%*	32%*
Services	36.3 %	36.4%*	36.2 %	34.4 %	43.4%*	47.1 %	36.3 %	35.1%*	32.8 %	30.2 %
Conglomerates	42.2 %	45.5 %	40.4%*	42.5%*	40.3 %	53.0 %	42.7%*	37.3 %	39.9 %	41.1 %

**Denotes statistical significance at a confidence interval of 95%*

Section 4: Satisfaction with Pay & Career Progression Expectations

The GCC continues to concentrate on financial rewards, pay and benefits as a key incentive to attract and retain talent. This has especially been the case in the public sector with high double and even triple digit pay increases in most GCC countries across all elements of pay, without the necessary impact on productivity. In the GCC, it is estimated that the average salary for 'Western' expatriates in administrative professions is US$12,215 per month on average. Arab expatriates earn slightly less at US$10,500 per month on average, and Asian expatriates earn the least (Gulf Business, 2013). Though the average pay levels would vary significantly in places like Oman & Bahrain, compared to the UAE & Qatar, highly differentiated salaries in the region are a manifestation of a segmented labor market. However, it absolute terms, it can be assumed that compared with many other parts of the world, employees in the region receive fairly competitive wages, more so, in a personal income tax free environment.

The *Qudurat* data shows that 30.1% of employees were completely satisfied with their level of pay, agreeing to the statement that they believe they are paid fairly for the effort they put into their jobs. However, by contrast, only a slightly higher group, 34.4% were completely dissatisfied, with the remaining one third indicating moderate levels of satisfaction. Surprisingly, there were no noticeable differences between expats and nationals and by gender either. Another notable observation was that the satisfaction with pay for nationals working in the public sector was reported at 32.3%. Though this is approximately 10% higher than that of the private sector, the difference is not as large as one would expect. It is often stated that pay is one of those aspects that no one will ever be completely satisfied with, no matter what the absolute amounts may be, and this seems to be the case in the GCC as well, where employees are typically earning competitive wages. This is further substantiated by the data from Egypt, where satisfaction with pay is not vastly lower than that of the GCC, although their absolute average salary levels are.

Saudi Arabia's satisfaction with pay levels was visibly lower for nationals at 16.1%. The wage conditions, especially for Saudi nationals in the Kingdom, are already beginning to change with the *Nitaqat* legislation. There is an increasing 'war for national talent' amongst organizations in order to meet its minimum Saudisation quota under the new, fairly stringent guidelines, lending to a demand in escalating levels of pay and benefits to attract Saudi nationals. Clearly, top talent are considered a rare commodity and wage levels are projected to increase at the same time as unemployment levels remain persistently high amongst nationals within different segments of the same markets. Hence, in the immediate term, there is likely to be a rapid change in the compensation structure and quantum of salaries for Saudi nationals, which could impact the reported satisfaction with pay.

Table 12 Satisfaction with Pay (2012) (% who believe they get paid fairly for the amount of effort they put into their jobs)

	Overall			Nationals (N)			Expats (E)		
	High	Medium	Low	High	Medium	Low	High	Medium	Low
GCC	30.1 %	35.4 %	34.4 %	29.7 %	33.2 %	37.1 %	30.6%*	37.8 %	31.6 %
UAE	35.6 %	33.0 %	31.4 %	39.3 %	29.7 %	30.9 %	32.1%*	36.2 %	31.8 %
KSA	20.8 %	34.5 %	44.7 %	16.1 %	29.5 %	54.4 %	24.2%*	38.0 %	37.7 %
Qatar	35.4 %	38.1 %	26.5 %	37.1 %	35.8 %	27.2 %	33.7 %	40.6 %	25.7 %
Bahrain	31.3 %	36.2 %	32.5 %	28.3%*	36.7 %	35.0 %	44.4 %	34.0 %	21.6 %
Oman	37.0 %	37.5 %	25.5 %	39.3%*	35.2 %	25.5 %	29.8 %	44.7 %	25.5 %
Kuwait	32.6 %	41.2 %	26.2 %	30.3 %	50.0 %	19.7 %	32.8%*	40.4 %	26.8 %
Egypt	29.2 %	33.6 %	37.3 %	29.3%*	33.4 %	37.3 %	21.4 %	50.0 %	28.6 %
GCC Public	33.4 %	34.9 %	31.6 %	32.3%*	34.7 %	33.1 %	39.1 %	36.1 %	24.9 %
GCC Private	25.7 %	36.1 %	38.2 %	21.6 %	31.6 %	46.8 %	27.7%*	38.3 %	34.0 %
GCC Semi-Govt	34.2 %	34.8 %	31.0 %	33.6%*	33.1 %	33.2 %	34.9 %	37.3 %	27.8 %
Energy	47.0 %	32.7 %	20.3 %	47.2%*	32.0 %	20.7 %	45.7 %	36.2 %	18.1 %
BFSI	28.2 %	34.6 %	37.2 %	27.7%*	31.9 %	40.4 %	29.4 %	40.6 %	30.0 %
Manufacturing	38.4 %	38.3 %	23.3 %	41.3 %	39.3 %	19.3 %	36.6%*	37.7 %	25.7 %
Services	28.3 %	33.4 %	38.2 %	23.6 %	33.1 %	43.3 %	36.1 %	33.9 %	30.0 %
Conglomerates	22.7 %	36.1 %	41.2 %	20.4 %	30.3 %	49.3 %	23.9%*	39.3 %	36.8 %

	Overall			Males			Females		
	High	Medium	Low	High	Medium	Low	High	Medium	Low
GCC	30.1 %	35.4 %	34.4 %	29.6 %	35.8 %	34.6 %	31.8%*	34.3 %	33.9 %
UAE	35.6 %	33.0 %	31.4 %	36.1 %	34.3 %	29.6 %	34.8%*	31.0 %	34.2 %
KSA	20.8 %	34.5 %	44.7 %	20.9%*	34.6 %	44.5 %	17.1 %	29.3 %	53.7 %
Qatar	35.4 %	38.1 %	26.5 %	37.6 %	37.4 %	25.0 %	30.8 %	39.4 %	29.8 %
Bahrain	31.3 %	36.2 %	32.5 %	32.9 %	36.6 %	30.5 %	28.8%*	35.5 %	35.7 %
Oman	37.0 %	37.5 %	25.5 %	35.7 %	39.3 %	25.0 %	40.4 %	32.7 %	26.9 %
Kuwait	32.6 %	41.2 %	26.2 %	31.6 %	41.9 %	26.5 %	36.3 %	38.9 %	24.8 %
Egypt	29.2 %	33.6 %	37.3 %	29.7%*	33.8 %	36.4 %	25.3 %	31.6 %	43.2 %
GCC Public	33.4 %	34.9 %	31.6 %	33.9 %	34.6 %	31.5 %	32.8%*	35.3 %	31.8 %
GCC Private	25.7 %	36.1 %	38.2 %	25.4%*	36.4 %	38.2 %	27.8 %	34.0 %	38.2 %
GCC Semi-Govt	34.2 %	34.8 %	31.0 %	34.3 %	35.4 %	30.3 %	33.8 %	33.3 %	33.0 %
Energy	47.0 %	32.7 %	20.3 %	44.8 %	34.8 %	20.4 %	53.9%*	26.0 %	20.1 %
BFSI	28.2 %	34.6 %	37.2 %	28.5 %	32.5 %	39.1 %	27.8%*	38.1 %	34.1 %
Manufacturing	38.4 %	38.3 %	23.3 %	38.6%*	38.1 %	23.3 %	37.4 %	39.5 %	23.1 %
Services	28.3 %	33.4 %	38.2 %	28.3 %	33.9 %	37.7 %	28.2 %	31.6 %	40.2 %
Conglomerates	22.7 %	36.1 %	41.2 %	22.4%*	36.3 %	41.3 %	24.6 %	34.7 %	40.7 %

**Denotes statistical significance at a confidence interval of 95%*

It is expected that private sector organizations may continue to grapple and be required to adopt a reactive strategy to managing their payroll costs in the short to medium term as they continue to compete with the public sector for national talent in particular. This is definitely counter-productive to the GCC's focus on significantly increasing the attractiveness of the private sector as the major source of employment. However, there is some opportunities for places like the UAE and Qatar to increase their private sector employment in the lead up to world events such as the Expo 2020 and World Cup 2022 respectively. According to a recent report by The Talent Enterprise in the Expo 2020 (Al Masar, 2014), careers in retail, hospitality, event management, media and advertising, real estate, the arts, publishing etc. will look increasingly promising and exciting for young nationals.

One of the other findings from the *Qudurat* data was that on average, 8 out of every 10 employees in the region, nationals and expatriates alike, have reported high to moderate expectations to get promoted within 12 months, with approximately 50% stating this as a given. The impact is a demonstration of rent-seeking behavior in action, as opposed to the concept of the 'rentier state' in theory alone. Remarkably, there are also no differences in the stated expectations between men and women and amongst the younger and older generations of employees, overturning pre-conceptions that the younger generation is more ambitious or men are more career-driven than women and so forth.

In many organizations within the region, gaining a promotion is the only way that someone can achieve an increase in their earnings or have access to better benefits. Aspects such as job title, size of office and formal progress within the rungs of the organization are perceived to be extremely important. In some instances, national talent prioritize a promotion and a better sounding job title over a pay increase or even more interesting or meaningful work. Also, on the other hand, organizations and HR practioners in the region seem to place a tremendous amount of emphasis on vertical movements within the organization, where lateral or horizontal movements and opportunities are not fully explored or encouraged.

The implications of these findings suggest that first, it is critical to communicate and set tangible goals with employees and hold them accountable to performance, so that they are more realistic with regards to their growth expectations. Second, it is imperative that organizations create and explore other avenues for career movements and doing more to manage an appropriate 'sense of progress' amongst nationals, so that there is more clarity and transparency to achieve the same.

Section 5: Organizational Leadership and Managerial Effectiveness

Jones & Punshi (2013) state that "increasing levels of employee engagement and harnessing the power of the collective at work has everything to do with leadership. This is not an overstatement. Leadership that extends not just to the topmost individual in the organization, but leaders at all levels". Findings from the *Qudurat* data show that employee's confidence in the most senior leadership within their organizations is low at 44.4%. This implies that a smaller proportion of employees believe that their senior leadership is making the right decisions in running the company and managing its employees. Confidence in public sector leadership was also reported as being lower than that of the private sector. Lowest scores with reference to organizational leadership were reported by national employees in Oman at 31.7% and Bahrain at 32.9% and higher levels were seen in UAE at 47% and Qatar with 50.2%.

GCC national talent reported approximately 10% lower confidence in their leaders as compared to their expatriate colleagues. These differences are significant. Initial indications from the *Qudurat* data seem to suggest that employees have much higher expectations from their senior leaders as compared to many other parts of the world. Culturally, the "region is a more collectivist and traditionally patriarchal society, with a dominant leader (or head patriarch) who is traditionally expected to look after the needs of people. There is also a very strongly defined hierarchy within social structures. These cultural norms seem to extend to the world of work and employees in the region, especially for national talent" (Aon Hewitt, 2011). They have a greater sense of entitlement in demanding more direct communication and oversight from the most senior leaders within the organizations. National employees also expect management to have increased levels of involvement while making decisions related directly to their span of work. The same extent of expectations do not hold true for expatriate workers, who prefer to communicate more directly with their managers and would like greater control over decision making when it comes to immediate work concerns.

This lack of confidence in leadership is a definite concern, keeping in mind that this factor has the highest potential positive impact on increasing the level of employee engagement. Organizations need to closely examine whether their existing recruitment strategies are attracting the right type of leaders required in today's circumstances and whether they are spending their training dollars wisely in developing their leaders effectively. Leaders themselves need to be more directly invested and committed to their employees. Increasing channels for genuine formal and informal communication with staff would be highly impactful. Crucially, the sometimes unrealistic expectations of employees from their leaders need to be managed and middle and supervisory levels should benefit from greater empowerment in making decisions and managing teams.

The lack of confidence in leadership extends to perspectives on managerial effectiveness as well, shedding light on a concerning gap of leadership and managerial impact. Only 40.5% of GCC employees believe that they receive ongoing and adequate managerial support and this percentage drops further to 36.4% for GCC nationals. There are no significant differences in terms of the perceptions amongst males and females; however, the 25-34 year cohort reports the lowest levels of satisfaction with their managers.

Table 13 Confidence in Organizational Leadership (2012) (% of employees who believe that their senior leaders are making the right decisions in running their organizations and managing their employees)

	Overall	Nationals (N)	Expats (E)	Males	Females	Under 25	25-34	35-44	45-54	55 above
GCC	44.4 %	39.9 %	49.4%*	45.2 %	41.9%*	44.5 %	40.1 %	43.9 %	53.4%*	59.0%*
UAE	50.0 %	47.0 %	52.8%*	52.5 %	45.9%*	51.2 %	45.7%*	49.1%*	62.0 %	64.8 %
KSA	41.0 %	37.5 %	43.6%*	41.2%*	35.4 %	41.3%*	38%*	39.0 %	51.9 %	58.2 %
Qatar	51.7 %	50.2 %	53.4 %	52.0 %	51.1%*	52.8 %	48.4 %	50.2 %	60.6 %	62.8 %
Bahrain	36.2 %	32.9%*	50.6 %	38.3 %	32.8%*	35.0 %	30.1 %	35.1%*	44.3%*	52.3%*
Oman	34.4 %	31.7%*	42.6 %	32.9 %	38.5 %	62.5 %	26.8 %	33.3 %	56.0 %	13.3 %
Kuwait	52.3 %	40.9 %	53.4%*	53.8 %	46.5 %	52.8 %	43.8 %	53.4%*	58%*	69.4%*
Egypt	34.9 %	34.8%*	42.9 %	35.5%*	30.5 %	44.2%*	30.9%*	33.9 %	42.3 %	51.9 %
GCC Public	36.5 %	33.9%*	48.7 %	37.6 %	35.2%*	42.9 %	30.8 %	34.5 %	45.9%*	56.7%*
GCC Private	44.9 %	39.6 %	47.5%*	45.2%*	43.2 %	43.1%*	41.3%*	44.6 %	54.1 %	60.6 %
GCC Semi-Govt	49.3 %	46.1%*	54.0 %	49.4 %	49.1%*	47.3 %	45.5 %	49.2%*	58.1 %	58.6 %
Energy	55.7 %	53.9%*	66.1 %	54.9 %	58.3%*	57.3%*	48.4 %	58.0 %	68.0 %	63.5 %
BFSI	45.9 %	41%*	57.2 %	46.2 %	45.5%*	48.3 %	42.6%*	45.1%*	59.2%*	57.1 %
Manufacturing	50.3 %	49.2 %	51%*	50.8%*	47.2 %	48.3 %	47.5%*	49.7%*	55%*	61.2%*
Services	41.1 %	33.8%*	53.3 %	41.3 %	40.5 %	38.1 %	35.2 %	43%*	50.8%*	57.3%*
Conglomerates	43.1 %	40.5 %	44.6%*	43.1%*	42.9 %	43.4%*	40.9%*	40.1 %	51.8 %	57.9 %

**Denotes statistical significance at a confidence interval of 95%*

Table 14 Managerial Support with Organizations (2012) (% of employees who believe they receive adequate managerial support)

	Overall	Nationals (N)	Expats (E)	Males	Females	Under 25	25-34	35-44	45-54	55 above
GCC	40.5 %	36.4 %	45.1%*	40.8 %	39.8%*	42.1 %	37.7 %	41.0 %	44.9%*	47.3 %
UAE	44.5 %	38.2 %	50.5%*	46.1 %	41.9%*	43.8 %	42.4%*	43.6%*	52.1 %	53.1 %
KSA	40.5 %	39.2 %	41.4%*	40.6%*	34.1 %	43.1%*	37.9%*	41.3 %	45.3 %	47.9 %
Qatar	37.0 %	33.4 %	41.7 %	36.9 %	37.1 %	37.5%*	31.0 %	39.5%*	44.7%*	41.0 %
Bahrain	37.5 %	34.3%*	51.2 %	37.5 %	37.5%*	40.3 %	34.2 %	37.5 %	39.8%*	45.2%*
Oman	35.9 %	31%*	51.1 %	33.6 %	42.3 %	50.0 %	32.9 %	33.3 %	40.0 %	40.0 %
Kuwait	40.6 %	39.4 %	40.8%*	39.2 %	45.9 %	41.7 %	34.8 %	43.6%*	44.8%*	45.8%*
Egypt	36.5 %	36.6%*	28.6 %	36.1%*	40.0 %	36.5 %	35.6%*	36%*	39.4 %	46.3 %
GCC Public	37.4 %	34.9%*	49.1 %	37.7 %	37%*	48.7 %	35.0 %	34.3 %	43.1 %	40.9 %
GCC Private	42.4 %	39.4 %	43.83%*	42.38%*	42.3 %	42.7 %	39.27%*	44.4 %	47.5 %	48.0 %
GCC Semi-Govt	40.0 %	35.45%*	47.5 %	39.5 %	41.6%*	37.2 %	37.1 %	41.1%*	42.6 %	51.07%*
Energy	38.0 %	35.5%*	52.0 %	38.2 %	37.3%*	38.5%*	31.2 %	43.9 %	38.8 %	52.4%*
BFSI	36.5 %	35.6%*	47.2 %	33.1 %	43.4%*	51.4 %	32.2 %	39.0 %	38.9 %	58.3 %
Manufacturing	42.1 %	39.8 %	43.6%*	41.8%*	44.6 %	34.5 %	40.7%*	42.2%*	48.1%*	42.7%*
Services	38.9 %	34%*	46.9 %	38.2 %	41.2%*	32.6 %	36.5 %	40.2 %	44.3 %	47.9 %
Conglomerates	42.5 %	41.2 %	43.2%*	42.6%*	41.3 %	45.9%*	39.8%*	42.8 %	46.3 %	50.9 %

**Denotes statistical significance at a confidence interval of 95%*

Increasing Employee Engagement: Priorities & Actions

Although the overall level of employee engagement in 2012 was 49% on average, another 28% of employees can be classified as nearly engaged. These are the fence-sitters and with the right actions, there is a significant and compelling opportunity to increase levels of engagement within the GCC labor markets and workplaces.

Increasing the absolute level of employee engagement is a complex task, with many inter-related dependencies, including an urgent reform in the very structure of the GCC labor market and education system driven at the national level. This needs to be supported by more mature, effective and innovative human capital practices and policies developed by employers, both in the private and public sectors. At the same time, the individuals need to play an important role towards their own levels of motivation and productive contribution to the workplace. Although this paper cannot do complete justice to all possible priorities and actions to significantly increase the levels of employee engagement, performance and productivity within the region's workplaces, some key recommendations have been listed below.

1. Continue to adopt an evidence-based, research-led approach to understand the distinct triggers for engagement and productivity amongst the various demographic segments and have the courage to build locally relevant solutions.
2. Another key area for reform is to re-boot the current, traditional approach to nationalisation focussing largely on quotas and numbers. An updated version, nationalisation 2.0 (Jones & Punshi, 2013) is the need of the hour which focuses increasingly on contribution and productivity, rather than quotas. It calls for a need to match the 'right' people to the 'right' jobs, by having a better view on the needs of the labor market, and understanding the aspirations, strengths and abilities of individuals. Most importantly, such policies need to be increasingly focused on encouraging individuals, organizations and nations to make more effective investments in developing their human capital endowments.
3. The third distinct area for action would be to drive greater educational reform and to increase the relevance of schools and higher education curriculum to the needs of the workplace. There is a need to bridge the gap between education and employment, by having key stakeholders from both sides work together in designing curriculum and programs, and offer opportunities for internships, traineeships, apprenticeships etc. Further, as discussed previously, fostering employability or life skills such as functional skills required for the job (business English, IT etc.), and other aspects such as communication, team-work, work ethics, problem solving, decision making, resilience, grit, self-confidence etc would enable development. Finally, skill

development, especially a focus on vocational education, is the need of the hour.

4. A related aspect would be to provide on-going career guidance and counselling support, whereby there is a greater awareness of the world of work and a matching of the right jobs, to individual strengths, skills and aspirations. Setting more realistic expectations amongst the younger generation is key.
5. From an organizational perspective, the *Qudurat* data demonstrates that the following factors have the highest positive and negative impact on engagement, and hence, these factors should be enhanced or sustained respectively. Organizational leaders and HR professionals need to be attentive and cognizant to the needs of their key constituent groups, to attract, engage, develop and retain their talent as a source of competitive advantage.

Figure 3 Engagement Factors, Impact Analysis

Factors that have the highest positive impact on engagement	**Factors that are critical to sustain current levels of engagement**
Confidence in Leadership	Pride at Work
Career Growth	Sense of Accomplishment and Meaning
Learning & Development	Fairness at Work
Managerial Effectiveness	Level of Trust
Pay & Benefits	Physical Work Environment
Supportive Work Culture	
Being Valued and Recognized	
Positive Relationships at Work	

6. Finally, from an individual perspective, there would be clear benefits to invest in one's own human capital development and a clear and demonstrable commitment to increasing personal levels of work motivation and performance, with a lowering of rent-seeking behavior, amongst both expatriate and national talent.

Critique of the Current Model of Employee Engagement and Recommendations for the Future

One of the sharpest and compelling critiques of current approaches and models to measure employee engagement have been voiced by the leading academic researcher, Prof. Arnold Bakker (2010). According to Bakker, "the truth is that engagement is a concept and a very appealing, marketable 'product' popularised by consulting firms". Often there is very little academic rigour. He substantiates that "an Internet search on 'employee engagement' yielded almost 650,000 hits. Narrowing the scope to scholarly publications – many of them from the grey area (e.g., whitepapers, fact sheets and consultancy reports) – reduced the number of hits to less than 2000." He further establishes that "the impressive number stand in sharp contrast to the dearth of publications on engagement included in PsychInfo, the leading database of academic publications in psychology, which revealed approximately 100 publications. Finally, the most restrictive search in any peer-reviewed international journal yielded only about 30 hits."

Bakker (2010) also adds that virtually all major human resources consulting firms are in the 'business' of improving levels of work engagement, without any credible academic substantiation. Although most claim that their models are different, a closer review reveals that they mostly measure organizational commitment, discretionary effort or satisfaction with organizational resources, commonly known as engagement 'drivers'. Bakker (2010) states that "the way these leading consultancy firms conceptualise engagement comes close to putting old wine in a new bottle."

Another critique by Jones & Punshi (2013) is that most current approaches to engagement are rather one-sided. "The onus for engagement lies completely with the organization. This is based on the assumption that the responsibility of motivating employees rests with the employer, management and HR. That by improving work resources, such as greater training and development opportunities, better leadership support, more pay and benefits, greater work-life balance and so on, employees will naturally become more engaged. However, though these factors are extremely critical and do contribute to engagement, they only provide half the picture at best".

What completes the equation is the fact that each individual chooses whether he or she wants to be engaged and maintain consistent levels of motivation, sometimes irrespective of what the organization provides. Shifting the focus away from the individual can fuel unrealistically high expectations, creating a cycle of dependence on the latest HR initiative to improve employee engagement.

To increase and sustain levels of engagement and work motivation in the Arab World and indeed globally, there is a need to adopt a more balanced approach, defined by how engagement (organizational and personal) is impacted by work resources as well as individual strengths or psychological resources. Work resources can be broadly understood by what the organization provides such as leadership support, managerial effectiveness, learning and development, career advancement, pay, recognition etc. Personal resources include strengths such as levels of optimism, self-efficacy, resilience, hope etc. along with aspects such as attitudes, expectations and a positive mindset.

Figure 4 A More Balanced View of Engagement, Focus Both on Individual and Organizational Factors

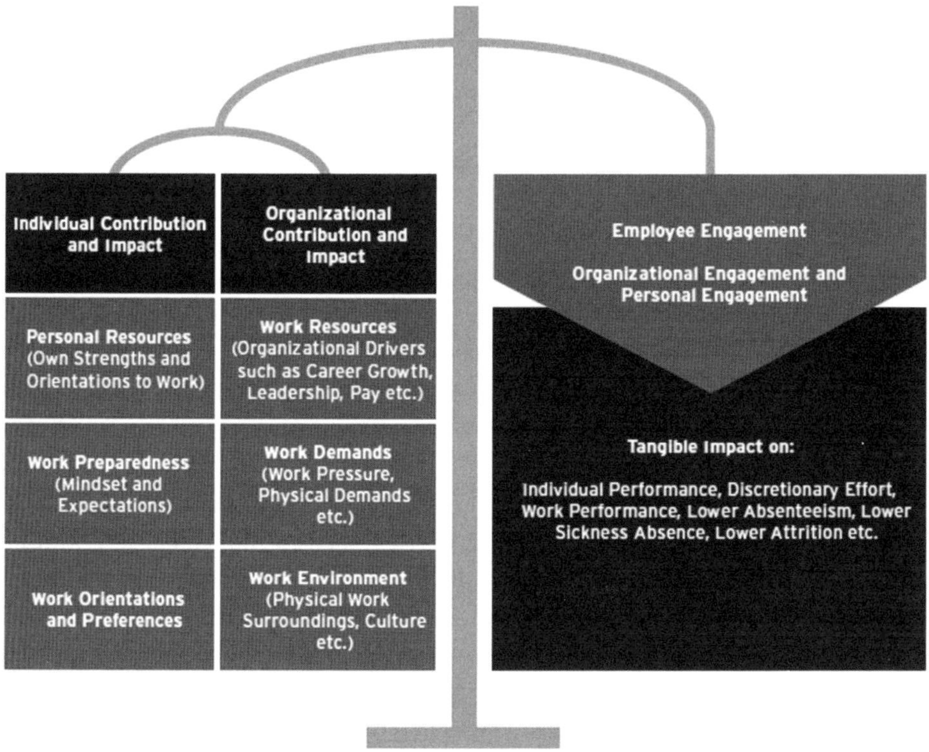

Source: From Unlocking the Paradox of Plenty, Jones & Punshi (2013)

Limitations of the Study and Future Research Imperatives

- A key drawback of the study was that it did not include responses from blue-collar workers, who are such a core part of the region's labor market. Their level of work motivation, concerns and consequences should definitely be closely examined.
- Further, sample sizes from Kuwait and Oman were quite limited at 731 and 192 respectively in 2012. These countries were also not adequately represented in 2010.
- One of the most interesting patterns from the source data analysis was the general degree to which respondents resident in the GCC were typically more guarded in their responses than those from other regions. GCC nationals, and expatriates to a slightly lesser extent, typically display a response pattern which is more collapsed towards the mean than a standard "normal" distribution, often assumed in many research projects. More research needs to be conducted to fully understand the salient nature

of this phenomenon as a keystone of robust research within the GCC for the future. Studies may need to be calibrated to account for this differential response patterns and parametric statistical assumptions need to be questioned going forward. Interestingly, GCC nationals responding in Arabic were significantly more guarded than those choosing to answer the study in English and expatriates typically became more guarded in their response patterns the longer they had resided within the GCC. These observations warrant further research and analysis as a methodological and ontological priority.

Conclusion

More than 150 years ago, nobody had considered that Japan would develop a unique approach to work, its own management model and 'modern' approach to economic development post-Meiji Restoration, which would enable it to become, and arguably remain, the leading manufacturing and technology producer in the world. There is no reason why a distinctly Arab or Gulf approach to work and organizational development cannot be built to establish an enduring and meaningful competitive advantage for the region going forward. Orthodoxies need to be questioned and 'best practices' imported from elsewhere and actions need to be on local evidence gathered from robust and relevant research conducted within GCC. During the twentieth century, the GCC became renowned for its endowments of fossil fuels. In the twenty-first century it must become recognised for the capabilities of its human resources if it is to continue the transition towards becoming a knowledge-based economy.

This research indicates that the unintended consequences of the traditional approach to nationalisation and the quota-driven positive discrimination it is based on are amongst the most significant challenges to the region going forward. '*Wasta*' and rent-seeking behavior lie at the heart of unlocking this paradox of plenty, and addressing them directly within the region's workplaces, remain priorities.

Future actions must include how to initiate a genuine two-way conversation to improve employee engagement in the GCC. The region should urgently address how to build better bridges between education and employment, improve labor mobility and break down barriers between the highly sclerotic and segmented labor markets, as well as deliver a more sustainable alignment between pay and productivity in the region. A continuation of some of the highest average wage levels, particularly amongst the top segments of the local labor markets, along with some of the lowest labor productivity metrics anywhere in the world does not bode well for the genuine achievement of sustainable knowledge-based economies going forward. What steps the region takes to improve employment opportunities for those who are currently disadvantaged, the next generation of young workers, for the region's women, for expatriates, to favor the development of more successful, independent commercial organizations, including flourishing small businesses, towards promoting the future growth and economic vibrancy of the GCC. All of these are critical in determining how successful GCC will be in building and then transferring a lasting legacy to the next generation from the opportunities the region has benefitted from so far.

The GCC has been fortunate to inherit a financial bounty that enables and fuels the investment in building the physical infrastructure of member nations. The built environment of the GCC and the pace and ambition with which it continues to be built is dizzying. It is easy to forget that financial resources and physical infrastructure alone, are not sufficient in isolation to build an enduring economic future for the region. The region now needs to prioritize similar levels of development in their collective human capital, develop the talent landscape and invest in strengthening the psychological capital so that both can work together more effectively and deliver sustainable growth. The GCC has witnessed a remarkable and accelerated economic revolution in the last century. There is now a need to deliver an even faster, deeper and more successful psychological revolution in order to secure the promise of a shining example to the rest of the world in the rest of the century ahead.

All the ingredients are in place for a future based on the talent and enterprise available to us within the GCC – the decades ahead will prove whether the region can be successful in getting the recipe right.

Table 15 2012 Sample Information

Survey Sample		Nationality	Participation Count
Total		Total	15,865
		Nationals	8,274
		Expats	7,591
Nationality	GCC Nationals	Total	6877
	Other Arabs	Total	4172
	Indian Subcontinent	Total	3334
	Expats from other Asian Countries	Total	731
	Expats from North America	Total	106
	Expats from South America	Total	10
	Expats from Western Europe	Total	220
	Expats from Eastern Europe	Total	51
	Expats from North Africa	Total	70
	Expats from Sub-Saharan Africa	Total	63
	Other Expats	Total	231
Gender	Male	Total	12,018
		Nationals	5,656
		Expats	6,362
	Female	Total	3,847
		Nationals	2,618
		Expats	1,229
Industry	Government	Total	3,409
		Nationals	2,464
		Expats	945
	Semi-Government	Total	4,024
		Nationals	2,467
		Expats	1,557
	Private	Total	8,432
		Nationals	3,343
		Expats	5089
Role with the Organization	Top Management	Total	161
		Nationals	110
		Expats	51
	Senior Management	Total	743
		Nationals	367
		Expats	376
	Middle Management	Total	1,997
		Nationals	907
		Expats	1,09
	Team Leader/Supervisor	Total	2,345
		Nationals	1,271
		Expats	1,074
	Professional Employee (not a Manager)	Total	4,092
		Nationals	2,227
		Expats	1,865
	Team Member/Front-Line Employee	Total	3,829
		Nationals	2,591
		Expats	1,238
	Intern (including student interns)	Total	296
		Nationals	281
Age	Under 25	Total	1,46
		Nationals	1,196
		Expats	264
	25-34	Total	7,331
		Nationals	4,128
		Expats	3,203
	35-44	Total	4,193

6

A Strengths-Based Approach to Enhancing Youth Motivation and Employability: Research and Practice from the GCC, with a Focus on Bahrain

Radhika Punshi, Cameron Mirza, and Gauri Gupta

Setting the Context: Youth Employability & Motivation in the GCC

The Middle East and North Africa (MENA) region, including the Gulf Cooperation Countries (GCC) are witnessing an unprecedented growth in their local population. Undoubtedly, this has far-reaching implications in terms of the region's economic, socio-cultural and indeed political future. At a time when most other populations in the world are in decline, the Arab world's population is expected to double by 2050 to reach 278 million from the current 145 million (UNDP, 2010). By 2020, the GCC's population forecast is expected to increase by one-third, to 53 million people (Economic Intelligence Unit, 2010).

A huge proportion of the increase is attributable to the growth in the youth population. "The number of children and youth is at an all-time high in the region. The increase in the proportion of 15 to 24 year olds in the total population, referred to as the 'youth bulge' combined with the growth in the overall population has resulted in the most rapid growth in the number of young people in the region's modern history" (UNDP, 2010). More than 60% of the region's population under the age of 30 years in the Arab World (IFC, 2011) and 50% in the GCC (United Nations, Department of Economic and Social Affairs, Population Division (2013) & The Talent Enterprise research (2014)).

Hence, the region has a compelling opportunity to tap into its demographic endowment due to its 'youth bulge' along with supporting the broader integration of women into the workforce. However, having a young working age population is a necessary but not a sufficient condition for enhancing productive capacity required to drive economic growth.

***Table 1* Proportion of Youth Population to Total Population in the GCC by 2015**

Country	Youth Population Under the Age of 30 by 2015	Total Population in 2015	%Youth Population
Bahrain	673,000	1,360,000	49%
Kuwait	1,817,000	3,583,000	51%
Oman	2,550,000	4,158,000	61%
Saudi Arabia	15,867,000	29,898,000	53%
Qatar	1,023,000	2,351,000	44%
UAE	4228000	9,577,000	44%
GCC	**26,158,000**	**50,927,000**	**51%**

Source: Research by The Talent Enterprise (2014) & United Nations, Department of Economic and Social Affairs, Population Division (2013)

Their energy and aspirations need to be channelled in the right direction in terms of developing their skills and providing positive and productive work opportunities (Jones & Punshi, 2013).

Facing more competition from peers than their parent generation, the youth in the Middle East experiences a growing frustration to find employment that allows them to reach the normal milestones in life: marriage, a household and family. (WEF, 2012).

The economic impact of youth unemployment to the Arab world is estimated at between 40 to 50 billion dollars annually (PwC, 2013). "On the eve of the Arab Spring, regional youth unemployment stood at nearly 24%, the highest of any region in the world and almost twice the international average, a pattern that started and has persisted since the early 1990s. While securing a first job is always a challenge for young people entering the labour force, unemployment for many youth in the region has become a state of normalcy" (WEF, 2012). As an example, in Saudi Arabia, four times as many young Saudis under the age of 30 are unemployed compared to the older generations. In Bahrain, 33% of those aged 25 to 29 are unemployed (Booz & Co, 2010).

For GCC countries in particular, it is counter-intuitive for significant levels of unemployment to persist amongst its young citizens. In a recent report on the UAE, it was noted that "high levels of unemployment persist despite the country's economic strength and the 'paternal state' system in which citizens are provided with extensive benefits and, often, secure public sector jobs". (International Council on Security and Development, 2010). Paradoxically, the GCC countries also continue to have a significant level of dependence on foreign workers for taking on white collar and blue collar jobs that the local talent supply is unable or unwilling to cater to. Of the world's 20 countries with highest proportion of international migration, 9 are in the Arab world, with Qatar (87%), UAE (70%), Oman and KSA (28%) (UNDP, 2010).

It is important to stress that youth unemployment is a global concern. Worldwide, young people are three times more likely than their parents to be out of work (The Economist, 2013). However, in contrast to global patterns, what is most concerning for the region is the nature of unemployment. In most parts of the world, the duration of unemployment is shorter for youths than for adults, reflecting the natural tendency of youth to more frequently move between jobs. In most MENA countries, youth unemployment appears to be the result of waiting for the 'right' job. During school-to-work transition in the Middle East, long unemployment durations are common. As an example, in Bahrain, youth are willing to wait up to 8 years to find the 'right job' (Booz & Co, 2010). This trend is prevalent across the larger Arab World. Half of unemployed Syrian youth have been searching for a job for more than one year and in Egypt, those between the ages of 20 and 24 reported searching for an average period of 34 months (WEF, 2012). To a large extent, this extended state of unemployment reflects a misalignment between the expectations of the younger generation and the quality of jobs available, as well as a historical preference to work in the public sector. Further, according to various studies, the socioeconomic background of a young person has been shown to affect their waiting times and choices. Youth from middleclass, urban backgrounds are generally slower to enter the labour market than both the poor and the rich (WEF, 2012). Young people from poor backgrounds are likely to enter the market more quickly, but often engage in lower quality jobs at the expense of completing formal education (WEF, 2012).

It is also critical to highlight that there is also a prevalence of underemployment, where GCC nationals are employed with low expectations in terms of their productive output. Another serious concern is that the region continues to face some extraordinary challenges with regards to motivating its young population. As compared to other parts in the world, nationals in the GCC report some of the lowest levels of workplace engagement or motivation, as compared to their expatriate colleagues. Of all the age cohorts, younger nationals (those aged 25 to 34) have consistently reported the lowest levels of engagement for over 3 years at 40.1% (Aon Hewitt, 2011). Further, a significant decline in engagement levels has also be reported for nationals under the age of 25 at 47.7% (compared to 64% in 2010) and 43.4% for the 35 to 44 age group (which was at 49% in 2010) (Aon Hewitt, 2011). These mediocre levels of engagement amongst the younger citizens of the Gulf countries is highly counter-productive to growth, and needs to be addressed in earnest by key stakeholders in a sustainable and urgent manner.

Hence, there is an onset of an 'early–mid career' crisis in the Arab world, seen almost a decade earlier than most other parts of the world, where a more typical mid-career crisis in the forties would prevail. The strikingly low levels of youth engagement significantly impacts personal well-being, long-term health and performance. It has a detrimental effect on organisational performance (Jones & Punshi 2013).

A combination of various factors, such as the ones listed below, may be leading to lower levels of motivation and engagement amongst the younger generation. Further research and evidence-based practice is required to establish these links further.

- Accelerating regulatory amendments towards nationalisation may have unintentional consequences such as an over-emphasis by employers on achieving quotas, without adequate consideration for aligning the skills and aspirations of youth to the right jobs. According to Jones & Punshi (2013) national talent sometimes report a degree of 'tokenism', in particular within the private sector.
- Further, national youth are typically used to a more traditional and rigid method of education and instruction which tend to be largely didactic and based on rote learning. This focus on highly supported learning extends as national talent enter the workplace. In most organisations, private or public sector, young GCC nationals usually participate in structured 'nationalisation' or graduate programmes where they continue to receive highly structured 'remedial' training and development. Further, most of these training programs are based on instructor-led, class-room based training with limited real-world application. Hence, it is assumed that due to the nature of instruction within the educational system and their extension in the way of employer-led nationalisation programmes leads to national youth struggling with real-world application and practical knowledge to be successful within their jobs.
- Unfortunately, there is a general lowering of expectations with regards to GCC nationals, both within their own community and also among expatriate counterparts. Both outcomes are regrettable and need to be addressed as a matter of urgency. On the one hand, national talent tend to get preferential priority with regards to recruitment or accelerated career opportunities through policies of quota-based hiring. Over time, this quota-based hiring has encouraged a sense of entitlement and expectation in the workplace, effectively reducing the individual's incentives to invest the consistent effort required to enhance their own performance and productivity. However, on the other hand, more subtle negative perceptions and biases are rife in terms of undermining the self-confidence and perceptions of local talent and their contribution (Jones & Punshi, 2013).
- In line with the social and cultural expectations and norms, the local population also tends to successfully reach other important milestones in the transition to adulthood like marriage and household formation (WEF, 2012) which leads to taking on additional social and familial responsibilities, which may be impacting the early-mid career crisis in some way.

- National talent tend to struggle in coping with the day-to-day pressures of their working lives. They display lower levels of workplace resilience (ability to deal with setbacks) and self-efficacy (belief in the impact of your own actions). These foundational life skills are (usually) not emphasised at all as part of the education or employment training (Jones & Punshi, 2013).
- Finally, due to the limited exposure to the world of work prior to completing their education and joining a 'full' time job, there seems to be mismatch in terms of expectations and a sense of entitlement from work. Workplaces in the GCC have developed rapidly and employees have become habituated to accelerated growth opportunities. As an example, in many organisations, 80% of employees, both nationals and expatriates working in the public or private sector are expecting a promotion within a year (Jones & Punshi, 2013).

The region can no longer afford to take this generation for granted. As the recent past has demonstrated with the onset of the Arab Spring, a young, working age population that is unemployed, lacking in skill sets or disengaged is a recipe for social and economic volatility. Notably, across the region, the Arab Awakening has been a movement predominantly led by youth and the main drivers for many of the protests were centered on high and persistent unemployment and lack of opportunity. (Jones & Punshi, 2013).

The Need to Develop a 21st Century Skills Agenda

Needless to say, the concerns around youth unemployment and de-motivation are detrimental to the region's growth and progress. Therefore, creating positive and productive work opportunities for the younger generation is arguably the single largest priority for policy-makers in the GCC. To meet the growing demands of a fast accelerating population and to move towards a more diversified, competitive, knowledge economy, the onus is now largely on the private sector to create the estimated 85 million jobs by 2020 across the Arab world (IFC, 2011).

However, despite the stated demographic surplus and current availability of youth due to high levels of unemployment, one of the essential factors inhibiting employment of young nationals is that that private sector employers believe that young people do not have the required skills for the workplace. These skills are often referred to as employability skills. Broadly, employability refers to a person's capacity to gain and maintain employment and meet changing job requirements. This necessitates employees or potential employees to possess the formal qualifications required for particular positions in the workforce; and the other skills that employers are looking for in addition to formal qualifications.

Hence, the current education to employment system is not adequately aligned for most employers and young people, particularly in the Arab world, but also in many other regions across the world. According to a global study (Mc Kinsey, 2012), less than half of the students (45%) and employers (42%) believe that the education system has prepared them for the workplace. Ironically, 72% of educational providers believe that the students are adequately prepared for the workplace. However, students report that the relevance of their education to the job market is insufficient. Fewer than half of the students are confident that they would study the same subject, if they were given a choice again. Furthermore, most students need to wait six to twelve months to find employment and more than half are unable to do so in their chosen area of study (Mc Kinsey, 2012).

These same global trends are being witnessed in the GCC region as well, and arguably, the situation may be even more alarming. Only 22% of young nationals believe their country's education system helped prepare them (or is preparing them) to find a job (Booz & Co, 2012). Only 29% of GCC employers feel that education prepares students with necessary technical skills and only 19% agree that it prepares young people with the right attitude for work (EY, 2014). The term 'appropriate skills' however requires deconstruction. What is meant by appropriate skills?

As an example, within Bahrain, over 500 companies in the private sector were asked whether graduates were sufficiently prepared for the position for which they were hired. Survey results show only half of the private sector find graduates have the skills required. Specifically 49% lacked the 'soft skills' (e.g. team work, communication skills, problem solving) required, 44% lacked 'hard skills' (e.g. specific vocational training, language skills, mathematics) and 42% did not have a satisfactory level of 'work ethic' (e.g. motivation and professional conduct) (Bahrain Chamber of Commerce and Industry, and the Economic Development Board, 2012).

Importantly, this research also identified that graduates from many tertiary education programmes were not 'work ready.' Local companies reported that Bahraini graduates lacked the ability to communicate, participate in a team, use their initiative, problem solve and to think critically. Similar gaps in skills are reported by employers across the GCC. Considering the above, the case for prioritising employability skills or 'twenty first century skills' for MENA youth is clear.

Enhancing Employability and Youth Motivation through a Strengths-Based Approach

The importance of fostering foundational employability and life skills to GCC youth cannot be stressed enough. Skills such as communication, teamwork, resilience, self-confidence, negotiation, self-expression etc. can be incorporated into the curriculum or added on top of the formal instruction within education curriculum. It is also equally critical to focus on youth motivation, inculcate work ethics and establish the right incentives for the younger generation to focus on their personal and professional development.

Current advances in behavioural sciences, especially the fields of Positive Psychology and Positive Education may be able to significantly contribute to the research and development of evidence-based practices in enhancing employability and life skills. Positive Psychology is the scientific study of the strengths and virtues that enable individuals and communities to thrive (Seligman, 2002). Positive Education focuses on specific skills that assist students to strengthen their relationships, build positive emotions, enhance personal resilience, promote mindfulness, and encourage a healthy lifestyle. Positive Education attempts to rebalance education's aims away from a sole focus on traditional academic skills, towards education which builds life skills associated with greater engagement and well-being (Geelong, 2012).

The major orientation of Positive Psychology programmes, including within the educational context, is to focus on a strengths-based approach. This helps students identify their signature character strengths and encourages students to use of these strengths in day-to-day life.

Previous research studies have established that aspects such as self-discipline and grit are some of the most important predictors of student performance and achievement (Duckworth, 2005).

Those with high grit complete more years of education and also make fewer career changes over the course of their lifetime. Further, on a longitudinal study of adolescents, strengths predicted school performance and achievement, school social functioning and well-being (Shoshani & Slone, 2012). Character strengths such as self-regulation, perseverance were predictive of school success (Weber & Ruch, 2012b). Positive Education programming which heavily involves character strengths assessment and intervention led to improved student school skills and greater student enjoyment and engagement in school (e.g., improved curiosity, love of learning, and creativity; Seligman et al., 2009).

As an example of Positive Education in practice, the Penn Resiliency Program (PRP) has been designed to increase the ability to handle day-to-day stressors and problems that are common for most students. The PRP was developed at the University of Pennsylvania and focuses on aspects such as optimism, problem solving, self-efficacy, self-regulation, emotional awareness, flexibility, empathy, and strong relationships. It was originally developed as a school-based training programme for students in late childhood and early adolescence. In addition, another programme titled the Apex project has focused on preventing depression and anxiety in college students. Research with the PRP has also demonstrated that teachers who are trained in the PRP can, in turn, teach PRP skills effectively. That is, when the Penn curriculum developers trained educators to teach PRP skills to their students, the students showed fewer symptoms of depression and behavioural problems. This demonstrated efficacy with a 'train the trainer' model is an important element of the PRP (Seligman et al, 2009).

Hence, along with fostering formal education, there is a critical need to understand, assess and foster psychological, employability and life skills and a positive mindset for GCC youth, as these impact not just academic performance, but also future success, motivation and performance at the workplace.

Research Background

The Talent Enterprise designed, developed and validated the GCC's first indigenous psychometric assessment tools to evaluate the strengths and work orientations of adults and youth. Known as the Employee Thriving Index (ETI for working adults) & Youth Thriving Index (YTI for youth), the questionnaires are based on a robust theoretical foundation of Positive Psychology and have been developed through an extensive process of test validation and an extensive review of literature (Jones, Punshi and Gupta, 2014).

All factors and sub-factors assessed in this research are 'state-based' measures, i.e. can be changed with the right guidance, training and support versus being 'trait-based' which are fixed attributes, such as personality, that cannot be changed. This is a crucial differentiator for the research, as specific training programmes or interventions can be developed to foster and build these strengths with youth across the GCC based on the findings from the results.

The survey questionnaire, includes 89 questions and all data was collected online. The questions were administered in English and Arabic. The sample size for the entire dataset (ETI) is n = 2301, with n = 1008 GCC nationals and n = 1293 expats. The youth data (YTI) has a sample size n – 451 with n = 263 for GCC national youth (under 25) and n = 171 for expat youth (under 25).

The YTI measures ten factors listed below, along with the sub-factors within each:

Mindset: Flexibility – Growth – Problem Solving
Fortitude: Bouyancy – Determination
Efficacy: Control – Confidence – Preparedness
Vitality: Drive – Energy – Optimism
Achievement: Absorption – Ambition – Mastery
Accountability: Ambiguity – Conviction – Responsibility
Affiliation: Autonomy – Empathy - Teamwork
Ingenuity: Analytical – Creativity - Curiosity
Motivation: Extrinsic – Intrinsic – Extra Role Responsibility
Integrity: Ethics – Values

GCC national youth report the lowest scores on control (16%), flexibility (26%), curiosity (33%), efficacy (37%), autonomy (38%), affiliation (39%), empathy (40%), absorption (40%), ethics (43%) and confidence (47%). Arguably, each of these strengths are critical

Key Findings

Figure 1 Highest and Lowest Strengths for GCC National Youth

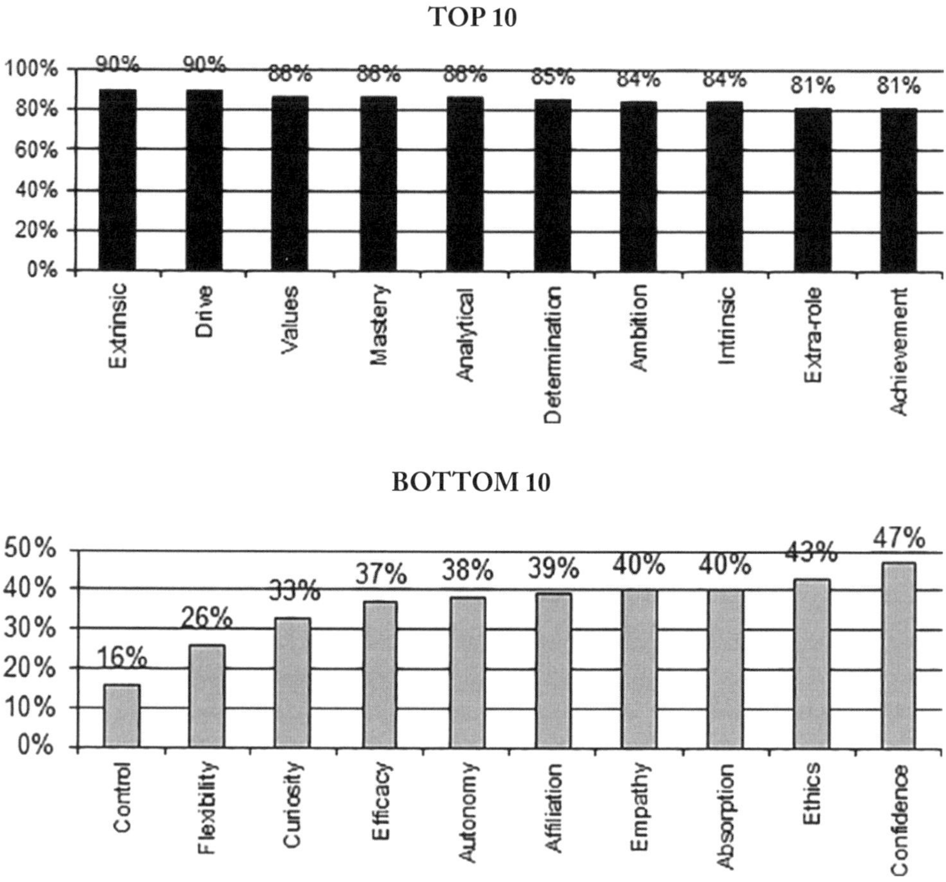

from a life and employability skills perspective and it would be critical to design and deliver work-based programmes to foster and build these strengths amongst national youth.

One of the most notable insights from the highest strengths show that GCC national youth have high levels of extrinsic motivation (90%) as well as significant levels of intrinsic motivation (81%). Hence, aspects such as external rewards, recognition and validation are as critical for the younger generation as a feeling of purpose, belonging and contribution to developing themselves, their communities and their nations. It would be assumed that both extrinsic and intrinsic motivation would exist on a continuum, i.e. if one was high, the other would be low, however, the data shows that both aspects can be high at the same time.

With reference to Table 2, 69% of the youth population feels higher on conviction as opposed to 57% of the other age groups. On the other hand, more number of people in the remaining age group feel higher on preparedness (73% vs 61% youth), teamwork (53% vs 43% youth), responsibility (59% vs 51% youth) and zest (71% vs 59% youth).

Table 2 YTI™ & ETI™ Scores for Youth (Below 25 years) and Others (25+ years)

ETI Factor/Sub-Factor	Overall Youth	Overall Others	Difference
Sample Size	**451**	**1850**	-
Accountability	63%	63%	0%
Ambiguity	19%	35%	16%
Conviction	69% B	57%	-12%
Responsibility	51%	59% A	8%
Affiliation	33%	41% A	8%
Autonomy	37%	41%	4%
Empathy	45%	48%	3%
Teamwork	43%	53% A	10%
Authenticity	72%	81% A	9%
Ethics	45%	50% A	5%
Values	76%	84% A	8%
Achievement	72%	72%	0%
Absorption	39%	48% A	9%
Ambition	77%	74%	-3%
Mastery	81%	80%	-1%
Drive	79%	86% A	7%
Extrinsic	81%	86% A	5%
Intrinsic	74%	74%	0%
Extra-role	71%	77% A	6%
Efficacy	31%	44% A	13%
Control	16%	14%	-2%
Confidence	42%	52% A	10%
Preparedness	61%	73% A	12%
Fortitude	69%	74% A	5%
Buoyancy	47%	55% A	8%
Determination	77%	78%	1%
Ingenuity	66%	67%	1%
Analytical	82%	79%	-3%
Creativity	69%	75% A	6%
Curiosity	33%	32%	-1%
Mindset	43%	48% A	5%
Flexibility	24%	39% A	15%
Growth	57%	53%	-4%
Vitality	59%	68% A	9%
Zest	59%	71% A	12%
Energy	60%	62%	2%
Optimism	52%	58% A	6%
Social Desirability	54%	69% A	15%

Note: ***Statistical significance testing has been done at a 95% confidence interval and has been denoted using alphabetical characters.***

In Table 3, which looks at trends amongst GCC nationals, youth are significantly higher when compared to the other age groups for a significant number of factors. For instance – youth are significantly higher on accountability (by 11%), conviction (by 12%), achievement (81% vs 74%) and determination (85% vs 77%).

***Table 3* YTI™ & ETI™ Scores for National Youth and National other Age Groups**

Factor/Sub-Factor	National Youth	National Other Age Group	Difference
Sample Size	**263**	**745**	-
Accountability	73% B	62%	-11%
Ambiguity	60%	18%	-42%
Conviction	71% B	59%	-12%
Responsibility	57%	56%	-1%
Affiliation	39%	38%	-1%
Autonomy	38%	45%	7%
Empathy	40%	38%	-2%
Teamwork	48%	52%	4%
Authenticity	78%	77%	-1%
Ethics	43%	43%	0%
Values	86%	82%	-4%
Achievement	81% B	74%	-7%
Absorption	40%	41%	1%
Ambition	84%	83%	-1%
Mastery	86%	81%	-5%
Drive	90%	86%	-4%
Extrinsic	90%	87%	-3%
Intrinsic	84% B	75%	-9%
Extrarole	81%	76%	-5%
Efficacy	37%	39%	2%
Control	16%	16%	0%
Confidence	47%	49%	2%
Preparedness	61%	59%	-2%
Fortitude	75%	72%	-3%
Buoyancy	52%	50%	-2%
Determination	85% B	77%	-8%
Ingenuity	72%	66%	-6%
Analytical	86% B	77%	-9%
Creativity	75%	71%	-4%
Curiosity	33%	32%	-1%
Mindset	51%	44%	-7%
Flexibility	26%	33% A	7%
Growth	62% B	51%	-11%
Vitality	69%	64%	-5%
Zest	71%	66%	-5%
Energy	69% B	59%	-10%
Optimism	54%	53%	-1%
Social Desirability	65%	72% A	7%

Note: ***Statistical significance testing has been done at a 95% confidence interval and has been denoted using alphabetical characters.***

The trend of GCC national youth reporting higher scores from their older cohort of nationals seems to show the exact opposite while comparing expat populations. As shown in Table 4, within the population comprising of expats, individuals from other age groups are significantly higher when compared to youth for many factors. For instance – expats over 25 years are higher on zest (by 31%), preparedness (by 23%), extra-role motivation (by 23%), responsibility (18%) and achievement (11%).

Table 4 YTI™ & ETI™ Scores for Expat Youth and Expat Other Age Groups

Factor/Sub-Factor	Expat Youth	Expat Other Age groups	Difference
Sample Size	**188**	**1105**	-
Accountability	49%	63% A	14%
Ambiguity	10%	39% A	29%
Conviction	67% B	56%	-11%
Responsibility	44%	62% A	18%
Affiliation	24%	44% A	20%
Autonomy	36%	38%	2%
Empathy	52%	55%	3%
Teamwork	37%	53% A	16%
Authenticity	63%	83% A	20%
Ethics	48%	55%	7%
Values	62%	85% A	23%
Achievement	60%	71% A	11%
Absorption	37%	53% A	16%
Ambition	67%	69%	2%
Mastery	74%	80%	6%
Drive	64%	86% A	22%
Extrinsic	68%	85% A	17%
Intrinsic	60%	74% A	14%
Extrarole	56%	79% A	23%
Efficacy	24%	48% A	24%
Control	15%	13%	-2%
Confidence	35%	53% A	18%
Preparedness	60%	83% A	23%
Fortitude	62%	75% A	13%
Buoyancy	41%	58% A	17%
Determination	65%	78% A	13%
Ingenuity	57%	68% A	11%
Analytical	76%	81%	5%
Creativity	62%	77% A	15%
Curiosity	34%	32%	-2%
Mindset	33%	51% A	18%
Flexibility	21%	42% A	21%
Growth	50%	54%	4%
Vitality	44%	71% A	27%
Zest	43%	74% A	31%
Energy	47%	64% A	17%
Optimism	49%	62% A	13%
Social Desirability	22%	67% A	45%

Note: *Statistical significance testing has been done at a 95% confidence interval and has been denoted using alphabetical characters.*

Further information, insights and trends are available to download on the website (www.thetalententerprise.com). This includes additional data on nationals and expatriates, males and females, youth and others etc.

Limitations of the Current Research

The current research is a significant step forward in an effort to create a regionally based assessment and solution to evaluate the strengths, work orientations and mindset of youth across the region. However, further research, including longitudinal research is needed to clearly establish the relationship of these strengths to job and employment outcomes. Further, additional data would be required from Saudi Arabia, Kuwait and Bahrain.

Implications and Recommendations

The challenges faced by the Arab world preclude unilateral efforts. While innovative solutions may be identified, created and even implemented in isolation, ensuring that these actions are sustainable and extended to meet the scale of the region's challenges requires a wholly different level of partnership. It requires cooperation and support from the governments, the educational sector and private enterprises, each working on a different but related mandate (Jones & Punshi, 2013).

Some suggested strategies and actions to ensure that the region realises the productive potential of youth in the region include:

1. Relevance of education and focus on vocational training: Policy-makers, educational providers and the industry can work in closer partnership to improve the relevance of formal education to the world of work. In an ideal world, macro-level skill and demand estimation should precede investments in economic sectors and growth industries, which is largely absent in most GCC countries. The necessity to reform education is not just pertinent to higher education, but also across primary and secondary levels. Also, with relatively low levels of interest and current enrolment in vocational education, there is a need to professionalise skilled and semi-skilled work and afford it the status it receives in other parts of the world as an honourable craft.
2. Fostering employability and life skills: The importance of fostering foundational workplace and life skills for youth cannot be stressed enough. Skills such as communication, teamwork, resilience, self-confidence, negotiation, self-expression etc. can be incorporated into the curriculum or added on top of the formal instruction. Nations such as the US, UK and Australia are taking the lead in this regard by investing in character education and positive education, driven by compelling research and the application of positive psychology and positive education. The region has a very distinct opportunity here if the necessary changes are made early on. To make

this happen, all stakeholders need less of a focus on human resources development and more of a focus on developing resourceful, self-driven human-beings.

3. Updating current approaches to career guidance: Career planning and development is one of the most vital aspects of a student's life. At the individual level, career decisions involve long range commitments and influence one's thoughts, feelings and actions for years to come. At a macro level, educational choices and career decisions impact the economic engine and can have a disproportionate effect on aspects such as employment, underemployment, overall engagement and productivity. The most effective solution is in ensuring that educational institutions provide effective and meaningful career guidance to their students and, importantly, build capability amongst career counsellors. The use of tools, including relevant pre-employment assessments, psychometrics and technology will also help in addressing the private sector challenge in identifying skilled workers. Currently, there is a visible lack of systematised information on the employability of available applicants, along with the inability to assess the validity of purported skill sets or information from employers. Setting up accurate and objective nationwide labour market information databases would be a positive step in this regard.
4. Provide opportunities for internships, work–study and co-op programmes: There is a visible lack of internship, apprenticeship, co-op and work–study opportunities in the region. Though some of this can be attributed to the legislative environment due to an absence of laws supporting part-time employment, visa restrictions and so on, much of this has to do with the misalignment between employment and education. Providing opportunities for alternate jobs works for both students and employers. Students gain the much needed exposure and experience that is strongly lacking with formal education. And employers have an early preview into future candidates.
5. Encourage a mindset to explore entrepreneurship opportunities: Young people from the region are more likely than in other regions to indicate an interest in starting their own businesses. However, at the same time, youth in the region are less likely than their counterparts elsewhere to actually take steps to start a business (Jones & Punshi, 2013). Thus, while the entrepreneurial spirit is alive among Arab youth, it remains constrained by a variety of barriers. Access to sustainable forms of finance and effective business support services would encourage further entrepreneurial ventures. Psychometric assessment tools can also be introduced to identify potential for entrepreneurship early on and then groom and mentor these skills via structured programmes.
6. Encourage learning through experiential action-based approaches: Young people entering the labour market in the Arab world not only lack marketable skills; they also lack relevant experience and knowledge of the working world. Hence, further classroom training through structured national development programmes may not be the only answer. Action-based, experiential learning would be very instructive

and lead to longer term behavioural and attitudinal change. Building confidence along with competence is just as important for young GCC nationals. Learning approaches which develop psychological capacity and personal strengths are becoming recognised as an ever higher priority.

7. Build careers: Career advancement opportunities, more than earnings or any other single driver of engagement, is the single most important source of motivation for GCC nationals (Jones & Punshi, 2013). However, career progression as an end in itself is not recommended and must be clearly linked to competence, performance and contribution.

Lessons from Bahrain – Bringing Higher Education & Employers Closer Together

In 2013, the Higher Education Council (HEC) of Bahrain instigated a policy change and created an employability agenda designed to reverse the trends outlined in earlier sections of this paper. It was clearly established that higher education needs to be aligned to the Bahrain labour market and also the wider GCC labour market. As part of system wide reform Bahrain is now capturing up to date labour market data, but more importantly gaining a forecast to future market needs. A new annual skills survey has been launched for both public and private employers so that policy makers can understand in detail the ongoing skills needs of employers.

A key element of reform is the development of a new tiered higher education sector with the introduction of new institutes that focus more on technical and vocational provision with the emphasis on applied learning. This fusion between higher education and vocational learning has been branded as a technical university with the expectation that a more technical tertiary offering will help close the gap with employer's needs.

Working closely with employers has been significantly ramped up with the creation of a Higher Education and Industry Steering Committee. The committee is represented by the large employers in Bahrain, SMEs and the academic community with a clear mandate to work sector by sector to drive out and disseminate sector specific skills and competencies. However, this new relationship has meant that universities have had to develop new skills if they are to succeed in developing high value partnerships with employers. These include strategic leadership skills to determine how the institute best fits with the economy and having a clear strategy on how to engage with employers.

Curriculum design and teaching methods are an intrinsic part of the skills for the 21st century agenda, having already created a joint steering group with employers at a national level, the key is to create an employer led ecosystem. The HEC has taken an active role in becoming a catalyst to allow employers and the higher education sector to intersect rather than operate in parallel worlds. Employers from all sectors are now are working closely with institutes to make curriculums more relevant to the needs of industry with a focus on sector specific technical and soft skills acquisition. However, having relevant curriculum is only part of the solution, the faculty member must be able to deliver curriculum in the classroom in such a way to encourage students to solve problems, think critically, work in teams and to be able to communicate effectively.

The key aspect of reform is to build capacity in teaching and learning and this is being done by the development of a first national professional development framework for faculty in Bahrain. Often underestimated is the focus on giving faculty the skills to deliver a curriculum effectively to allow students to develop a skill set rather than memorising notes, the role of faculty is more than ever a role of facilitator. The professional standards framework will focus on developing teacher's core skills, core knowledge and professional values with the expected outcome being that students have improved 21st century skills. Taking teaching a step further universities are now being encouraged to ask industry to teach modules and to supply adjunct professors to universities in order to strengthen the link and gain real time industry insight.

Universities must act through a variety of different and innovative methods. One method is currently being piloted is where students are assessed against employability skills by assessment and then subsequent improvements measured over time as a result of a series of considered interventions. The object of this pilot is to eventually move the sector to a point where skill acquisition is considered just as important as gaining a qualification, the development of a skills portfolio for each student is considered a medium term policy objective for the country.

According to the World Bank (2010) among the disparate contributing factors that have led to the supply and demand mismatch is the dearth of soft skills that young people, educated in more traditional systems and lacking practical experience, never develop. As a result, Bahrain has now introduced a new policy measure to combine classroom training with an internship period for all students including postgraduate. By linking with industry, SMEs, the public sector the higher education council has been able to provide a national internship programme and by 2016 all students are expected to experience a quality internship period linked to their academic studies through a project completed with an employer with some clear intended outcomes for the student.

A number of studies have called into question the quality of education provided to students in the Middle East, these studies have highlighted the rigidity of the education system and poor career guidance at the expense of students of honing student's critical thinking and soft skills. The question facing Bahrain is how to integrate the initiatives mentioned above into a more holistic framework and to embed the new relationship with employers into the heart of the education system.

In order to do this, by 2015, Bahrain will introduce accreditation for all higher education institutes, with key elements focusing on employment engagement, teaching and learning methods, curriculum design, capturing skills development of students, offering informed career guidance and work based learning opportunities for all students. Accreditation is the vehicle to drive change in the sector and moves towards an education system that stimulates student's abilities to think, challenge and be creative. If these are the skills required in students by employers then the education system in Bahrain must also adapt, learn and change and by implementing new policy the expected outcomes for students will improve. In order to assess impact of the HEC strategy, all universities will be required to capture destination data for all graduates for a minimum of 2 years after graduation.

Also, from 2016, an elective module in entrepreneurship will be made available to all students regardless of what they are studying. Enterprise and entrepreneurship training can provide students with leadership, confidence and the tools to think in an innovative and creative way.

Closing Thoughts

With the expected demographic and financial surplus forecasted for the Gulf region over the next decade, each GCC country has a unique and compelling opportunity to provide work opportunities for its younger generation and focus on job creation and employment in the private sector. However, as a result of the current mismatch between education and employment and the resultant skills gap, all stakeholders, policy-makers, education providers and employers need to work together to understand, nurture and develop critical employability and life skills for GCC youth. The region can benefit from the latest developments in fostering life skills, well-being and engagement using a strengths-based approach, based on advances in Positive Psychology and Positive Education. This research paper takes an evidence-based approach in assessing the strengths and work orientations of GCC national youth, using the ETI & YTI, the region's first psychometric assessments that have been validated and developed in the region, tested on both local and expat populations.

Strengths such as efficacy, flexibility, curiosity, autonomy, affiliation, empathy, absorption and confidence need to be developed by integrating applied learning and character education in the current curriculums. Even within organisations, employers need to develop the mindset and psychological strengths of their youngest employees, along with focusing on technical and functional skills. Finally, this paper highlights some of the initiatives underway in Bahrain based on the agenda outlined by Bahrain's Higher Education Council.

7

The Two Universes of Entrepreneurship in the United Arab Emirates: An Answer to the Gulf Employment Conundrum?

Joachim Kolb

Introduction

One of the most pressing challenges for Gulf policy makers is to find ways of ensuring gainful employment for the national workforce, and balance this with developmental visions and the need to accommodate an important, sometimes majoritarian, international segment of the population. The attendant problems are well-known: while it may have been possible to maintain the entire national population in style during the 1970s, this is increasingly problematic in the face of rising population numbers and expectations on the part of a younger generation of Gulf nationals that has grown up taking material blessings and extraordinary returns to employment for granted.

Policy makers thus face a trilemma, two sides of which have already proven problematic: Other than the employment of additional nationals in the public sector or successfully encouraging them to work in the private sector, entrepreneurship represents the only option of dealing with this crisis. Becoming entrepreneurs, Gulf nationals are supposed to set out on their own, thus pulling themselves out of the swamp of national underemployment by their own initiative.

In the UAE labor market, the problem is set to get more pressing, with the number of young Emirati applicants considering labor market entry set to rise from under 20,000 p.a. today to well over 30,000 p.a. by 2030.

Both the expansion of the bureaucracy and nationalization policies appear not to be infinitely scalable due to the limited absorptive capacity of the GCC public sector, the unwillingness of many companies to nationalize their work force, and ultimately the sheer cost of both processes to the public-sector institutions and private-sector employers implementing them. By contrast, there is no basic limit to the ability of GCC entrepreneurs to take charge of their destinies, and this third solution thus appears more promising and expandable than the other two.

Figure 1 Emirati Births by Year

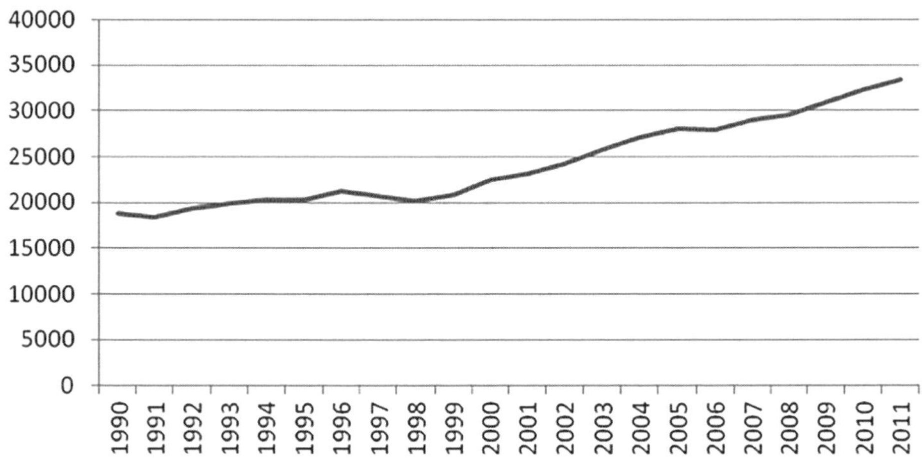

Source: National Bureau of Statistics (NBS, http://www.uaestatistics.gov.ae)

It is hence unsurprising that in the UAE, possibly the economically most innovative Gulf state, an active discourse on entrepreneurship should have emerged, with a large number of stakeholders in academia, policy making and public administration. But to what extent are the expectations that are voiced realistic with regard to the role entrepreneurship can play for the national workforce?

In order to answer this question, this paper first reviews the global discourse on entrepreneurship in Section 2, which is followed by some remarks on entrepreneurship in the Gulf in Section 3. On this basis, the following two sections explore the institutional embedding of the Emirati entrepreneur and the expat entrepreneur in Sections 4 and 5, including a discussion on an existing corpus of Emirati SMEs and its relevance for the developmental potential of startups in the region and the role of nationals in their creation. Section 6 concludes.

The Global Discourse on Entrepreneurship

While Entrepreneurship has been linked to variety of concepts, including risk and uncertainty (Frank H. Knight), arbitrage (Kirzner), and the coordination of economic resources (Mark Casson), discourses on entrepreneurship are most often traced to the central concepts of innovation and the resulting economic growth, which took center stage in the writings of Josef Schumpeter in the early 20th century. At that time, the entrepreneur was perceived as an extraordinary individual who would create opportunities and propel economic development forward. An entrepreneur thus transcended the world he had found and put a new one in its place. He could retain his exalted status precisely because others would not and could not compete with him: the very success of Henry Ford as an entrepreneur consigned thousands of others to the secure monotony of the assembly line that promised them relative prosperity, but also guaranteed a working life largely devoid of creative spark.

The situation at the beginning of the third millennium is rather different. Throughout the world, social welfare levels have come under pressure as state resources declined from the 1970s onwards, a tendency exacerbated by the economic crisis that started in 2007/08. As a result, the figure of the entrepreneur has gone from being a cultural hero standing apart from the grand mass to being held up as a role model for all, and particularly for those in urgent need of a job. A couple of examples may illustrate this:

- In 2010, the US State Department launched its Global Entrepreneurship Program (GEP), which aimed at encouraging entrepreneurship and addressing the youth bulge in the Muslim world through the channel of startup formation and increased entrepreneurial activity. Global Entrepreneurship Summits linked to the program were held in Washington in April 2010 and in Istanbul in 2011.
- This resonates with discourses within the business community. In 2011, Booz and Company and the World Economic Forum released their report on *Accelerating Entrepreneurship in the Arab World*, which propagated the ubiquity of entrepreneurship discourse in education, business and government: "Discuss entrepreneurship every day and generate hype around a handful of success stories." (Booz et al. (2011:6)).
- In continental Europe, since the 1990s, German state-owned companies shed employees by forcing them into subcontractor relationships, a process justified by a rhetoric of entrepreneurship, but often limited to work for a single client, their former employer. A couple of years later, the German federal bureaucracy set out to encourage the unemployed to become entrepreneurs, supporting their initial steps into entrepreneurship so as to wean them off benefits, a strategy already adopted in Britain during the Thatcher era (Andersson & Wadensjö (2006); Bundesministerium (2011)).

Whether this has indeed led to a linear and continuous increase in entrepreneurial activity worldwide is another question, with entrepreneurship apparently subject to cycles of bust and boom, much like other areas of economic activity.

The discourse of entrepreneurship can thus accommodate many stakeholder groups, including policy makers, administrators, supranational bureaucracies, educational institutions, pundits, consultants, and other talking heads, private-sector companies, and the individual entrepreneur himself.

Figure 2 **Historic Activity in the Entrepreneurship Field**

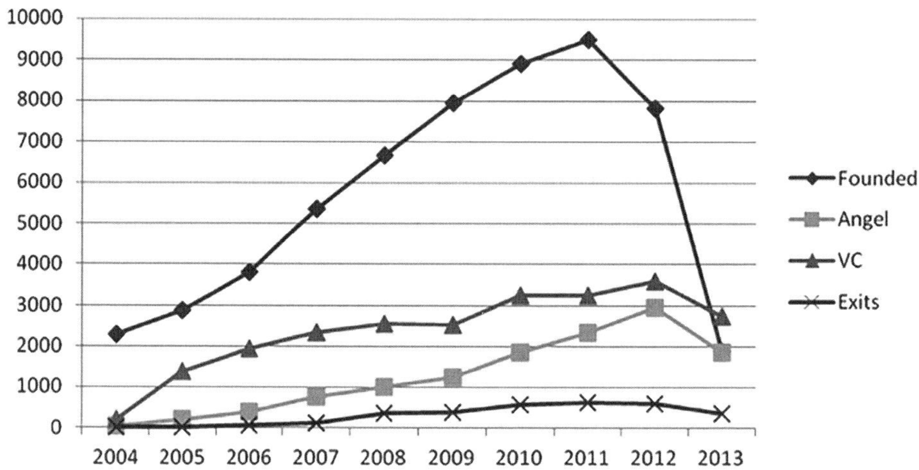

Source: www.seedtable.com, accessed 2014/5/24

Beyond its immediate concern with entrepreneurship, this discursive system provides an upbeat way of presenting societal challenges, including questions of equity and political power, as solvable problems relying primarily on individual activity.

Entrepreneurs are active in almost all economies, but the specific differences between different locations tend to be overlooked: in academic studies of the system, the American paradigm often takes the place of a standard model. This is understandable in the light of the fascination Silicon Valley exerts on students of entrepreneurship worldwide. Features of the American standard model include the following points:

1. Entrepreneurs are distinguished by their superior insight into technical and business opportunities. They operate in a competitive market economy where access to capital depends on the attractiveness of their ideas to primarily private-sector financial backers. In this economic ecosystem, failure is an undesirable, but acceptable outcome that is seen as a natural by-product of the process of creative destruction, and is celebrated rather than stigmatized.
2. At different stages in the process, private-sector actors make their support available to the entrepreneur. They include

    a. incubators and accelerators that promote the development of a nascent venture by providing facilities, support, and ideational input,

b. angel investors, meaning individuals who support early-stage ventures with their own money, provide financial input and guidance,
c. venture capitalists, who invest in more mature projects with a view to holding them until they are sold.

3. Successful exits are either achieved by a private sale or an IPO, providing attractive payouts to entrepreneurs, their senior employees, and early-stage investors.

Some underlying factors that enable its functioning include (a) a strong scientific and educational system providing highly skilled entrepreneurs with high value-added, cutting edge entrepreneurial concepts, (b) strong protection for individual property rights, including a system of intellectual property rights that makes high-tech startups calculable risks, (c) an early-stage investment infrastructure that provides sufficient entrepreneurial interest in start-up entrepreneurs, and (d) deep and well-developed capital markets that reliably provide exit options to entrepreneurs and early-stage investors alike.

While the stars of the American entrepreneurial system are globally celebrated and lessons are learnt from the American paradigm in entrepreneurship courses worldwide, these four underlying factors have proven hard to replicate, with even otherwise similarly developed OECD economies unable to make full use of the model's features. For example, accelerators are heavily concentrated in the US, with the lion's share of the remainder concentrated in the UK and other stalwarts of the Anglo-Saxon world (www.seed-db.com, accessed 2014/5/24). For the MENA region, Booz et al. (2011:6) already warned: "Do not imitate Silicon Valley. Identify and leverage your country's own unique resources."

The Development of Entrepreneurship in the Gulf and the UAE

Openings for entrepreneurial activity in the Gulf were already a fact of life during the period of British dominance, during which relationships between what were to become the GCC states and India were close, and a considerable influx of Indian traders occurred. A number of biographies of entrepreneurial individuals and their firms have been published, portraying such enterprises and individuals as the Bin Laden conglomerate, Al-Waleed b. Talal, or the Kanoo family enterprise in Bahrain and beyond (Coll (2008); Kanoo (1997); Riz (2005)).

In the UAE, entrepreneurial activity in the pre-oil era developed through a small number of channels, including trade and the pearling industry, which involved a limited number of families in transnational transactions and financing of the pearl trade and the pearling fleet. Particularly after the collapse of the pearl trade in the 1930s, the lack of a monetary economy, harsh environmental conditions and generalized poverty meant that there were limited outlets for entrepreneurial activity (Al-Fahim (1995)). Whoever did have any commercial experience, however, found it in high demand once oil boom set in (Al-Fahim (1995: 138)).

Early on in the boom, the government put significant amounts of money into the hands of its citizens and enabled them through legal provisions privileging its nationals to profit directly from the immense rise in economic productivity by making the involvement of an Emirati majority owner imperative in any business venture.

These privileges for nationals in business have since been integrated into UAE company legislation, with Article 10 of the UAE Company Law requiring every on-shore company to be majority owned by a UAE national. In particular, through the acquisition of exclusive agency agreements for the local distribution of imported goods, UAE nationals could enter business arrangements that assured them of a secure stream of revenue, often without the need for any marketing effort.

In this environment, entrepreneurial activity was destined to succeed, almost irrespective of the field. Investing alongside an enlightened leadership implementing a clear developmental vision, Emiratis and expatriates alike learned that trust in the government's vision paid off, and that an incremental additional investment was always a good decision. In what reads almost like a Biblical simile, Krane (2009: 93f.) tells about a Kuwaiti investor who, when offered patches of desert that were to become prime Dubai real estate, failed to make use of the opportunity and missed out on a bonanza. The message is clear: investing in Dubai has always been a good idea.

However, in the course of time, a number of factors changed: in the place of informal largesse and a Wild West marketplace, elaborate institutional structures emerged to accommodate and regulate business activity. With the emergence of special economic zones and a sophisticated infrastructure supporting entrepreneurship, the overall landscape now presents a very different picture from the boom time innocence of the 1960s and 1970s.

Some information about the situation of entrepreneurship in the UAE can be gleaned from survey results. Here, the UAE Labor Survey 2009 provides valuable information on the demography of entrepreneurs, as well as the relevant reports of the Global Entrepreneurship Monitor (GEM) and the Global Entrepreneurship Development Institute (GEDI). Regarding the prevalent level of entrepreneurship in the UAE, the 2009 Labor Force Survey provides a snapshot of the situation in 2009:

Assuming a labour force of around 4.9mn in 2009, this appears to imply that there were around 156,000 employers and 35,300 self-employed individuals in the UAE in 2009 (NBS (2013)). With moderate growth in the intervening years, the total number of employers and self-employed could then be assumed to be around 200,000 in the UAE. The level of full-time entrepreneurial engagement is hence very limited at less than 5%

Table 1 **2009 Labor Force Survey 1: Distribution of the Employed Population**

	Nationality Group								
	Nationals			Foreigners			Total		
In %	**Male**	**Female**	**Total**	**Male**	**Female**	**Total**	**Male**	**Female**	**Total**
Employer	3.2	0.7	**2.6**	4.2	0.9	**3.6**	4.1	0.9	**3.4**
Self Employed	0.7	0.0	**0.5**	1.1	0.4	**1.0**	1.0	0.4	**0.9**
Paid Worker	96.0	99.3	**96.8**	94.7	98.5	**95.4**	94.9	98.6	**95.6**
Unpaid Worker	0.1	0.0	**0.1**	0.0	0.2	**0.1**	0.0	0.1	**0.1**

Source: 2009 Labour Force Survey, Table (16: Distribution of Employed Population (15 Years +) by Nationality Group and Sex according to Employment Status and Occupation

of the workforce. The most comprehensive information about the income of this group is also due to the 2009 Labor Survey, which also contains information on the distribution by income level (Table 31of the Survey) and the mean and median income of entrepreneurs and employers (Table 35).

While there are no comprehensive data on the number of companies in the UAE, World Bank data tell us that company formation is at a moderate level per head of the population, but rising in absolute terms: In 2012, there were 1.38 limited liability companies established per 1000 inhabitants, corresponding to 10,814 companies (www.doingbusiness.org, accessed 2014/5/26). While the index of LLC foundations per 1000 inhabitants dropped from its initial high of 2.18 to bottom out at 0.92 in 2009, before recovering somewhat to reach 1.38 in 2012, this reflects the rapid population increase in the UAE, mainly consisting of low-skilled migrants, rather than a drop in entrepreneurial activity. Actual establishment figures have risen over the period from 6,626 in 2004 to 10,814 in 2012, although not monotonously: after reaching an interim high of 9,127 in 2008, the figure dropped to 6,068, its lowest value during the period, in 2009 before starting a gradual recovery.

In the UAE context, it would be highly desirable to complement these data with figures on other corporates such as joint stock companies, and particularly on the corporate life in the free economic zones that remain outside the UAE legislation and allow full ownership by foreigners. Unfortunately, the zones themselves do not publish these numbers, and no comprehensive figures on numerical developments are available. There are, however, some numbers on aggregate licensing activities published at the level of the Emirate, with the most detailed information available for Dubai, where the Department of Economic Development makes licensing information available by license type, if not by legal status of the entity.

Table 2 **2009 Labor Force Survey 2: Monthly Income Levels of Employers and the Self-Employed**

Occupation	**Monthly Income Levels (AED)**					
	=> 5000	**5001-10000**	**20000-10001**	**40000-20001**	**+ 40000**	**Total**
Legislators, senior officials & managers	14.1	27.0	28.7	19.0	11.2	100.0
Professionals	2.4	17.3	32.8	29.9	17.5	100.0
Technicians and associate professionals	35.3	38.2	11.8	2.9	11.8	100.0
Clerks	41.7	58.3	0.0	0.0	0.0	100.0
Service workers & shop & market sales workers	64.3	23.5	11.2	0.0	1.0	100.0
Skilled agricultural and fishery workers	33.3	33.3	33.3	0.0	0.0	100.0
Craft and related trades workers	54.9	23.9	9.9	5.6	5.6	100.0
Plant and machine operators & assemblers	69.4	26.5	2.0	2.0	0.0	100.0
Elementary occupations	66.7	0.0	33.3	0.0	0.0	100.0
Total	19.4	23.5	26.0	19.3	11.8	100.0

Source: 2009 Labor Force Survey, Table (31): Monthly Income Levels of Employers and the Self-Employed

Table 3 **2009 Labor Force Survey 3: Mean and Median Income Levels of Employers and the Self-Employed**

Characteristics	Mean (AED)	Median (AED)
BY EMIRATE		
Abu Dhabi	22482.46	10000.00
Dubai	28540.67	20000.00
Sharjah	27377.22	15000.00
Ajman	13178.33	8000.00
Umm Al Quwain	17356.66	14301.24
Ras Al Khaima	24993.66	3022.76
Fujairah	8896.78	5074.04
GENDER DIFFERENCES		
Males	25572.76	15000.00
Females	19798.97	12000.00
NATIONALITY		
Nationals	64441.82	25277.83
Non-Nationals	22117.64	15000.00
FIELD OF ACTIVITY		
Legislators, senior officials & managers	29857.85	15000.00
Professionals	29513.34	20000.00
Technicians and associate professionals	25179.06	8000.00
Clerks	6900.69	5807.67
Service workers & shop & market sales workers	6105.25	5000.00
Skilled agricultural and fishery workers	9294.34	11531.28
Craft and related trades workers	9859.97	5000.00
Plant and machine operators & assemblers	5178.96	3500.00
Elementary occupations	6368.81	3230.44
EDUCATION		
Illiterate	6112.10	3000.00
Read & Write	18143.89	6362.71
Primary	13026.11	7000.00
Preparatory	19872.99	7000.00
Secondary	20269.52	13000.00
University & Above	34269.25	20000.00
Total	25264.87	15000.00

Source: 2009 Labor Force Survey, Table (35): Mean and Median Income Levels of Employers and the Self-Employed

What the tables show is not unexpected: incomes are highest in Abu Dhabi and Dubai and lower in the Northern Emirates, higher for men than for women, higher for the educated than for the unskilled, and higher for nationals than for expatriates. Interestingly, all average values are higher than the corresponding values for employees (2009 Labour Market Survey, Table 36).

Table 4 **World Bank Entrepreneurship Data for the UAE**

Number of Limited Companies Registered in the UAE

Year	Per 1000 Population	Number of LLCs
2004	2.18	6626
2005	2.14	7036
2006	1.96	7756
2007	1.83	8810
2008	1.61	9259
2009	0.92	6086
2010	1.06	7700
2011	1.19	9127
2012	1.38	10814

Source: World Bank Data accessible at http://www.doingbusiness.org/data/exploretopics/entrepreneurship, accessed 2014/5/26

More light is shed on the demographic profile of entrepreneurs in the Emirates by the Global Entrepreneurship Monitor (GEM) Survey (El-Sokari et al. (2013)). The report reproduces participation rates in the adult UAE population, distinguishing between different developmental stages of company involvement: it distinguishes between nascent and baby businesses, which together account for the total early stage entrepreneurial activity (TEA).

For all of these groups, the GEM numbers record a rise of entrepreneurial activity between 2006 and 2009, with, however, a marked drop in early entrepreneurship in 2011. Throughout, a marked differentiation of involvement in entrepreneurship as a function of geographic provenance can be observed: Arab expatriates constitute the most active group, followed by Emirati nationals, with Western expatriates and Asian expatriates for less active as a share of the respective populations. The two latter groups were also the only ones to desist almost completely from startup involvement in 2011.

For the period 2006-2011, the development of involvement in TEA is also available for four main categories: Emirati, Western, non-GCC Arab, and Asian entrepreneurs, as well as detailed information on discontinued businesses.

The openness of the UAE business environment is reflected in favorable survey scores. The Heritage Foundation's 2014 Index of Economic Freedom allots an overall very positive 28th place to the UAE ("*Mostly free*"), but considers the 49% foreign ownership limit for onshore companies in the UAE repressive. According to the World Bank (2013), the UAE lead the Arab World, taking 23rd place globally, but fall short on a number of metrics

Table 5 GEM UAE Entrepreneurship Participation Rates 2011

UAE Entrepreneurship Participation Rates 2011

GEM Category	Emirati Participation Rate	Expat Participation Rate	UAE Participation Rate	Innovation Driven Economies Participation Rate
Nascent	4.6%	3.3%	3.9%	4.0%
Baby Business	6.0%	2.3%	4.0%	3.0%
TEA	10.4%	5.6%	7.8%	6.9%
Established Business	5.0%	2.5%	3.6%	7.2%

Source: El Sokari, van Horn, Huang & Al Awad (2013:13)

Table 6 GEM UAE Early Entrepreneurship Rates 2006-2011

Owns and Manages a Business up to 42 Months Old

Year	Emirati	Arab Expatriate	Asian Expatriate	Western Expatriate	UAE Average
2006	1.7%	3.6%	1.2%	3.2%	2.2%
2007	4.7%	7.1%	2.0%	1.3%	4.1%
2009	12.0%	9.7%	4.0%	6.6%	7.4%
2011	1.7%	5.2%	0.7%	0.0%	2.6%

Source: El Sokari, van Horn, Huang & Al Awad (2013:15)

that include investor protection, access to credit, enforcing contracts and resolving insolvency, all of which are of relevance to SMEs. On the other hand, they lead the world regarding the ease of dealing with their tax system. The Global Entrepreneurship and Development Institute (GEDI) portrait of the Emirati business environment ranks economies on 15 variables of relevance to entrepreneurship. While the UAE once again leads the Arab World in this ranking, GEDI, a Washington-based private research institute, finds shortcomings on a number of metrics: in particular, start-up skills are very low, and risk-acceptance, gender issues, process innovation and technology also do not appear to rate very high. According to GEDI, all of the efforts to improve the system are currently being directed to the cultivation of start-up skills.

The institutional features of the UAE entrepreneurial ecosystem rise the question to what extent the institutions of the American Standard Model outlined in Section 2.1 are relevant to the UAE.

The scientific and educational landscape in the UAE has experienced a drastic qualitative and quantitative expansion over the past decades, with the country now home to a regionally leading academic infrastructure, particularly in Abu Dhabi and Dubai. Nevertheless, caveats remain: As a percentage of GDP, research expenditure reached just 0.2% of GDP in 2012, and even at universities, it tended to stay below 1%. Patent grants have long not been statistically traceable. Regarding protection for property rights, some criticism regarding investor protection, access to credit, enforcing contracts and resolving insolvency, has already been recorded in section 3.2 above. While the discussion of details is beyond the scope of this paper, it has to be noted that there appears to be no consensus that foreign investors' property rights are sufficiently protected, particularly since their presence depends on temporary visas that may be revoked.

Regarding the early-stage investment infrastructure, both state and non-state actors have to be considered. Within the business community, there are at least two UAE-based accelerators, both located in Dubai, iAccelerator360 (http://i360accelerator.com/) and Seedstartup (http://seedstartup.com/), both of which appear to have a modest footprint. Seedstartup appears to have raised USD 50,000 to fund a total of 7 projects. No comparable information is available on i360accelerator, whose involvement with state-owned logistics giant DP World in the TURN 8 accelerator does, however introduce an interesting business model: mostly international entrepreneurs are invited to pitch early-stage ideas and, if successful, receive funding and support for a 120-day accelerator period that is to take them to the venture capital stage. A similar model is pursued by another accelerator, AFKAR (www.afkar.me), with both of these accelerators concentrating on IT-entrepreneurship and led by individuals with strong connections in Western tech and telco startup ecosystem.

With respect to angel investors, UK-based Angel's Den crowdsourcing platform is apparently active in Dubai. Another institution, Arab Business Angels (ABAN) was founded in 2008 with Dubai International Capital, part of the Dubai Holding, as its lead investor and linked up with the Clinton Global Initiative. However, while there are traces of activity in 2009, it appears to have discontinued its activities since. As for Dubai

International Capital itself, a major debt restructuring to the tune of USD 2.5 bn became necessary in the aftermath of the financial crisis. It has exited a number of investments, most of which were outside the UAE. The UAE investments tend to be of substantial, money-spinning companies (retail, steel production, etc.), rather than startups.

There are venture capital firms in the UAE, but their focus is not necessarily on the UAE market. For example, MEVP (www.mevp.com) is a Lebanese-owned firm concentrating on investments in Lebanon, with the UAE a location for raising, rather than providing, finance.

Table 7 **The GEDI Assessment of the UAE Entrepreneurial System**

The GEDI Assessment of the UAE Entrepreneurial System

	GEDI Score	**Percentage of total new effort for a 10 point improvement in GEDI score**
Start-up Skills	0.07	100%
Gender	0.36	0%
Tech Sector	0.37	0%
Risk Acceptance	0.43	0%
Process Innovation	0.5	0%
Competition	0.51	0%
Networking	0.61	0%
Opportunity Startup	0.64	0%
Opportunity Perception	0.68	0%
Cultural Support	0.78	0%
Internationalization	0.8	0%
Product Innovation	0.81	0%
Risk Capital	0.99	0%
Human Capital	0.99	0%
High Growth	1	0%

Source: http://www.thegedi.org/countries/united_arab_emirates, accessed 2014/5/26

This leaves the more informal forum of the Dubai chapter of Impact Hub for entrepreneurs in search of an investor.

Entrepreneurial listings have tended not to happen on Emirati capital markets, with relevant companies such as Al Nur Hospitals, NMC Hospitals and Damac opting for an external listing, for example on the London Stock Exchange. Listings on the NASDAQ Dubai, which currently boasts eight listed securities, have been few and far between, and it is unlikely to take on the role of its New York namesake in the region.

To the extent that these players display dynamism and activity, they tend to focus on IT and telecommunication, to be associated with a very limited number of regional VC heavyweights, most prominently the Abraaj Group, and, as Schroeder (2013) illustrates, to have strong links to the US startup scene.

Together with private-sector players, public-sector actors and parastatals are at the center of the entrepreneurship ecosystem in the UAE and provide a rich infrastructure, partly directed at providing a home to international entrepreneurial ventures in the UAE free economic zones, be it through TECOM and its sister companies in Dubai or through other ventures, partly through support program largely directed at potential entrepreneurs with Emirati passports.

Free economic zones were originally created in Dubai, but have now become commonplace in practically all Emirates, including in Abu Dhabi. Offering their tenants an off-shore business platform for a fee, they are most prominently represented by TECOM Investments in Dubai, in turn a subsidiary of Dubai Holding.

Institutions paving the way for Emirati entrepreneurs include the following, which will be discussed at greater length in Section 4:

- The *Khalifa Fund in Abu Dhabi*, offers loans and logistical support for would-be Emirati entrepreneurs from Abu Dhabi,
- *Dubai SME*, part of the Dubai Department of Economic Development provides training and services for entrepreneurs, including the *Intelaq* program for UAE entrepreneurs:
- The *Sheikh Saud Bin Saqr Program for Young Business Leaders*, encouraging the growth and development of Emirati youth projects, based in Sharjah,
- The *Ruwad Establishment* encouraging the growth of SMEs in Sharjah,
- The *Istishara Program*, introduced by the Western Region Development Council in collaboration with specialists from both the Government and the private sector.

In addition, universities are eager to jump upon the entrepreneurship bandwagon, hosting entrepreneurship forums, and organizing lectures on the topic. The UAE GEM report has been produced at one of the three federal universities in cooperation with a senior representative of the Khalifa Fund (El-Sokari et al. (2013)).

For actors in this entrepreneurship ecosystem, there is thus more than one motive for getting involved, with payoffs at once in the economic and in the political realm. In a complex discourse of entrepreneurship, from a political perspective, four different objectives can be distinguished, although it may not be possible to establish objectively in every case which one is being pursued.

In channeling its youth into supported entrepreneurial activity, the Emirati state, often represented by the ruling families of the individual Emirates, continues to fulfill its part of the societal bargain, although no longer through the direct provision of work in the bureaucracy. While regulating the labor market for all comers in the SME sector, it takes care to maintain a support function for nationals that these have come to expect from their state.

At the same time, the entrepreneurship discourse allows for communication with external audiences, positioning Dubai in particular as a modern locus of entrepreneurial activity in line with the different developmental visions (*Abu Dhabi 2030, Dubai 2015, UAE*

Figure 3 Political and Economic Dimensions of Entrepreneurship in the UAE

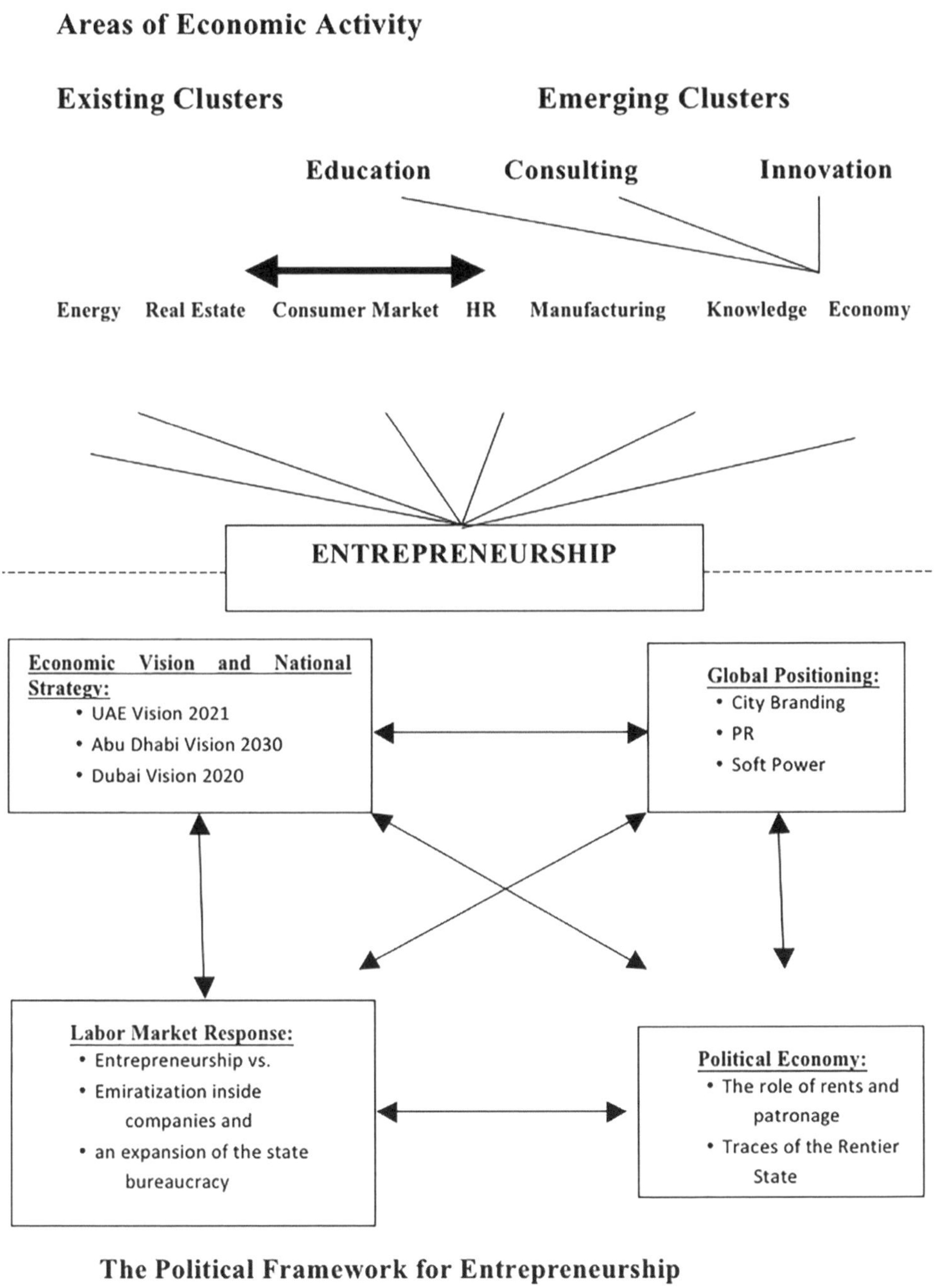

Vision 2021, etc.) officially adopted. Here, it has to be shown that a modern, innovative SME sector is on the way to providing the innovative businesses that the country needs to prosper in its post-oil future, and that it hence makes sense for the potential entrants to set up shop in the Emirates and be part of the dream.

Nevertheless, the proof of the pudding will remain in the eating: unless economic returns justify the engagement, there will not be takers either among nationals or among expatriates for what is on offer. In this perspective, it needs to be asked in which areas entrepreneurial activity can be expected to be successful: are entrepreneurs more likely to react to market incentives in pragmatic, but ultimately not very innovative ways, or are they likely to spawn the kinds of innovation that comes out of Silicon Valley, with its Googles and Facebooks?

In the former case, entrepreneurship can be expected to react primarily to country specific impulses, catering to the consumer sector, and servicing the existing labor and HR requirement of the UAE labor market. In the second case, we will see them go beyond a reaction to market signals, and introduce genuinely new products that can initiate revolutionary change in the UAE business system and beyond. The following three sections will gather evidence towards an answer to that question.

The Emirati Entrepreneur

The Emirati entrepreneur is a Janus-faced being. On the one hand, he is a member of a core group of nationals who are party to a ruling bargain in which they have been assumed to trade support for the ruling family for the participation in the rent flows accruing to the state. On the other hand, he (or she) enters a marketplace in which he may expose himself to international competition and the workings of market mechanisms. As will be seen, however, it is not necessarily clear where rent-seeking ends and the dead heat of competition starts.

This ambiguity of Emirati entrepreneurship is illustrated graphically by Krane's (2009:177f.) account of a visit of Sheikh Muhammad bin Rashed of Dubai to Zayed University, where the ruler was so pleased at the sight of a bazaar where ZU students were selling different products that he gave the students a financial reward of more than $1 million.

The ruler's reaction would have been instantly understandable to an Abbasid court poet of the 9th century, whose artistic output would have been as much pitched at triggering his patron's munificence in the guise of instant pecuniary gratification. But in conforming to the classical calque of august behaviour to deserving subjects, the Sheikh's reaction also fed into a discourse of entrepreneurship and self-reliance that was at marked contrast with expectations of life-long employment in the state bureaucracy which had been prevalent in the previous generation.

In addition, the Emirati entrepreneur has other institutional advantages. As a young Emirati passes from the education system into the job market, there are several specific resources available to him that support a possible entry into an entrepreneurial role:

1. He can tap the general financial resources of the Emirati state and the Emirate through a number of organizations (Khalifa Fund in AD, Intelaq licenses in Dubai (Dubai SME), etc.). These programs also provide training and support.
2. He can tap social networks inside the Emirati community, to which, due to its large degree of insularity and social isolation from foreign business communities, international entrepreneurs have only limited access. This is likely to open up contacts across the divide between the Emirati bureaucracy and businesses.

A number of foundations support entrepreneurial activity by Emirati nationals. These include the Khalifa Fund in Abu Dhabi, the *Intilaq* initiative under the umbrella of Dubai SME in Dubai, the Sheikh Saud bin Saqr Program for Young Business Leaders in Ras al-Khaimah, the Ruwad Establishment in Sharjah, and the Estishara Scheme in the Western Region of Abu Dhabi (El-Sokari et al. (2013:14f.)).

Established in June 2007, the **Khalifa Fund** supports Emirati entrepreneurs with advice, mentoring, and loans at highly preferential conditions. With a fund volume of AED 2 bn in 2011, it funds suitable Emirati projects, taking an active part in contributing to the success of the application process: "When a business idea is initially approved, the applicant must provide a business plan. If required, Khalifa Fund will provide a business plan template and assist the applicant in preparing it," as the fund's website explains. If they are successful, applicants then can obtain preferential loans, as well as help in finding premises and fee waivers that make use of specific agreements the fund has with different authorities.

Loans start from micro-finance loans of AED 100,000 and can reach AED 5,000,000 in the *Ziyada* program. With the latter program, there are some restrictions on the sectors that can be funded, with some of the more obvious start-up ideas excluded: the owners of embryonic construction companies, cafes and restaurants, car rentals, real estate brokerages, health and beauty ventures, or securities trading firms need not apply. The Khalifa Fund has separate programs for women, prison inmates, persons with disabilities and inhabitants of Abu Dhabi's Western Region, adding a social and developmental perspective. Although it is known to have financed more than 240 projects, the Khalifa Fund has not published any detailed repayment and profitability data until now, and has a reputation as an accessible place for Emiratis to obtain funds for businesses. Together with Zayed University, the Khalifa Fund constitutes the UAE country team producing the Global Entrepreneurship Monitor reports for the UAE, thus feeding both into the entrepreneurial activities themselves and into the discursive system reflecting them.

The **Intilaq Initiative** is run by Dubai SME, in turn part of the Dubai Department for Economic Development, and strives to "assist Emiratis residing in Dubai to take their first step into the world of entrepreneurship" (http://sme.ae/services, accessed 2014/05/26). Support includes "licensing, training courses as well as financial, legal, marketing, technical support, and consultancy," with the corresponding license priced competitively at AED 1060 and allowing the Emirati applicant to set out as a freelancer. With an Intilaq license, the budding entrepreneur may not hire staff, but may purchase services from outside providers. Funding and training via the Dubai Entrepreneurship Academy, also run by Dubai SME, as well as incubator services are equally available from the same provider, as is access to the Government Procurement Program (GPP) in Dubai. Regarding this program, Dubai SME states:

> All Dubai Government departments allocate at least 5% of their annual purchasing budget to participants of the Government Procurement Programme (GPP). This enables UAE Nationals who own and operate small and medium-size businesses to compete with larger companies and sell their products and services to government departments. Since this programme was established in 2002, GPP members have sold more than AED 1 billion worth of goods and services to the Dubai Government. (http://sme.ae/services#funding, accessed 2014/5/26)

Compared to the Khalifa Fund of Abu Dhabi, Dubai SME thus concentrates less on funding and more on enabling and providing access to knowledge, licenses, and networks for Emirati start-up entrepreneurs. According to the Dubai Department of Economic Development (2014c), 224 Intilaq licenses were issued in 2013.

In Ras Al Khaymah, the **Saud bin Saqr Program for Young Business Leaders** was established in 2008 under the umbrella of the Ras Al Khaymah Chamber of Commerce and Industry (RAKCCI) in order to facilitate entrepreneurship and encourage the establishment of new businesses and projects by UAE entrepreneurs, with the main emphasis on small and medium enterprises. The program offers Emirati entrepreneurs comprehensive fee waivers. The chamber of commerce also liaised with different banks in the emirate to facilitate funding for local entrepreneurs, and with the RAK Department of Economic Development, which apparently intends to offer licenses along the lines of the Dubai Intilaq license to young RAK natives, encouraging them to set up businesses they can run from home.

Ruwad is an initiative based at the Sharjah Chamber of Commerce to promote entrepreneurship. It backs entrepreneurship education in Sharjah and apparently follows the RAK model in concentrating on fee waivers. An incubator has been established by the Sharjah Chamber of Industry.

It would thus appear that much relevant activity still remains at the Emirate, rather than at the national level, with Abu Dhabi and Dubai having dedicated institutions to support entrepreneurship, with considerable funding available for this purpose, particularly in Abu Dhabi, while in the Northern Emirates, this function tends to be located at the chambers of commerce and industry, with the emphasis more on fee waivers and start-up licenses and general start-up facilitation than on direct financial support.

In all GCC countries, the only individuals who can go into business without the need of a local partner have traditionally been GCC nationals. Foreigners, at least those who do not hold the nationality of another GCC state, have had to enter into joint venture arrangements, in which control of the business remains formally with the local partner, who owns no less than 51% of it. Even without substantial inputs of time and material resources, Emirati entrepreneurs have thus traditionally been able to profit from the participation in business ventures conceived, established, and run by others, receiving either a fixed fee or a share of the profits.

Given the strong Emirati presence in the bureaucracy and the relatively limited social contacts between Emiratis and expats in the UAE, Emirati entrepreneurs will have a stronger endowment when it comes to doing business with Emirati institutions and parastatals. Thanks to the declared priority given to empowering nationals in UAE policy making, an Emirati bidder, or a bid including an Emirati partner, will have an advantage in any tender process, all other conditions being equal.

The recent passage of a new SME law reinforced this trend. Federal Law No 2 of 2014, approved by the president in April 2014, exempts SMEs from customs tax for equipment, raw materials and capital goods. They are also exempted from bank guarantees that companies have to deposit for every new worker. In addition, the law stipulates that federal authorities and ministries have to award at least 10 per cent of their procurement budget for purchasing, servicing and consulting to SMEs. Parastatals and other firms of which the federal government owns 25 per cent or more are similarly constrained to award 5 per cent of their contracts to SMEs.

If these provisions in themselves can be seen as a clear boost to Emirati entrepreneurs, who are more likely to own a locally registered SME than foreigners, this is all the more true of certain additional provisions. According to Sultan Al-Mansuri, the UAE Minister of the Economy, "Emirati entrepreneurs falling under the small and medium classification will benefit from a number of incentives offered by the council, including credit and funding facilitation, financing, marketing and reduced licensing costs" (Gutcher et al. (2014)).

A new SME Council is to be established in accordance with this law in order to implement these support measures.

The GEM study provides further information about Emirati startup entrepreneurs. Regarding gender balance, Emirati men are 30% more likely to engage in entrepreneurial activity than Emirati women, with 11.8% of Emirati men, but only 7.6% of Emirati women engaging in early-stage entrepreneurial activity. With established businesses, the contrast is even more pronounced, with 7% of Emirati men, but only 0.9% of women owning established businesses (El-Sokari et al. (2013:39)). The study also points out that small households are more likely than large households to harbour an entrepreneur, that the well-off are more likely than low income earners to set out on their own, and that the age cohort between 25 and 34 has the largest share of entrepreneurs.

Interestingly, "over four of five Emirati entrepreneurs are employed while they start-up their new venture. Just over eight in ten Emirati entrepreneurs are also employed in full-time employment in addition to their SME activities. As we know that the majority of the

Emirati workforce is employed by the different levels of government, this would indicate that a large percentage of Emirati entrepreneurs are in fact government employees as well" (El-Sokari et al. (2013:19)).

In other words, most Emirati entrepreneurs survey the dead heat of the competitive marketplace from the comfort of a civil service position, may have preferential access to funding via organizations such as *Intelaq* or the *Khalifa Fund*, and are likely to find a market for the produce thanks to the provisions of the SME law and general procurement practices. In spite of their generally positive stance to Emirati entrepreneurship, Sokary and her co-authors remark: "However, high-growth and high-impact enterprise formation and development require more than full-time commitment, which would seem to be difficult if the entrepreneur were also employed full time. ... One of the key challenges is that the security and generous benefits afforded to Emiratis working in the public sector are difficult to give up for the insecurities and risks commonly associated with the entrepreneurial process."(ibid.). When a choice has to be made between entrepreneurial success and its alternatives, Emirati entrepreneurs appear to be more likely than the other groups to abandon their business venture: While Arab expatriates are the most likely to establish enterprises, between 2006 and 2011, Emirati entrepreneurs have consistently been the most likely group to discontinue a business, doing so at twice the average rate for entrepreneurs in the UAE (El-Sokari et al. (2013:29)).

Table 8 GEM Discontinued Business in the Past 12 Months (2006-2011)

Discontinued Businesses in the Past 12 Months

Year	Emirati	Arab Expatriate	Asian Expatriate	Western Expatriate	UAE Average
2006	9.5%	5.4%	2.5%	3.2%	4.7%
2007	8.6%	6.3%	1.8%	2.0%	4.7%
2009	7.5%	5.9%	0.7%	3.0%	3.7%
2011	4.5%	3.5%	0.7%	0.0%	2.2%

Source: El Sokari, van Horn, Huang & Al Awad (2013:29)

In the UAE media, Emirati entrepreneurship is regularly highlighted, with features about Emirati startups and entrepreneurs a regular feature in media reporting. Articles introduce young Emirati women selling pre-owned designer handbags (Salem (2010)), the Emirati entrepreneur who bought his university's canteen as a second-year student (N.N. (2012)), or the first-year student in Sharjah who, in spite of having only recently turned eighteen, has already several ventures to his name (Ghazal (2014)).

Although such articles are both entertaining and uplifting, the depth of coverage is generally limited and does not allow generalize beyond the individual case. In particular, they provide relatively little information about the general employment impact to be expected from Emirati entrepreneurship.

The Expat Entrepreneur

Globally, expat entrepreneurship is not a new phenomenon, but there are some peculiarities to the UAE setting (Godley (2006)). Here, the expat entrepreneur is sitting on the fence and will remain there. Permanently denied citizenship in the destination country, his decision to locate his business in the UAE is necessarily based on the strategic assessment that this location is more advantageous than either staying at home or relocating to a third destination. With the Emirati entrepreneurs privileged in their home market, this is a decision to enter a business environment in which he will always be faced with a handicap and compete in a skewed marketplace, facing higher costs and more restrictions than his local competitors.

An analysis of his situation has hence to consider three different factors. Push factors include a perceived unattractiveness of the home country, be it with respect to the cost of doing business, the quality of the infrastructure, the regulatory framework, or the tax system.

Pull factors include specific allures of the UAE market, such as the availability of certain factor inputs (labor, energy) and consequently a premium being put on the entrepreneur's skills, market opportunities such as servicing the vibrant consumer market, or the massive market for imported labor, or specific advantages of the UAE with respect to the cost of doing business, the quality of the infrastructure, the regulatory framework, or the tax system.

Eventually, configurational factors include advantages related to international business and access to international networks that can be put to use thanks to being in the UAE, rather than in the country of origin, but may not be specific UAE resources, such as the ability to tap bilateral migration networks.

Some forms of expat entrepreneurship arise out of the very legal and social situation that the expat entrepreneur finds himself in. Expat entrepreneurship, understood as the activity of individual foreigners in the country, may be differentiated around the axes of formality, technological sophistication, and whether or not they engage primarily with the local UAE marketplace or with the international market.

Informality is the condition of those who lack the funds of setting up a legitimate business. Prime examples of this are those mostly subcontinental workers who people the labor camps and may remit over 100% of their limited monthly wages to their home country. This is achieved by engaging in extracurricular work, engaging in odd jobs, washing cars in parking lots, conducting petty trade, or the setting up informal markets (Ahmad (2014)).

Furthermore, individuals may establish themselves as brokers/social workers (*dalal*), combining the apparently altruistic provision of services to recent arrivals with a broker function undertaken primarily for the sake earning provision income. In their analysis of the Indian *dalal* system of getting things done, as opposed to the more hierarchical Arab concept of *wasta*, Osella & Osella (2012:120f.) provide numerous illustrations of how migrants develop informal entrepreneurial activity and manage to develop solid networks over time that strengthen their *de facto* position in their communities, although their legal status does not change significantly from the moment they first obtain a visa to the day they leave the country again. Some of these activities are against the spirit, if not the letter, of the law.

In the case of these migrant entrepreneurs, informality arose under conditions of a formal integration into the labor market, albeit one which did not reflect the real role of the individual concerned. Nevertheless, this activity will be at best tolerated, probably only temporarily, and cannot be transformed into a legitimate enterprise.

Historically, expat entrepreneurs could achieve eminent positions as entrepreneurs in Gulf trader communities. In the UAE context, early arrivals such as Youssufali M.A., the chairman of the EMKE group, illustrate just how far business-savvy foreign entrepreneurs could advance at the time. Youssufali's Lulu Hypermarket has opened stores throughout the GCC, and, in addition to several awards, he was honoured by the election to a director's position at the Abu Dhabi chamber of commerce. Youssufali remains proudly Indian, and his operations characteristically span the subcontinent, and particularly his native Kerala, on the one hand and the Gulf on the other.

In his business ventures, his ethnic identity is a major source of his success. In his native Kerala, he participated in the establishment of a Smart Village in cooperation with TECOM, the free zone operator from Dubai. On the other hand, in the UAE, it is largely the very sizable Indian community that patronizes his hypermarkets.

For more recent arrivals, such arrangements are hardly within reach, but more institutional options are on offer. The fundamental decision to be taken is whether to establish an offshore, free zone company or stay onshore and share control with a UAE national who will have a majority stake in the business.

For an entrepreneur considering entry, the elementary choice is between an onshore and an offshore presence.

If the former is chosen, there will have to be an Emirati individual as majority owner of the company (at least 51%). This does not deter some expat entrepreneurs, who insist that their Emirati partner is definitely a very nice man, contents himself with a modest fee, and does not interfere in the business. This might be relatively riskless as long as the business is, e.g., a translation agency or a restaurant, where the physical assets limited, managerial know-how largely determines success, and expropriation of minority owners is thus less of an issue. At the same time, where exponential growth of the business value is expected that is not linked to the labor input of the principals, there might be understandable reluctance

Figure 4: **The Expatriate Entrepreneur: Decision Tree for Company Design**

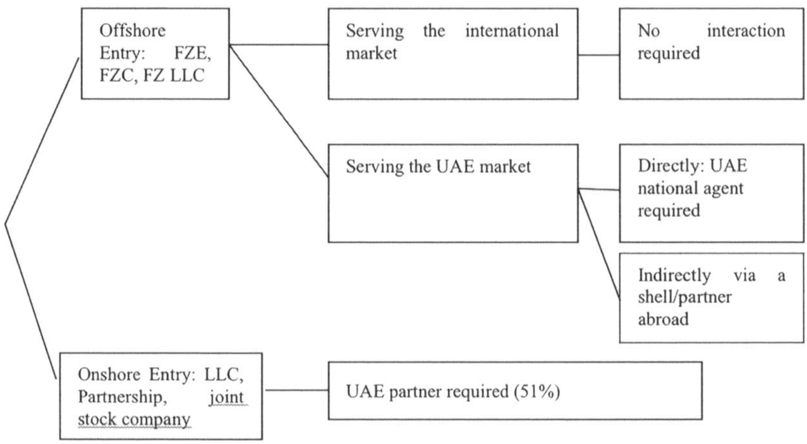

to engage in such an arrangement if the next hot IT startup company were to be founded onshore in the Emirates, it would necessarily create an Emirati billionaire, irrespective of who originally provided the intellectual input and did the actual work.

If an offshore company is chosen, administrative fees can be expected to be higher, possibly including a rental agreement for premises within the free zone. The advantage is the possibility of 100%-ownership. This is, however, a blessing that can be best leveraged effectively if there is an international client base. If a national one is targeted, the necessity of employing an Emirati agent arises, although this does not compromise ownership of the company itself. A way around this might that was mentioned occasionally would be to use a foreign company as a conduit for selling into the UAE market. This would, however, not allow the entrepreneur to sell to the important group of UAE government clients, who only accept bids from locally registered company. The choice for international entrepreneurs is thus between a complete engagement in offshore markets and arrangements including significant involvement with Emirati onshore partners.

As noted above, there is a significant asymmetry between the behaviour of Arab, Asian, and Western expatriates, with the former Arab expatriate group apparently far more active than any other group of entrepreneurs (El-Sokari et al. (2013:15)). Although he is far more likely than the Emirati entrepreneur to have opened a business over any given time, he is less likely to have closed one over the period (El-Sokari et al. (2013:29)). A strict causal interpretation cannot be given on the basis of the available data, but the phenomenon is compatible with regulatory arbitrage by Arab entrepreneurs between their home and their target environments: since the UAE is both accessible to Arab entrepreneurs and far stronger than their home countries in terms of governance indicators, they have greater motivation to engage in entrepreneurial activity in the UAE. A positive story about the involvement of Arab entrepreneurs in UAE markets may represent it as a triumph of regulatory quality, allowing the release of Arab entrepreneurial energies that remain handicapped in their home countries.

The same does not apply to Western expatriates, who have the option of improving the quality of the regulatory environment by returning to their home countries for entrepreneurial purposes, leaving the UAE behind. They also tend to have better paid positions and thus a higher reservation wage in the UAE, explaining their relatively low involvement.

The explanation does, however, fail to account for the relatively low involvement of Asian entrepreneurs in UAE entrepreneurship, although they, too, could profit from regulatory arbitrage. It should be kept in mind, however, that the relatively low percentages of Indian entrepreneurship in the UAE correspond to sizable absolute numbers due to the size of a resident subcontinental population far in excess of the Arab or Western communities. It may be lower incomes, more than anything else, that are keeping the lion's share of the Indian population from pursuing formal entrepreneurial activities. A reported eagerness to engage in informal entrepreneurial activity certainly suggests that this may be relevant.

This outline has illustrated the basic legal and pragmatic frameworks in which the UAE expat entrepreneur can be expected to engage. While it has made an argument as to why the next GOOGLE may just not come out of an expat run onshore company in the UAE, concrete pointers as to the kinds of choices made by Emirati and foreign entrepreneurs have not to date been discussed.

A locally conducted beauty contest for entrepreneurs that provides some pointers as to what best practice actually looks like in this entrepreneurial ecosystem is the 2013 edition of the Dubai SME 100 competition, released in early 2014, and the report on entrepreneurship in Dubai, equally published in early 2014. With the 100 companies having been chosen by Dubai SME out of a pool of 3041 applicants on the basis of growth performance, financial soundness, innovation, human capital development, international orientation and corporate governance, they can certainly be expected to present a clear indication of what is within reach for SME and startup activity in Dubai, although they cannot be taken to be representative for the larger pool of firms that make up that entrepreneurial ecosystem.

The SME report documents a revival of entrepreneurial activity and reports aggregate numbers and financial ratios for SMEs in Dubai. Critically, it notes the relatively weak role of research and development in the Dubai business system, with only 8% of the businesses it surveys having a dedicated R&D budget (Dubai SME (2014:34)).

Collectively, the top 100 SMEs provide some reason for optimism on commercial grounds. Between 2011 and 2012, this elite group of enterprises managed to expand revenues, profit, employment and productivity per employee dramatically, as the following table illustrates.

Table 9 **Dubai SME 100: Revenues and Profits, Employment and Productivity**

Collective Impact	**2011**	**2013**	**Increase**
Total Revenues (AED mn)	2,248	4,521	101%
Total Profits (AED mn)	219	434,5	98%
Employment	4,319	7,105	65%
Productivity per employee (AED)	520,542	636,349	22%

Source: http://www.dubaisme100rankings.com/2013/, accessed 2014/05/26

Although the importance of this sample should not be exaggerated, a couple of stylized facts emerge:

- Among chosen Dubai SME 100 companies, a significant number are system integrators, combining technology sales with consultancy and potentially training. This corporate format conforms to expectations regarding expat entrepreneurship, combining the attractions of selling high value-added products into the Gulf market with relatively little need for large-scale investments. These companies are likely to be located at one of the free economic zones, and to be largely or exclusively expat-run.
- Some of the Emirati companies in the group explicitly specify the importance of Emirati institutions and private Emirati-run corporations for business, illustrating how societal networks may be of importance for entrepreneurial success.
- The highest-ranked SME of the list, the internationally expanding ethnic fast-food chain *Just Falafel*, appears to have a more positive story of engaging stakeholders. Combining Indian, Arab and Emirati know-how that came together in the Emirati marketplace, this Emirati-Lebanese joint venture looks set to list on the NASDAQ Dubai in the near future, thus becoming one of the first Emirati enterprises to experience the whole entrepreneurship cycle form startup to IPO less than a decade (Al-Sayegh (2013); Sleiman (2013)).

Conclusion and Future Perspectives

In pursuing the link between the Gulf national employment trilemma, internationalized discourses on entrepreneurship and actual start-up activity in the UAE, the preceding pages have highlighted a number of nascent opportunities and structural problems, as well as reviewing resources on the ground.

On a positive note, the ground is well prepared for an entrepreneurship eco-system in the UAE, contributing significantly to the dynamism of the business environment. International surveys rank the UAE quite highly on the entrepreneurship scale.

That said, entrepreneurship discourses in the UAE can be self-referential and out of touch with the economic reality on the ground, with global discourses on entrepreneurship recycled with often very limited adaptation to local circumstances. Mechanisms of rent-seeking may persist in individuals that claim to be in pursuit of entrepreneurial opportunities, particularly in the case of nationals: in order to wean them away from the reliance on the bureaucracy as the traditional employer of last resort, entrepreneurship itself may be facilitated to a degree that tends to push young national entrepreneurs into ultimately familiar modes of rent-based interaction.

Data are murky. Some existing databases, such as the SME100, do provide relevant information, but are only helpful up to a point and have to be used strategically. In the academic exploration of entrepreneurship in the Gulf, greater efforts are hence needed to construct more helpful datasets and case studies that take into account the specific terrain on which both expatriate and national entrepreneurs interact.

In the practical pursuit of entrepreneurial activity in the Gulf, the differing constraints and incentive structures highlighted here should be kept in mind and, where possible, used strategically with a view to

a) maintaining realistic expectations regarding the possible impact of entrepreneurial activity on economic growth, employment, and in particular national employment,
b) making entrepreneurial activity more attractive for international entrepreneurs, and hence creating more vibrant a mix for the domestic market, and
c) sensitizing Emirati and GCC entrepreneurs to mechanisms that allow them to make use of the split entrepreneurship universe through combining strengths and weaknesses.

8

Rents, Start-Ups, and Obstacles to SME Entrepreneurialism in Oman, Bahrain and Qatar

Jessie Moritz

Introduction

Gulf states have long discussed the necessity of small and medium enterprises (SMEs) – companies with fewer than 100 employees – to the long-term sustainability of their economy. As governments find themselves overstretched in an attempt to provide employment for citizens in the public sector, the employment potential of private sector SMEs cannot be overlooked. It also presents an opportunity to encourage the kind of worker motivation and entrepreneurialism among nationals that, if business guides are to be believed, has been lacking in the region for some time. Yet most Arab states of the Gulf have struggled to create the incentives necessary to support SME growth and entrepreneurialism of nationals. Proceeding from a basis that obstacles to entrepreneurialism are political, structural, and removable, this chapter focuses on the major obstacles to SME development in the post-2011 period. SME growth is not in itself an end; rather, it is the potential for SMEs to encourage increased employment of nationals in appropriate positions in the private sector that is of interest.

Termed *SME entrepreneurialism*, this chapter focuses on policies encouraging SME development by nationals, not FDI or SME growth by non-nationals that will not, ultimately, reduce citizen dependence on the public sector. Further, while policy in the Gulf states tends not to differentiate between micro, small, and medium enterprises, the focus of this chapter is on micro (less than 10 employees) and small (less than 50 employees) enterprises, and particularly on start-up enterprises utilising new technologies: these are exactly the type of enterprises that can offer high-wage and high-skill opportunities to Gulf nationals and therefore represent an ideal type of entrepreneurship.

The Gulf is also a diverse region, and that which frustrates SME entrepreneurialism in, say, Kuwait may be very different to obstacles to entrepreneurialism in the UAE, or Oman. As an underlying purpose of this research is to investigate the impact of rents on

SME entrepreneurialism, this chapter discusses three case studies – Qatar, Bahrain and Oman – that fit the classical definition of a 'rentier state' (oil or gas exportation provides at least 40 percent of government revenue and a sizeable portion of GDP), yet face diverse economic development challenges. Oman is a late developer with low oil and gas wealth relative to the rest of the GCC, Qatar is a capital-rich rent economy which has benefited from phenomenal gas wealth over the past decade, and Bahrain started diversification very early but must contend with post-peak oil reserves and dependence on the Saudi Arabian economy. They thus represent the diversity of the Arab states of the Gulf even as they conform to the general parameters of a 'rentier state'.

To explore the challenges these states face in increasing entrepreneurialism, this chapter draws from a series of semi-structured interviews completed with over 120 citizens of Qatar, Bahrain and Oman in 2013 and early 2014, including ministers, development experts, members of major business families, SME managers, and youth entrepreneurs.[i] These interviews discussed, among other topics, the development trajectory of the state, challenges to SMEs, entrepreneurship, personal motivation in joining either the public or private sector, and perceptions on worker productivity, the intention being to draw out similarities in responses across Qatar, Bahrain and Oman, and support a comparative analysis of SME entrepreneurialism.

The second purpose of the interviews was to consider practical responses to entrepreneurialism in light of an influential literature on the 'rentier state', which has colored perceptions of Gulf development since the 1970s. This literature outlines a number of characteristics that, theoretically, rentierism encourages in the domestic political economy, and this chapter draws particularly from a revisionist phase in the literature where the state plays a deliberate role in private sector employment growth yet is still strongly influenced by rentierism. Existing support programs, discussed in the second section of this chapter, also indicate tangible attempts to encourage entrepreneurialism, and highlight that although they face similar challenges in increasing national participation in the private sector, the current environment for SME entrepreneurialism varies enormously within the Gulf. The remainder of the chapter draws from the interview data to outline remaining challenges to SME entrepreneurialism as identified by citizens of Qatar, Bahrain and Oman. These challenges have occurred at three levels: at the practical or day-to-day level, including difficulties obtaining finance and bureaucratic inefficiencies; at the market level, including discussion of market monopolies, skill mismatches, and the persistence of a 'rentier mentality'; and at the policy level, where disharmony and duplication between economic policies and poor implementation of vague economic visions have affected private sector participation.

Most critically, these states have faced political pressures since 2011 that force them to balance political responses aimed at addressing societal discontent with longer-term goals of economic diversification. Ultimately, the underlying obstacles to SME entrepreneurialism are shown to be political in nature and stem largely from the rentier structure of the political economy. To succeed in increasing SME entrepreneurialism, the governments of

Qatar, Bahrain, and Oman will need to overcome these political obstacles and escape the development traps encouraged by rentierism.

Rentier State Theory and Theoretical Obstacles to Entrepreneurialism

Despite ancient histories of trading and entrepreneurialism in the Arab states of the Gulf, an influential literature dominant since the 1970s asserts these traditions have been overwhelmed by *rentierism*, the influence of economic rents from the exportation of oil, gas and other lucrative natural resources. Classic RST (1970 – mid-1990s) emerged as a response to resource-driven development strategies of the 1950s and 60s, identifying a connection between rent abundance and political and economic stagnation (Mahdavy 1970). For Hazem Beblawi, the key difference was the *rentier mentality* fostered by the distribution of rents from the state to the population, breaking the work-reward causation and eliminating the incentive to be a productive member of society (1987, p.87-88, 52). Giacomo Luciani, by comparison, explored the notion of an allocative state, limiting the concept to cases where at least 40 percent of government revenue comes from resource exportation or other foreign earned rents. The classic literature focused on elaborating the typical characteristics of a 'rentier state', including an absence of political pluralisation, poor development performance, an over-extended bureaucracy and citizen reliance on state distributions.

While classic RST has been criticised as overly simplistic and deterministic, the literature is far from static. Where criticisms were accepted theorists now offer more nuanced understandings of RST, contributing to a revisionist phase in the literature. The determinism of classic RST has been largely debunked, with more recent works observing a conditional effect of rents dependent on context (Dunning 2008; Herb 2005). Far from the early assumption that rentier states would avoid creating coherent economic policy, this chapter is informed more by conceptions of rent-rich states as influenced by entrepreneurial state capitalism, where the state remains central to the economy yet uses its influence to guide economic development and underpin private sector growth (Gray 2013). Still, however, the literature emphasises an absence of entrepreneurialism among nationals as a result of the rentier political economy.

In practice, rentier practices continue to pervade business across the Arab states of the gulf, especially as the private sector remains clustered around government, dependent on lucrative government contracts or on the petro-sector itself (Bizri 2013, p.198-203). Even where some shift to productive enterprise via economic free zones has occurred, this has not necessarily increased private sector employment of nationals, instead expanding expatriate employment. The Gulf states appear to be following a mixed method of Martin Hvidt's 'Dubai Model' (using regulatory zones to encourage growth of productive enterprises in the private sector) and traditional rentier allocative strategies (2011). The use of free zones, or what this chapter terms 'bubbles of efficiency' – referring not only to specific zones for investment such as Doha's Education City, or Salalah Free Zone, but also to government bodies with markedly different business practices, such as the Economic Development Board in Bahrain – is intended to avoid embedded inefficiencies and reveals an interesting challenge to traditional RST. Yet even these bubbles have been, thus far, unable to overcome broader challenges to SME entrepreneurialism, resulting in the current situation where micro and SMEs constitute the vast majority of enterprises in the Gulf – including 98 percent of Oman's companies, 98.6 percent in Bahrain, and over 75 percent in Qatar[ii] - yet employ only a minority of nationals (Hertog 2010). However, the potential of these enterprises to play a leading role in national entrepreneurship and reduce the employment burden on the state situates them at the core of any economic development strategy. Importantly, this chapter situates government policy – as the most powerful creator of incentives to support or dissuade SME entrepreneurialism – as central to the success of these programs.

Existing Support Programs in Qatar, Bahrain, and Oman

SME and entrepreneurship support programs have proliferated in the Gulf since the 1970s as part of a broader strategy of economic diversification. Some are promising, although it is exceedingly difficult to measure success when information on program outcomes is only rarely published. This section outlines some of the major government support programs designed to promote SME entrepreneurialism, with the intention of differentiating between the environment in Qatar, Bahrain, and Oman. As SME programs are fragmented and not systematically documented in the Gulf, these should be taken as a broad survey of examples, not an exhaustive list of all programs available.

Qatar

A number of SME and entrepreneurship support programs have been initiated so far in Qatar, including Enterprise Qatar, Qatar Science and Technology Park (QSTP), and programs from the Qatar Development Bank, a state-owned bank specialised in SME funding. A number of smaller initiatives have also received support, such as the Roudha Center for Entrepreneurship and Innovation (targeting female entrepreneurs), and Silatech (youth entrepreneurs). As is the case in most Gulf states, ostensibly 'private sector' programs are intricately linked to the ruling apparatus. Silatech, for example, is technically private yet the Board of Trustees includes Chairperson of Qatar Foundation Sheikha Moza bint Nasser al Misnad, the Minister for Information and Communications Technology Dr. Hessa Sultan Al Jaber, CEO of Qatar Development Bank Abdulaziz bin Nasser Al Khalifa, and several other influential Qataris with strong ties to government (2014). In this vein, programs supported by entities like Qatar Foundation – such as QSTP – are considered in this chapter as *indirectly* state-guided programs, especially as they are so closely linked with government development strategies.

Young Qatari entrepreneurs interviewed also identified the Qatar Leadership Program (QLP, also known as the Current and Future Executive Leaders Programme from the Qatar Leadership Center) as critical to their personal success in the private sector, and several had bounced from one program to another – for example from QLP to the ICT Qatar Incubation Center. Universities in Education City have begun to offer courses in entrepreneurship, such as the Department for Entrepreneurship at Virginia Commonwealth University and the Entrepreneurship Center at the College of the North Atlantic. Of greater import for the access it provides to Qatari students is the Center for Entrepreneurship at Qatar University, which runs training programs and a business incubation centre for students and faculty. The universities work with other government-funded projects to support innovation; Carnegie Melon, for example, offers a nine-month course on Technology Innovation and Entrepreneurship in partnership with QSTP (2014).

Many programs are very small – QLP, for example, accepts only 25-35 students, and entry is highly competitive (2012). Initiatives preference Qataris and some are exclusive to nationals but others, such as QSTP, target expatriates, presumably in the hope that innovation will spread throughout society. Qatar Statistics Authority (QSA) data suggests moderate success, showing an increase of Qataris in the private sector from 3,362 in 2006 to 7,664 in 2012. Yet this growth remains fragile; although official data is not available after 2012, Remy Rohani, the Director-General of Qatar Chamber, placed the percentage of Qatari nationals in the private sector at only 8 percent in April 2014, a decrease from 2012 (Pathak 2014).

Figure 1 **Growth of Qataris in Private Sector**

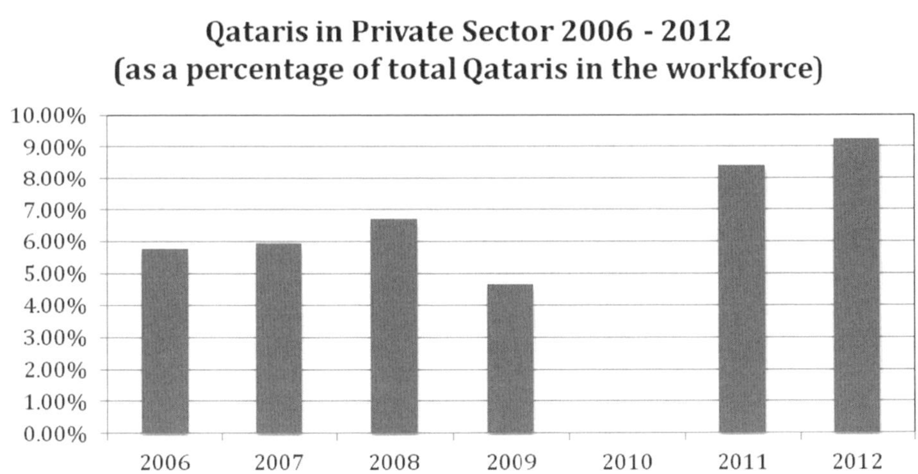

Source: Qatar Statistics Authority

The government has also set a number of Qatarisation goals. In 2000, the government announced an ambitious five-year goal of 50 percent Qatarisation in the Energy and Industry Sector – which includes state-run companies such as Qatar Petroleum. As of 2005, however, the industry had reached an average of only 31 percent (al-Attiyah 2005). Qataris as a share of the overall workforce have actually decreased in recent years, from 14 percent in 2001 to 6 percent in 2009 – a reflection of the current construction boom that has attracted large numbers of expatriate workers. Problematically for a country aiming to become a knowledge-based economy, from 2006-2011, Qatar filed approximately 14 patents per year, compared with over 5,000 in countries like Norway and Singapore, and in 2009, only 2 percent of Qataris managed or invested in their own businesses (Qatar General Secretariat for Development Planning, p.99, 149, 151). More recently, the government announced a target of 15 percent Qatarisation in the private sector, and the Ministry of Labour and Social Affairs is pushing for 20 percent, although it is unclear how this will be achieved (Walker 2014). As of 2013, Qataris comprise less than 1 percent of the private sector workforce, a considerable distance from the level desired by government (QSA).

Thus, there has been a measurable increase in the number of Qataris in the private sector in recent years, but this increase remains fragile and far below levels desired by government. Qatari-owned and managed companies like iHorizons (website design), Qartoon (animation), ibTECHar (education technology), and Girnaas (gaming) also demonstrate the potential for SME entrepreneurialism in Qatar even as they remain a tiny minority. Data on the number of Qatari-run start-up companies is not available, but it worth noting that the majority of Qatari entrepreneurs interviewed in this research were very recent start-ups, starting in 2012 or 2013, and were almost all linked to government-run support programs, indicating some tangible success in increasing entrepreneurialism. Some youth entrepreneurs interviewed claimed to be posting profits as of their second year, although without public data on the number of Qatari enterprises that survive past their third year, it is impossible to determine whether these are aberrations or indicative of a broader trend in Qatari entrepreneurship.

Several companies in the ICT Qatar Digital Incubation Centre have been formed from winners of technology or innovation competitions such as QITCOM, held annually in Doha, or Stars of Science, a Qatar Foundation-funded television competition. Key to SME entrepreneurialism in Qatar is the presence of technology oriented, high value-added enterprises: these are the type of SMEs most likely to offer employment acceptable to Qatari nationals. Their employment potential should not be overstated, as most remain micro or small enterprises requiring specialist skills, and the selection of new enterprises from competition winners is also hardly replicable in large-scale. Yet with such a tiny national population, estimated at 250-300,000 in 2014,[iii] small-scale programs aimed at Qatari citizens can have an outsized effect on entrepreneurship. "I was a product of a process," said one Qatari entrepreneur in 2013. "I am not an exception; there are many like me".

Oman

Oman has similarly had some success with small-scale entrepreneurship support programs, although its larger citizen population and lower rents make this a less viable long-term strategy. Support available to Omani SMEs include business incubators and training from the National Business Centre, policy management and training from the Public Authority for SME development, and a host of funding opportunities and innovation centres. The Knowledge Oasis Muscat, founded in the late 1990s but opened in 2003, has a Technology Park and Incubation Centre for technology-based SMEs, and like QSTP attracts largely foreign companies whose innovations then (theoretically) spread throughout Omani society. The Sharakah Fund for Development of Youth Projects was similarly founded in the 1990s, and offers funding, workshops and guidance for Omani and expatriate SME projects across the country. Since 2008, over 30 businesses have received Sharakah support, although again the majority are expatriate enterprises.

As in Qatar, youth entrepreneurs in Oman tend to benefit from more than one government support program – one example is the Mazoon Environmental and Technological Services, which moved from incubation in the Knowledge Oasis to obtain Sharakah funding (Sharakah 2014). There are also a number of public-private partnerships such as Shell's Intilaaqah program, where graduates of the program are connected with major Omani private sector powerhouses like the W.J. Towell Group (Pourhammadi 2014a).

The Omani government recently made a concerted effort to expand finance options for SMEs. In late 2013, the Central Bank of Oman announced that at least 5 percent of commercial bank lending must be directed towards SMEs, more than doubling the current pool of finance available (Oxford Business Group 2014). A host of new funding schemes have emerged, from the Al Raffd Fund that replaces the former body, Sanad, to the Oman Development Bank, which funds 4,500 to 5,000 entrepreneurs per year in SME and micro-enterprises (James 2014). In May 2014, a new SME development fund, Al Namaa Fund, was launched (Prabhu 2014). While simply expanding funding will not resolve all obstacles to Omani entrepreneurialism, the funds do signify tangible commitment to SME development.

Oman has pursued Omanisation since 1988, and in 2003 Sultan Qaboos set a number of requirements for private sector Omanisation depending on sector and profession, from 60 percent for transport, storage and communications, to 15 percent for contracting (Omanuna 2014). Thus far, there remains a clear gap between targets and actual outcomes, particularly since only around a third of employed Omanis work in the private sector (Ennis and al-Jamali 2014, p. 3-4). As of March 2014, Ministry of Manpower figures showed only 217,578 Omanis working in the private sector compared with 1,597,552 expatriates, meaning Omanis form only around 12 percent of the private sector workforce (Pourmohammadi 2014b). Of that number, only a minority – 8.3 percent in 2013 – work in micro enterprises (National Center for Statistics and Information 2014a). Even fewer work in high-skilled positions, a reflection of Oman's late-developer status, and the majority, some 55 percent in July 2014, earn less than OMR300 in basic monthly wages (National Centre for Statistics and Information 2014b). Most troubling for SME entrepreneurialism, however, has been a recent de-Omanisation of the private sector at a rate of around 1,800 per month from September 2013-2014 (al-Shaibany 2014b). This movement is a clear response to policies expanding the availability and appeal of government employment, highlighting the centrality of government policy in determining the incentives (or disincentives) for entrepreneurialism.

Bahrain

Unlike late-developer Oman, Bahrain was the first in the Arabian Peninsula to establish formal education. It was also the first to export oil, and the first to substantially deplete its reserves, which, combined with Bahrain's status as the leading regional financial hub in the 1980s, encouraged greater GDP diversification and left Bahrain's private sector in a stronger position than that of Qatar or Oman.

The Bahraini government, particularly the Economic Development Board (EDB), has initiated a host of programs designed to expand and support SME employment. The most crucial body in terms of SME entrepreneurialism is Tamkeen, founded in 2006 at the behest of the EDB and designed to offer training and support to Bahraini enterprises and workers, including support for feasibility studies, accounting training and marketing assistance. Both Tamkeen and the Bahrain Business Incubation Center, a subsidiary of the Bahrain Development Bank (BDB), provide incubation for fledgling companies, and the Bahrain Institute for Entrepreneurship and Innovation, another BDB subsidiary, provides technical training (BDB 2012; Tamkeen 2014). Other government departments focusing on SMEs include the Ministry of Industry and Commerce's Small & Medium Enterprises Unit, which helps new companies conduct feasibility studies and marketing research, as well as international organisations such as ARCEIT, the Arab Regional Center for Entrepreneurship and Investment Training (ARCEIT 2014). The Bahrain Chamber of Commerce and Industry (2014), the main body for Bahrain's business elite, opened the SME Development and Support Centre in 2012, running workshops on business skills and connection to funding bodies and service providers like Zain Bahrain, Ebtikar Society, and the Arab Investment and Export Guarantee Corporation. Funding for SMEs generally comes from the BDB, which focuses almost exclusively on SME enterprises, and the Tamkeen Labour Fund, which provides a 50 percent loan guarantee for SMEs borrowing from private banks. By 2014, Tamkeen had supported 31 new enterprises through its own start-up support scheme and from 2005-2012 the Bahrain Development Bank had disbursed just under 240 million Bahraini Dinars, the majority between 2009-2012 (Bahrain EDB 2013, p.68).

The evidence for increasing SME entrepreneurialism as a result of these programs is unclear. Bahrainis are certainly active in the private sphere; as of 2012, Bahraini citizens own 98 percent of all private sector companies and a majority of citizens work in the private sector (see Figure 2).

Figure 2 **Bahrainis in Private Sector 2003-2014**

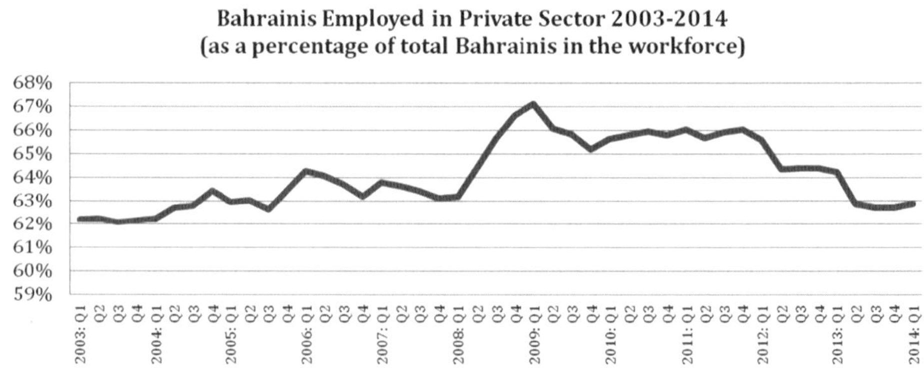

Source: Labour Market Regulatory Authority (LMRA), Kingdom of Bahrain, based on data from Bahrain Labour Market Indicators website http://www.lmra.bh/blmi

The sudden increase in 2008 of Bahrainis in the private sector as shown above is most likely due to the introduction of a levy on expatriate workers in 2008, which has funded the Labour Market Regulatory Authority (LMRA) and Tamkeen's activities. Yet a downward trend since 2009 (particularly from late 2011, when the levy was suspended) suggests this has not been enough to overcome obstacles to further Bahrainisation of the private sector. Moreover, the vast majority of Bahrainis in the private sector (87 percent) are employed in large companies, not SMEs or micro-enterprises. This means that some 99 percent of companies, which produce 77 percent of all jobs, are not creating the type of employment attractive to Bahraini nationals. This is particularly true for micro-enterprises, where Bahrainis form only 9 percent of the employee pool (by contrast, 39 percent of the workforce in large private companies are Bahrainis, particularly in trade and finance) (Bahrain EDB 2013, p. 65-67).

To some extent, this is unsurprising; the majority of enterprises in Bahrain capitalise on low-cost workers in labour-intensive positions, and the Bahraini economy has been designed to create an attractive location for these activities, offering low levels of business taxation and cheap (expatriate) labour. Yet with increasing pressure on the economy since the start of the Bahraini Uprising in 2011 - itself linked to inequality within society - there is certainly a need for improvement in this area.

The potential to increase SME entrepreneurialism by nationals certainly exists and has particularly been identified in the Information Communication Technology and other high value-added service industries (Dun & Bradstreet 2008). The number of new economic units (national and non-national) have increased, with 9,844 in 2013 compared to 6,187 in 2009, suggesting opportunities are expanding (Bahrain EDB 2013). The challenge, then, is to ensure Bahrainis can capture an increasing share of the SME market, and SME employment can compete with higher wages and job security offered by public or large private sector firms.

Overall, then, the governments of Bahrain, Qatar and Oman have demonstrated a clear focus on SME entrepreneurialism, particularly in the last decade. Support programs have proliferated, opportunities for government and private sector finance have expanded, and efforts to localise the workforce through Omanisation, Qatarisation and Bahrainisation policies continue. Support programs also do not operate in isolation; rather they operate as an interconnected network, with entrepreneurs moving from one support system to another (and, theoretically, eventually into independence).

Yet the paucity of statistics on the outcome of SME support programs makes evaluation exceedingly difficult. Despite billions in investment and program support, nationals still display a strong preference for employment in the public sector (or, in the case of Bahrain, large private sector firms), indicating that obstacles to SME entrepreneurialism have not yet been overcome. The remainder of this chapter turns to the remaining challenges for SME entrepreneurialism, differentiating between those that impact SMEs on a practical level, market level and policy level.

Remaining Challenges: Practical

Practical challenges are those that affect the day-to-day workings of the micro or small enterprise, not wider features of the market that create less tangible obstacles. They are usually the easiest to diagnose and some have already been at the heart of policy reform. However, the challenges outlined here are those identified in interviews within the last 24 months, and the repetition of near identical challenges in early 2014 as before policy reform suggests these obstacles remain an issue.

Finance and Start-up Requirements

With few exceptions, citizen-entrepreneurs across all three case studies identified finance as the greatest challenge to their business goals. Most felt they needed to rely on personal wealth or loans from family to support their enterprise and did not think private lending was easily available.

The Gulf is not unique in this regard; access to finance remains a key challenge to SMEs worldwide and is especially difficult in emerging markets. However, lending in the Gulf region is geared towards personal loans, yet personal wealth – as a result of generations of rent-distribution schemes supporting interest-free housing loans and land allocations – is often tied up in property and unsuitable for use as collateral (Hertog 2010). Instead, start-up entrepreneurs rely on personal networks to obtain finance, limiting the potential pool of entrepreneurs to those with sufficient personal finances or who manage to join state-funded support programs. "How do you raise equity finance in the Gulf?" joked a Qatari involved in entrepreneurialism support. "Through the three F's: Family, Friends, and Fools".

Financial requirements for business registration can often be expensive and particularly incompatible with the needs of micro or technology-oriented companies, stifling emerging types of entrepreneurialism and resulting in a larger informal SME market outside the control of the state. Comparison between Bahrain, Qatar and Oman's start-up requirements is revealing: despite their differing levels of economic development, they require similar levels of paid-in capital to be deposited into a bank account before company registration is possible – 20,000 Bahraini Dinar, 200,000 Qatari Riyal and 20,000 Omani Riyal respectively, or between USD52-55,000. For Qatar, this represents 62 percent of income per capita – although the associated costs of leasing office space and accommodation for employees in Doha should not be understated. For Bahrain and Oman, however, these requirements constitute over 200 percent of income per capita, a significant cost for nationals and a stark contrast with business-oriented United Arab Emirates, which has no requirement for paid-in capital at all (World Bank 2014).

Another requirement in all three states is the lease of a physical office space in preparation for starting operations. While this may be appropriate for traditional businesses, it limits more innovative ideas that operate outside a traditional office. WhatsApp entrepreneurs in the Dhofar region of Oman selling handbags and small goods via social media, for example, noted that Omani start-up requirements don't deal well with businesses that work entirely online and do not require offices, and as a result, they prefer to remain in the informal sphere. This is particularly key to increasing female entrepreneurship in Oman as this type of enterprise can operate in the privacy of home and provides more flexible socially acceptable working hours than typical private sector employment. Critical to note here is that the majority of Omani women interviewed who preferred *public* sector employment cited socially acceptable working hours and flexibility to explain their decision. Considering that these technology-oriented enterprises are an ideal place to expand formal local employment, especially for women, the mismatch between their needs and current start-up regulations is troubling.

Visas and Bureaucratic Inefficiencies

Disharmony between policy and the needs of SMEs can also affect existing enterprises, as can inefficiency in wider state bureaucracy, even where the enterprise is based in a free zone or bubble of efficiency. Qatar's expatriate worker visa process provides a revealing example of this issue and the tension between political and economic needs. To ensure a politically acceptable demographic balance the Qatari government enforces quotas of each nationality that may be granted working visas each year. To hire an expatriate – which all the companies interviewed had needed to do – the company must first identify which nationalities will be able to obtain work visas that year, and then recruit an individual from that country. For jobs requiring a very specific skillset, this is problematic. As a Qatari youth entrepreneur noted:

"our problem is that some of the jobs that we require, requires certain skills. For example gaming, gaming building, it is not taught at the schools here and I don't think anywhere in the region…so it's tough to find someone like that and we cannot afford to have a visa before having the person." While anecdotal evidence suggests some visa issues can be resolved through informal connections, in the long term Qatar will need a more sophisticated and formal solution.

Bahrain similarly limits work visas on the basis of preserving a demographic balance, although entrepreneurs did not specifically discuss them when asked what they felt were the major challenges facing their business. Oman does not have limits *per se*, although it recently limited movement of expatriate workers between employers, making hiring an expatriate worker accustomed to the Omani working environment more challenging. In Oman's case, the policy is explicitly designed to encourage Omanisation, but also limits labour market flexibility needed for high-skill, technology intensive enterprises (Times News Service 2014).

Entrepreneurs from all three states identified bureaucratic inefficiency as a key challenge to entrepreneurialism. "The bureaucracy kills business opportunities," a Qatari researcher claimed. An over-extended bureaucracy, symptomatic of a rentier economy, can result in complicated, costly and time-consuming procedures that can restrict the competitiveness of new enterprises. Even well managed support programs cannot insulate the enterprise from broader inefficiencies in the economy. In Qatar, entrepreneurs praised the responsiveness and support within their incubation centre, but described delays and mismanagement when dealing with wider government bureaucracy. Overall, said a Qatari entrepreneur: "It doesn't work for a government to own an incubation…it just doesn't work. Because there's a lot of bureaucracy around the government, a lot of papers need to be written, a lot of things need to be approved, and then you have a start-up that needs to be agile".

As with work visas, interviewees overcame bureaucratic inefficiencies through personal networks rather than official pathways. Informal links between business and government in the Gulf have long been embedded in the political economy and are used simultaneously with official procedures, providing two pathways to access the state. Historically, this system advantaged nationals, who tend to have stronger social ties to the state than new expatriate managers. However, the difficulty comes not with having informal pathways to the state, but when basic bureaucratic processes are impeded *without* recourse to these pathways; this was a central frustration for entrepreneurs from all three states – indeed for most it was a central reason for their initial preference for the private sector, which they perceived as having more of a meritocracy.

Remaining Challenges: Market Environment and the Rentier Mentality

Entrepreneurs also face broader challenges from the market environment and a tenacious rentier mentality. Major market-level obstacles to SME entrepreneurialism identified in interviews include continued skill mismatches between the education system and labour market needs, a persistent rentier mentality, and the role of major business families in either supporting SME entrepreneurialism or crowding out new competition.

The Skill Gap

The market structure and skill composition of nationals in Qatar, Bahrain and Oman is not uniform, yet all three suffer from a structural imbalance between the skills and training of the national population and the private sector employment available, denoting a weak alignment of the education sector with labour market needs. A major Omani businessman, for example, noted that despite his company's efforts to hire more locals, the vocational training model in Oman is not appropriate or effective, and he usually had to retrain Omanis after they came out of the vocational schools. Sheikh Mohammed bin Abdullah bin Hamad Al-Harthy, Chairman of the Oman Economic Association, shifted responsibility from Omani society to government policy, arguing:

> Is the problem that the skills are not matching the market requirements? Or is it the problem that when the government is doing their overall five-years planning, it's not matching their manpower capabilities?...We are creating new jobs. But we are not creating jobs [for nationals] - maybe 2/3rds of the new jobs we are creating - we are creating for non-Omanis.

Government data on the composition of national labour and skill creation is not widely published, with the notable exception of Bahrain. Nevertheless, opinions obtained during interviews align with the results of international surveys, such as a 2009 survey of Arab CEOs across the Middle East, which found that only 12 percent of Bahraini CEOs felt there was a sufficient supply of qualified national labour emerging from the education system, compared with 17 percent and 26 percent in Oman and Qatar respectively (Mohammed bin Rashid Al Maktoum Foundation and Price Waterhouse Coopers). The skill gap is not identical between the three states; in Bahrain, for example, the private sector requires large numbers of unskilled workers (with low pay) and highly skilled workers (with advanced computational skills, for example) that do not fit the skillset of most Bahrainis (Allens 2009; Deloitte 2010, 12-17). Bahrainis tend to have higher average levels of education than Omanis, yet in both countries (and Qatar) interviewees from government support programs identified an absence of technical skills and vocational training as key to a continued skill gap and underemployment of nationals.

Private sector wage levels, historically well below those of the public service, also remain a key obstacle, one which simply replacing expatriate workers with nationals as was announced in Oman in early 2014 will not resolve (Haque 2014). When asked if they would consider moving to the private sector if employment were available, Omanis in the public sector noted the costs of supporting a family in Oman is high relative to private sector wages; they felt they could not compete with similarly skilled expatriates who remit wages back to other countries. Low private sector wages play two roles: they lower costs for existing SMEs but also dis-incentivise entrance into the private sector among nationals, and here government must determine whether lowering costs for existing enterprises or encouraging entrance into the private sector should be accorded preference. Overall, across all three states, low private sector wages combined with inadequate national skills were identified as central obstacles to attracting greater numbers of nationals into the SME sector, and these issues will not be resolved by simply increasing the quota of nationals required in the private sector.

Business Elites and Market Monopolies

Major business families, nationals who own large enterprises and often have close ties with government (or are even *in* government), can play an important role in the employment of nationals in the private sector. Opinions on the major Omani business families – such as Al Zawawi, Al Zubair, Al Bahwan, and Sultan (W.J. Towell) – were disputed, with some Omanis interviewed claiming the families promoted SMEs and others arguing the oligarchs undercut SMEs and forced new competitors – even Omani ones – out of business. When asked if large companies are genuinely committed to local SME entrepreneurialism or simply "ticking boxes", the response of two major business leaders is instructive:

> Let me give you an example of how we are addressing this from a grassroots level. We recently established a new brand called Itharaa. We wanted it to be a platform to showcase Omani talent and Omani products. During the launch of the brand, 95 per cent of things used was from local companies. We looked at the things that we need for our hotels and are trying to outsource them to local companies.
>
> - *Wael Al Lawati,*
> *CEO of OMRAN.*

> The experience that we have had is that when we decide to work with an SME, it usually starts on the basis of supply. Unfortunately, a number of SME initiatives remain in the area of trading and a big challenge is to come out of trading and to try and add locally … then they will be embraced by industry.
>
> - *Gerf Hoefman, CEO, Oman Cables Industry*
> *(Oman Economic Review 2014).*

Their responses imply an important point: major business leaders clearly wish to portray commitment to local SMEs, yet may, as the second quote indicates, have difficulty in practice sourcing local products in appropriate areas. Their responses aligned with major Omani business leaders interviewed for this research, all of whom claimed that Omani SMEs did not yet match the needs of large private sector businesses while simultaneously emphasising their own improving levels of Omanisation. Their difficulty connecting with Omani-run SMEs is problematic as major business families dominate the private sector economy and are responsible for most large-scale infrastructure projects: they therefore represent an ideal opportunity to promote local entrepreneurship.

The potential for major business elites to support SME entrepreneurialism is also relevant given the substantial influence these families have over development and economic policy. In Oman, for example, business elites were crucial to the creation and implementation of Oman's 2020 Vision, and some continue to play prominent roles in government (US Embassy Muscat 2009). Yet business elites in government must balance private financial requirements with those in the public interest, and this balance is not always easily maintained. This became particularly clear in Bahrain, when the business elite – national and foreign – lobbied strongly against LMRA levies that funded Tamkeen's SME support programs, resulting in their suspension in April 2011 and partial re-introduction in mid-2013. The government decision to suspend LMRA levies was, according to Bahraini interviewees in government and society, a political one. It was driven by the reinvigorated political influence of the Bahraini business elite as government struggled to calm society as well as by a dispute between two government factions, yet also indicates the tension between short term pressures and longer-term goals of diversification.

Persistence of the Rentier Mentality

Job opportunities, however, mean little if nationals are uninterested in taking up private sector positions. A study by Qatar's Silatech and Gallup (2009) found that 73 percent of Bahrain's youth would prefer to work in the public sector, assuming the pay and work conditions were similar. 63 percent of Qataris also selected the public service, although this number seems exceptionally low relative to government research where 75 percent of unemployed Qataris would *not* consider working in the private sector (Doha News 2013). Oman has even seen de-Omanisation of the private sector since 2011 (Oman Observer 2013). Many entrepreneurs interviewed simultaneously held public and private sector employment; they were *part-time* entrepreneurs, with full-time employment in government ministries. They expressed reluctance to commit to full-time work in their own company, noting it was more profitable to remain there only part-time. For some, of course, their enterprise is designed as a part-time project, yet having a large class of 'entrepreneurs' who receive the majority of their salary from the state is an ultimately unsustainable strategy.

In part, entrepreneurs face societal resistance over why an individual might choose the riskier entrepreneurial path over the security of the public sector. A Qatari entrepreneur who quit a secure public service job to focus on his new company, for example, found that the reaction from friends and family was shock: "You are Qatari, why [on earth] would you want to leave your job?" Societal resistance to entrepreneurial risk-taking does not suggest a cultural disinclination for work, but the continued impact of incentives on worker motivation, stemming from the rentier structure of the economy. For all that respondents across the Gulf emphasised the uniqueness of their country's development, the description of the rentier mentality as a core challenge to entrepreneurship was strikingly similar across all three case studies. "Oil acts like a drug," said a Bahraini private sector businessman, while a public servant claimed: "they want to be spoon-fed," noting that the most common reaction to any challenge in Bahrain was to look for government support rather than, for example, forming societal support groups. In Oman: "we don't like to talk about it," said a senior public servant, "but [the rentier mentality is] very strong". In Qatar, most respondents identified motivation as a major development challenge. "I'm really worried about the younger generation, because of the wealth and support and the opportunities, they are not enough motivated, really, to do well," said one Qatari.

This is hardly promising for states looking to develop an independent entrepreneurial spirit. However, it is crucial to distinguish between the persistence of a rentier mentality due to political and economic incentives, and the *inevitability* of a rentier mentality. In the most direct criticism of the idea of an inevitable rentier mentality, prominent Bahraini businessman Khalid Al Zayani claimed the idea that rents produce unproductive workers is: "absolute nonsense. Train them well, pay them well and treat them well, and Bahrainis will work very hard".

What this suggests is that while the rentier mentality has a continuing impact on worker motivation, it is caused by the political and economic incentives created by government policy and the wider political economy, not inherent characteristics of Gulf workers. Youth entrepreneurs, describing long working hours, hardly fit the rentier mould; nor did the Qataris, Omanis or Bahrainis who had entered the private sector looking for more challenging professional opportunities and a chance to excel.

Remaining Challenges: Policy and Political Pressures

Government policy thus emerges as critical to SME entrepreneurialism; it is government policy that most powerfully shapes incentives for productivity, entrepreneurialism, and innovation among nationals. The major challenges for SME entrepreneurialism policy discussed here include the gap between vision and implementation, duplication of support programs, and government factional infighting. Most importantly, the post-2011 period has forced states to balance political responses aimed at deflecting pressure from the Arab Spring with long-term economic sustainability. Many of these moves demonstrate the tension between short and long-term social needs, where the reactive nature of policymaking since 2011 has undermined previous efforts at creating a comprehensive 'Vision' to guide the state towards sustainable economic, social and political development.

Vision and Implementation

The economic Vision plans are worthy of some analysis in themselves, forming one of the most revealing challenges to RST and the basis for SME support programs and government policy.

Qatar 2030, Bahrain 2030 and Oman 2020 represent ambitious but theoretically achievable 'visions' of where development should lead and contradict directly with classic RST's assumption of an absence of economic policy as a result of rentier wealth. At the same time, the Visions do align with recent RST work such as Gray's entrepreneurial state capitalism, even as other facets of rentierism – such as a bloated bureaucracy – have created challenges for their implementation (2011).

The Visions are broad and vague in detail, but are supplemented by shorter-term strategies, such as the Qatar National Development Strategy 2011-2016 (QNDS). A number of innovative programs have emerged from the QNDS 2011-2016, however the targets for entrepreneurship are not easily measurable and the absence of any clear repercussions should these targets not be met is problematic. Qatari views on the plan were mixed. The plan itself and intentions behind it were lauded yet they noted that the Vision had not been effectively translated into practical outcomes. Said one Qatari involved in SME support: "The *challenge* is always by connecting strategy, or the vision, the plans and the projects…if it's not synchronized, if they're not aligned together, you will find a lot of waste happens." Particular issues noted were the absence of concrete development goals for economic planning, the need for clear-cut evaluation methods, and, in practice, constantly shifting smaller goals (Al Kuwari 2012).

Oman faces similar challenges in synchronising a broad vision with policy. Oman's 2020 Vision was completed far earlier than that of either Qatar or Bahrain, covering the period 1996-2020, and preparations are currently underway for the formulation of the next Vision (2040). Despite continued efforts, however, diversification has not yet been successful. One of the central goals of the Oman 2020 Vision, for example, was to increase the share of non-oil GDP from 62.4 percent in 1991-1995 to 81 percent by 2020, yet since 1995 the share of non-oil GDP has actually *decreased*, falling to 52.9 percent in 2010 (Mansour, n.d.). The implementation gap between vision and practice has been a significant challenge in Oman, especially as the central architects of the 2020 Vision, Qais bin Abdul Munim Al-Zawawi and Mohammed bin Musa Al-Yousef, are no longer in government.

Bahrain, too, published and released an economic strategy designed to guide the country's economic, social and political development. Bahrain's Vision 2030 was launched in 2008, and focused on sustainability through the creation of medium and high-income jobs for Bahrainis in high value-added industries in the private sector (especially the financial sector) (Bahrain EDB 2014). Like other Gulf states, the Vision provides overarching goals and strategy, while shorter-term national plans (such as the National Economic Strategy 2009-2014) elaborate specific targets. Despite the EDB's efforts, however, most Bahrainis interviewed felt the 2030 Vision – particularly its third pillar on 'fairness' – had not been implemented effectively, especially following 2011 Bahraini Uprising. Even as the strategy and actions of EDB affiliated programs like Tamkeen indicate some level of co-ordination between Vision and practice within Bahraini bubbles of efficiency (see for example Tamkeen 2010), the wider political economy and political events since 2011 have diminished the likelihood that the Vision will be implemented in time to achieve its goals by 2030.

Duplication

New SME programs across the region often duplicate or overlap with existing programs, resulting in confusion, inefficiency, and ultimately competing with each other, rather than co-ordinating to achieve the ambitious targets set in the Visions. Both Tamkeen and the Ministry of Labor, for example, manage programs for hiring unemployed Bahrainis whereas it would obviously be more efficient to consolidate resources in one (well-run) program; the major obstacle to this, according to Bahrainis in economic policy planning, was political, not logistical. Oman and Qatar also suffered from duplication in SME programs and more generally across government ministries and services (Fadhli 2014). It is unclear, for example, what distinguishes new Omani financing funds like Al Raffd, Oman Development Bank Schemes, and Al Nemaa from previous programs such as Sanad. As Saleh Al Shaibany wrote in early 2014:

> The Al Raffd Fund for the small to medium enterprises (SMEs) is welcome but my concern is that all that the new fund will do is to substitute the former financing schemes such as Sanad, rather than move forward to meet the real needs of the businessmen. Like the old funds, Al Raffd will prove too large to be policed or managed and the whole effort may end up tangled in bureaucratic shamble, leading to the familiar lip service we are used to.

To some extent, SME entrepreneurialism is an emerging field for the Gulf states; dedicated government agencies for SME development have only recently been established in most Gulf states and their influence on policy has fluctuated since 2011. Yet the key challenge is not time, but a tendency for rent-rich states to paper over inefficiencies with new distributions, creating new programs rather than dealing with the difficult and protracted task of reforming existing ones. This is particularly relevant considering the tendency for entrepreneurs to move from one program to another; to be effective at the lowest cost to the public purse, entrepreneurship support programs must function as an integrated and synchronized network, not as competitors.

Government Factionalism

Inefficiency of previous programs is not the sole cause of program duplication; disputes internal to government can also affect the implementation of SME support strategies. Internal government factions exist in varying levels across the Gulf: some Qataris perceived divisions between individuals supporting and opposing reform yet there is little public evidence; in Oman, it is less a matter of *factions* negotiating on SME development than *individuals* moving to protect their personal interests; in Bahrain, however, divisions within the ruling family have been clearly apparent since 2011 with detrimental implications for SME entrepreneurialism.

For example, Bahrain's EDB faced resistance within government due in part to the radical nature of the reforms they recommended, but also because the EDB's activities were viewed by some as representative of a broader power struggle between the reform-oriented Crown Prince Salman bin Hamad bin Isa Al Khalifa and conservative Prime Minister Khalifa bin Salman Al Khalifa. There was a strong perception among Bahraini interviewees that the suspension of LMRA fees in 2011 was not only a result of private sector lobbying but also a power play by the Prime Minister, seeking to stymie economic reforms and, through them, the position of the Crown Prince.

Figures affiliated with government and the rentier elite expressed frustration at internal government division. Steve Harrison, in particular, noted that drawing a distinction at all is:

> Extraordinarily damaging and divisive, because we're all here in Bahrain on a small island…if there are good things that are going on, then they should be supported, but a number of people will count out against anything that, say, the LMRA do because 'it's the Crown Prince's', or 'the Prime Minister's'.

These factions, and the tensions behind them, have been increasingly apparent in the post-2011 period, where heightened political and social pressures have complicated economic development and tested government commitment to SME entrepreneurialism.

Post-2011 Policy Pressures

Although the Arab states of the Gulf have faced *less* political pressure as a result of the Arab Spring than other Middle Eastern states like Egypt or Syria, they have by no means been immune. Several responses to the Arab Spring in the Gulf have counteracted strategies in place to encourage SME entrepreneurialism, demonstrating the tension between short and long-term social needs.

All three states raised public sector wages in response to regional political pressure. In September 2011, for example, the Qatari government announced a pay increase of 60 percent for most of the public sector, 120 percent for senior military and security personnel, and 50 percent for other military and security employees, with similar hikes for pension payments (Tuomi 2011). The pressure on new start-up companies, which, as discussed earlier, already identify high salaries and finance as major challenges, also increased as a result of the wage hikes.

The Bahraini government, facing active and widespread social protest, also raised wages in an attempt to placate protesters and strengthen traditionally loyal sections of society. Combined with the suspension of the LMRA levy on expatriate workers, the percentage of Bahrainis employed in the private sector has markedly decreased (see Figure 2), contrary to the goals of Bahrain's 2030 Vision. Prioritising short-term security over longer-term economic sustainability may seem rational considering the intensity of protest in Bahrain since 2011. However, if the protests themselves are based on economic inequality within society, then reforms in line with the 2030 Vision – in other words, those designed to increase the real wages of all Bahraini families – should not be undervalued. Ultimately, struggling to contain a restive society, Bahrain has focused on short-term security-driven measures that have weakened incentives for local entrepreneurship.

Oman has similarly struggled to balance policies responding to short-term political and social demands with longer-term SME entrepreneurialism, facing far less social unrest than Bahrain (but more than Qatar). It is a complex dilemma: the government must remain responsive to society and since 2011 several Omani groups have called for wage increases, yet by doing so the government creates difficulties for Omani entrepreneurs, who may not be able to afford the higher salaries. In early 2013, for example, the Omani government raised the minimum wage in the private sector to OMR 325 per month, in an effort to make the private sector more attractive to nationals (Al Shaibany 2013). Later in the same year, however, the government responded to a series of strikes by announcing the unification of all *public* service salaries – effectively, wage increases across the public service - counteracting the incentive for movement into the private sector and demonstrating the reactive nature of policy. These changes come at high cost to the public purse; the new measures cost an estimated RO800-900million annually, a monumental 39 percent increase in the salary allocation section of the Omani government budget (Muscat Daily 2013).

More problematically, some Omani policy changes since 2011 respond to political pressures without considering the long-term impact. In mid-2011, for example, the government responded to high levels of youth unemployment (linked to the skill mismatch in the Omani economy noted earlier) by massively expanding the availability of government-funded scholarships (Gulf News 2011). Expanding access to education can be an effective way to boost human capital and encourage entrepreneurship. However, in this case there has been little discussion of the long-term strategy to ensure Omani graduates will find employment *after* their graduation. An excerpt from an interview with an Omani economist involved in consultation for the Oman 2040 Vision is instructive here:

Author: So one of the recent decisions has been to provide more scholarships to Omanis who finish high school-

Interviewee: It was already there, it just got expanded.

Author: So does that mean…in three or four years when those students return, when they finish university and re-enter the job market, is the government looking at making sure there are jobs available for them?

Interviewee: No.

Author: So what's going to happen then?

Interviewee: I don't know. Nobody knows. It's a serious challenge.

In essence, this means the structural challenges of the Omani labour market are simply being delayed, not resolved. Oman, Qatar, and Bahrain will need to move from short-term, myopic and reactive policies to the genuine implementation of their long-term economic strategies if SME entrepreneurialism is to be successful.

Conclusion: The Political Determinants of Economic Success

The exploration of SME entrepreneurialism in Qatar, Bahrain and Oman in this chapter suggests the ultimate determinants of success in SME policy-making are, in fact, political. Despite continued attention and massive government investment, rent-driven political challenges continue to create obstacles for SME entrepreneurialism.

Yet it is important to remember GCC states are not only struggling to increase human capital in the private sector labour market, but that large sections of government are un-practiced in this type of economic reform. Their successes thus far should not be undervalued, nor should some emerging indications that entrepreneurship among Arab youth in the Gulf is increasing – such as a recent survey finding over 60 percent of GCC youth felt their generation was more likely to start a business than those of previous generations (ASDA'A Burson Marsteller 2014, p.17).

To succeed in increasing SME entrepreneurialism, Qatari, Omani and Bahraini governments will need to overcome the political obstacles stemming from the rentier structure of their economy. Specifically, they need to ensure greater harmony between SME regulations, skills created in the local labour market through alignment with the education sector, and the needs of SMEs, avoiding 'quick-fix' policies that address short-term needs but will be detrimental to long-term goals. Moreover, rather than duplicating existing programs, governments must tackle the challenge of reforming existing institutions and addressing underlying management deficiencies. This is not an easy task. Addressing these issues will mean challenging political structures embedded and reinforced by the rent-based economy and will require broad political will within government; there is no room for factionalism if SME entrepreneurialism is to be successful.

Yet despite these issues it is clear that all Gulf governments are well aware of the importance of SME entrepreneurialism to the long-term sustainability of their economy and are willing to commit significant financial resources. Developing greater private sector participation of nationals is a collaborative process, requiring constructive links between the public and private sectors that are, as a result of the entrepreneurial state capitalist approach, already in existence. Rentierism may encourage policy obstacles, but it does not make them inevitable.

If the obstacles identified in this chapter can be overcome through cohesive government and private sector leadership, this would greatly enhance the potential for increased employment of nationals in the private sector. If successful, the expansion of

SME entrepreneurialism would reduce the employment burden on the state, encourage an innovative and financially independent society and support the long-term sustainability of the Gulf economies.

Notes

i Some non-national experts were also interviewed as a part of this project, but the focus was on perceptions of development from citizens. The name and expertise of the interviewee is included only where permission has been obtained to do so.

ii Official data in Qatar only differentiates between companies that employ up to 10 individuals, or more than 10 individuals – in other words, between micro enterprises and all other enterprises.

iii There are no official statistics on the number of Qatari nationals, but this range is where most academic estimates fall.

9

Saudi Manufacturing: Can *Monozukuri* Take Root in the Kingdom?

Makio Yamada

Introduction

This paper will discuss the prospects of, and challenges facing, the development of manufacturing industries in Saudi Arabia, using both macro and micro approaches. In the macro approach section, the paper will frame industrialization in Saudi Arabia as "production with rentier characteristics", and will compare it with the experience of Japan's early industrialization. In particular, it will highlight the importance of the *social underpinnings* of industrialization, arguing that Saudi Arabia needs to reform its "rentier society" and build an industrial society as a precondition for developing labor-intensive manufacturing industries. In the micro approach section, the paper will analyze the current situation of relevant policies in Saudi Arabia, particularly education and labor market reforms. Finally, the paper will make practical proposals for those reforms which may help Saudi Arabia to build an industrial society.

Background: Why Manufacturing in Saudi Arabia?

Developing manufacturing industries to produce more "Made in Saudi Arabia" products is one of the major goals of Saudi policymakers today. For this purpose, the National Industrial Strategy (NIS) was announced in 2010. The NIS is in line with the *Vision 2020*, which calls for progress in economic diversification by 2020. The NIS set the following targets for the decade between 2010 and 2020:

1. Double manufacturing from 11% to 20% of GDP.
2. Double national industrial employment from 15% to 30%.
3. Double industrial exports from 18% to 35%.
4. Double technology-based manufactured products from 30% to 60%.

The implementation of these goals has been entrusted to the National Industrial Clusters Development Program (NICDP), a program jointly run by the Ministry of Commerce and Industry and the Ministry of Petroleum and Mineral Resources. The NICDP targets five industrial sectors in particular: (1) automotive; (2) minerals and metals processing; (3) solar energy; (4) plastics and packaging; and (5) home appliances.

The NICDP practices a two-step strategy for developing these five sectors: first, creating the production base in the country by inviting foreign direct investments; then, "Saudizing" the production over a number of years, through transfer of knowledge and skills from the foreign investors to Saudi technologists.

These ambitious projects are primarily driven by Saudi policymakers' deepening concern regarding the country's youth unemployment problem. The majority of the population in Saudi Arabia is under the age of 30, and the youth unemployment rate among is estimated to be over 35% (*The Economist*. Saudi Arabia: Out of the Comfort Zone. 3 March 2012). The magnitude of the problem is likely to increase in years to come as nearly 600,000 new graduates enter the job market every year (*Arab News*. 600,000 Saudis Flood Job Market Yearly. 27 March 2014). In theory this means that the country needs to create almost 10 million job opportunities by 2030. Nevertheless, the public sector, which has been a prime employer of Saudi nationals over the past decades, is already bloated and is reportedly capable of absorbing only an additional one million national workers before 2030 (*Arab News*. Most SMEs in Saudi Arabia 'Are in Red and Yellow Zones'. 5 October 2011). Thus, the vast majority of young Saudi nationals will have to seek jobs outside the public sector. Saudi policymakers are attempting to cope with this challenge through the development of labor-intensive manufacturing industries, which create a number of opportunities for private businesses, particularly small and medium sized enterprises (SMEs).

Conceptual Transition: From the Production-Rentier State Dichotomy to "Production with Rentier Characteristics"

The analysis of this new development in Saudi Arabia requires us to create a new analytical framework which will enable us to understand the Saudi economy not only as an oil-centred economy but as an "industrializing economy with abundant oil rents". Nearly a quarter of a century ago, when the Gulf economies were still significantly underproductive, Giacomo Luciani presented us with an insightful conceptual dichotomy of the "production state" and the "rentier state" (Luciani 1987). At that time the economic policies of the states in the Gulf region seemed to consist exclusively of allocation policies, as the petrochemical industry, which is an exemplar of competitive industry in the region today (Yamada 2011), was still in its infancy. Nevertheless, the Gulf governments' attempts at economic diversification have become more visible in recent years, to the degree that the image of the unproductive Gulf has been modified by many researchers. For instance, Matthew Gray argues that Gulf economies have evolved to the "late rentier" stage characterized by oil-driven – rather than oil-centred – state-capitalism (Gray 2011). Luciani himself also argues that Gulf economies today enjoy a "resource blessing" and actively invest in economic diversification (Luciani 2012).

With economic diversification increasingly becoming a norm rather than a novelty, the research question that is most worth asking today is not that which was asked in the past: it is no longer *whether or not* a rentier economy industrializes, but *what* the industrialization in a rentier economy *is like*. Just as was witnessed in the past in the rise of catch-up economies in East Asia, which showed different features of industrialization from those in the West, we are observing today the rise of new types of industrializing economies in the Gulf region which, due to the presence of abundant oil rents, show distinctive features of development. Such "production with rentier characteristics" may form an independent analytical category in our knowledge of development. The experience of Gulf economies' industrial diversification should therefore be compared with the experience of previous industrializations, rather than being "othered" as economies trapped in dependency and a resource curse.

In particular, making comparisons with East Asian economies should generate useful insights which will help us to understand Gulf development in more depth. East Asian economies – Japan, Taiwan, South Korea, and China – all developed competitive labor-intensive industries, becoming global manufacturing powerhouses. In addition, they are all catch-up industrialisers, from the non-Western world, and show different models of state–business relations to those that exist in the West. Their industrializations are often understood as "state-led", "state-sponsored", or "state-capitalist", although in reality the patterns of state–business relations vary among them (Clark & Jung 2004), and it remains debatable whether the state's heavy hand has promoted industrialization or has actually hindered the growth, preventing the economy from exploiting its even greater potential (Pei 1994).

Industrial Diversification: Comparative vs. Competitive Advantages

Yet another reason why comparing the Saudi and East Asian industrializations should be useful is that it seems that their development strategies are, perhaps surprisingly, likely to converge in the years to come (Yamada 2015). At the early stage of development catch-up economies tend to capitalize on what economists call "comparative advantages", advantages with which they are endowed naturally, such as geography, natural resources, and population (Gilpin 2001: 210–214). Thus, different types of comparative advantages with which they are endowed create substantive diversity in their development strategies. Resource-scarce, agriculture-based East Asian economies took advantage of the presence of abundant labor and developed labor-intensive light-industries, such as textiles and basic manufacturing products. On the other hand, labor-scarce but resource-abundant Gulf economies succeeded in the development of capital-intensive heavy industries in which they took advantage of oil rents and a great feedstock advantage. In the petrochemical industry the Gulf region has become a new hub of production, with Saudi Arabia alone accounting nearly 10% of the global petrochemical production and its state-owned enterprise, Saudi Arabian Basic Industries Corporation (SABIC), being one of the largest petrochemical producers in the non-Western world (*Saudi Gazette*. Saudi Arabia to be World's 3rd Largest Exporter of Petrochemicals by '15. 18 November 2013).

However, in order to move on to the second stage of development, they need to harness what are referred to as "competitive advantages": artificially acquired advantages, such as skills, knowledge, and technologies, in addition to their comparative advantages (Gilpin *Ibid.*). Those advantages are also called "human resources" or "human capital", and an economy equipped with a high degree of competitive advantages is often called a "knowledge-based economy" – which is, indeed, a buzzword among Gulf policymakers today (Ulrichsen 2012). To achieve a transition to a knowledge-based economy, appropriate investment must be made in human resources development (HRD), which includes not only education but also research and development (R&D) and the promotion of entrepreneurship (Etzkowitz et al. 2000). The rationale is clear – competitive industries must be supported by a sufficient number of competitive industrial workers who are equipped with the right skills, knowledge, and technologies and who are able to add value to production.

In this regard, the development of HRD institutions in Saudi Arabia is still a work in progress. The pool of qualified national industrial workers is still not large in comparison with the scale of industrialization that Saudi policymakers are pursuing. There are some anecdotal evidences for this. For instance, one of the truck assembly plants in Saudi Arabia has recently achieved a 30% rate of Saudization. However, most national employees in the plant work in the administrative section, with only a few deployed on the factory floor as technicians – leaving most of the production lines in the hands of expat workers. A manager of the plant wants to increase the production in the coming years while maintaining the Saudization rate (which is today required by the country's labor nationalisation policy). Thus, the firm currently funds students at one of the technical training colleges so that more qualified national technical workers will be deployed on the factory floor in the near future (Anonymous, interviewed by author, 2014).

In this manner, Saudi Arabia today still remains in the situation of "industrialization without industrial workers". Nearly three decades ago, pioneers of SABIC envisioned the creation of a "dynamic technological society" by making the company seek to "train talented young Saudis to run it" (Pampanini 1997: 63). SABIC has become a beacon of the country's technological progress today, by achieving a markedly high Saudization rate of over 80% (Achoui 2009: 43). Nevertheless, outside SABIC and a few private petrochemical firms, the fruits have yet to be widely seen. The development of labor-intensive industrialization requires sufficient social underpinnings: Saudi Arabia needs to build an *industrial society* as a precondition for achieving manufacturing growth.

The Monozukuri Tradition: The Industrial Society in Japan

In thinking how an industrial society can be built, examining the case of Japan should be useful. Japan was the first successful industrialiser in East Asia (and in the non-Western world): it implemented rapid modernisation in the period of the Emperor Meiji (1867–1912) as the basis for full-blown industrialization after the First World War. While other East Asian economies are still in the process of fully achieving a transition to a knowledge-based economy today, Japan achieved that transition in the final quarter of the twentieth century following the period of post-WWII rehabilitation, high growth in the 1960s, and a stagnation caused by the oil crisis in the 1970s, which urged a transition in the Japanese economy. The Japanese economy is characterized by the presence of competitive SMEs specializing in high-tech manufacturing that produce industrial products components and supply them to large firms both in Japan and other countries. This advantage has historical roots: many economic historians assume that the major distinction between industrialization in Japan and that in the West is that the Japanese industrialization was more labor-intensive than the West while the Western industrialization tended to be more capital-intensive than Japan (Kawakatsu 1991; Nakaoka 2004).

The source of that difference is primarily attributable to the difference in the size of population. In spite of its long backwardness, Japan's population at the beginning of the twentieth century was already around 42 million: it was larger than the population of the UK and France at that time – around 38 million each – which were the world's two most industrialized countries. Indeed, British and French industrialists then faced a chronic problem of labor shortage due to their countries' small population in comparison with the scale of their industrial activities. This, in turn, made the form of their industrial production capital-intensive: they had to invent machinery in order to compensate for the labor shortage and to increase production. In addition, the labor shortage also resulted in the improvement of management methods, in order to enhance organisational efficiency through standardisation – which were later developed by American industrialists into the mass production system.

Such a course of development did not take place in Japan. The country's large population (and population density) enabled Japanese industrialists to recruit workers from cities and villages at low-costs as there were a number of young educated citizens queuing for jobs (some of them even went to Americas to search for jobs). Thus, Japanese productions tended to rely more on human power than on machinery. Likewise, individual workers' knowledge and skills were considered more important than the system of standardization. This gave birth to the human-oriented tradition of manufacturing activities, which is described as *monozukuri*. Monozukuri ("making things") literally means manufacturing, but it implies a certain cultural value as well. Some contemporary Japanese industrialists consider monozukuri to be a "vocation of the Japanese, their way of life, and their pride" and believe that its full exploitation is the only way to survive in today's world of cutthroat competition (Kimura 2009: 12).

Like many other Japanese terms, the conceptual contours of monozukuri have not been defined strictly in social scientific terms. Nevertheless, the concept may represent the following three things: first, excellence of industrial workers in knowledge and skills, especially of those technologists who work on the factory floor, is highly appreciated. Second, at the societal level, a high degree of respect is paid to industrial workers who possess sophisticated technical skills and the spirit of invention. Third, prominent engineers-cum-owners of a SME provide role models to the country's young citizens. For instance, engineers such as Soichiro Honda (a founder of the Honda motor company) and Konosuke Matsushita (a founder of Panasonic) still remain icons for young Japanese citizens today, together with Thomas Edison and Steve Jobs. Careers in engineering are favoured by talented students, despite the fact that they are not as stable as government jobs and do not necessarily offer as great financial rewards as white-collar professions. In many cases, young engineers instead value the psychological reward, especially the positive self-image of pursuing professionalism – or what the Japanese call *shokunin katagi* (the spirit of a true artisan) – represented by character traits such as an uncompromisingness, frontier-spiritedness, and self-confidence.

Certainly, monozukuri has its weaknesses too. The maximization of individual productivity is sometimes privileged over organizational efficiency, making overall productivity underexploited and the level of standardization weak (Kimura 2009: 99–101). Thus, some Japanese firms absorbed Western management methods and created a new style of management called *kaizen*, through the conflation of the Western management methods with the monozukuri tradition. Kaizen ("improvement") is often translated as "continuous development of process". Combining the principles of Taylorian management methods, kaizen encourages the constant overhaul of workflows and elimination of waste in order to achieve a leaner production process. However, kaizen also humanises that process, by calling for the participation of all workers in the firm in the improvement activities, rather than implementing it in a top-down manner.

In particular, *genba* (also written *gemba*), or the factory floor, is considered to be the most important venue in the firm, being the location where value-adding activities take place. Workers at the genba are especially encouraged to voluntarily detect problems in the process, suggest possible solutions, and implement them through consultation with their supervisors. Such proactive participation in the improvement activity enables the genba workers to develop their independent problem-solving capacity and communication skills, as well as increasing their motivation (Imai 1997; Wakamatsu 2007). The role of management in kaizen is to support these genba workers by reducing constraints as much as possible (Imai 1997). Thus, managers are encouraged to visit the genba on a regular basis in order to listen to workers' opinions and to update his/her understanding of how values have most recently been created in the workplace. Japanese managers have a great advantage in this regard as many of them have worked as genba workers themselves in the early stages of their career.

One of the important aspects of the human-oriented monozukuri tradition is a high level of basic education. One estimate suggests that over 50% of Japanese males were already literate before the modernisation in the Meiji period (Hayami 2004: 28). There were private schools in almost all villages to teach farmers' children (around 80% of Japanese people were farmers at the time) reading, writing, and basic mathematics skills (Takahashi 2007: 20). This early spread of educational institutions was driven by socioeconomic changes before the nineteenth century. In the long peace under the Tokugawa samurai regime (1603–1868), Japan's agricultural output greatly increased, leading to population growth and the accumulation of capital. Because arable lands were limited due to Japan's geography, capital was invested in industrial and commercial activities in villages, which were labor-abundant and where labor costs were cheaper than in cities. Thus, the demand for education among farmers increased: for their children not all of whom could inherit lands from their parents, acquiring literacy and engaging in industrial and commercial activities were the only means of survival. Supported by educated labor in villages, Japan came to see proto-industrialization in the late eighteenth and early nineteenth century (Shimbo & Saito 2004: 341). Thus, when Japan, under the modernist Meiji government, began modernization in 1868, a pool of educated workers prepared for industrial production was already present.

Saudi Arabia in Comparison: The Barriers Posed by a "Rentier Society"

Those two socioeconomic factors – the labor-abundance and the spread of education – are increasingly seen in today's Saudi Arabia. The population of Saudi Arabia has increased five-fold, from around 6 million in 1970 to 30 million today: comprising approximately 20 million nationals and 10 million expat workers and their dependents (*Arab News*. Population of Country 30 Million. 18 February 2014). This is almost the same population size as Japan had at the time of early manufacturing development. Saudi Arabia's education standard has significantly improved in the past decades as well. While only 15% of males and 2% of females were reportedly literate in 1970 (*Arab News*. Kingdom Tops World in Education Spending. 2 January 2013), the literacy rate has reached 96% today (*Arab News*. Kingdom Achieves 96% Literacy Rate. 10 September 2013). As a result, there has emerged a pool of educated workers who are not absorbed into the traditional economic sectors such as the public sector and the oil industry. Thus, in theory, Saudi Arabia should be in a more advantageous position today than in the past to develop labor-intensive industries and, hence, to nurture a culture of monozukuri. Likewise, Saudi industrialists should be able to recruit qualified national workers more easily today than in the past when the pool of educated workers was significantly smaller and a handful of qualified workers were taken either by the government or the oil company. However, in reality, technical professions outside prestigious state-owned enterprises like Saudi Aramco and SABIC do not seem to attract young Saudi citizens. In general, private firms remain dominated by expat workers who hold no less than 86.6% of the private sector jobs today (*Arab News*. Expat Workers Hold 86% of Private Sector Jobs. 9 September 2013).

What are the barriers to the employment of nationals? This paper considers that barriers are created by the unique nature of development in Saudi Arabia, which this paper refers to as a "rentier society". A rentier society is defined as a society that remains underproductive because of the presence of abundant oil rents. As for the causal linkage between oil rents and an underproductive society, the following points are assumed.: First, abundant oil rents led to the institutionalization of job preference among national citizens, with a high priority given to public sector jobs. Oil rents supported the continuing expansion of the public sector between the 1950s and the 1990s. While the rentier state theory assumes a political logic behind this expansion, it also had a practical reason: the country's HRD institutions were still significantly underdeveloped then and many were unable to find jobs elsewhere if they were not employed by the government. In fact, although the country's rapid modernization after the oil boom period in the 1970s created a large number of work opportunities in the private sector, most of these opportunities did not go to nationals but to expat workers. At the beginning, receiving a few million expat workers was considered by policymakers to be only a temporary measure, until the country's HRD caught up with the pace of modernization and more nationals became employable in the private sector. However, generous entitlements in the public sector, in terms of salary, work hours, and social services, made private sector jobs much less attractive than public sector ones, resulting in the institutionalization of nationals' job preference over the years. Accordingly, the choice of a job became a matter of social status. Young nationals tend to shy away from private sector jobs *both* because of their lower payment *and* for fear of being looked down upon by their national peers (*Arab News*. Saudi Youth Need to Expand Career Options. 31 January 2014): they fear the possibility of facing difficulties in social relations, including marriage (Ramady 2013: 485).

This does not mean that Saudi Arabia lacks a national business community. The country, particularly the Hejaz region, has been home to vibrant commercial activities. Before the beginning of oil production, the Saudi state was financially dependent upon the taxes paid by Hejazi merchants. Nevertheless, most of the businesses those merchants engaged in were not industrial but were either trade or *hajj* (pilgrimage)-related services, such as hotels, restaurants, and transport. In addition, the rise of the state as a mainspring of development and the increase of foreign investments after the oil boom period resulted in the proliferation of private businesses that Sharaf Sabri has called "commission entrepreneurs" (Sabri 2001: 18–19). Commission entrepreneurs reap profits from businesses, such as sponsorships, commissions, contracts, sub-contracts, and speculation in real estate, rather than taking risks and creating value on their own. Moreover, the high purchasing power of Saudi consumers supported by oil rents made import businesses more lucrative for national entrepreneurs than the production of cheaper but lower-quality imitations, while import-substitution through imitation formed the first step of catch-up industrialization in East Asian economies.

Due to low oil prices after the 1980s the expansion of the public sector eventually ceased in the 1990s and the government began encouraging young nationals to take jobs in the private sector. The entry of Saudi nationals into the private sector was, however, described as "mudir syndrome", which refers to the Saudi nationals' tendency to only look for *mudir* ("manager") positions in private firms (Henry & Springborg 2001: 181). Many young nationals considered that they deserved only managerial and supervisory positions in the firm and that technical genba work should be carried out by expat workers (Szyliowicz 1979: 366–367). This has become somewhat an overstatement today, with Saudi nationals starting to take many non-managerial jobs too. Probably it would be more precise to refer to "thawb syndrome" today: Saudi nationals prefer jobs in which they wear *thawb*, a traditional Arab garment, and eschew ones in which they have to wear uniforms (except for security apparatus jobs), as one Saudi journalist told the author.

In fact, the achievements of labor nationalization policies have largely been limited to thawb jobs: according to the Central Department of Statistics and Information in Saudi Arabia, 53% of all workers in the service sector (3.9 million out of 7.4 million) are Saudi nationals. However, the figure is only 22% (696,000 out of 3.19 million) in the manufacturing sector (*Arab News*. Manufacturing Sector Has Few Saudi Workers. 23 August 2013). In terms of profession, 85.7% of managerial posts and 97.8% of administrative jobs in the private sector are already held by Saudi nationals, but less than 10% of engineering jobs have been Saudized: there are only 149,000 Saudi national engineers, in comparison with over three million expat engineers (*Arab News*. Expat Workers Hold…). This shows that the division of labor between thawb-wearing Saudi administrative workers and uniform-wearing expat technical workers remains a norm in the private sector. Monte Palmer and others had already warned about the division in 1984, saying: "If the indigenous populations do not become psychologically involved in the development process, they may be transformed into a prodigal luxury class, totally dependent on rents and foreign labor" (Palmer, Alghofaily & Alnimir 1984: 21). To achieve a transition to an industrial society, more Saudis will have to wear a uniform.

Reforming the Rentier Society

In fact, many senior Saudi nationals recall the past – the period before the oil boom – and deplore the transformation of Saudi society. They tend to share the feeling that, due to the oil rents, Saudi society became "abnormal" in terms of people's attitude towards work. Abdulhady Taher, a former governor of Petromin (the national oil company created before the nationalisation of Aramco) once said:

> Fifty or sixty years ago, people in Saudi society worked at everything that was legal according to their capacities and the resources available at that time. They worked as builders and artisans, using mud bricks and the leaves and trunks of

> the palm tree; they were shepherds and camel owners and skilled workers such as carpenters and plumbers and I can testify to that. (Taher 2011: 164)

Thus, it may be more appropriate to describe Saudi society as a "rentierised society" than as a rentier society: its unproductive traits should be understood as *a posteriori* constructs rather than the inherent nature of the society itself (although there may be regional divergences in people's attitude towards work – Taher was from the Hejaz region). Interestingly, this "nostalgia for normalcy" felt by senior Saudis is also often expressed in a future-oriented manner: they expect that normalcy will (should) be restored by the right government policies which make people less dependent on foreign labor. Certainly, whether the rentier society is structurally determined or reformable by human agency is a no easy question to answer. However, if it is possibly reformable, two policy fields seem to be the key to change: education and labor market reforms.

Education reforms should be conducive to enhancing young Saudi citizens' employability in the private industrial sector, by providing them with the right knowledge and skills required in the labor market. In addition, such reforms could change their preferences for professions if schools collectively succeed in instilling students with a love of engineering and technical work. On the other hand, labor market reforms should provide Saudi nationals with the right incentive to gain (and keep) jobs in the private sector. Given the strong cost advantages of expat workers vis-à-vis national workers, it may be somewhat inevitable that the reform takes some uneconomic measures. In fact, Saudi policymakers (especially the Ministry of Labor) think that labor nationalisation can only be pursued by dint of political will, at the expense of short-term growth. In some sense, it is considered to be a "leftover" of the decision made in the oil boom period: then, swift modernisation of the country was prioritised and privileged over the preservation of national homogeneity in the society (Braibanti & Al-Farsy 1977: 17).

Nevertheless, if labor nationalization policies end up stalling industrial diversification, educated national workers will not be able to find the right work opportunities. There must be a well thought through coordination across industrial, educational, and labor policies to enable schools to meet the demands in industry and to supply appropriately qualified workers to the labor market, who propel, rather than slow down, industrial growth and achieve *both* industrial diversification *and* labor nationalization at the same time. This is no easy task and requires effective communication mechanisms among relevant policymaking institutions.

Education Reforms

Education reforms have, in fact, been given a high priority in policymaking in Saudi Arabia in the past 15 years: nearly a quarter of the state budget has been allocated to HRD ever year. Education expenditure in Saudi Arabia today amounts to almost 10% of the country's

GDP, double the global average (*Arab New.* Kingdom Tops World in Education Spending. 23 January 2013). In particular, remarkable progress has been seen in the expansion of higher education infrastructure. The number of universities, which was only eight in 2001, has quadrupled in a decade, to 32 (24 public and eight private universities). Currently, there are over a million students at universities, 60% of whom are female (Ankari 2013: v). With an increase in the capacity of universities to accommodate students: no less than 86% of high school graduates (337,000) were reportedly enrolled at universities in 2013 (*Arab News.* Most High School Grads Enrolled in Universities. 20 September 2013).

The newly-created universities include the King Abdullah University for Science and Technology (KAUST), the country's first co-ed university, specialising in R&D, located in Thwal. Established by an initiative of King Abdullah and with funding from Saudi Aramco, the KAUST has established research collaboration with a number of advanced foreign university laboratories, such as Stanford, Cornell, and Oxford. Under its Global Research Partnerships program, the KAUST funds research at those laboratories in return for their cooperation in developing research programs at the KAUST in the same field (Shobakky 2008). In addition, other universities have been reinforcing their R&D capacity and infrastructure for commercializing research outcomes for industrial use, through the creation of "centres of excellence" and "techno valleys". Some universities are today emerging as launching pads of manufacturing activities. For instance, a team from the King Saud University in Riyadh assembled the first "Made in Saudi Arabia" automobile, named *Ghazal-1*, in June 2010, through a collaboration with several Western firms, such as Mercedes-Benz and Motorola (*Arab News.* King Unveils First Saudi-Made Car. 14 June 2010). Likewise, in January 2014 the King Fahd University of Petroleum and Minerals (KFUPM) in Dhahran unveiled the FABLAB Dhahran, a special fabrication laboratory modelled after the original FABLAB at the Massachusetts Institute of Technology (MIT). The lab is open to students and businesspeople interested in high-tech manufacturing (*Arab News.* Aramco, KFUPM Set up Design and Manufacturing Laboratory. 25 January 2014). In addition to these developments at domestic universities, the King Abdullah Scholarship Program, launched in 2005, offers full scholarships to Saudi students studying at foreign universities. To date, over 150,000 Saudi students have been sent to universities in 46 countries under the program, and 55,000 have already returned to Saudi Arabia (*Arab News.* Most High School Grads…).

Nevertheless, in spite of such remarkable *quantitative* achievements, there is still large room for *qualitative* development in higher education institutions in Saudi Arabia. In particular, the mismatch between school curricula and the skills required in the labor market is one of the greatest challenges facing these institutions today. The number of university students majoring in subjects related to industry is still low. Out of 101,700 university graduates in 2010, only 4,800 (5%) majored in engineering, and 4,200 (4%) in maths – in comparison with 19,600 (19%) in humanities, 18,000 (18%) in Islamic studies, and 12,800 (13%) in business management (*Arab News.* Only 5 percent Saudis Study Engineering.

6 April 2014). As a result, a large number of jobless degree holders exist. No less than 48.2% of university graduates are reportedly unemployed currently (*Arab News*. Long Work Hours, Low Salaries Keep Saudis Away from Private Sector Jobs. 1 March 2014). In addition, the exceptionally high university enrolment rate means that technical and vocational training are quite unpopular among young Saudi nationals. While 41% of high school graduates in the OECD countries attend technical and vocational training schools, the figure is only 9% in Saudi Arabia (*Arab News*. Why Technical and Vocational Training is an Urgent Need for KSA's Future. 19 June 2014).

While higher education in Saudi Arabia is administered by the Ministry of Higher Education (with the exception of the independently-run KAUST), technical and vocational training schools fall in the administrative turf of the Technical and Vocational Training Corporation (TVTC), under the Ministry of Labor. In recent years the TVTC has attempted to attract more high school graduates to its schools. A significant move was the launch of 10 special training colleges, named "Colleges of Excellence" (CoEs), in 2013. The CoEs differ from previous colleges in that they are all run by foreign operators and their curricula are taught in English. In addition, the length of their courses is three years – a year longer than the courses at standard colleges. By emphasizing their international character and raising high expectations regarding the employability of their graduates, the TVTC attempts to make the CoEs a game-changer (A TVTC official, interviewed by author, 2013). The TVTC plans to open 100 CoEs by 2020: together with the standard colleges, the number of students accommodated by TVTC schools is planned to quadruple from the current 110,000 to over 450,000 by then (*Arab News*. 27 More Technical Colleges Planned. 12 April 2014). The greatest challenges facing TVTC schools today is, however, the quality of students. Since technical and vocational training is currently unpopular among Saudi students, many of those attending TVTC schools today are those who have been unable to achieve grades high enough to be enrolled at universities. Thus, the TVTC will face a trial in the coming years: if the CoEs are able to demonstrate the high performance of their graduates in terms of employment, more talented high school graduates are likely to be drawn to them; if not, they may suffer from a vicious cycle of underperforming students and compromised post-graduation employment outcomes.

Nevertheless, the real problem behind the unpopularity of technical studies lies in the stage *before* tertiary education – education from primary school to high school. Saudi Arabia's primary and secondary education is administered by another ministry: the Ministry of Education. The ministry ran a ten-year strategic plan between 2004 and 2014, to overhaul the country's education system. Based on the outcomes of the overhaul it is currently implementing reforms of school curricula, to make them better able to prepare students for employment, by placing a stronger emphasis on mathematics, science and English, and by changing the style of teaching from traditional rote memorisation to a more communicative form that fosters students' critical thinking and creativity (*Arab News*. Kingdom Tops World…; Saudi Education Catching up with World's Best. 4 November 2013). A new education minister, Prince Khalid, who was appointed in December 2013, underscored the objective of the reform, saying: "Our academic programs must conform to labor market requirements" (*Arab News*. Educators Promised Incentives. 22 August 2014).

One of the greatest challenges facing the reform of primary and secondary education is, however, the quality of teachers. According to a survey conducted by the National Centre for Assessment in Higher Education (Qiyas), nearly half of the teachers in Saudi Arabia are not qualified to teach students, with a quarter of them not having a university degree (*Arab News*.'50 Percent of Teachers Not Qualified'. 19 December 2013). Many teachers are under-motivated as well (A Ministry of Education official, interviewed by author, 2014). This is mainly because of the strong "welfare" nature of employment in the Ministry of Education. Jamal Khashoggi, a Saudi journalist, points out that many teachers were employed by schools because they were not qualified enough to find jobs elsewhere (*Al-Arabiya*. Saudi Arabia's Education System in the Spotlight Again. 9 February 2014). According to Khashoggi, the Ministry of Education is the third largest ministry, after the Defence and the Interior, in terms of the number of nationals employed. Thus, the latest emphasis of the reforms has been on the retraining of teachers. In May 2014, a new endowment worth SR 80 billion ($21 billion) was approved by the king for the reform of the country's education system over the next five years: SR 5 billion ($1.3 billion) of the budget has already been allocated to the retraining of 25,000 teachers abroad (*Arab News*. SR80-Billion Education Overhaul Approved. 20 May 2014; Overseas Training of Teachers to Cost SR 5bn. 26 May 26 2014).

In addition, just like the KAUST in higher education, there have been attempts to establish independently-run education programs outside the purview of the Ministry of Education. These have taken an "island approach" – providing intensive educational training to selected groups of students. For instance, the King Abdullah Project for Public Education Development (Tatweer), an independently-run holding company, was created in 2006 with a SR 9 billion ($2.4 billion) endowment. The Tatweer is an experimental project creating 50 model secondary schools equipped with the latest technologies: these schools practice advanced curricula following the retraining of teachers and administrators (*Saudi Gazette*. SR9 Billion Tatweer Project Set to Transform Education. 19 August 2008). Saudi Aramco has run its own educational programs as well. It recently launched the "iThra Youth Program", aimed at offering opportunities to young Saudi nationals to familiarise themselves with STEM (science, technology, engineering, maths). Khalid Al-Falih, a CEO of Saudi Aramco, has announced the goal of offering training opportunities to two million Saudi children by 2020 (*Arab News*. Instilling Love of Science in Children. 4 March 2014). The iThra has recently been organising "education with entertainment" programs in multiple cities, which aim at instilling a love of science in children through family-friendly activities and workshops. In addition, the King Abdulaziz and His Companions Foundation for Giftedness and Creativity (Mawhiba) has been working on identifying gifted children across the country and offering them special intensive training. Saudi students recruited through the Mawhiba achieved the 29th and the 42nd positions in the International Math

Olympiads in 2012 and 2013, respectively, significantly improving the country's performance from 91st position in 2007 and 94th in 2008 (*Arab News*. Yanbu Students Win 4 Medals in World Math Contest. 31 July 2013). The KAUST also collaborates with the Mawhiba and invites talented Saudi high school students to its summer research camps (a KAUST official, interviewed by author, 2014). While these island approach projects are limited in their scope, they may influence the reforms in public schools by demonstrating what they can achieve and creating a sense of competition among them.

Labor Market Reforms

While education reforms are important in enhancing the employability of Saudi students, labor market reforms are needed to materialize supportive work environments in the private sector for these students. The focus has been on labor nationalization, called *sa'wada* ("Saudization"), or *tawteen* ("nationalization"). The Saudi government's labor nationalization policy dates back to 1995, when the target of an annual 5% increase of Saudi employees in private firms was set. Then, the proportion of Saudi workers in the private sector was around 10% (Ramady 2005: 359). That 5% target was replaced by a 25% target in 2001 (Looney 2004). To achieve the target, the Ministry of Labor and Social Affairs (split into the Labor and the Social Affairs in 2004) set various sectoral quotas for national employment and created the Human Resources Development Fund (HRDF) to financially assist private firms employing Saudi nationals, providing 75% of the salaries for their Saudi employees in the first two years of employment, with a cap of SR 2,000 ($530) per month. Nevertheless, the quotas were not met in many cases (Hertog 2012: 92–93), and the proportion of Saudi nationals in the private sector was almost unchanged at the end of the first decade of the twenty-first century, at around 10%.

In order to revamp the labor nationalization policy, the Ministry of Labor, under the initiative of the minister Adel Fakeih (2010–present), implemented a legally-binding Saudization program called the *Nitaqat* ("zones") in 2011. The program established four "zones" into which private firms were classified in accordance with the degree of their achievement in Saudization. Those four zones are: premium (over 27%), green (10-27%), yellow (4-10%), and red (below 4%). The program imposes certain penalties on the firms in the yellow and red zones while rewarding those in the premium and green zones (Ramady 2013). In addition, as there were a number of undocumented expat workers in the country, the Ministry of Labor raised a campaign to correct their status in 2013, resulting in the deportation of 900,000 illegal workers by the end of that year (*Arab News*. Over 900,000 Undocumented Expats Deported since Beginning of Amnesty. 14 December 2013). These policies changed the business landscape in Saudi Arabia to a certain degree: while nearly 200,000 private firms, or 10% of all private firms in the country, have been closed down (*Arab News*. Nitaqat: 200,000 Firms Closed Down. 5 August 2014), the private sector achieved a 15% rate of labor nationalisation, or 1.5 million national workers, by the end of 2013 (*Arab News*. 1.5 Million Saudis Now Work in Private Sector. 11 August 2014). The number of firms in the green zone doubled from 40% in mid-2011, at the time of the implementation of the Nitaqat, to over 80% (*Arab News*. Companies Fire 70,000 Expats in Two Years. 2 April 2014). In particular, the number of female national workers in the private sector quadrupled in two years, from around 100,000 in 2011 to 400,000 in 2013. However, due to the increase in the overall size of the private sector, the number of expat workers and their dependents has also increased in the same period, surpassing 10 million in 2014. That the country hosts more expats while over one-third of young nationals are jobless is considered by the Ministry of Labor to be a problem which must be tackled by stricter policies. The ministry is currently discussing further legal measures for labor nationalization, such as placing a cap on the duration of stay of expat workers in the country (*Arab News*. 8-Year Expat Cap Plan under Review. 26 May 2014).

Many private firms that have benefitted from the availability of cheap skilled expat workers in the past decades have been reluctant to comply with those legal requirements for labor nationalization. Thus, an illegal practice of *tasattur* ("cover-up" or "fake Saudization") is widespread: many firms register on paper the names of Saudi nationals who do not show up to the workplace in reality (*Arab News*. "Cover-Up Businesses Cost Economy Dearly. 18 February 2012). Some firms also recruit expat workers from the underground labor market where "visa mafias" set up ghost firms to import them and make profit by selling them to other firms (Hertog 2012; *Arab News*. Expat Visa Trader Arrested. 1 May 2014). One of the major problems facing labor nationalization is that many private firms count their national employees merely as a numerical asset for fulfilling the quota set by the Nitaqat, rather than as substantive human resources. With such a negative attitude on the part of the management towards national workers, many national workers seem to find their workplace unmotivating, leading to premature quitting of their jobs. The attrition rate in the private sector in Saudi Arabia is currently not available but it is supposed to be high (*Arab News*. "Shoura 'Disappointed' at TVTC Performance". 17 April 2014). In fact, the majority of the TVTC school graduates have reportedly ended up joining the military instead of staying in their jobs in the private sector (*Arab News*. "TVTC 'Ensure' 75,000 Graduates in 5 Years". 2 March 2014). An instructor at one of the technical training schools suggested that only 10–20% of the school's graduates seemed to stay in the job they obtained after their graduation (Anonymous, interviewed by author, 2014). In order to reduce early quitting by national workers in the private sector, the HRDF is currently planning to create a scheme to offer financial rewards to those who have stayed at a job for a certain period of time (*Arab News*. Saudis Who Find and Keep Jobs to Receive Rewards. 3 April 2014). The scheme would apply to those who have found jobs using its *Hafiz* ("incentive") Program, a matchmaking scheme between job-seekers and prospective employers. (The Hafiz, implemented in 2011 following the Nitaqat, offers registered job-seekers a stipend of SR 3,000 ($800) per month for up to one year, in addition to services such as a CV database for prospective employers, skills development programs, and mass interviews. By the end of 2012, 1.9 million job-seekers had registered with the Program, 80% of whom were female. Among them, nearly 200,000 have found jobs in the private sector (*Arab News*. Hafiz: Inspiration for Job Seekers. 15 May 2012)).

The dissatisfaction of national workers with the work environment of private firms risks further discouraging young nationals from taking up private sector jobs. To some extent the source of dissatisfaction is a financial issue. Private sector jobs are generally lower-paid than public sector ones: indeed, 86% of expat workers earn less than SR 2,000 ($530) per month (*Arab News*. KSA Has 9.2 Million Expatriates, Says Study. 11 October 2013). In order to prevent tasattur, the Ministry of Labor implemented the minimum wage of SR 1,500 ($400) per month in February 2013, and also designed the calculation system for the Nitaqat to count one national employee in a case where an employee is paid more than SR 3,000 ($800): in a case where the employees is paid less than SR 3,000, he/she is only counted as 0.5, and in a case where the payment is less than SR 1,500, he/she is not counted (*Arab News*. Firms, Idlers Connive to Beat Nitaqat. 17 January 2013). In addition, in order to encourage Saudi nationals to join the private sector an unemployment insurance scheme was introduced in August 2014, under which the unemployed under the age of 60 are provided with 50–60% of the previous salaries he/she received in the past two years, within the range of between SR 2,000 ($530) and SR 9,000 ($2,400), for up to one year (*Arab News*. Job Security for 1.5 Million Saudis. 7 January 2014; Unemployment Insurance Scheme to Start of Aug. 31. 13 July 2014).

However, underpayment is not the only barrier to national employment in the private sector. National technical workers often find their workplace not comfortable to work in: since many workplaces have long been designed exclusively for expat workers, they remain unsatisfactory for national workers, in terms of safety standards, cleanliness, and comfort (many workplaces are without air conditioning). In addition, many national workers find their relationships with their expat colleagues and supervisors hard to manage: the lack of trust and respect from them is, in fact, one of the major reasons national job-seekers avoid private sector jobs (*Arab News*. Saudi Job Seekers Hesitant to Take Private Sector Jobs. 15 January 2014). Expat workers' negative attitudes towards their Saudi colleagues are considered to be shaped by multiple factors. One of these derives from the labor nationalisation policy itself. Since the Nitaqat began eroding the job security of expat workers, many of them now fear that they will lose their current jobs if their national co-workers acquire sufficient knowledge and skills and become ready to replace them (*Arab News*. Job Security Remains Expats' Major Concern. 8 June 2012). Thus, unless their employment is assured, it is in their interest not to transfer knowledge and skills to their national colleagues (A TVTC official, interviewed by author, 2013). The insufficient level of trust between national and expat workers at the genba poses an impediment to the practice of kaizen and deprives firms of opportunities to add value to production. Thus, some firms attempt to help them build mutual trust by providing a monthly bonus to expat workers who effectively assist their national co-workers at the workplace.

In other cases, expat workers find their national colleagues not qualified enough for their work. In fact, many firm managers complain that the schools they graduated from did not provide them with appropriate knowledge and the skills required in the labor market. However, it is difficult for schools to rightly identify these elements: since the feedback mechanism from industry to education is still not well-developed, collective data indicating what knowledge and skills are needed in the labor market are insufficient. In order to overcome this shortcoming, the TVTC currently attempts to improve its capacity to survey the labor market, through its *mursad* ("observatory") (*Arab News*. Shoura Critical of 'Slow' Data Collection by Labor Observatory. 22 October 2014). In addition, the Ministry of Labor is now in the process of developing its research capacity, as the Hafiz Program has begun providing data about the skills match/mismatch between job-seekers/finders and private firms (A Ministry of Labor official, interviewed by author, 2014). Stories about what national workers are experiencing in their workplace in the private sector still remain largely anecdotal and more data must be generated in the coming years. Universities also express their desire for more firms to invest in education and provide them with data so that they can understand the labor market better (*Arab News*. KSA Universities 'Not Aligned with Jobs Market'. 20 November 2014). How to establish effective communication mechanisms between industry and education will be a policymaking challenge in the years to come.

Conclusions

While Saudi policymakers are attempting to develop labor-intensive manufacturing industries as a way to provide a solution to the country's deepening youth unemployment problem, industrial development in Saudi Arabia still lacks sufficient social underpinnings. Emerging labor-abundance and the spread of education today creates a pool of educated workers in Saudi Arabia which, in theory, puts the country in a more advantageous position than in the past for the development of manufacturing industries – as the experience of Japan's industrialization suggests. In reality, however, the country's rentier society (or "rentierised society"), a society in which people tend to remain underproductive because of their dependence on oil rents and foreign labors, continues to pose barriers to national industrial employment. Private technical professions are undervalued by Saudi nationals – who prefer thawb jobs to uniform jobs – and continue to be dominated by expat workers. As a precondition for the development of labor-intensive manufacturing industries, this rentier society must be reformed and transformed into an industrial society where technical workers receive a sufficient degree of respect in the society and talented young citizens aspire to engineering careers.

Education and labor market reforms are considered to be the key to that transformation. In the field of education reforms, Saudi Arabia has achieved a remarkable expansion of higher education infrastructure in the past 15 years. However, the mismatch between school curricula and the skills required in the labor market still remain great because only a small segment of students specialise in industry-related courses. Likewise, technical and vocational training still remains unpopular among Saudi students. While universities and technical training schools must make efforts to attract more high school graduates to the technical studies required for industrial employment, the reform of primary and secondary education is also indispensable. The Ministry of Education is currently working on improving curricula, to place more importance on mathematics, science and English, and on retraining teachers to achieve reform. In addition, an increasing number of independently-run education projects for training selected groups of students are also taking place outside the purview of the ministry. How those developments will unfold in the coming years remains to be seen.

In the realm of labor market reforms, stricter labor nationalization policies in recent years have brought more Saudi nationals to the private sector. However, while labor nationalization has been relatively successful in thawb-wearing administrative jobs, it has been greatly insufficient in uniform-wearing technical professions. The attitude of many private firms towards the labor nationalization policies still remains one of "reluctant compliance", as the proliferation of the illegal practice of fake Saudization suggests. Managements' negative attitudes towards national employees – counting them as more of a numerical asset for fulfilling the Saudization quota than as substantial human resources – seem to be causing a demotivation of national employees, leading to their early quitting of jobs. In addition, many national workers tend to be dissatisfied with the level of financial rewards in the private sector, the fact that work environment falls short in terms of safety and comfort, and with their relations with expat workers. Evidence in this regard, however, largely remains anecdotal, and more data about work environments surrounding national workers must be generated. These data should also help schools understand the requirements of the labor market better as many firms also complain that national workers are not appropriately educated or trained.

Proposals

Based on the above analysis this paper offers practical proposals regarding education and labor market reforms in Saudi Arabia.

Proposals for Education Reform

This paper believes that the Ministry of Education's recent moves towards placing a stronger emphasis on mathematics and science in primary and secondary education and retraining teachers for that purpose are positive. Based on these policies, this paper makes a further suggestion regarding the reform. This paper believes that national industrial employment in Saudi Arabia will greatly benefit from the introduction of technical classes at all levels of schooling, from primary school to high school. In order to convert knowledge and skills into industrial uses, students must learn how to apply them to practical operations. Among STEM, "T" (technology) and "E" (engineering) are as important as "S" (science) and "M" (mathematics). It is desirable for Saudi students to discover the joy of using their hands and carrying out designing and engineering activities at early stages of education. For instance, students at primary school can start with playing with simple paper crafts or clay crafts. Then, at higher grades, they may be able to carry out slightly more complex operations, such as creating toys made of different materials or simple furniture, like a chair and a bookshelf. Then, at the high school level, they may be able to expose themselves to further complex activities, such as assembling electrical gadgets. This kind of gradual and progressive learning of technical operations will enable students to prepare for professional technical education and training at the tertiary level. In fact, the Saudi Electronics and Home Appliances Institute (SEHAI), one of the TVTC schools, runs a "Monodzukuri Lab" [sic] (*ma'mal al-tarkibat*) at the beginning of the two-year course, in which students familiarise themselves with the act of engineering by assembling machines using *Lego* blocks. Instructors at the institute have found this introductory lab to be effective in developing students' motivation for further learning (An instructor at the SEHAI, interviewed by author, 2013). Such an entry point can be established at much earlier years of schooling.

One concern regarding implementing such technical classes at primary and secondary schools is the ability of teachers: it is likely that (re)training of teachers will be required at the beginning. After (re)training, selected teachers may first run technical classes on an experimental basis in some model schools and they may then disseminate their know-how to other teachers and schools. Another concern is a possible objection to a further reduction of the hours dedicated to religious teaching, which currently occupy nearly one-third of the total hours in primary and secondary education. This paper suggests that technical classes should be effectively *integrated* with classes on religious teachings, taking advantage of the fact that Islam serves as the foundation of Saudi society. To prepare students for industrial employment, the morals, ethics, and discipline that technical workers should apply to their work should be taught, along technical operations. Islam is a "religion of work" which teaches virtues such as quality (*jawda*), justice (*'adl*), sincerity (*khulus*), diligence (*jihad al-nafs*), and paying respect to workers by treating them like one's brothers (a Saudi instructor at the Technical Trainers College, Riyadh, interviewed by author, 2014). Such integrated teachings should help Saudi students learn how to put the principles (*mabadi*) of Islam into practice (*tatbiq*) as professionals.

Proposals for Labor Market Reforms

Regarding labor market reforms, this paper proposes that labor nationalisation in Saudi Arabia will greatly benefit from the government and private firms building a dialogue-based constructive relationship that *empowers* private firms to fully exploit the potential of national workers, since only exercising coercive power towards them, in imposing quotas for labor nationalization, risks creating an endless cat-and-mouse game. The government may be able to assist private firms in practising genba-oriented management methods of kaizen by inviting experts and organising workshops, from which the management of firms can learn how to offer a supportive work environment for their national employees. Improvement of the work environment will lead to an increased motivation on the part of national workers to work and learn, and also will enable firms to recruit qualified national workers in the future. The minimum requirements seem to be a sufficient level of safety and comfortable conditions in the workplace, including sufficient air conditioning. In addition to these, what kaizen theorists call the "5S" may be improved. 5S are: (1) *seiri*, or the elimination of the unnecessary; (2) *seiton*, or the organization of the necessary; (3) *seisou*, the maintenance of cleanness; (4) *seiketsu*, the maintenance of hygiene; and (5) *shitsuke*, building discipline (Imai 1997). Firms' managers are encouraged to make frequent visits to the genba to listen to workers' voices and think about how to assist workers further. Such regular direct communication will help national workers build a sense of trust and self-confidence. They may be rewarded psychologically as well as financially for their performance, by honours and prizes.

It is also desirable for firms to conduct a survey of the workplace, together with the schools from which their national employees have graduated. By doing so, schools will be able to have a clearer idea of how they should improve their curriculum in order to match it with the skills required in the labor market. (Presenting successful cases of national employment to current students as role models should help inspire them as well.) The management of firms will benefit from the survey by acquiring a deeper understanding of the psychology of their national employees and the problems facing them. Media can also be more greatly involved in raising the awareness among firms and schools about industry–education collaboration. Recently a TV program entitled "Jobs on Air" was launched by the state-owned Al-Danah TV. The program documents the stories of jobless Saudi men and women who receive training and get jobs in private firms (*Arab News*. New TV Program to Help Young Saudis Find Jobs. 3 September 2014). Such moves should form a step forward towards establishing effective communication mechanisms between firms and schools. It is also desirable that representatives of institutions relevant to national industrial employment (such as the NICDP, the Saudi Council of Chambers, the Ministry of Labor, the HRDF, the TVTC, the Ministry of Higher Education, the Ministry of Education, and others) meet regularly, for instance at a special committee devoted to this issue, in order to design and check policy coordination among them.

10

The Anthropological Elements of Failed Saudization: Historicism, Image, Islam and Tribe

Tanya Cariina Newbury-Smith

Introduction

Research into the underlying causes of the unemployed/underemployed condition Saudi Arabia experiences reveals a paucity of documentation with no serious enquiries as to its cultural history as an underlying factor. Whilst a significant body of work exists on the affect of official policies over time, root causes outside of statistics must be included. The ethics and history of the Saudi culture have direct bearing upon national employment and growth.

This paper attempts to analyze factors that may provide a deeper observation of the Saudi ethos, both present and past, to better judge the strengths and weaknesses of unemployment in the Kingdom. With ten years of ethnographical and accumulated first-hand materials from Saudi Arabia, archival materials, and personal interviews within the general population, officials, ministers and members of the royal family, this paper also draws upon research in Riyadh from January to May 2014, as well as previous quantitative responses from a survey this author conducted on Saudi students' attitudes in June 2007 (Hsu *et al.*, 2007). Although interviewees agreed to be quoted directly in some cases, several requested anonymity considering a cultural resistance to criticism of those in leading positions of influence.

The first section explores the Saudi employment policy, development of '*Saudization*' and *Nitaqat* (ranges), and ethics of the young-adult generation in relation to work and aspirations. The second section of the paper analyses the impact of deep historical traditions, both tribal and Islamic. Finally, the third section takes into account particular complex cultural attitudes towards time and intentions. The paper suggests in its conclusion that economic trends and analyses are insufficient if historical perspectives are ignored, with quantitative solutions offering temporary progress at best.

Threat to the Kingdom

The greatest threat posed to the Kingdom today is not an external challenge to security or regional political instabilities. Instead it is the looming crisis of Saudi underemployment that alone stands as a bigger challenge than any terrorists from neighboring states (Kabuli, 2014).

Saudis are frequently dismissed as unwilling to work hard and disdainful of manual labor. Although largely accurate in the present day, this would be false when considering the past. It is misleading to create a general narrative that describes Saudis with an historical monolithic characteristic. They have survived since ancient times despite the harshest of conditions, without laborious commitments to ensure survivability. Some of these endemic traits remain entrenched in society steeped in nostalgia, whereas others have been discarded: what worked in the desert no longer applies to the air-conditioned offices of urbanization.

The oil-generated revenues of the seventies produced a society flush with cash as well as quickly decreasing employment ambitions. Foreign labor had been imported for so long that there was little reason for Saudis to remain in low-wage blue-collar jobs: oil revenues created a bountiful welfare state that provided for all. The generation that followed the years of excess had a different concept to their parents with regard to work ethics, as even personal experience with daily chores — a normal precursor to self-reliance in any culture — was eliminated when domestic staff became standard in most homes. The Kingdom's reliance on foreign workers to fill a void in manual and private sector jobs allowed the majority of the Saudi population to take government sector positions, healthy with perks no longer sustainable. In 2014, 78% of professional Saudis indicated they received a basic salary, plus housing allowance, transport, children's education, medical insurance for the family, annual personal airline tickets and an end-of-service gratuity. Almost half also expressed dissatisfaction that their wages were insufficient (Albawaba, 2014). An attempt to repatriate Saudis into the workforce whilst reducing Saudi reliance on foreign workers was discussed by a few Saudis who raised the subject of quotas over the years, and only within the last decade was a formal plan of '*Saudization*' announced.

By not conveying negative consequences should Saudis not re-adjust workforce expectations, nothing changed, and instead worsened. As was revealed in a Wikileaks cable from the American ambassador in Saudi Arabia, *Saudization* as proposed then was not viewed as a solution to the national unemployment problem, and King Abdullah instead ordered the labor policy back to the status quo, excepting four sectors of the economy: education, hospitals, industry, and construction (Wikileaks, 2006). The Saudi government's initiative to overhaul the unemployment situation was from all angles a failed policy, certainly regarding implementation to date. It is a "vicious cycle of private-sector employment with low wages and low productivity that will be unsolvable," said Riyadh investment strategist John Sfakianakis (Sfakianakis, January 2014).

It is insufficient to look at the process of *Saudization* and hypothesize as to its outcomes without understanding the root causes. *Why* has the unemployment situation amongst Saudis reached a tipping point? Examining anthropological causes, it is difficult to observe a positive outcome unless institutional changes and overhauls are undertaken to change attitudes, bureaucracy, corruption and false pride.

Employment in Saudi Arabia

During the seventies, revenues were directed overwhelmingly to construction and development industries, and the government injected massive amounts into sending waves of Saudis overseas to be educated in the West. The aim was to liberalize Saudis away from a traditionally conservative culture into a more democratic society, intellectually and professionally prepared for modern world challenges. Economic growth produced a petrochemical-based welfare state that provided 'cradle to grave' benefits: education, housing, health care, retirement, and generous salaries. Hejazis dominated the mercantile sector, a preponderance of Meccans and Qassimis prevailed in Islamic scholarship, and the Al Saud controlled government ministries and industries. Even though the trading and private sector families were Saudis, they preferred not to hire Saudi nationals since they demanded high wages. The answer to employment requirements was always "find a foreigner!" (Freeman, 2014).

Soon Saudis became contemptuous of blue-collar workers who performed the jobs they assumed they would never need to work in again. Foresight to address twenty-first century expectations were overlooked in government budgets, and few allocations were made to build training and vocational schools and colleges for the strengthening of human resources. Instead of the gradual development of a system to provide appropriate skills for Saudis no longer reliant on traditional agrarian and subsistence economies of a nomadic society, industrialization arrived "pre-packaged" and purchased with the sudden advent of enormous oil wealth (Fakeeh, 2009).

Also overlooked was how the inevitable pendulum swing from a conservative to liberal society might be viewed domestically. More than a generation of unemployed Saudis coupled with economic frustrations created a potential clash of young and old, tensions not lessened by recent revolutions in surrounding states.

Saudization

The nineties ushered in a period of budget deficits and high rates of unemployment. To promote full employment, the government set a target rate for national hires in the private sector at 75%. A new deadline was set in 2002, of 25% Saudi national private sector employment, and in 2005 altered the figure again, to 30%. Employment trends are far below expectations, as foreigners still dominate 90% of private sector jobs in 2012. In June 2011, the *Saudization* program was replaced by the *Nitaqat* program, although the terms are used interchangeably and most people use *Saudization* as the default descriptor. *Nitaqat* meant that the government would evaluate private sector performance based upon new targets, calculated by the number of Saudis employed by the firm. This led to bureaucratic chaos: the Ministry of Labor created 180 different quotas for business entities of various sizes and sectors, leading to confusion across the country (Saudi Hollandi Bank, 2012). Rather than alleviating unemployment, Saudi unemployment in 2012 was even greater compared to 2001 (SAMA Chart, Saudi Hollandi, 2012).

Complicating matters further, in February 2014, the *Majlis Ash-Shura* proposed reducing weekly working hours from 48 to 40 to parallel the West, and several private sector Saudi businessmen opposed the move on the grounds that it would have a negative impact on the economy. The private sector has always preferred cheap and hardworking foreign laborers and has at times actively discouraged worker training programs. They argued that foreign workers did not complain about long hours and six-day weeks. According to Abdul Rahman al-Zamil, president of the Riyadh Chamber of Commerce, "things would be worse" for the economy and diminish private sectors achievements. Another businessman argued that giving workers an extra day off would send a negative message to employees "to relax and ask for more" (Al-Mukhtar, 2014). Paying Saudis four or eight times as much as a foreign worker, however, cannot work long-term; the priority has been to *not* effectively build up the country and not prioritize increased production, yet increase salaries nevertheless. According to Sfakianakis, the private sector can pay Saudis SR 10,000 instead of the SR 2,000 a foreigner would receive for the same job, as long as productivity increases. "Give him a machine, he sweeps the streets clean in an air-conditioned and dignified manner," said Sfakianakis ("SUSRIS, 2014"). Aspiring economies need to migrate from low-productivity low-wages, to high-productivity high-wages, but administrative measures must also be applied and enforced.

The declining economic situation presents itself on a more personal level for young Saudis. Increasingly unable to afford housing and begin a new family, they feel helpless. Fully cognizant that wages are rising in other Gulf nations, Saudis inevitably compare themselves and maintain aspirations of duplicating their high living standards. Thus, they continue to demand even higher wages and increased benefits at home (Al-Zamel, 2014).

Prospects for change remain dim. According to a 2011 survey on the willingness of Saudis to undertake such employment, the vast majority fully reject working in private sector jobs. By far the key integrator was prestige and status. Almost all (97%) felt they had a high level of status consciousness that prevented them from accepting an opportunity they perceived as beneath them. The same percentage agreed or strongly agreed that they actively viewed status as the predominant factor in suitable employment, and realized that their focus on prestige was in and of itself a driver of unemployment. Rather than hold themselves accountable they blamed others: the government, their family and peers, and society. When asked if they felt they could perform as well as foreigners, 70% of Saudis felt they could work as hard, and 93% felt they could replace ex-pats in both public and private sectors. Key to their willingness to work in typically foreigner-dominated position was the compensation package provided. However, even with a fixed minimum salary, only 68% of respondents said they would take such jobs (Al-Anazi, 2011: pp. 56–80). How did this sense of elitism become so pervasive?

Kashkha: The Importance of Image

Presentation is essential in Saudi Arabia. The image the Kingdom presents remains paramount, and newspapers are the best source to generate a snapshot of the culture. Pages are filled with accounts of accomplishments carried out under the patronage of a leading member of the royal family or due to the benevolence of the king. Photographs publicize officials presenting or accepting awards, trophies received for a commission about to be formed, or a meeting that intends to address important issues; in almost all cases officials will have little involvement with these processes directly. Far from discretion and anonymity, great emphasis is placed upon *kashkha,* the image of prestige, recognition and accolades. Congratulatory future tense articles cement news that the Kingdom expects, anticipates, forecasts, pledges and promises to make something happen. Rarely does news announce the building of a vocational school or training solutions to help Saudis in skills required in the present. This juxtaposition between image and reality was illustrated in the *Arab News* on 28 April 2014: "Nine Golden Years of Prosperity and Stability" under King Abdullah on one page, it was followed on another by the unwelcome news that turnover amongst Saudi employees was significantly on the rise due to clear differences in expectations between employer and employee (Arab News, 2014). Even Nitaqat categories are presented akin to a line of luxury services: the most compliant *Saudization* companies are granted 'VIP' status in media reporting (Wahhab, 2011).

As frequent as award ceremonies are the announcements of mega-plans for new offices and hotels costing billions of dollars, Saudi Arabia leading the MENA region with a portfolio of projects in the works valued at $8 billion (Schellen, 2014). In 2014, the government announced its intention to double the tourism sector by 2020, generating SR200 billion. Yet, promises of tourism industry growth have been advertised for ten years and still the Kingdom lacks the basic infrastructure and development or available tourist visas to meet any demand. Tourism instead refers almost exclusively to Hajj and Umrah visitors, unable to leave Mecca or Medina and explore the Kingdom. Certainly, luxury hotels are being built at a rapid clip all around the Kingdom but they cater to business travellers who rarely leave the confines of the city. Still no progress has been made in areas around historical sites such as Maiden Saleh, Taif or Sakaka, plans for Red Sea tourism seem on hold, and tourist coaches, affordable hotels, guides, multi-lingual museum information and clean toilet facilities are all but absent. The Saudi Tourism Commission goes to great lengths to promote Saudi Arabia in a first-class global publicity campaign and sponsors impressive museum exhibitions of Arabian natural treasures worldwide, *kashkha* on display.

Kashkha image-projection is opposite to *niya*, the modesty propagated by Islam. Instead of encouraging restraint, moderation and empathy among young Saudis, *kashkha* has not engendered empathy, nor does it encourage restraint and moderation. Instead, it has led to a generation of apathy and unrealistic expectations.

Ethics of a Young Saudi Generation

Until the eighties, 90% of Saudis had no shame about their class, nor embarrassment and lack of dignity over manual labor. Since then ethics have changed dramatically and by the nineties approximately 80% of Saudis refused manual work (Al-Obaid & Al-Ateiah, 2003. Madhi & Barrientos 2003, pp. 70–77). The view that manual labor is degrading is a relatively new phenomenon not borne out by history, and evidenced within the most profitable industry in the Kingdom. (Aramco and SABIC, both petrochemical giants, have remained committed to not only hiring the best Saudis, but also have established training programs and teaching opportunities for the next generation. As government owned industries [Aramco 100%, SABIC 70%] they are outliers in the Kingdom. However, their management is structured in line with international corporate practices, having begun as foreign-influenced companies.) Not only are manual laborers denigrated, so are service professions such as driver, craftsman, barber or shopkeeper. Coupled with "the bad behavior of paying a premium to nationals," as retired US Ambassador Chas Freeman explained, this illustrates current social problems. "The answer was to pay 15% more — a hardship burden if you will — to persuade foreigners to live and work in Saudi Arabia".

There are 9 million foreign workers in Saudi Arabia who provide the world's second biggest remittance source, sending $27.1 billion in expatriate remittances to their home countries (Saudi Hollandi, 2012). Since the push towards *Saudization* outbound remittances have doubled (Saudi Hollandi, 2012). Foreigners also have the skills and willingness that make them hard to replace, but without a change to the unemployment situation the problem will magnify. This 'economic leakage' will cause per capita GDP levels to fall and living standards to decline, and undermines growth and job opportunities for nationals (Shediac & Samman, 2010: pp. 4–28). With the Nitaqat system this appears a contradiction. Although the government is stricter regarding visa allocations with enforced terms, fixed professions, and limits to their duration in country, for all the discussion regarding capping *iqamas* (work permits), the Kingdom cannot force change without a risked implosion. The system also targets those proved the most loyal to the country, as foreigners will have to leave after a few years. Currently new work visas have a contract date of two years that must be completed before switching positions, but without the approval of the sponsor, transfer to another company is not possible.

Saudi nationals' demand for status and recognition is evidenced in the failure of *Saudization* to adequately address social concerns, and one of the most profound challenges is the mismatch between expectations and suitability. Perhaps one comment in the *Arab News* recently best summarized the young Saudi work ethic:

> Objective statement in the résumé would read: *"Looking for an entry level position in the top ten* organizations, *as a Manager, Vice President or a Senior Executive, with a basic salary of 20k [per month] and a package of 35k, with my own working hours and little contribution to the job. Willing to quit anytime without notice."*

Employers consistently report a lack of motivation from Saudi employees, reporting prayer times used only for long coffee and cigarette breaks on top of two-hour lunchtimes. With such obstacles, many employers resort to *sawda wahmiah*, or 'fake *Saudization*' (Knickmeyer 2014). Steffen Hertog regards these as "just temporary teething problems," although rising labor costs are reducing profits as firms hire more, better-paid, Saudis which "create incentives to game the system," he said (*Ibid*). Since potential employers regard Saudis largely as unskilled, this only compounds the unemployment problem: the long-term unemployed who are unable to make compromises necessitate increased training and education requirements to reintroduce them into the workforce (Fakeeh 2009). Non-productivity due to a resistant potential workforce drains the nation's financial resources and merely cements a dependence on foreign workers, continually necessary to meet requirements. The more Saudis demand a service-based economy wherein they are *magror* (snobbish) to those serving them, the more they distance themselves from ever rectifying the problem.

The unemployment crisis is not alleviated by the generosity of unemployment benefits: in 2011 the unemployment benefit was just under SR 2,000 ($533) per month, and increased in 2014 to a minimum of SR 2,000, with a cap of SR 9,000 ($2,400) per month (Al-Suhaymi 2014). Although the Labor Ministry intends benefits be provided for only one year, it can be assumed — given up to 40% of Saudi adults are currently unemployed — that this is a temporary bandage to an unsustainable wound. As a comparison, Bahrain provides a model: census figures from 2001 reveal that 13% of unemployed Bahrainis had still not worked after eight years of unemployment (Shediac & Samman, 2010: pp. 6–28). With unemployment benefits that equal an average teacher's salary, this does little to alleviate sustained voluntary unemployment.

Dependence upon parents reinforces a lifestyle of ease, the primary income-earner (inevitably the father) feeling greater pressure to generate further income to support increasing expenses. Soviet economist Alexander Chayanov termed this theory the Consumption-Labor-Balance Principle. That is, the higher the ratio of dependents to workers in a household, the harder the workers have to work. Chayanov proposed that labor will increase until it meets (balances) the needs (consumption) of the household; a family works to maintain a living but not for profit (Sterk Gemengd, 2009). Wrote Abdullah Al-Anezi "Saudis choose to remain unemployed instead of doing something worthwhile to bring added revenue to their families" (Al-Anazi, p. 81). Rather than relocate in search of better opportunities — often a reason to 'reinvent' oneself and leave status and peer pressure behind — Saudis are the least likeliest to move overseas for employment despite qualifications affording greater opportunities, enabling them to earn salaries they could return to the Saudi economy.

Rewarding unemployment exacerbates and prolongs the employment dilemma. This was the option taken by King Abdullah in early 2011 when, with increased tensions in neighbouring Arab states a potential model for a frustrated, idle and more vocal younger generation, he announced a massive package of benefits. In February, $37 billion was provided including pay rises of 15% to public sector workers, increases in education funding, and the promise of affordable housing; a month later the king added another $94 billion, for a total of $130 billion — 21% of the country's GDP or 56% of the nation's actual budget expenditure the year before (Kukemelk, 2011). There is no guarantee, however, that protests will remain external. If the status quo is maintained in the face of *hope*, the Kingdom will face an overwhelming fiscal liability that risks destabilizing the country, no foreign threat the factor.

Peer Pressure and Social Media Influences

The Kingdom has unwittingly produced a generation comforted by a lifestyle of consumption, ease, dependence upon foreign labor, and reliance upon family and state (Al-Anazi, p. 83). With strong peer pressure in a culture of excessive consumption habits coupled with unrealistic desires to join elite social and professional networks, a rise in online entertainment as a 'full-time occupation' compounds unhealthy habits.

Social media in Saudi Arabia is understandably a lifeline to young Saudis. The exponential growth of various digital platforms such as YouTube, Facebook, and WhatsApp — and an insatiable appetite for the latest iPhones and computers — has propelled Saudi Arabia into the top spot for the most active country in the world on Twitter (Radcliffe, 2014). The ability to access content from anywhere has generated an explosion in technologically perceptive unemployed youths with much time on their hands. There is little indication they use these platforms towards searching for employment opportunities, e-learning, or training enhancement. An example is the particularly flawed official Saudi websites e.g., the Ministry of Foreign Affairs (MOFA) portal, consistently devoid of basic information such as telephone numbers or email addresses. MOFA is the first point of contact with Saudi Arabia for many potential visitors; there is no excuse to remain second-class. With an entire unemployed body of skilled Saudi Internet users willing to improve such sites, more than a decade after an online presence these areas remain barely addressed.

This is illustrative of a larger problem: absorption in a digital world has permeated traditional home life as more time is spent using a computer or mobile phone at the dining room table instead of family. This erosion of the social fabric affects families globally, but in Saudi Arabia, the family relationship is particularly acute. A Saudi will insist that his family is his priority, but using one's family as an argument for distancing-behavior because they share the same living space has weakened. Time unconnected continues even during visits to the desert as mobile phones reach farther every day, lessons from the elders a thing of the past (Collins, 2014).

From an enigmatic country with closed borders a decade ago, Saudis can now interact with anyone anywhere on the planet at the expense of cultural traditions. This has direct bearing on values they claim today: on the one hand they cherish the past and feel passionate about their history; on the other their actions belie a different code of conduct. They find little problem remaining attached to social media for hours; they do have a problem with a time-value-production in the workplace. One mother remarked, "Our men are soft-bellied and weak. Serving in the armed forces for a determined amount of time should put some muscle back in their bodies and heads. Get them to do things for themselves. This will also teach our young men and hopefully also women ... in an honourable way" (Al-Maeena, January 2014). Her solution of incorporating discipline with cultural traditions is increasingly common in the older generation keenly aware that a country steeped in nostalgia now has a generation that does not marry well with twenty-first century employment requirements.

The question remains whether Saudis are newly apathetic. Understanding the collective Arabian character permits a broader understanding of the dominant traits of the past in comparison to today's trends.

Historical Attitudes in Arabia

Nietzsche wrote that history belongs to the living person: "it belongs to him as an active and striving person; it belongs to him as a person who preserves and admires; it belongs to him as a suffering person in need of emancipation…the problem to what degree living requires the services of history generally is one of the most important questions and concerns with respect to the health of a human being, a people, or a culture" (Nietzsche, 1873). Image, ethics, intentions and time can be better understood if these traits can be observed in historical Arabia.

Examining the Arabs of ancient Arabia, character traits that have developed for thousands of years cannot be ignored in relation to the Saudis of today. What worked in the desert is ill suited to urban air-conditioned towers today; a culture suited to the slow pace of Bedouin life met opposition when brought into a fast-paced information age.

Tribe

Although Saudi Arabia uses Islam as justification in how the country is run it still operates more in a continuation of the tribal system from top to bottom. Islam emphasizes equality, yet the reality is that of hierarchy and class that prevents those outside of the royal family or with connections to leading officials from the most senior positions. In historical tribal fashion this ensures absolute loyalty to the leader and takes precedence over qualifications and ability. Within the royal family, princes who are born of non-tribal mothers, foreigners or slaves rarely rise to prominence: the announcement that Prince Muqrin bin 'Abdul 'Aziz was named as third-in-line to the throne has been met with controversy, as his mother was a Yemeni slave. Prince Bandar bin Sultan is another exception to the exclusion of mixed-heritage offspring gaining power; his mother was an African slave yet he was the Saudi Ambassador to the United States for twenty-two years and recently departed Head of Saudi Intelligence. Whereas young Saudis aspire to be included in the category of those who 'beat the system', the odds are stacked against them. The image, *kashkha*, will dominate for the foreseeable future. Khalid Al-Dakhil, Saudi writer and professor of politics, argues that tribalism will take several decades to disappear as the state "uses tribal mechanisms for political ends" (Al-Dakhil, 2013).

Tribes had a class structure that remains infused in the Saudi culture: Bedouins looked down upon their *senaa* (manual laborers), leaders and their families neither intermingling nor marrying them. Bedouins held two competing values with regard to manual work: if a man voluntarily dug a trench to gather water for his family, this was admired and respected. Were he to do the same work for someone else, this was looked down upon lest he be viewed as a *senaa* member of society. The same work had two interpretations (A-Anezi, p. 84). Fighters were the most elite of Bedouins, but even they had levels of hierarchy. Above the regular forces of the tribe were the *hajanah* camel riders who normally earned twice that of a regular soldier, above him was the *khalayalah* (cavalry rider) who earned almost twice as much again, and the most elite were the 'chosen ones', the *al-mangeyah* (Mack, 1976: p. 17).

Tribal affiliation and hierarchy remain reasons for discrimination in the workforce today, preventing the most well-educated university graduates from suitable careers perhaps based solely upon his family name, which identifies his lineage, tribe, family background or historical profession. For example, the surname Obaid means 'little slave', Saatchi means 'watchmaker' and so on. Sometimes collective punishment can be taken against a sub-set of the population because of lineage: in 2005 Qatar revoked the citizenship of the entire Al Ghafran clan of the Al Murrah tribe claiming they had lived there illegally for 70 years.

After seventy-five years of a dominantly tribal ethic determining progress whilst marginalising large portions of Saudi citizens, fully aware that they can never truly integrate into top positions, there are rumblings of a return to tribal-loyalties over state patriotism.

"Bedouin culture is growing back and gaining strength, and people are returning to the roots and returning to family," said Faisal, a prominent member of the Ru'ala tribe of Northern Arabia. "Bedouins are the most resistant to pressures to conform to a uniform mentality, whereas the *hadar* (settled Arabs) were the most susceptible and weakest of the population. It is for this reason that they pose the most threat, the most likely to fall into the trap of the government of divided loyalties" (Al-Rueli, 2014). With three generations of promises of integration and equality for all Saudi citizens, if policies do not change in the short-term, the long-term backlash could be severe. The government may have already sensed this as they are actively seeking certain tribal members for key executive positions. By intentionally selecting those of the lowest ranks of the tribe they know these are the ones who have the least to lose and most to gain, assuming they will be more loyal to king rather than tribe, and will therefore counter any potential threat. Faisal added that this "shows how 'schizophrenic' they have now become." This argument is supported by Sultan Al-Qassemi, political lecturer at Dubai Men's College who wrote, "tribalism is likely to pose a challenge to the Peninsula States in their quest to advance from being 'developing nations.' Loyalty to leaders of states that are mere decades old can come into question…tribalism is a sort of elite club that outsiders can never truly belong to" (Al-Qassemi, 2014).

The Bedouin ethic has permeated Saudi culture to an extent undiluted in everyday matters. Even attempts by officials to communicate plans for the future are made during conference panel discussions that resemble *dewaniah*s rather than serious workshops. The tribal *majlis* (or *dewaniah*) culture became so important to Gulf states that it was one of the main launching pads of the civil society movement. Even the structure of parliament more often resembles the traditional *majlis* rather than effective parliamentary body. Tribal identity causes Saudis to look to pull away from the state in a reaction to economic prospects. "When the government causes the problems, they will be held accountable," Chas Freeman stated, and "a retreat to the tribe will occur. People will become sub-national and return back to their roots" (Freeman, 2014).

Islam

Dominant morals presented in Islam — of duty, hard work, responsibility, provision of sustenance and shelter — reinforced the essentials of Bedouin survivability. Equality superseded hierarchy, the prince no better than a pauper, and all men were considered capable of hard physical work unless sick or injured. The Prophet Muhammad was a shepherd and a merchant who worked for his wife Khadijah, his equally hard-working employer. After the new Muslims' emigration (*Hijra*) to Medina in 622 CE to escape persecution from the Meccans, the years were fraught with decreasing odds of survival. An anecdote recounts that the Prophet toiled so exhaustively to build the Muslims' new city that he tied slabs of stone onto his stomach to compress feelings of hunger (Ibn al-Qayyim, Vol. 1: 147). He urged Muslims to work to earn a living, reportedly saying: "Nobody has ever eaten a meal better than that which he has earned from working with his own hands." He further emphasised motivation and ambition stating, as narrated by Abu Bakr Al-Bazzar, "Help from Allah comes to the servant according to his diligence."

To impart the importance of personal responsibility, Anas ibn Malik related the story of the man who came to visit the Prophet on his most prized camel. Muhammad asked why he did not tie the animal securely, to which the man answered that he put his trust in Allah. The Prophet then responded, "Tie your camel first, and *then* put your trust in Allah".

Understanding the two inter-related issues of tribe and Islam enables comparison of the past to the present in order to devise a stronger policy direction for the future. Ambassador Chas Freeman commented on the distortion of Islamic values by adding, "If the state claims to be an excellent example of Islam, they should represent excellence as a state. King Abdullah talks about returning to pure Islam then do so. Return to the Salafi way, or hard work and virtuous labor. Reinterpret the Salafi narrative" (Freeman, 2014).

As Islam teaches the value of responsibility, ethics, hard work, diligence and sacrifice, only after all these efforts are exhausted can one be excused from blame. It is fallacious for Saudis today to therefore blame the lack of satisfactory jobs on external factors whilst excusing their own responsibility, and at the same time claim high standards of religious piety themselves.

Intentions, Pledges and Promises

Islam permeates almost every aspect of Saudi life at some level, and one of the most identifiable expressions is in his speech pattern. Intentions in the Arab world take on a different meaning that they would in the West. A Saudi often prefers *insha'Allah* (God willing) as an affirmative response to a question because, as narrated by Al-Mu'minin there is a chance that God might take him before he can deliver on his promise. Since God has ultimate control over events it can often be painful for many pious Saudis to confirm 'yes' in response to a simple commitment. Consequently his pride and religious commitment are at stake. This is significant as it is often misinterpreted, and the term can be over-utilised to avoid responsibility or deflect blame; many times it is genuinely in concern of blasphemy. Westerners particularly have trouble interpreting a Saudi's intent, as hearing *insha'Allah* can lead to frustration when they require a yes or no. It is necessary to gauge the person saying *insha'Allah*: he might mean yes, no, maybe, or never. This can only be determined in a face-to-face assessment to judge proximity, eye contact, gestures, tone and reliability, signalling nuances and subtleties in meaning that can lead to misunderstanding. The high context Arab communication style relies upon body language, touch, gesture, face-to-face interactions and volume to signal information, evident in its delivery and physical presentation. By contrast, the Westerner employs a low context style of clarity and precision that appears too straightforward and harsh to Gulf Arabs in particular. Arabic is florid and expressive whereas English is muted and precise. Imposing Western styles of communication to analyse Saudi intentions would be misguided. When interpreting Saudi leaders' promises for plans for the future, Saudis might maintain scepticism whereas Westerners might already be drawing up proposals to meet potential needs on their behalf, running budgets and booking plane tickets.

Americans interviewed for a study held that Saudis were incapable of expressing an idea "clearly and concisely" (Adelman & Lustig, 1981; *op. cit.* Feghali, 1997, pp. 345–378). Arab delivery styles are often circuitous and indirect, preferring pleasant and agreeable — perhaps less relevant — conversation rather than a factual direct response that can be embarrassing and distressing to deliver. This can be problematic: Arabs do not respond to direct questions easily, seen as a sign of confrontation, and silence serves as a psychological retreat so as to contemplate a measured response. Americans' direct 'let's get down to business' style can cause significant discomfort for the Saudis, and has resulted in turbulent intercultural professional relations over the decades (Cohen, 1987; *op. cit.* Feghali, pp. 345–378). Westerners visiting the Kingdom mistake *Insha'Allah* as an indication that they may be forgotten, often leaving the Arab world angered after a long expensive journey without an agreement, unable to understand why their Arab counterparts are loathe to commit. Interpreting Saudi announcements that promise the completion of a project with a specific time will inevitably lead to revision by the Westerner perplexed that commitments cannot be made within a specific time. The Saudi sees nothing wrong in his behaviour, as he was hospitable, gracious, and polite, and gave the businessman his valuable time. His intention was pure; his follow up commitment is dubious. The Saudi, when he has made his decision, will let the Westerner know when it is final and, he might assume, this will be well received. Meanwhile, the Westerner will have written a lengthy report on his annoyance at having wasted his time in Saudi Arabia, now prepared to take his business elsewhere because 'time is money'. When the Saudi has considered, debated, and ruminated on the proposal, he finds he is too late and his project is delayed whilst he searches for another contractor to fulfil the promise he has already announced publicly.

Time Perception

Time to Arabs is a reference point only, and in Saudi Arabia is measured at a glacial pace. Although Westerners are often impressed with Arab generosity, the greatest gift an Arab can grant a visitor is time. Western businessmen, for example, often find an expected confidential meeting frequently interrupted with telephone calls or visits from a secretary or even another visitor, and is put off by the Saudi attitude towards delaying his own pre-scheduled time.

Individual attitudes towards time are learnt from personal experiences, collectively attitudes towards time influence national destinies. Psychologist Philip Zimbardo, known for his Stanford Prison Experiment, has long examined various concepts of time, culminating with his analysis in *The Time Paradox: The New Psychology of Time.* (Zimbardo, 1972 & 2007; Zimbardo *et al.*, 1973) In the late eighties, Zimbardo and his team initiated an experiment on Time Perception (Zimbardo, 2008). Testing four-year-olds as to their powers of patience and gratification, he gave them a simple quiz and offered them one sweet immediately, or two sweets if they could wait and not eat the first for a few minutes.

The overwhelming majority of children were simply unable to delay gratification and ate the first sweet immediately. Fourteen years later the same children were evaluated to determine if their concepts of time affected their characters (Zimbardo, 2010). Those who had waited for their rewards scored an average of 258 points higher on their SAT scores, were self-reliant and confident, co-operative, worked well under pressure, and exhibited "all the necessary traits of the most successful candidates for future professional success." From this early test, Zimbardo's study divided people into six Time Perception zones (Past Positive, Past Negative, Present Positive, Present Negative, Future Positive, and Future Negative), which can be applied to nations and populations to determine how they behave.

Zones of Time Perspective Inventory (ZTPI)

Past Positive	Past Negative
Happy, friendly, grounded, high self-esteem	Nostalgia overrides present
Nostalgic, ritualistic, patriotic, religious; Strong identity to family and ancestry	Prone to guilt, depression, trauma
Focused on stories and poetry, victories in wars, fate (e.g., *insha'Allah* / God wills it); Little urge to act or initiate change today	Retaliatory, vengeful
Creative, cheerful; Thinks 'outside the box'	Hedonistic, indecisive, risk-taking; Low-impulse control, angry, over-reactive
Improvisational, embraces challenges	Easily addicted to drugs, alcohol, gambling, cigarettes Prone to high anxiety, depression, aggression, jealousy and envy
Puts stock in 'wings of hope'	Generally financially poorer, lives in the present relying upon 'hope'
Controls impulses and ego, non-aggressive, energetic, non-sensation seeking	Low control of ego, low energy, low emotional development
Keeps promises, conscientious, consistent, social, explorative	Wary, isolated, little regard for others
Decisive, strategic, persistent; Delays gratification	Lives in the negative past to shape future events (i.e., what happened before cannot be repeated)
High achievers, future planners; Problem solvers, anticipates consequences	Controlling, dominant, high depression and anxiety rates, pressure of expectations

The children who delayed reward all fell into the Future Positive category as young adults. Future oriented people — or nations — are the most successful as long as there were optimal balances between other zones. *Past Oriented* people distance themselves from the realities of the present or future, are conservative, mistrustful of strangers or foreigners, focus on collective or personal commitments (cultural or tribal obligations), employ rituals, and as a group tend to be dependent rather than competitive. Other determining factors amongst *Present Oriented* people include a focus on emotions and feelings, and emphasis instant gratification and emergent needs of the present. The hedonistic era of the sixties' hippie generation and its drugs, alcohol, live-for-the moment movement that spread in the West exemplifies the Present Oriented. Only *Future Oriented* people succeed despite obstacles, as they conceived responsibility, efficiency and hard work optimized future outcomes whereas distractions and wasted time diminish accomplishments. This group also saves their resources and takes care of their long-term health.

Using Saudi Arabia's collective and established traits as a nation in a rudimentary experiment to generate a snapshot of the culture — which Zimbardo clarifies is as possible as with individuals — test results show a substantial imbalance in its characterization of Time Perception and inverse to the average Present time balance. Compared to optimal outcomes where Past, Present and Future Positives score highly, Saudi Arabia has a proportionately opposite score on Present Positive perceptions of time, whereas most Westerners (and nations) drop sharply into the Past Negative zone. Scores revealed the Kingdom controlled by an overwhelming lack of focus on Future concepts, instead deeply rooted in the past. So drastic where the results, they had to be re-run twice to plot more accurate levels (ZTPI. 2008). Without knowing Zimbardo's precise scaling method, it is nevertheless possible to estimate perceptions:

Time Perspectives — Normal vs. Saudi Arabia (Theorized)

Ranges: PN Low to High 1.4–4.7; PP 2–4.56; PrN 2.67–4.65; PrP 1.11–4.67; F 1.31–4.15; FP 1.4–5

Normal Average:		**Saudi Arabia's Average:**	
Past Negative	2.1	Past Negative	2.7
Past Positive	3.67	Past Positive	4.56
Present Negative (Hedonistic)	4.33	Present Negative (Hedonistic)	4.07
Present Positive (Fatalistic)	1.67	Present Positive (Fatalistic)	4.67
Future	3.69	Future	1.31
Future Positive (Assumed)	3.4	Future Positive (Assumed)	5

Source: http://www.thetimeparadox.com/surveys/

It can be of no surprise that a weighted score on the Past Positive is evident, although the significantly below expected Future Oriented result is troublesome. Test results did not generate a Future Transcendental score but this category is defined to include those who are fatalistic, spiritual, religious, and base life on the belief that there is an afterlife. It is safe to assume this trait dominates in the case of Saudi Arabia and would thus produce a significantly high score. This enterprise demonstrates the benefits of an investment in detailed research into the psychology of Saudis and the contrasts and similarities between tribal, Islamic and modern-era traits that influence modern cultural behaviors and policy decisions today.

Nostalgia is an admirable trait in nations as long as other factors are observable and it is self-evident that Saudi Arabia is proud of its history. Nevertheless, as Nietzsche also observed, "An excess of history harms the living person."

China as an Example of Cultural Reversal

Comparisons to other countries are worth considering as international ethics and time perceptions are helpful when considering a country's functionality, and German economic sociologist Max Weber — who coined the phrase 'Protestant Ethic' to describe the hard work and self-reliance of the more prosperous Protestant countries — is well known. This paper will only introduce one example of a nation that successfully reversed its traditional work ethics.

In the nineteenth century China had similar work ethics to the Saudis today, with their motto 'just about' similar to the Arabic *insha'Allah.* In order to compete globally the country realized it had to force change upon itself. By employing harsh measures to reverse a potential catastrophe, China switched to a system of efficiency, punctuality and responsibility. This was a choice during an era of socialist labor reforms but before Communism, to prevent a sizeable and increasing population from deprivation. The Chinese began a mass effort to denigrate the intellectuals of society and promote manual labor. Although the bourgeoisie were shunned, literacy and intellectuals were not: China has always placed a high value on literature.

Every Chinese man and woman experienced this work ethic transformation, the young keenly aware of the efforts their parents contributed to society, the values instilled into this generation. Consequently the new overnight post-Communist millionaires — like their Soviet peers — understood the reward granted hard labor, whether in a field, factory, or future construction project. Wages are now increasing rapidly because of this infused diligence and the country is growing economically into a powerhouse.

Saudi Arabia in the present can learn from the strengths and weaknesses of these other cultures, and retain the positive ethics of the past to apply relevant lessons to today. Status should not be exclusive to the elite, and instead should be gained from merit and active middle-class citizenship. "The change should be built around Islamic virtues, traditional virtues, family virtues, but clearly it isn't and hasn't been," said Chas Freeman.

Education

One of the root causes of underemployment in Saudi Arabia is the lack of education. It is not a shortage of university graduates; it is the fact that 46% of them are unemployed. More than two-thirds of undergraduates hold theoretical academic degrees that offer no vocational skills, the remainder science graduates (Fakkar 2013). With 63% of Saudi universities focused on the social sciences and Islamic studies, they are left ill equipped for the labor market upon graduation (Sfakianakis, March 2014). Many represent 'diplomatitis' — earning the diploma to gain social status but failing to acquire practical abilities for the private sector (IMF Survey 2014). As ambitious as many Saudis are at university, the dearth of prospects upon leaving produces a 'youth bulge'. In 2010, Saudi nationals accounted for just 2.7% of auxiliary basic engineering jobs, and 6.9% of industrial, chemical or food industry jobs (Saudi Hollandi, 2012). This confirms the misplaced extraction from the economy as it directs funds towards more universities when the country urgently requires building vocational schools and colleges instead. A better solution would be to lessen the importance on personally named mega-universities and converting them into more practical training facilities. "The greatest schools in the world are not necessarily those housed in plush buildings," wrote general manager of Al-Arabiya television Abdulrahman Al-Rashed. "The world's most important universities are not as fancy as ours, which are more akin to five-star hotel" (Al-Rashed 2014).

During this process foreign workers will still be required perhaps for the next 30–40 years, which Saudis may perceive as highlighting their failure to address the situation earlier. As it stands, only 9% of high-school graduates are enrolled in technical or vocational training colleges compared to a global average of 40% (Sfakianakis, March 2014). These options are still viewed with disdain, as a second-class choice, advertising a 'failed' status within the community.

Saudi national oil company Aramco, and petrochemical manufacturer SABIC have led the way on training qualified nationals in the Kingdom, and are investing in training programs of state owned enterprises. Yet more 'academies', joint international training ventures, internships and scholarships programs are required to establish a nation of technicians and managers. Additionally, in a conservative culture, online training can circumvent much embarrassment registered by Saudis, especially for women. To date, out of an education budget of SR 211 billion ($56 billion), only SR 1 billion has been allocated towards e-learning. Al-Rashed believes, "the real crime in education lies not in the attempt to hijack it, nor in the dilapidated buildings in which it takes place—it is worse than that. It is the neglect of development, whether due to the ignorance of those responsible for education, or the lack of attention paid to it. Progress stopped such a long time ago that it has become part of history, a part not in harmony with the sciences and the needs of modern times (Al-Rashed, 2014).

A massive injection of funds was, however, granted to increase full foreign scholarships for students, currently exceeding 120,000, half for study in the United States. Under the

King Abdullah Scholarship Program, full tuition, a monthly stipend for the student plus any spouse and children, medical and dental coverage, annual round-trip tickets for the students and their family, private or additional academic tuition costs, textbook allowances, and special needs assistance if required, is provided. The cost for one undergraduate for four years in an American university ranges from $80,000 to $160,000 for university expenses alone, depending on whether a public or private school (US Dept. of Education 2012). The Kingdom has thus apportioned approximately $12 billion for the 151,000 full scholarships in 2014, which contributes more than $3 billion into the US economy per year (Hsu *et al.*, 2007).

Impediments to Reform in Saudi Arabia

Considerations must include some of the most challenging impediments to a national attitude change. Bureaucracy, fraud, *wasta*, women's roles, and increasing living costs demand immediate solutions that are outside the scope of this paper. In brief, examples are provided.

Bureaucracy

Perhaps the greatest impediment to changing the dynamic of youth unemployment and motivation is bureaucracy, as at every level inefficiency and endless delegation prevents the country from performing at optimal conditions. Hertog referred to these bureaucracies as 'pathologies', and wrote that state owned enterprises were overstaffed, sluggish, and corrupt, and muddled in accounting, politicisation, and chronic inefficiencies (Hertog, 2012; pp. 124, 126). Primary jobs in well-paid government positions are a magnet, ensuring the least work with the greatest stability, and remain the most sought after by 97% of the Saudis surveyed (Al-Anazi, 2011 pp. 56–80). Nepotism is often used to secure positions not gained through academic qualifications, and *wasta* (favours) is routine. Saudis understand that this is a price to pay for assistance and connections.

The Arabian habit of not being critical perpetuates the problem due to the backlash to those who report corruption: the proximity of those in powerful positions is unknown. With non-existent transparency or accountability, the message communicated to Saudis is one that more intensely drives them to refuse any but a lucrative public sector position — not for the perquisites afforded, but the corruption opportunity it affords. There is validity to the argument that within a culture unused to public critique, any favoritism or benefits would be removed by the government if real debate and analyses on these matters took place, as has been shown to occur on a frequent basis.

Fraud

The sale of fraudulent diplomas is a thriving business in the Kingdom, easily purchased for less than the cost of a mobile telephone. A Bachelor's degree costs approximately SR1,000, a Master's degree SR 1,200, a PhD can be purchased for SR 1,400, and SR 1,600 will provide

Professor certification. Public exposure of corruption and private sector fraud occurs on a daily basis due to the anonymity offered by social media (Al-Maeena, February 2014). Recently, 30 private schools were found to be involved in fabricating false statistics. Their records indicated that the schools employed over 2000 Saudi teachers to meet *Saudization* employment quotas, although none actually existed. The government paid the schools SR 2500 per month in assistance per Saudi employed, plus an average monthly salary of SR 2000 for the invisible teachers (Knickmeyer 2014). Where is the SR 165,000 going instead and why is this not a priority?

Many Saudis too often find it 'acceptable' to plagiarise from the Internet, pay professionals to complete student work assignments, use phones or hide notes to cheat during exams, and copy from other classmates (Al-Maeena, February 2014). Parents abet in some cases, and pass on their own notes from their own degrees to their children, who are awarded their own degree for the same subject. Some teachers are bribed (under *wasta*) by students for passing grades; teachers likewise can select students to fail if they so choose.

The state must be transparent, accountable and fair, and consequences must be implemented to those perpetuating the practice of corruption or cheating.

Rising Cost of Living Expenses

A shortage of affordable housing and rapidly rising living costs ranks high on the list of concerns for young adults. With little low to middle-class housing available, 70% of Saudis cannot afford to marry and start a new life (Al-Maeena, February 2014). Pressures for expensive weddings and dowries require years of saving, yet 30% of Saudis have no savings at all (Albawaba, 2014). Government pledges to alleviate housing shortages have produced little: King Abdullah ordered $70 billion to be allocated towards the construction of entry-level homes in 2011, yet after three years there has been almost no evolvement in this construction.

Those who own homes increasingly find expenses stretched to their limits, and even with two incomes per household couples find it hard to make ends meet (Al-Maeena, March 2014). Electricity usage in the Kingdom now registers as the highest in the world, the average household consuming twice that of international counterparts (Peninsula Times, 2014). There is also a shortage of natural gas, SABIC regularly complaining that it cannot get enough to meet demand (Woertz, 2013). With virtually no public transportation in Saudi Arabia, car costs are high, fuel prices are increasing by 4% per year, and the Kingdom now consumes 25% of its oil production annually. Infrastructure cannot keep pace with traffic flow demands, thus petrol is wasted from idling on clogged roads. Since women cannot drive, a second car plus a foreign driver must be provided to transport her, with the added cost- burden to the ex-pat of wages, accommodation, food, and travel expenses. Second and third vehicles also present an even greater challenge as the country tackles energy costs, from both an economic and ethical basis.

Female Employment

Despite their high levels of education and career-orientation aspirations, unemployment disproportionately affects women, and the most educated suffer the greatest cost (Shediac & Samman, 2010 6–28). Capable and aware, few incentives are available for the more than 70% of female university graduates; jobs available tend to be confined to the health and education sectors. Moreover, women earn between SR 5,000 and SR 9,000 per month, on average 20% less than their male counterparts (Aziz, 2014). Women comprise 50% of the labor market in Kuwait, close to the world average of 56%; by contrast in Saudi Arabia only 18% are employed (Shediac & Samman, 2010 10–28). All those interviewed by this author agreed that women are more willing to work than their male counterparts, complained less, and held a stronger work ethic. Despite the assumption, women do not need permission from a male guardian for employment, nor to travel within the country. On the positive side the reality of economic problems confronting young Saudis today ought to prompt the government to reconsider its lukewarm encouragement of women's participation in all sectors, and accommodate traditional sensibilities that comport to a conservative Islamic culture.

Conclusion

The United Nations estimates that the Saudi population will explode from 28 million (2010), to 54 million by 2050, requiring hundreds of thousands of new jobs (Shediac & Samman, 2010 4–28). *Saudization* and Nitaqat have failed to impress thus far, and the Kingdom cannot afford to return millions of foreign workers and expect unwilling Saudis to meet the void. There is a mismatch between qualifications and demand for highly ranked jobs based upon a false notion of status and culturally endemic expectations and communications that hinders economic growth. The slowness of reform is not aided by the strong adherence to past tribal ethics at the expense of future generations. Both young and old Saudis believe that if they do not achieve high status in the workforce they will cease to become effective or respected members of Saudi society. This sense of superiority over others was ideally to have eroded with the advent of Islam, but concerning employment, it is apparent that tribalism remains the driving ethos.

Female employment is a ready-made partial solution, but the culture has far to go before their inclusion becomes acceptable despite their academic achievements lest they exemplify 'diplomatitis'. Pouring billions of dollars into scholarships for overseas study must be met by guaranteed jobs upon students' return or a least a serious effort to modify their skills with further training. With little openness or transparency the Saudi system from bottom to top will further deteriorate; there must be an efficient transformation to punish corruption and reward transparency. The argument that 'this is the way it has always been done' cannot survive. One Saudi businessman cogently asserts, "Saudi Arabia is not ready for prime time at any level. The culture is unfit for modern times".

Whether root causes are due to lack of connections, the *wasta* system, family name, tribe, status-desires or lack of employment ethics, the failure to address the issue of underemployment and unemployment decades ago has magnified the problem to such an extent it is difficult to see a reassuring short-term outcome to the quagmire long ago created. In sum, without radical economic changes the Kingdom faces radical threats to its very survival.

11

Setting the Agenda for Global Dialogue: A Theoretical and Practical Approach to Business Ethics in Saudi Arabia

David Cowan

Introduction: The Saudi Challenge

I take as my starting point Saudi Arabia in order to ground the discussion in a concrete way, but the themes and actions discussed here are relevant across the Gulf region and indeed the Islamic community as a whole, and address the alignment and conflict of values that present themselves in our era of globalization. Saudi Arabia is a nation that recognizes, as others in the region do, that the future presents some very specific economic challenges, and companies are planning for the next 10 years and beyond in the face of twin pressures of changes to the economic base and the need to support a growing population. Major companies in Saudi, like Dallah Al-Baraka Group, the Kingdom Holding Company, the Saad Group, SABIC and Saudi Aramco are aware they face great challenges as companies operating on an international scale, with some sensing the need to make changes which will make them global companies based in Saudi rather than Saudi companies with an international business.

Part of being a global company today involves demonstrating leadership as a global corporate citizen, and this in turn means embracing a set of values and ethics that are deemed normative by international standards, and they must reach deep into the organization. A major aspect of how these values and ethics are to work is engagement with the employee base. To become a Saudi company that stands equally with other global companies therefore requires a workforce that embraces a set of international values and ethics. I believe this presents a challenge for Saudi companies. Company values and ethics will only work if employees feel connected to the values and ethical standards of the company, and achieving this is not as straightforward as one might think, because at the individual level employees may have their own values, ethics and faith outside of the workplace, and at the organizational level a company operates within the context of national laws, values and norms.

In this paper, I will first look at the notion of a global corporate citizen and examine this question in the context of Saudi Arabia. I will examine business ethics and morality by questioning the normative status of business ethics, and how different cultures and religions, in this instance Saudi and Islamic, engage with business ethics. I want, in part, to understand whether an Islamic approach challenges notions of what is in fact normative, and whether there is an arrogant assumption that "West knows best."

Globalization of the "Good Corporate Citizen" Concept

Corporate Social Responsibility, known as CSR or simply CR, is a growing area in the business world, with positions often filled by people who have been protesting from the outside as NGO employees and activists. It is part of an expectation today that businesses will seek to be good corporate citizens and be ethically responsible, meeting a range of legal, ethical and economic demands placed on them by various stakeholders, not just their shareholders. Businesses today are expected to show leadership in the community by raising standards of living and the quality of life in the communities in which they operate, while still staying in business. This has become part of "the brand" and impacts their share performance and customer loyalty. Being socially responsible has also become part of the appeal to employees. This is a significant step change in capitalist economies, where hitherto the simple focus has been on profitability, often at any price. There is not time here to engage in the question of what the balance should be between CSR issues and profit, but for Saudi and other countries like it, and those in the developing world, building a business now also means being a CSR company, being ethical and being a good global corporate citizen. This puts the question of the role of ethics central to the discussion of business in our globalized economy, especially in light of the recession of 2008/09, but what does this mean in fact?

On Our Best Behaviour: Normative Ethics

To answer this I want to look first at to what extent international business ethics are normative, and assess how this fits with behaviour in organizations and cultures in practice. Theory, as we all know, is a beautiful thing. In business, in practice, there is a difference between the theory of business ethics and the way it is understood and implemented in the business setting. In my experience working with many different business organizations globally, business ethics is programmatic, undertaken literally as the implementation of a specific program. It often involves ticking the boxes, and setting up various committees which take the whole thing very seriously only to find there is little organizational appetite or enthusiasm for what they are doing. The ethics, CSR and communications people send out a message, put up a poster and create a process. However, it is sporadic, with the occasional outburst of enthusiasm by the leadership for the topic, but generally does not translate so well into actual decision-making and internal behaviours. Beyond awareness campaigns that ensure people know at least there is a policy in place, most managers and employees don't want to spend a lot of time thinking about it beyond the knowledge it exists.

Much of what does get traction in business ethics is really the more tangible stuff. By which I mean, the legal requirements, the audit trail and compliance needs. The stuff that can be readily implemented and understood, and failing to comply or obey might just find you out of a job. We may happily conclude this is no bad thing. After all, organizations are places of rationality and utility; places of duties and obligations. What is most robust in business organizations is the legalism, the playing by the rules as much as one has to, but it does not necessarily translate into a behavioural pattern in organizations. It is much more of an intellectual assent or conformance to legalism. Business ethics are not part of the DNA of the business strategy, except perhaps as part of the mission and values statement of the organization or the PR needs. What I am saying is that no-one is really agonizing over ethics. In short, my view of business ethics and CSR in organizations is a little like Dr Johnson's remark about a dog walking on its back legs: it is not done very well, but one is surprised it is done at all. My observation may appear cynical, perhaps even unfair, but I would say the same is true of many ethical messages and their intended audiences, it's got a name: lip-service.

Theories of Business Ethics

The roots of modern business ethics lie in the 1970s, so it is still a developing discipline. It is a discipline that coincides with postmodernity and the pluralism of ethical standards. To analyse this question, business ethicists have developed a theoretical base, with the core debate in business ethics being the shareholder/stakeholder debate. I want to explore this debate through the lens of three normative theories (Arnold, Audi, and Zwolinski, 2010; and Hasnas) that have been proposed to answer this question. They are:

1. Shareholder theory (Friedman, 2009)
2. Stakeholder theory (Freeman, 1984)
3. Social Contract theory (Donaldson, 1982)

The **Shareholder theory** looks at business organizations as economic organizations of people and interests, and the objective is to achieve shareholder value according to the overall direction of shareholders and the board, leaving managers to act under this direction and achieve these objectives. I would also call this the economic realist approach. This approach assumes positively the economy benefits from the aggregated and nebulous outcome of all this economic activity, in part explained by Adam Smith's oft-quoted but equally oft-misunderstood "invisible hand."(Grampp, 2000). Business ethicists today do not like this theory, and for most it is put forward as a straw man to provoke a more "enlightened" view of business ethics, which happens to be whatever position they advocate.

The **Stakeholder theory** covers how managers should approach balancing the interests of various stakeholders in the business, which includes the general public as well as employees, political bodies and others in addition to the shareholders. It is posited that others have a stake in the firm because it affects their community, the environment, power structures, and so on. The interests of various stakeholders may often conflict, and at base the shareholder desire for a profit may conflict with the interest of the local community in terms of jobs, pollution or other concerns. More radical versions of this theory argue there is a societal dimension to the utility of the business, which is fulfilled by business being a true partner with pubic bodies and civil society.

The **Social Contract theory** shares much of what is said of the stakeholder theory, but proponents go further and suggest there is essentially an obligation that business should enhance the welfare of society. In this view, business is given legitimacy by society at large and in return they should provide employment, look after the natural resources and support the community.

Having suggested the practical problems, I want to highlight that these theories suggest there is a conflict about what it is a business is supposed to do, which will determine what we think the ethical demands of business consist of. The shareholder theory highlights the interests of the owners of capital and business, operating legally and rationally to create a successful and sustainable business. The stakeholder theory suggests there is balance between the business interests and the welfare of various stakeholders, internal and external to the organization. The social contract theory puts the business at the service of society, the reversal of the shareholder theory. I suggest in practice, most business leaders operate according to the shareholder theory, but allow for the stakeholder theory out of pragmatic awareness of image and reputation. The social contract theory is one embraced by those who oppose the market capitalism of our era. I do not intend to adjudicate on this issue, simply to highlight them at this stage (see Beekun, Badawi, 2000).

A Global Business Ethic?

Today, we live in a globalized, interconnected international market system that makes the concerns we are addressing even more complex, and probably even less prosaic. If we are uncomfortable with the shareholder theory and a business world left to its own devices, we should not exaggerate the current situation. Businesses are subjected to many laws and rules, and greater transparency is expected of them than we see in government or civil society. Businesses accept this and even Milton Friedman accepted the need for a regulatory role, albeit more akin to a referee ensuring fair play rather than an interventionist approach. This is not to absolve business of wrong-doing or defend the great scandals of recent times, only to put them in some context. The reality is that these scandals came to light, not because of protests or idealism, but because of the less prosaic actions of internal processes, external auditors and market reaction. The protests came after. Our global economy is one in which it is now expected big companies will sign up for a raft of international standards of law, compliance and ethics. The flagship activity is the UN Global Compact, though one can ponder whether this essentially amounts to companies simply agreeing to a very broad shopping list of legal, compliance and ethical standards. To what extent companies sign up for the Global Compact, or other such voluntary ethical standards, for reasons of PR and popular pressure, rather than a conviction, is moot.

The Compact consists of ten principles, in the areas of human rights, labor, the environment and anti-corruption which enjoy universal consensus and are derived from the Universal Declaration of Human Rights, the International Labor Organization's Declaration on Fundamental Principles and Rights at Work, the Rio Declaration on Environment and Development, and, the United Nations Convention Against Corruption. To quote the UN Global Compact directly, they ask companies "to embrace, support and enact, within their sphere of influence, a set of core values in the areas of human rights, labor standards, the environment and anti-corruption."

I will raise two concerns here. First, my own experience of working with CEOs of multinational companies is that these things are certainly secondary to the business of profit-maximisation. There is an increasing trend among CEOs to argue sustainability means not so much CSR and ethics but keeping the business around for the next ten years and beyond. At best, we may say the business approach is aligned with the stakeholder theory, under pressure from a civil society that pushes the social contract theory. The second concern with these standards is they ignore or gloss over the competitive realities of doing business. They are insufficient in dealing with the disconnect between the norms of the actor's home country and the country in which they are doing business, thus they do not really cross the boundary unless both domestic sets of laws are akin. In respect to developing and related nations, the global rules tend to privilege the notions of justice and right that exists in developed nations. For an American company doing business in Western Europe there is likely to be agreement, but for the American company doing business in Saudi Arabia then there will be a difference to consider, and global rules will favor America over Saudi.

However, the two are getting closer together. Since 2006, the Emirates Environmental Group (EEG) has been engaged as a focal point in extending the influence and membership base of the Global Compact in the Arabian Gulf Region. The top businesses in Saudi, such as SABIC and Saudi Aramco, have signed up for the UN Global Compact. Yet, if we take a closer look at the UN Global Compact standards as they apply to Saudi Arabia, we can see that international bodies are critical of Saudi Arabia as a nation, especially in respect to human rights and gender. The 2013 Amnesty International Report on Saudi Arabia states:

> The authorities severely restricted freedoms of expression, association and assembly and clamped down on dissent. Government critics and political activists were detained without trial or sentenced after grossly unfair trials. Women were discriminated against in law and practice and inadequately protected against domestic and other violence. Migrant workers were exploited and abused. Sentences of flogging were imposed and carried out. Hundreds of people were on death row at the end of the year; at least 79 people were executed (Amnesty International, 2013).

The question becomes, to what extent are companies culpable? The flip side, is to ask to what extent companies as good citizens can make change in their home country? Business is not going to solve these problems directly, especially in a place like Saudi where the major businesses are either part government-owned or have close ties to government and the royal family. Things are difficult enough at the political level, as a 2014 visit to Saudi Arabia by President Obama (Shear, 2014) demonstrates, where it was reported that the President ended his trip to Saudi with a brief private ceremony in which he presented an International Women of Courage award to a Saudi woman who works to prevent domestic violence in the kingdom. This "came a day after the president chose not to raise the issue of human rights during a two-hour discussion with King Abdullah of Saudi Arabia" (Shear, 2014). What hope has a business?

Equally, if a foreign business is operating in another country, to what extent do they respect the local norms and culture? This is quite clear as an issue in the case of gender in Saudi. From a global stance, women have a severely limited role in business. They cannot drive to work. They generally cannot work alongside male colleagues, instead having a partitioned section for their offices. Often basics are not well provided for, such as restrooms which may be some distance away from an office or meeting room. Women are required to wear the abaya and hijab to work. Foreign women are excused some of this control, but even then they are severely limited compared to the freedoms they are used to at home or in most other countries, and need to be chaperoned by male colleagues. This is changing a little, but it is slow. This presents a problem for foreign companies operating locally, both in the locality and at home. To illustrate this difficulty, we can look at a story involving the Swedish furniture multinational IKEA (Quinn, 2012), which ran into trouble in KSA when they released a local version of their catalogue which photo-shopped women out of the global catalog. This became known in Sweden and the news went viral, causing the company to apologize and explain that excluding women from the Saudi Arabian version of the catalog was in conflict with the IKEA Group values (Wharton, 2012). What was right in Saudi was condemned by public opinion in their home nation and abroad. So, let us look a little more deeply into culture and Saudi.

Building Organizational Culture in Saudi Arabia: The Challenges

Global companies are trying to build culture, but we can ask which culture? In which case, does a Saudi company impose a Saudi culture on its global operations or impose a global culture on its Saudi home base? Happily, we do not need to opt for an either/or solution, because I argue there is no such thing as a corporate culture, only cultures within the body corporate:

> The monolithic idea of a corporate culture is undermined by the reality that there are a range of issues of personality, class, education, religion, other beliefs, interests and self-interests which are simply too large and impactful to delude us into thinking there is such a thing as corporate culture (Cowan, 2014).

What a company has to do is create a harmony of values and ethics amongst cultures within the organization, and hence my advice to Saudi companies is to strike a cultural balance. The global challenge is to recognize the need to harmonize a set of different cultures that exists within an organization at all levels and geographically. A headquartered Saudi company presents challenges in terms of entrenching values in a global company, and also in creating dialogue globally across the organization in order to create a coherent set of cultures. It also presents problems in respect to the other parts of the world which are reporting to it as the summit of leadership. This is particularly obvious in areas such as gender issues, but also in terms of empowerment and leadership. There are challenges that are both practical, such as skill shortages, and in certain behaviours, such as time management of project delivery and the sense of Inshallah. Harmonizing cultures connects to the issue of being a good corporate citizen, and can be an effective way to build employee interest as a means to connect the cultures, whilst enabling differences to remain. If one realizes a monolithic culture is not the goal then we can find a truly multicultural organization that will resonate with employees.

However, aiming to become a good global citizen also means recognizing there remain some norms and conflicts globally which need to be addressed. This paper has highlighted the problem of ethics, and in the conclusion I will propose in outline some avenues for dialogue, which recognizes the range of cultures, or sub-cultures, that exist within an organization. In the Saudi context it is, I suggest, essential to understand that business ethics as understood by most international companies and in the vast array of business schools are grounded in a Christian vision which have undergone a process of secularization. This begs the question, what will happen with Islamic ethical ideas that are rooted in different soil or sand? I do not propose to offer final answers to such complexity; rather I want to set out a five point agenda for dialogue about global ethics and religion in business that may take us closer to these answers.

Where the West looks to ethics without religion, in Saudi religion is at the heart of ethical discussion. The Saudi constitution is clear and the "Basic Law of Governance"

(Royal Embassy of Saudi Arabia, 2013) sets out the legal basis of the Kingdom. It states in Article 1:

> The Kingdom of Saudi Arabia is a sovereign Arab Islamic State. Its religion is Islam. Its constitution is Almighty God's Book, The Holy Qur'an, and the Sunna (Traditions) of the Prophet (PBUH). Arabic is the language of the Kingdom. The City of Riyadh is the capital.

In this respect, regard for the rule of law, in the form of Sharia, is high. when it comes to activities such as drug smuggling and terrorism, and activities directed against the state or the royal household, one can quickly find law and process overridden by state action. For our purposes specifically, the interesting part of the Basic Law is how it defines the economy. Article 22 of the Basic Law states "Economic and social development shall be carried out according to a fair, wise plan."

As stated at the outset, there is a lot for Saudi to worry about economically, yet the law demands economic challenges to be handled "according to a fair, wise plan." The current plan is an interesting one that seeks to grapple with some fundamental problems, such as a growing younger population that is less skilled and used to a welfare principle that cannot possibly support them much longer. It's obvious, but the source of Saudi's wealth is oil. However, there is concern that oil will become less dependable as a wealth creator. Saudi has, because of the oil wealth, been able to subsidize a great many things in society, and the population has been used to them. Imagine the former Soviet Union with wealth, and you might get the picture. Like the Soviet Union, there is a danger of implosion, albeit it at a much slower rate. The plan horizon is not Stalin's five year plans, but 2020 and 2025, which represent timelines that converge between the demands on the economy by the growing and young population, the pressing problems of food and water to sustain the population, and, the perceived impact of alternative energy sources to challenge oil. Ahmed Zaki Yamani, the one-time Oil minister, quipped that the Stone Age didn't end because of a shortage of stone, meaning that the oil age, and certainly Saudi's privileged position because of oil, will not end because of a shortage of oil but because of other factors (qtd. in Lippman, 2012).

Concerns about 2020 and 2025, and if not the end of the oil age at least a more competitive environment, are creating a dynamic of tension. To change requires a more international outlook, but does it mean it has to become more Western or less Islamic? Saudi Arabia is attempting to establish a modern business culture while grappling with globalization's challenges to Islamic teaching and Arabic social values. Saudi political and businesses leaders are acutely aware that the Saudi economy needs, on the one hand, to diversify, while on the other needs to become more self-reliant, in terms of skills and resources. As a wealth creation resource, oil was found and extracted by foreigners. My reason for mentioning this is that the Saudis basically had oil-based wealth handed to them on a platter, which suggests there was no sense of pioneering for wealth or manifest destiny of national growth, and there was no Protestant work ethic. They have long relied on expat expertise and management, and it is only comparatively recently they have sought increased self-reliance.

To illustrate further the challenges Saudi faces, I want to draw attention to four specific dynamics, namely:

1. Saudization
2. Gender
3. Inshallah
4. Religion

This is not an exhaustive list, but one that draws out some key practicalities.

Saudization

Since the discovery of oil wealth, Saudi has had a high level of dependency on expatriate skills, knowledge and workers. The policy in Saudi today is to decrease this dependency and build its own skill base, and many young people have been funded to go to foreign universities, principally in the US, to gain the skills and knowledge necessary for a new generation of Saudi leaders and managers. Another policy goes under the name of Saudization. This is the process of ensuring all businesses in Saudi employ Saudis, based on a percentage formula according to size; a similar process is going on elsewhere in Qatar, UAE, etc. It dates back to 2004, but was stepped up in 2013, with tens of thousands leaving voluntarily or being deported, encouraged with an amnesty offered to many workers; hence 5.2 million expats legalized their status during the amnesty period. Most of those who left or were deported were laborers, so the immediate effect was that many public works projects were halted temporarily because they didn't have the labor force to work on the.

The idea is to create self-reliance, but in reality there is a great skills shortage, and of course there are many jobs the Saudis don't wish to do. Saudis in the private sector amount to 1.26 million employees out of a total 8.7 million, that's one-eighth of the working population, and only a minority of this is women. The education minister Prince Faisal bin Abdullah has admitted that "Saudization and employment is not the solution... The solution lies in creating job opportunities. How can we do that? By developing the economy and expanding areas of work for Saudis to become productive" (Albawaba, 2013). Saudization, however, continues and the Ministry of Labor and the Council of Saudi Chambers (CSC) have constituted a high-level joint panel aimed at boosting the Saudization drive and increasing the efficiency of the labor market (Saudi Gazette, 2014). Many private companies are achieving their Saudization quotas through the so-called false employment of Saudis that experts say is damaging the local economy, and involves tactics such as employing Saudis to stay at home just to make up the numbers. What will help Saudi change will be training, skills and Saudi women.

Gender

Saudi Arabia's Princess Ameerah al-Taweel said in 2013 on a panel discussion at the World Economic Forum in Jordan that many conservative men in Saudi say "we don't want women to work, we want her to maintain her dignity... I think the main reason is fear from women and not for women, because they are afraid of women. We know that women are stronger than men in our society because they're a minority and the minority usually wants to prove itself" (Trenwith, 2013). However, The WEF's annual Gender Gap Index for 2014 now ranks Saudi Arabia ninth among Arab countries in terms of gender equality, stating that Saudi Arabia has improved the income of Saudi women compared to their male counterparts, with higher levels of political and economic participation, and improvement in education, health and living standards (Arab News, 2014).

Yet, there remain concerns that women must obtain permission from male guardians to work, travel, study, seek medical treatment or marry, and that the Saudi labor code, which came into force in 2006, incorporates an earlier stipulation decreeing that in line with article 4 of the code, which requires adherence to Sharia, "women shall work in all fields suitable to their nature" (article 149). The Committee on the Elimination of Discrimination against Women (CEDAW) in 2008, argued that this principle of "imposing the guardianship of a male over the woman all her life in Saudi Arabia is linked to the inferior look to women and her traditional role in society and family."

High profile stories have been reported which draw attention to the status of women in Saudi. One is that on October 26, 2013, more than 60 Saudi women's activists got behind the wheel of their cars protesting against a ban on women driving. Another is the story of a Saudi student at a woman's university in Riyadh, 24-year-old Amena Bawazir, who died of a heart attack after waiting for nearly two hours because male medical staff were not allowed to attend her (RT.com, 2014). What you won't get in Saudi is a sudden turnaround. However, pressure does seem to have some effect, and international observers may conclude it seems largely a matter of time, which brings me to the next dynamic.

Inshallah

Like elsewhere in the Arab world, the Inshallah is a constant in Saudi. It is a key to understanding this intriguing and changing nation. It will punctuate conversations, and will frustrate foreign visitors trying to get something done. Its' specific meaning is not always adequately grasped by foreigners: God has willed it, but also the one uttering the saying is recognizing that God wills it, not our individual will. It is part of the Islamic submission to God's way. The Koran reveals what God's way is, and hence the believer needs to obey what the Koran has revealed. However, some Saudis will joke Inshallah means "if the boss wills it."

Inshallah also reflects a sense of time that is quite different from the capitalist business culture of being very time sensitive, after all time is money we say. In Saudi time is more open, and it is God's time to dictate and not ours to second-guess. The prevalence of Inshallah indicates to me there is a level of efficiency in our Western business model that I do not believe is accepted and possibly not even desired in the Saudi business culture. Which brings us back to the role of religion, and the balance between economics and faith in Saudi and Islam.

Religion

The major companies of Saudi Arabia have very large mosques, often much larger than many of the neighborhood mosques their employees normally attend. They tend to be at the heart of the building complex, and are well-used. It is hard to imagine the average American company, like Exxon or Coca-Cola, having such Christian church facilities. It is also hard to imagine the work day stopping in its tracks to allow the workforce to attend to their prayers, or to have a meeting interrupted or scheduled to allow a manager to go down the corridor and set down a prayer mat to pray. It is not completely regimented, meetings do go on at prayer times and a manager will make up prayer time at another time. Religion is everywhere in Saudi, but this is not to say that religion is all-pervasive.

In the business context, it is influential but it does not rule the roost, and its position may be evolving. Kayed and Hassan have undertaken a detailed study which argues that Saudi Arabia in business terms is driven by Western economic dynamics, principally profit maximization, rather than Islamic prescriptions (Kayed, Hassan, 2011, 2010). However, this needs some clarification, because the Islamic and cultural influences make Saudi companies appear still quite different from their western counterparts. Superficially, seeing employees at prayer in a corridor or the centrality of the mosque may give a misleading impression of religion in the workplace.

To conclude on these challenges, I would argue that, from a Western business perspective the religious aspects of Saudi are not the challenge. The challenge for Saudi companies is that, because of the gender issue, the attitude of *Inshallah* and Saudization, Saudi business in a purely economic consideration of the challenge, is being run at a sub-optimal performance level. Which brings me to consider the Islamic business ethic.

An Islamic Business Ethic?

As Capitalism and Western liberal society developed, received wisdom assumed the secularization thesis which suggested that religion was a private affair, largely irrelevant to public life. The rise of a number of religious movements globally, but chiefly Islam, has forced many in the various fields of intellectual endeavor to play catch-up in the last decade or so, seeking a greater understanding of religion. However, talk of a "clash of civilizations" and other fanciful notions has not been helpful, but unfortunately has been influential in both intellectual circles and the *vox populi*. The secular worldview of the West is very much a part of global capitalism, and underpins business ethics and employee's own values. It is thus almost alien to consider the influence of religion on business ethics, but in the Islamic context it is part of an often poorly explored conflict of values, which is not the same as a clash of values, and dialogue will be essential to addressing these inherent differences.

We can start by understanding that essentially, and without making a value judgment here, that Capitalism is a disruptive force in religion. For example, long gone in Western Capitalist societies are the quiet Sundays, set aside mainly for worship; the peace replaced by busy roads and church bells replaced by ringing cash tills. This was driven by the desire of people to be able to shop on their Sundays, and do other leisure things on both Saturday and Sunday. Likewise, we can ponder whether the Saudi daily rhythm that allows for prayer times will give way to the ever-pressing needs for discipline and speed to deliver products. Capitalism is a challenge for, though not necessarily antithetical to, religious life. It is not simply the materialism, but also the imaginative and aspirational qualities of Capitalism that challenge religious values and way of life. We see this aspirational element reflected in the advertising approach, such as MasterCard's "There are some things that money can't buy. For everything else there's MasterCard" and competitor Visa's "It's everywhere you want to be." Capitalism doesn't just seek to feed the stomach, it seeks to feed the soul, and we can express ourselves through Capitalism, whether it is wearing Nike's "Just Do It" or caring for our skins with Clairol's "Does she or doesn't she?"

In response to this disruption, Western ethics and much of Christian literature on Capitalism have historically looked upon business and trade negatively; indeed, in the 20th Century you will be hard pressed to find a major Christian theologian who had a good word to say about Capitalism until the fall of Communism. This is not quite the same case for Islam. According to Islam, Allah blesses trade and investment and the world of business, which is for the benefit of society. Indeed, the Prophet was himself a trader, as was his first wife. As the 14th Century writer Ibn Khaldun explained, if people stop doing business then civilization itself will slump. The activity of business, however, is judged by intention and not the results. It is not only acceptable, but required, to have lower profits with the right intention rather than maximum profits by bad intention and breaking the commands of faith.

In Ali, Aali & Owaihan, the authors argue the Islamic view of the market is that it is based on justice, transparency and fair dealing, with the absence of exploitation. They contend that profit maximisation, which lies at the heart of market capitalism, is not sanctioned by Islam and thus not the goal of an ethically guided business. Their argument is that no action in business can be separated from the social context, stating "Islamic ethics refers to specified rules that govern individuals and organizational conduct and seek to insure generosity, openness, and accountability in behavior and actions, while safeguarding societal interests" (Ali, Al-Aali, Al-Owaihan, 2013). Ali identifies four foundations of Islamic ethics that not only meet with international standards but, the authors argue, exceed them as well: *ihsan* (goodness and generosity), relationship with others, equity and accountability.

Fair dealing is an everyday command, even in an Arab culture renowned for its market haggling where there are rules set by Islamic teaching. The object is to reach an agreeable price, not for one party to get the upper hand on the other. The Koran states "He that doeth good shall have ten times as much to his credit. He that doeth evil shall only be compensated according to his vice" (Koran 6:160). Hence, the warning "buyer beware" and other seemingly aggressive aspects of trading and capitalism are also ruled out by the Islamic business ethic.

There are also forbidden products, much like the ethical investment requirements familiar in the West, whereby the drive toward profit is overridden by ethical demands. Hence, alcohol, arms, gambling and tobacco products are forbidden or *haram*. The Koran states "They ask thee concerning wine and gambling. Say: in them is great sin, and some profit for men; but the sin is greater than the profit" (Koran 2:219). Gambling and speculation are jointly forbidden because they involve getting monetary gain without proper effort and also attempting to predict what the outcome is, when that is God's will. A similar concern leads to the ban on usury, though Islamic countries do generally allow interest-based banking. However, there is a growing Islamic banking and insurance market, though it remains something of a niche market, and I have long argued this area is problematic when it comes to the intent.

Countries like Saudi Arabia adopt global standards in business ethics, but they often run counter to their political record and cultural norms, more than they do to Islamic ideas. On one level, we can say that the UN Global Compact and Islamic principles are in harmony. Williams & Zinkin in their study find no substantive conflict between the tenets of Islam and the UN Global Compact (Williams and Zinkin, 2010). In fact, they go further and argue that "not only is Islam fully in accordance with the CSR agenda as codified in the UN Global Compact, but it goes further in ways that could potentially lead to understanding between Islam and the West" (Williams and Zinkin, 2010). They conclude that Islam exceeds the requirements for three principle reasons:

1. Wider in scope in respect to transparency and ethics of business transactions.
2. A clear codification of what is haram and halal.
3. An explicit mechanism in the *Shariah*, community enforcement and accountability in face of the day of judgment.

Much work has been done to articulate a broader socio-economic system based on Islam, pointing to the specifics in the Koran and other teachings such as rules on contracts, pricing, fair trading, taxation, speculation and charging of interest. It is difficult to construe simply an individualistic version of Islam, it is driven by a social vision. From an Islamic perspective, business is rooted in society and as such it is subject to the ethics of Islam as much as any other person or persons. Actions and decisions have to be undertaken through what Muhammad Umer Chapra calls the "moral filter" of Islam (Chapra, 1985). In practice this means that business is part of the needs of society, not a temptation, which means rampant consumerism is forbidden. Islam places consumption before consumerism, prioritizing necessities (*daruriyyat*), conveniences (*hayiyyat*) and refinements (*tahsiniyyat*). A study by Bhuian et al. (2002) examined Saudi Arabian consumers' attitudes toward ethical business practices, government regulations, and consumers' rights. Their findings revealed that in practice Saudi consumers exhibit positive attitudes toward ethical business practices related to advertising, product quality, government regulations, and perceived status of consumer rights.

What the business and consumer share in Islam is the core notion of trusteeship (Khilafah), whereby all people are regarded as trustees or guardians of the earth, acting as vice-gerent with God. We have responsibility together. The actions of a person, whether in business or not, is to fulfil the dual command to be a true servant of Allah and to act responsibility as a vicegerent of God. There is a balance or equilibrium (*'adl*) between these two missions. What Islam sets down are duties rather than rights.

There are many ways we could study an Islamic economic system, and there are many studies that do just that. There is just one last point to highlight, which matches concerns I have highlighted in the area of employee engagement, and that is bad and good behaviours in organizations originate from the top (Cowan, 2014). They are legitimated and copied within the organization. Al-Khatib et al, studied attitudes of employees in the Gulf region countries of Saudi Arabia, Oman and Kuwait. The authors argue that ethical attitudes affect business performance and they concluded from their study the issue is a critical one in the Gulf, as employees follow their leaders and because their superiors are unable to challenge some wrongs in the business, employees' ethical consciousness is relaxed (Al-Khatib, Rawwas, Vitell, 2004).

If we are vicegerents then this equally applies to hierarchy, and of course the wearing of thobes and abayas is rooted in a desire in Islam to show equality of all before Allah. Ostensibly, an Islamic company should reflect this attitude and have a more inclusive and cooperative view of employee relations, far from the Western model of boss versus employees, and of course the role of trade unions, which are forbidden in Saudi, though arguably not in Islam. Zulfiqar, in the context of writing a new labor code for Iraq, explains "Ideas of profit sharing, collective bargaining and even trade unions find justification in Islamic Law and have been instituted into the codes of many other Muslim countries" (Zulfiqar, 2007; see also Rehamn, 2010; see also Said, 1972; Al-Balagh Foundation, 1997; Possumah, et. al 2013; Elsaman, 2012).

On the basis of what I have outlined, admittedly in some broad brushstrokes, it is possible to construct an Islamic economy, financial system and business organization. However, it would come up against the same question that the more radical versions of the stakeholder theory and social contract theory come up against: would it work?

An Agenda for Ethical Dialogue

Williams & Zinkin added a caveat emptor of their own, they say (and many do) there is a difference between the teachings of Islam and the practice. This is no surprise. On the positive side, I suggest there is a shift towards the stakeholder/social contract view of business in the West, and as such Islamic tenets are compatible with the tenets of those who, rightly or wrongly, are pushing us to the edges of the stakeholder view or into the social contract view. However, the role of business ethics in Saudi, and Islamic countries generally, is akin to Western nations, whether we are talking about Western or Islamic notions of ethical demands. This is because Saudi companies have embraced the broad demands of international ethical standards, along with Islamic standards, which are in tension with the daily practicalities of doing business and the economic challenges they now face. There is an Islamic framework of ethics which can be looked to as a dialogue partner for change, and as such it would be similar to the discussions in the West between business and the more radical statements of stakeholder theory and those holding a social contract theory. I contend more so the social contract theory, except in the Islamic case it is a contract underwritten, so to speak, by Allah.

The more challenging aspects of Saudi today are the cultural ones, and the desire for skills and attitudes that will bring Saudi business closer to a Western economic model, leading us to ponder whether Islamic nations generally, and Saudi in particular, are simply absorbing Western-style capitalism and its ethics. Ali et al, quoted in the Kayed & Hassan paper, argue that in "Saudi Arabia…the private sector in the Kingdom is driven to profit maximisation rather than Islamic prescriptions" (Zulfiqar, 2007). I would suggest this is happening out of a sense of economic realism, which the nation certainly needs in facing the economic problems that lie ahead. This presents more of a challenge, because the challenges are behavioral. Economic life and religious life are both behavioral, and we have to unpack what this means in our economy, and we can also ponder whether the current landscape is one of Islamic societies going with the Capitalist flow and embracing objectives and the pace of change predicated on Capitalist assumptions, or if there is scope or appetite to offer an alternative economic vision. Perhaps it is too late in the day to be asking this question, but I don't think it is. Rather, more work needs to be done on the challenge I have posed. One thing is perhaps certain, that is Islamic thinkers ought to avoid the error of Islamic Socialism and equally the disorder of Islamic finance dressed up in Capitalism if there is to be a distinctive voice.

The challenges of materialism to religious life, as well as the way in which what we can buy plays a role in our identity, and begs the question of whether Islam offers an alternative system, is a fellow-traveler for Capitalism, or, will become more secular like Christianity has in in the West. This discussion presents us with a clear and fascinating agenda. Islamic thought suggests a different approach to the economic task, which aligns with the civil society approaches in the West, and as such they can be dialogue partners together in their challenge to global business and the shareholder view; though it also brings Saudi on a collision course with civil society globally due to the failures to comply with the global standards discussed. Another route for Islamic countries like Saudi is to take to more, not less, Islamizing of their economies.

In short, I propose a five point agenda to guide future discussion:

1. Create greater dialogue between Islamic and Western business ethicists, business schools, civil society groups and the like.
2. Have open dialogue amongst Islamic ethicists and business practitioners on the points of disconnect highlighted in this paper, such as gender, corporate values, human rights, and identify points of difference or alternative approaches in relation to "global standards."
3. Find more imaginative ways to promote dialogue within companies to understand diversity of culture and how people work together whilst remaining different in the source of their values and ethics.
4. Explore a clearer articulation of Islamic economic ideas and specific policies, and how they are distinctive in the context of globalization, other economic policy options and cultural settings.
5. Create a forum for all interested parties, Islamic and non-Islamic, to share approaches and discern how there can be harmony in the global economy based on acceptance of cultural and faith differences rather than fear and ignorance, so that we have a mosaic of ethical viewpoints that sustain rather than fracture the economic life of the world.

I leave this as an open agenda for all those interested in understanding Islamic thinking about economic ideas and their ethical implications, and also those interested in understanding ethical conflict in a world dominated, justifiably or not, by Capitalism. This paper and agenda are offered in the belief this agenda is an Islamic version of the same battle raging in the West between economic realism and those who would have business serve society rather than simply fund it.

Bibliography

Abdel-Fadil, M. (1987). "The Macro-Behaviour of the Oil-Rentier States in the Arab Region", in Hazem Beblawi and Giacomo Luciani (eds), *The Rentier State*, Croom Helm, London.

Abouammoh, A.M. (2012). "Higher education in the GCC states: Reforms and regulations". In Hertog, S. (ed.). *National Employment, Migration and Education in the GCC. The Gulf Region* (Economic Development and Diversification, 4), 265-286. Berlin: Gerlach.

Achoui, Mustapha (2009). "Human Resource Development in Gulf Countries: An Analysis of the Trends and Challenges Facing Saudi Arabia". *Human Resource Development International.* 12(1), 35–46.

Adler, N.J. (1997). *International dimensions of Organizational Behavior.* London: International Thompson Business Press

Ahmad, Anwar (2014). "It's a buyer's (and seller's) market. Laborers set up stalls at their camps to supplement wages," *The National*, 25 May 2014.

Ahmed, Ali (2011). "New Emiratisation regulations". *IFLR*, 3 March 2011, http://www.iflr.com/Article/2779603/New-UAE-emiratisation-regulations.html

Al Ahram, (2012). "Saudi Arabia Real GDP Growth at 6.6 pct in Fourth Quarter 2011", 14 Apr 2011. Cairo

Al Aiban, K.M. and Pearce, J.L. (1993). "The Influence of Values on Management Practices: A test in Saudi Arabia and the United States. *International Studies of Management and Organization.*, Vol. 23, No. 3, 35-52.

Al Ali, Jasim (2007). "Emiratisation: drawing UAE nationals into their surging economy" *International Journal of Sociology and Social Policy,* Vol. 28 No. 9/10, 2008. 365-379

Al Anazi, A. (2011) *Behavioral Attitude The Cause For High Unemployment In Saudi Arabia*, Kuala Lumpur: Open University of Malaysia.

Al Attiyah, A. H. (2005) *Address to the Qatarization Annual Review Meeting*, 3 May, Ritz Carlton, Doha, accessed 19 September 2014, http://www.qatarization.com.qa/Qatarization/Qatarization.nsf/40278ec4e9ade91c4325725d003bc463/3326f7d62f45085e432574c500386f00?OpenDocument.

Al Awar, M. (2012). "Heterogeneity of national culture and workplace values in the Arab region: a UAE national's perspective". *Interview between Masood Al-Awar and the author, held at Marriott Hotel, Marble Arch, London.* 16 February.

Al Balagh Foundation (1997). *Work and production: Selections on the labor law in Islam (Islamic concepts).* Al-Balagh Foundation.

Al Bawaba Business (2013) [online]. 30 Sept 2013. Available from: http://www.albawaba.com/business/saudization-education-523901.[Accessed 9 Nov 2014].

Al Bawaba (2014). "Saudi Salaries are Having a Tough Time Catching Up With the Country's Explosive Cost of Living", 9 June

Al Dakhil, Khalid (2013). *Personal Conversation*, 12 May, Riyadh, Saudi Arabia

Al Fahim, Mohammed A. J. (1996). *From Rags to Riches. A Story of Abu Dhabi.* London Centre for Arabic Studies, London.

Al Ghurair, AbdulAziz (2013). "Measuring Success of Emiratisation in the Banking Sector" *UAE Banks Federation*, http://www.uaebf.ae/News-&-Events/Chairman-Opinion-Pieces-/Measuring-Success-of-Emiratisation-in-the-Banking-Sector-78-Details.html

Al Jandaly, B. (2010). "UAE residency visa, labour card validity cut to two years". *Gulf News* [Online] Available from: http://gulfnews.com/news/gulf/uae/visa/uae-residency-visa-labour-card-validity-cut-to-two-years-1.725290 [Accessed: 12th January 2012[

Al Khatib, Jamal A., Rawwas, Mohammed Y.A., and Vitell, Scott J. (2004). "Organizational Ethics in Developing Countries: A Comparative Analysis," *Journal of Business Ethics*. P [309] of 309-322.

Al Kuwari, A.K. (2012). "The Visions and Strategies of the GCC Countries from the Perspective of Reforms: The Case of Qatar", *Contemporary Arab Affairs*, vol. 5, no. 1, 86-106.

Al Maeena, Tariq (2014). "Exposing the Corrupt in Saudi Arabia", *Gulf News*, 23 February.

Al Maeena, Tariq (2014). "Saudi Graduates Challenged in Labor, Housing", *Gulf News*, 13 March.

Al Maeena, Tariq (2014). "A Debate on Military Service", *Gulf News*, 25 January

Al Masah Capital (2011). *"MENA: The Great Job Rush."*

Al Mukhtar, Rima (2014). "Shoura Sword Hanging on Five-Day Week", *Arab News*, 3 February

Al Munajjed, Mona and Karim Sabbagh (2011). *Youth in GCC Countries: Meeting the Challenge*. Booz & Company

Al Nassar, S. and Dow, K.L. (2013). "Delivering High Quality Teaching and Learning for University Students in Saudi Arabia", in Smith, L. and Abouammoh, A. (eds.) *Higher Education in Saudi Arabia: Achievements, Challenges and Opportunities*, Dordrecht: Springer.

Al Obaid and Al-Ateiah, (2003). "Economy of Kingdom of Saudi Arabia: An Analytical Review", 1994 (in Arabic); cited in Madhi, Salah and Barrientos, Armando, "Saudisation and Employment in Saudi Arabia", *Career Development International*, Vol. 8, No. 2,

Al Ohali, M. and Burdon, S. (2013) "International Collaboration", in Smith, L. and Abouammoh, A. (eds.) *Higher Education in Saudi Arabia: Achievements, Challenges and Opportunities*, Dordrecht: Springer.

Al Omari, J. (2009). *Understanding the Arab Culture: A practical cross-cultural guide to working in the Arab world*. 2nd ed. Oxford: How to books

Al Omran, A. (2011). "Generational Divide in Saudi Arabia", *Saudi Jeans*. [Online] 6th February. Available from: 2011: http://saudijeans.org/tag/scta/ [Accessed: 26th April 2012.

Al Qassemi, Sultan, (2014). "Tribalism in the Arabian Peninsular: It's a Family Affair", *Jadaliyya Monthly, Arab Studies Institute*, 1 February

Al Rashed, Abdulrahman, (2014). "Developing Education", *Asharq Al-Awsat*, 2 June

Al Rasheed, Madawi (2003). *A History of Saudi Arabia*. USA: Cambridge University Press

Al Rueli, Faisal, *Personal Conversation*, 5 May 2014, Sakaka, Al-Jaouf, Saudi Arabia

Al Saud, Alwaleed, (2011). "A Saudi Prince's Plea for Reform", New York Times [Online] 24th February. Available from http://www.nytimes.com/2011/02/25/opinion/25alsaud.html?_r=0 [Accessed: 21st March 2014.

Al Sayegh, F. (1998). "Merchants' Role in a Changing Society: the Case of Dubai, 1900-90". *Middle Eastern Studies.*, Vol. 34, No. 1, 87-102.

Al Sayegh, Hadeel (2013). "Just Falafel brings in Arqaam Capital for IPO Guidance," in *The National*, 29 October 2013.

Al Shaibany, S. (2013). "Oman Raises Minimum Wages to Avert Future Protests", *Reuters*, 9 February, accessed 18 September 2014, http://www.reuters.com/article/2013/02/09/us-oman-employment-wage-idUSBRE91805A20130209.

Al Shaibany, S. (2014). "Fund for SMEs Needs Commitment, Not Lip Service", *Times of Oman*, 12 January, A1.

Al Shaibany, S. (2014b), "Sunday Beat: Why Thousands of Omanis Quit Jobs in Private Sector?" *Times of Oman*, 15 November, accessed 23 December 2014, http://www.timesofoman.com/News/42740/Article-Sunday-Beat-Why-thousands-of-Omanis-quit-jobs-in-private-sector?

Al Shamsi, F. (2008) "Implications of the GCC's Labor Nationalization Policies on Employment Opportunities for Indigenous Females." *Proceedings of Gender and Economics in MENA: From Theory to Policy Making*, Dubai, United Arab Emirates, Dubai School of Government.

Al Suhaymi, Obaid, (2014). "Saudi Cabinet Approves Benefits Scheme", *Asharq al-Awsat*, 7 January.

Al Waqfi, M.A. & I. Forstenlechner (2012). "Of private sector fear and prejudice: The case of young citizens in an oil-rich Arabian Gulf economy". *Personnel Review*. 41(5). 609-629.

Al Waqfi, Mohammed, and Forstenlechner, Ingo (2010). "Stereotyping of Citizens in an Expatriate Dominated Labour Market: Implications for Workforce Nationalization Policy". *Employee Relations*, 32, 364–381.

Al Waqfi, Mohammed; Forstenlechner, Ingo (2014). "Barriers to Emiratization: The role of policy design and institutional environment in determining the effectiveness of Emiratization". *The International Journal of Human Resource Management*, Vol. 25 No.2 167-189

Al Yahya, K. (2009). "Power-Influence in decision Making, Competence Utilization, and Organizational Culture in Public Organizations: The Arab World in Comparative Perspective". *Journal of Public Administration Research and Theory.*, Vol. 19, No. 2, 385-407.

Al Zamel, Essam (2014). "Saudi Labor Reform Opens New Opportunities for Economy", *Al-Monitor*, 5 January

Ali, A. (1986). "The Arab Executive". *American-Arab Affairs*. Vol.19,94-100

Ali, A. (1989). "Decision Style and Work Satisfaction of Arab Gulf Executives: A Cross-national Study". *International Studies of Management and Organization*, Vol. 19, No. 2, 22-37

Ali, A. (1990). "Management Theory in a Transitional Society: the Arab's Experience". *International Studies of Management and Organization.*, Vol. 20, No. 3, 7-35.

Ali, A. (1993) ."Decision-Making Style, Individualism, and Attitudes toward Risk of Arab Executives". *International Studies of Management and Organization,* Vol. 23, No. 3, 53-73.

Ali, A. (1995). "Cultural Discontinuity and Arab management Thought". *International Studies of Management and Organization.*,Vol. 25, No. 3, 7-30.

Ali, Abbas J., Al-Aali, Abdulrahman, Al-Owaihan, Abdullah (2013). "Islamic Perspectives on Profit Maximization." *Journal of Business Ethics* (Volume 117, Issue 3) p.469.

Ali, S. (2010). *Dubai: Gilded cage*. New Haven: Yale University Press

Allen Consulting Group 2009, "*Skill Gaps Research Study: Final Report – A Future Strategy for Bahrain (2009-2016)*"

Amnesty International (2013). "Annual Report 2013: Saudi Arabia." *Amnesty International* [online]. Available from: http://www.amnesty.org/en/region/saudi-arabia/report2013. [Accessed 9 Nov 2014.]

Anderson & Wadenssjö (2006). 'Do the Unemployed Become Successful Entrepreneurs? A Comparison between the Unemployed, Inactive and Wage-Earners". *IZA Discussion Paper*, Bonn, 2006.

Ankari, Khalid (2013). "Foreword". In: Smith, Larry. & Abouammoh, Abdulrahman. (eds.) *Higher Education in Saudi Arabia: Achievements, Challenges and Opportunities*. New York: Springer.

Arab News (2014). "Only 6% KSA engineers are Saudi", *Arab News* [Online] 20th September. Available from: http://www.arabnews.com/saudi-arabia/news/632801#.VB1D4RXNrKo.twitter [Accessed: 21st September 2014.

Arab News (2014). "Turnover Trend Among Saudi Staff 'On the Rise", *Arab News,* 28 April

Arab News (2014) "KSA Narrows Gender Gap." *Arab News* [online]. 30 Oct. Available from: http://www.arabnews.com/featured/news/652321. [Accessed 9 Nov. 2014.

Arab Regional Centre for Entrepreneurship and Investment Training (ARCEIT) c. (2014) "Launch of Manama Arab Capital for Entrepreneurship", accessed 5 June 2014, http://www.arceit.org/content/news/13-latest/69-manama2014.html.

Arabian Business (2012). Retrieved from http://www.arabianbusiness.com/84-surge-in-saudi-women-working-in-private-sector-558843.html

Arnold, Denis G., Audi, Robert and Zwolinski, Matt (2010). "Recent Work in Ethical theory and its Implications for Business Ethics," *Business Ethics Quarterly*, 20:4 (October 2010), 559-581.

Asda'a Burson Marsteller (2014). "We want to Embrace Modern Values", *Arab Youth Survey* 2014 White Paper.

Asger, M. (2011). "Stress taking heavy toll on UAE's workforce". *Gulf News*. [online]17 February. Available from: http://gulfnews.com/news/gulf/uae/employment/stress-taking-heavy-toll-on-uae-s-work-force-1.763448 [Accessed: 12 February 2012.

Askari, Hossein, (2014). "Islamicity Index", George Washington University, June

Assaad, R. & F. Roudi-Fahimi (2007). "Youth in the Middle East and North Africa: Demographic Opportunity or Challenge?", *Population Reference Bureau.*

Atwood, E. (2011). "Twitter usage rockets in conservative Saudi Arabia", *Arabian Business* [Online] 5th January. Available from: www.arabianbusiness.com/twitter-usage-rockets-in-conservative-saudi-arabia-371485.html [Accessed: 22nd March 2014.

Ayubi, N.N. (2001). "*Overstating the Arab State: Politics and Society in the Middle East",* London, I. B. Tauris

Aziz, Afshan (2014). "Women Employees Suffer in Prevailing Gender Pay Gap", *Arab News,* 8 May.

Bahrain Chamber of Commerce and Industry c. (2014), "SME Development and Support Center" accessed 19 September 2014, http://www.sme.bh./

Bahrain Development Bank (2012). *Annual Report*

Bahrain Economic Development Board (EDB) (2013). *Bahrain Financial Yearbook.*

Bahrain Economic Development Board (EDB) c.(2014). *Bahrain Vision 2030,* accessed 8 June 2014. http://issuu.com/economicdevelopmentboard/docs/bahrain_vision_2030.

Bakker, A.B., & Leiter, M.P. (Eds.). (2010). *Work Engagement: A Handbook of Essential Theory and Research.* New York, NY: Psychology Press.

Baldwin-Edwards, M. (2011). "Labour immigration and labour markets in the GCC countries: national patterns and trends. LSE Global Governance". *Kuwait Programme on Development, Governance and Globalisation in the Gulf States.* March 2011. No.15

Bambidge, S. (2010). "Saudi population stands at 27.1m, expats number 8.4m". *Arabian Business.* 5 August. [Online] Available from: http://www.arabianbusiness.com/saudi-population-stands-at-27-1m-expats-number-8-4m-340099.html [Accessed: 17th February 2012[

Barada, A. (2012). "National culture and Workplace values in the UAE". *Telephone conversation beetween the author and Ahmed Barada*: London-Abu Dhabi. [Personal communication, 14 February 2012]

Barnett, A., Yandle, B., and Naufal, G. (2013). "Regulation, Trust, and Cronyism in Middle Eastern Societies: The Simple Economics of 'Wasta'" *The Institute for the Study of Labor (IZA)*, Bonn, Germany, Discussion Paper No. 7201

Basu, Anuradha (2006). "Ethnic Minority Entrepreneurship," in *The Oxford Handbook of Entrepreneurship,* ed. Casson et al., 580-600. Oxford University Press, Oxford.

Beblawi, H. (1987). "The Rentier State in the Arab World", in Hazem Beblawi and Giacomo Luciani (eds), *The Rentier State*, Croom Helm, London.

Beblawi, H. (1990). "The Rentier State in the Arab World". In: Giacomo Luciani (ed.*), The Arab State.* London. 85-98.

Beekun, I. and Badawi, Jamal A. (2005). "Balancing Ethical Responsibility among Multiple Organizational Stakeholders: The Islamic Perspective," *Journal of Business Ethics,* Vol.60, No 2.

Bizri, O. (2013). "Research, Innovation, Entrepreneurship and the Rentier Culture in the Arab Countries", in Thomas Andersson and Abdelkader Djeflat (eds), *The Real Issues of the Middle East Arab Spring: Addressing Research, Innovation and Entrepreneurship,* Springer, New York.

Bjerke, B. and Al-Meer, A. (1993). "Culture's Consequences: Management in Saudi Arabia". *Leadership and Organization Development Journal.* Vol. 14, No. 2. 30-35.

Blanchard, C.M. (2006). *Islam: Sunni and Shiites* [Online] December 11. Available from: http://fpc.state.gov/documents/organization/78715.pdf [Accessed: 10th February 2012[

Bock, P.K. (1999). *Rethinking psychological anthropology,* 2nd edn. Prospect Heights, IL: Waveland

Bontenbal, M. & H. Aziz (2013). "Oman's tourism industry: Student career perceptions and attitudes." *Journal of Arabian Studies.* 3(2). 232-248.

Booz & Company & World Economic Forum (2011). "*Accelerating Entrepreneurship in the Arab World".* Geneva.

Booz and Co (2011). *Youth in GCC countries: Meeting the challenge.* [Online] Available from:http://www.booz.com/me/home/press_media/management_consulting_press_releases/article/49943632 [Accessed: 26 January 2012[

Booz and Company(2010). *Meeting the Employment Challenge in the GCC: The Need for a Holistic Strategy.*

Bosbait, M. and Wilson, R. (2005). "Education, School to Work Transitions and Unemployment in Saudi Arabia", *Middle Eastern Studies* 41(4), 533–46.

Bozeman, B. (1987). *All organizations are public.* San Francisco, CA: Jossey-Bass

Braibanti, Ralph. & Al-Farsy, Fouad (1977). "Saudi Arabia: A Development Perspective". *Journal of South Asian and Middle Eastern Studies.* 1(1): 3–43.

Brandenburg, T. (2013). "The Political Economy of Internationalization and Privatization of Higher Education in the Sultanate of Oman." In Wippel, S. (ed.*). Regionalizing Oman: Political, Economic and Social Dynamics,* 289-304. Berlin: Springer.

Bundesministerium für Arbeit und Soziales (2011). *Aus der Arbeitslosigkeit in die Selbstständigkeit – im Aufschwung Gründungen fördern.* Bonn.

Butenschon, N.A, Davis, A. and Hassassian, M. (2000*). Citizenship and the State in the Middle East: Approaches and Applications.* New York: Syracuse University Press

Casson, Mark & Yeung, Bernard & Basu, Anuradha & Wadeson, Nigel (eds.) (2006), "*The Oxford Handbook of Entrepreneurship*". Oxford University Press, Oxford.

Casson, Mark (1998). "An Entrepreneurial Theory of the Firm". Conference paper, available at http://www.druid.dk/conferences/summer1998/conf-papers/casson.pdf

Center for Advanced Human Resource Studies (2006). "Succession Planning and Identifying High Potential Talent: Focus on the Middle East", CAHRS [Online] Available from: https://est05.esalestrack.com/eSalesTrack/Content/Content.ashx?file=01f27854-8c25-4af3-bc4f-d5a9287c216d.pdf [Accessed: 5th October 2014].

Central Intelligence Agency (2014). "Saudi Arabia", *The World Factbook,* [Online] Available from:https://www.cia.gov/library/publications/the-world-factbook/geos/sa.html [Accessed: 4th October 2014.

Chaaban, J. (2011). *UNDP Arab Human Development Report. Job Creation in the Arab Economies: Navigating Through Difficult Water.*

Chapman, M. (1997). "Preface: Social anthropology, business studies, and cultural issues". *International Studies of Management & Organization*, Vol. 26, No. 4, 3-29.

Chapra, Mohammed Umer (1985). *Towards a Just Monetary System*, Islamic Foundation: Leicester, UK.

Chbani, N. (2012). "Heterogeneity of national culture and workplace values between UAE and KSA?" *[Telephone conversation] Between the author and Nabil Chbani:* London-Dubai. [Personal communication, 23 February 2012[

Checkel, Jeffery (2004). "Social constructivisms in global and European politics: a review essay", *Review of International Studies,* Vol.30, 229–244

Clapham, C. (1985). *Third World politics: an introduction.* London: Croom Helm

Clark, Cal. & Jung. Changhoon (2004). "The Resurrection of East Asian Dynamism: A Call to Look Beyond the Orthodoxies in Development Studies". *Asian Affairs.* 31(3): 131–151.

Cockburn, P. (2014). "Isis militants: Twitter provides one of the few forums in which Saudis can discuss what they really feel—and it says they blame the clergy for Isis", The Independent[Online]5thOctober. Availablefrom:http://www.independent.co.uk/voices/comment/twitter-provides-one-of-the-few-forums-in-which-saudis-can-discuss-what-they-really-feel--and-it-says-they-blame-the-clergy-for-isis-9774884.html?origin=internalSearch [Accessed: 5th October 2014.[

Coll, Steve (2008). *The Bin Ladens. The Story of a Family and its Fortune.* Allen Lane, London.

Collins, Katie (2014). "Wireless Broadband can Reach the Moon, and Maybe Mars", Wired, 23 May 2014. NASA and MIT recently demonstrated that data communication technology is capable of providing the moon and perhaps Mars with WiFi connectivity, including data transfers and high-definition video streaming.

Cooke, Mariam (2014*). Tribal Modern: Branding New Nations in the Arab Gulf.* University of California Press, CA.

Cowan, David (2014). *Strategic Internal Communication: How to Build Employee Engagement and Performance,* London: Kogan Page.

Cunnigham, R.; Sarayrah, Y. (1994) "Taming Wasta to achieve development", *Arab Studies Quarterly,* Vol. 16, Issue 3 p29-41

Cunningham, R.B. and Sarayrah, Y.K. (1993). *Wasta: The hidden force in Middle Eastern society.* USA: Praeger Publishers.

Darbouche, H. and Fattouh, B. (2011). "The Implications of the Arab Uprisings for Oil and Gas Markets". *Oxford Institute for Energy Studies,* University of Oxford.

Davidson, C. (2008). *Dubai: The Vulnerability of Success*". London: Hurst & Company

Davidson, C. (2009). *Abu Dhabi: Oil and Beyond.* London: Hurst & Company

Davidson, C. and Mackenzie Smith, P. (eds.) (2008). *Higher Education in the Gulf States: Shaping Economies, Politics and Culture,* London: Saqi/London Middle East Institute SOAS.

Davidson, Christopher (2009). "Abu Dhabi's New Economy: Oil, Investment and Domestic Development" , *Middle East Policy,* Vol16 No. 2, 59–79.

De Soto, Hernando (1989). *The Other Path: The Invisible Revolution in the Third World.* HarperCollins, New York.

Deloitte (2010). "Wanted: A National Labour Force. Labour Policies and Youth Unemployment in the Gulf Region", *A Middle East Point of View*, November, 12-17.

DeNicola, Christopher (2005*). Dubai's political and economic development: an oasis in the desert?,* Available from: http://library.williams.edu/theses/pdf.php?id=48[Accessed: 10 February 2012[

Dessi, A. (2011). "Algeria at the Crossroads, Between Continuity and Change". *Istituto Affari Internazionali.* September, 2011. IAI Working papers 11.

DLA Piper (2012). *Be Aware: Focus on Kingdom of Saudi Arabia.* Retrieved from http://www.dlapiper.com/files/Publication/8013ec0e-9213-4de5-93b1-769e55e29b70/Presentation/PublicationAttachment/c8a4d367-e2f0-4df4-83c4-8b94cf0e0e88/Be_Aware_Middle_East_June_2012.pdf

Doha News (2013*).* "Most Qatari Job-Seekers Don't Want to Work in the Private Sector", 24 August, accessed 8 June 2014, http://dohanews.co/survey-most-qataris-dont-want-to-work-in-the-private/

Donaldson, Thomas (1982). *Corporations and Morality.* New Jersey: Prentice-Hall.

Donno, D. and Russett, B. (2004.) "Islam, Authoritarianism, and Female Empowerment: What are the linkages*?*" *World Politics.*, Vol. 56, No. 4, 582-607.

Dresch, P. and Piscatori, J. (eds.) (2013). "Monarchies and Nations: Globalization And Identity" in *The Arab Gulf States*, London: I.B. Tauris.

Drucker, Peter F. (1986). *Innovation and Entrepreneurship.* New York.

Dubai SME (2014). "Dubai SME 100 Ranking". Dubai, UAE. Available at http://www.dubaisme100rankings.com/2013/

Dubai SME (2014). "The State of Small & Medium Enterprises (SMEs) in Dubai". Dubai.

Duckworth, A.L. & Seligman, M.E.P. (2005). "Self-discipline outdoes IQ in predicting academic performance of adolescents". *Psychological Science,* 16, 939–944.

Dun & Bradstreet (2008). "Study of the Key Problems and Challenges of SMEs in Bahrain", Report for Phase 1 of D&B and Tamkeen Engagement, October.

Dunning, T. (2009*). Crude Democracy: Natural Resource Wealth and Political Regimes,* Cambridge University Press, Cambridge.

Economist Intelligence Unit (2010). "The GCC in 2020: Resources for the future: A report from the EIU". Sponsored by the Qatar Financial Centre Authority.

Edarabia (2012). "Emirati Student bought Campus Canteen after First Year of Studie*s*," published on Edarabia.com on 7 June, 2012, at http://www.edarabia.com/29542/emirati-student-bought-campus-canteen-after-first-year-of-studies/, accessed 25 April, 2014

Eisenstadt, Shmuel N. (1973*). Traditional Patrimonialism and Modern Neopatrimonialism.* Beverly Hills: Sage Publications.

El Said, H., and Harrigan, J. (2009). "You Reap What You Plant: Social Networks in the Arab World-The Hashemite Kingdom of Jordan". *World Development* , 37, Vol. 7, 1235–1249.

El Saman, Radwa S. (2012). "Corporate Social Responsibility in Islamic Law: Labor and Employment," *New Eng. J. Int'l & Comp.* L. 97.

El Sokari, Hala & Van Horne, Constance & Huang, Victor & Al Awad, Muawiya (2013). *Entrepreneurship: An Emirati Perspective*. ISER, Zayed University, Dubai. (=GEM Country Report 2013, available online)

Emirates 24/7 (2013). "UAE GDP to grow by over 3%" 17 July 2013 http://www.emirates247.com/business/economy-finance/uae-gdp-to-grow-by-over-3-2013-07-17-1.514544

Emirates 24/7 (2010). "Expats make up over 88% of the UAE. Emirates" *24/7*. 17 April [Online]. Availablefrom:http://www.emirates247.com/news/expats-make-up-over-88-of-uae-population-2011-04-17-1.381853 [Accessed: 17th February.(

Ennis, Chrystal E. (2013). "Millenials and the State of Entrepreneurship in the Gulf, "panel presentation at the 2013 Deutscher Orientalistentag, September 2013, Münster, Germany.

EOS Magazine, (2009). "Sterk Gemengd", March

Ernst & Young. (2014). "Youth Perspectives on Employment". *Jeddah Economic Forum.*

Estrin, Saul & Meyer, Klaus E. & Bytchkova, Maria (2006), "Entrepreneurship in Transition Economies" in *The Oxford Handbook of Entrepreneurship,* ed. Casson et al., 693-725. Oxford University Press, Oxford.

Etzkowitz, Henry; Webster, Andrew; Gebhardt, Christiane; Terra, Branca; Cantisano, Regina, (2000). "The Future of the University and the University of the Future:Evolution of Ivory Tower to Entrepreneurial Paradigm". *Research Policy*. 29: 313–330.

European Commission (2008), *Entrepreneurship in Higher Education, Especially within Non-Business Studies.* Final report of the expert group, Brussels. Expert Group

Fadhli, R. (2013). "Duplication in Ministries and Institutions", *The Peninsula*, 5 December, accessed 8 June 2014, http://thepeninsulaqatar.com/qatar-perspective/Rashid-Fadhli/263383/duplication-in-ministries-and-institutions.

Fakeeh, Manal Soliman, (2009). *Saudization as a Solution for Unemployment: the Case of Jeddah Western Region,* Doctoral Dissertation: University of Glasgow,

Fakkar, Galal, (2013). "Foreigners Required in KSA 'For 40 More Years", *Arab News*, 9 May

Farah, Samer (2012). "Education Quality and Competitiveness in the UAE" Policy Paper No.2, *Al Qasimi Foundation*, Sheikh Saud Bin Saqr Al Qasimi Foundation for Policy Research, Ras al-Khaimah

Fasano, U. and Iqbal, Z. (2003). "GCC Countries: From Oil dependence to diversification". Washington: *International Monetary Fund*

Fasano, Ugo; Goyal, Rishi (2004). "Emerging Strains in GCC Labor Markets" *IMF Working Paper* 04/71 International Monetary Fund, Middle East and Central Asia Department

Feghali, Ellen, (1997). "Arab Cultural Communication Patterns", *International Journal on Intercultural Relations,* Beirut, Lebanon, Vol. 21, No. 3,

Field, A. (2005). *Discovering statistics using SPSS.* (2nd edn) London: SAGE Publications

Finnemore, Martha, and Sikkink, Kathryn (2001). "Taking Stock: The Constructivist Research Program in International Relations and Comparative Politics", *Annual Review of Political Science*, Vol. 4, 391–416

Forstenlechner, Ingo & Rutledge, Emilie (2010). "Unemployment in the Gulf: Time to Update the "Social Contract", *Middle East Policy*, 17, (2010), 38-51.

Forstenlechner, Ingo (2008). "Workforce nationalization in the UAE: image versus integration", *Education, Business and Society: Contemporary Middle Eastern Issues* Vol. 1 No. 2, 82-91

Forstenlechner, Ingo, Madi, Mohamed, Selim, Hassan and Rutledge, Emilie (2012). "Emiratisation: determining the factors that influence the recruitment decisions of employers in the UAE", *The International Journal of Human Resource Management*, Vol. 23, No. 2, 406–421

Forstenlechner, Ingo, and Rutledge, Emilie (2011). "The GCC's "Demographic imbalance- perceptions, realities and policy options" , *Middle East Policy,* Vol. 18 No.4, 25-43

Foster, N. (2004). "An unstoppable force meets a movable object? Assignment of rights in UAE". *Arab quarterly.* Vol. 19, No. 1/4, 169-190.

Fougere, M. and Moulettes, A. (2006). "Development and Modernity in Hofstede's Culture's Consequences: A postcolonial reading". *Lund institute of Economic research*: Working paper series

Frank, Andrea I. (2005). "*Developing Entrepreneurship Skills in the Context of Higher Education,*" Conference Presentation, Built Environment in Education Symposium, July, 2005.

Freeman, Ambassador Chas W. (2014). *Personal Conversation*, 28 May 2014, Bristol, Rhode Island

Freeman, R. Edward (1984). *Strategic Management: A Stakeholder Approach.* Boston: Pitman.

Friedman, Milton (2009). "The Social Responsibility of Business is to Increase Profits," *New York Times Magazine,* September 13th, 2009.122-125.

Fukuyama, F. (1989) "The end of history", in M. A. Genest (Ed.), *Conflict and cooperation,.* Orlando, FL: Harcourt, Brace, 320–329

Galani, U. (2011). "Gulf's liberal shift is more than sop to Arab spring". *Reuters.* [online] 27 September. Available at: http://www.arabianbusiness.com/gulf-s-liberal-shift-is-more-than-sop-arab-spring-422198.html [Accessed: 18th January 2012[

Gallant, M. & J.S. Pounder (2008). "The employment of female nationals in the United Arab Emirates: An analysis of opportunities and barriers". *Education, Business and Society.* 1(1). 26-33.

Gellner, E. (1990). "Tribalism and the State in the Middle East." in: Khoury, P.S., and Kostiner, J. eds. *Tribes and State Formation in the Middle East.* California: University of California Press

Ghazal, Rym (2014). "My UAE: It's Crafty Business for Young Entrepreneur Tariq al-Harmoudi" in *The National,* 14 February 2014.

Giersch, H. (1984). "The Age of Schumpeter". *The American Economic Review* 74, (1984), 103–109.

Gilpin, Robert (2001). *Global Political Economy: Understanding the International Economic Order.* Princeton: Princeton University Press.

Girgis, M. (2002). "Would nationals and Asians replace workers in the GCC?", Paper presented at *Fourth Mediterranean Development Forum.* Amman, Jordan (6-9 October) Mimeographed.

Godley, Andrew (2006). "Migration of Entrepreneurs", in *The Oxford Handbook of Entrepreneurship,* ed. Casson et al., Oxford University Press, Oxford, 601-610.

Grampp, William D (2000). "What Did Smith Mean by the Invisible Hand?" *Journal of Political Economy* Vol. 108, No. 3 (June 2000), 441-465.

Gray, M. (2011). "A Theory of 'Late Rentierism' in the Arab States of the Gulf", *CIRS Occasional Paper* no. 7, 1-44.

Gray, M. (2013), *Qatar: Politics and Challenges of Development,* Lynne Rienner, Boulder, CO.

Gray, Matthew (2011). "A Theory of 'Late Rentierism' in the Arab States of the Gulf" *CIRS, Georgetown University,* School of Foreign Service in Qatar

GSDP (General Secretariat for Development Planning) (2011). *Qatar National Development Strategy 2011–2016,* Doha: GSDP

Gulf Business (2012). "Over 1.3 Saudis on Unemployment Benefit" Retrieved from http://gulfbusiness.com/2012/09/over-1-3m-saudison-unemployment-benefit/#.UioacyVfrIU

Gulf Business (2013*).* "GCC Asian Expats Earn 26% Less than Western Peers". Retrieved fromhttp://gulfbusiness.com/2013/03/revealed-gccasian-expats-earn-26-less-than-western-peers/#.UirzcCVfrIW

Gulf News (2011). "Oman to Fund Record 28,400 Scholarships this Year", 14 August, accessed 8 June 2014, http://gulfnews.com/news/gulf/oman/oman-to-fund-record-28-400-scholarships-this-year-1.851378.

Gutcher, Lianne and Arnold, Tom (2014). "Landmark SME Law has Big Implications for UAE Economy" in *The National,* 13 April 2014.

Hakim Mohammed Said [ed] (1972). *The Employee and the Employer – Islamic Concept,* Dar al Fikr al-Islami, Pakistan.

Hall, E.T. (1976). *Beyond Culture.* New York: Anchor Press/Doubleday

Hammoud, J. (2011). "Consultative Authority Decision Making: On the Development and Characterization of Arab Corporate Culture". *International Journal of Business and Social Science.* Vol. 2, No. 9, [Special issue-May 2011]

Hanieh, A. (2011). *Capitalism and Class in the Gulf Arab States.* New York: Palgrave Macmillan.

Haque, F. (2014). "100,000 Expats to Lose Jobs in Omanisation", *Times of Oman,* 18 February, accessed 8 September 2014, http://www.timesofoman.com/news/29950/Article-100-000-expats-to-lose-jobs-in-Omanisation.

Harry, W. (2007). "Employment creation and localization: the crucial human resource issue for the GCC", *International Journal of Human Resource Management,* Vol. 18, No.1,132-146

Hasnas, John (1998). "The Normative Theories of Business Ethics: A Guide for the Perplexed", *Business Ethics Quarterly*, Vol 8, Issue 1, 19-42.

Hayami, Akira (2004). "Introduction: The Emergence of 'Economic Society", in: Hayami, Akira, Shimbo, Hiroshi. & Saito, Osamu. (eds.) *The Economic History of Japan: 1600–1990, Volume 1: Emergence of Economic Society: 1600–1859*. Oxford: Oxford University Press.

HEAC (2011*). The Annual Statistical Report of Higher Education in the Sultanate of Oman, 2010-2011.* Muscat: Higher Education Admissions Center.

HEAC (2012). *Summary of admission statistics: Academic years 2009/2010, 2010/2011, 2011/2012.* Muscat: Higher Education Admissions Center.

Heard-Bey, F. (2005). "The United Arab Emirates: Statehood and Nation-Building in a Traditional Society". *The Middle East Journal.* Vol. 59, No.3. 357-375

Henry, Clement & Springborg, Robert (2001*). Globalization and the Politics of Development in the Middle East.* Cambridge: Cambridge University Press.

Herb, M. (1999). *All in the Family: Absolutism, revolution, and Democracy in the Middle Eastern Monarchies.* New York: State University of New York Press

Herb, M. (2005). "No Representation without Taxation? Rents, Development, and Democracy", *Comparative Politics,* vol. 37, no. 3, April, 297-316.

Hertog, S. (2010). "Benchmarking SME Polices in the GCC: A Survey of Challenges and Opportunities", *Eurochambes,* Brussels, Belgium.

Hertog, S. (2011*). Princes, Brokers and Bureaucrats: Oil and the State in Saudi Arabia,* Cornell University Press, Ithaca.

Hertog , S. (2012). "A comparative assessment of labor market nationalization policies in the GCC". In Hertog, S. (ed.). *National Employment, Migration and Education in the GCC. The Gulf Region: Economic Development and Diversification,* 4, 65-106. Berlin: Gerlach.

Hertog, Steffen (2012). "Public Industry as Tool of Rentier Economy Diversification: The GCC Case", in Luciani, Giacomo (ed.) *Resources Blessed: Diversification and the Gulf Development Model*" Berlin: Gerlach Press.

Hertog, Steffen (2010). "Defying the Resource Curse: Explaining Successful State-Owned Enterprises in Rentier States". *World Politics*. 62(2): 261–301.

Hewitt, Aon (2011). *Qudurat Research Report.*

Hickson, D., and Pugh, D. (1995). *Management worldwide.* London: Penguin Books

Hofstede, G. (1980). *Culture's consequences: International differences in work-related values.* USA: SAGE

Hofstede, G. (1983). "The Cultural Relativity of Organizational Theories and Practices". *Journal of International Business Studies*, Vol. 14, No. 2, 75-89

Hofstede, G. (1994). *Cultures and Organizations: Intercultural cooperation and its importance for survival-software of the mind.* Great Britain: McGraw Hill

Hofstede, G. (2001). *Culture's consequences: Comparing values, Behaviors, Institutions, and Organizations across nations.* 2nd edition. USA: Sage Publications

Hofstede, G. (2002). "Dimensions do not exist: A reply to Brendan McSweeney", *Human Relations,* Vol. 55, No. 11

Hofstede, G. (2011). "Hofstede's Arab countries: methodology, respondents and advice". [Email] *Email received by the author from Professor Geert Hofstede*. [Personal communication, 25 November 2011.

Hofstede. com (2009). 'Hofstede: Arab world" [Online] Available from: http://www.geert-hofstede.com/hofstede_arab_world.shtml [Accessed: 20th November 2011.

Hopf, Ted (1998). "The Promise of Constructivism in International Relations Theory", *International Security* Vol. 23, No. 1 p914

Hourani, A. (1991*). A History of the Arab Peoples*. London: Faber and Faber

House, R.J. et al. (2004). *Culture, Leadership, and Organizations: the GLOBE study of 62 societies.* CA: SAGE

Hsu, Schwartz and Smith (2007). "Saudi Student Survey: Results and Analysis", *Institute for Research: Middle Eastern Policy* (IRmep), June 2007

http://www.arabianbusiness.com/saudi-princess-says-men-are-too-afraid-allow-women-s-rights-503045.html#.VFJeMfnF-uk. [Accessed 9 Nov 2014].

Human Rights Watch (2013). "World Report 2013: Saudi Arabia." Human Rights Watch [online]. Available from: http://www.hrw.org/world-report/2013/country-chapters/112341. [Accessed 9 Nov 2014.]

Hunt, D.M., and At-Twaijri, M.I. (1996). "Values and the Saudi Manager: an empirical investigation", *Journal of Management Development.*, Vol. 15, No. 5, 48-55

Hvidt, Martin (2011). "Economic and Institutional Reforms in the Arab Gulf Countries", *Middle East Journal*, vol. 65, no. 1, Winter, 85-102.

Hvidt, Martin (2013). "Economic diversification in GCC countries: Past record and future trends" *Kuwait Programme on Development, Governance and Globalisation in the Gulf States,* Number 27, London School of Economics and Political Science, London, UK

IFC (2011). *Education for Employment: Realizing Arab Youth Potential.*

Imai, Masaaki. (1997*). Gemba Kaizen: A Commonsense, Low-Cost Approach to Management.* New York: McGraw-Hills. Kindle Edition.

IMF Country Report (2013). "Saudi Arabia. Selected Issues." Report Number 13/230.

International Council on Security and Development (2010). "Unemployed Youth in the UAE, Personal Perceptions and Recommendation"s.

International Monetary Fund (IMF), (2012). "World Economic Outlook (WEO)", April

International Monetary Fund. IMF Survey, (2014). "Gulf Economies Should Diversify to Sustain Strong Future Growth", *Gulf Development Conference,* 3 June

International Monetary Fund. (2012). "IMF Country Report No. 12/272, Saudi Arabia: Selected Issues", Prepared by Ghada Fayad, Mehdi Raissi, Tobias Rasmussen, and Niklas Westelius, September 2012.

Ismail, M. (2011). "More Emirati Women marrying Foreigners", *The National.* [online] 10 April. Available from: http://www.thenational.ae/news/uae-news/more-emirati-women-marrying-foreigners#page2 [Accessed 18 December 2011[

Issawi, C. (2010*). An Economic History of the Middle East and North Africa.* New York: Routledge

Jacob, N. (2005). "Cross-cultural investigations: emerging concepts". *Journal of Organizational Change Management*, Vol. 18, No. 5, 514-528

James, A. E. (2014). "Oman Development Bank to Disburse OMR50m This Year to Fund SMEs", *Times of Oman*, 12 April, accessed 3 June 2014, http://www.timesofoman.com/news/32346/Article-Oman-Development-Bank-to-disburse-OMR50m-this-year-to-fund-SMEs.

Janardhan, N. (2009). "Expatriates — a Liability?" *Khaleej Times,* 14 December, 2009 http://www.khaleejtimes.com/kt-article-display-1.asp?xfile=data/opinion/2009/December/opinion_December85.xml&section=opinion

Jennis, C. and Al Jamali, R. 2014. "Elusive Employment: Development Planning and Labour Market Trends in Oman", *Chatham House Research Paper*, September.

Jones, D. (2014). "Employee Engagement and Productivity: A Longitudinal Study 2010 – 2012". *Cambridge University GRC Conference* (working paper).

Jones, D., and Punshi, R. (2012*). Unlocking the Paradox of Plenty. A Review of the Talent Landscape in the Arab World and Your Role in Shaping it.* Motivate Publishing.

Kabasakal, H. and Dastmalchian, A. (2001). "Introduction to the Special Issue on Leadership and Culture in the Middle East". *Applied Psychology: An International Review.*, Vol. 50, No. 4, 479-488

Kabuli, Saoud, (2014). "Saudi Arabia Faces More Immediate Threats Than Arab Spring", *Al Monitor,* 30 January.

Kamarva, Mehran (2012). "The Political Economy of Rentierism in the Persian Gulf" in *The Political Economy of the Persian Gulf,* Kamarva (eds) CIRS, Doha, Qatar.

Kanoo, Khaled M. (1997). *The House of Kanoo: A Century of an Arabian Family Business.* London.

Kantor, J., Roberts, C.B. and Salter, S.B. (1995). "Financial Reporting Practices in Selected Arab Countries: An Empirical Study of Egypt, Saudi Arabia and the United Arab Emirates". *International Studies of Management and Organization.,* Vol.25, No. 3, 31-50

Kapiszewski, A. (2001). *Nationals and Expatriates: population and labour dilemmas of the Gulf cooperation council states.* Lebanon: Ithaca Press

Kapiszewski, A. (2006). *Arab Versus Asian Migrant Workers in the GCC Countries.* United Nations, Population Division.

Karl, T. L. (2007). "Oil-Led development: Social, Political and Economic consequences". Working paper, *CDDRL.* Stanford University. No. 80

Karl, T. L. (1997). *The Paradox of Plenty: Oil Booms and Petro-States,* University of California Press, Berkeley, Los Angeles.

Karoly, L.A. (2010). "The role of education in preparing graduates for the labour market in the GCC countries". *RAND working paper.* Available online: http://www.prgs.edu/content/dam/rand/pubs/working_papers/2010/RAND_WR742.pdf

Kawakatsu, Heita (1991). *Nihon Bunmei to Kindai Seiyou.* Tokyo: NHK Books.

Kayed, Rasem N. and Hassan Kabir (2010). "A Case Study of Saudi Arabia". Journal of Developmental Entrepreneurship." *Durham Modern Middle East and Islamic World Series.* Dec 2010, Vol. 15 Issue 4, p. 379-413. London: Routledge.

Kayed, Rasem N.; Hassan Kabir (2011). "Islamic entrepreneurship." *Durham Modern Middle East and Islamic World Series.* London : Routledge.

Kent, R. (2007). *Marketing research approaches, methods and applications in Europe.* London: Thomson.

Khalaf, S. and Khalaf, R. (eds) (2011). *Arab Youth: Social Mobilization in Times of Risk,* London: Saqi Books.

Khan, Riz (2005). *Al Waleed: Businessman Billionaire Prince*, Harper Collins.

Khoury, P.S., and Kostiner, J. (1990). "Introduction: Tribes and the Complexities of State formation in the Middle East." in: Khoury, P.S., and Kostiner, J. eds. (1990) *Tribes and State Formation in the Middle East.* California: University of California Press

Kimura, Hidenori. (2009). *Monotsukuri Haisen.* Tokyo: Nihon Keizai Shinbun Shuppansha.

Kinninmont, J. (2013) "To What Extent Is Twitter Changing Gulf Societies?", *Chatham House,*[Online] Availablefrom:http://www.chathamhouse.org/publications/papers/view/189413 [Accessed: 6th February 2014]

Kirkman, B.L., Lowe, K.B., and Gibson, C.B. (2006). "A Quarter Century of 'Culture's consequences': A Review of Empirical Research Incorporating Hofstede's Cultural values framework". *Journal of International Business Studies*, Vol. 37, No. 3, 285-320.

Kluckhohn, F. R., & Strodtbeck, F. L. (1961). Variations in value orientations. Evanston, Illinois: Row, Peterson

Knickmeyer, Ellen, (2014). "Saudi Labor Market Overhaul Comes at a Cost", *Wall Street Journal*, 3 February 2014

Koen, C.I. (2005). *Comparative International Management*, London: McGraw Hill

Kostiner, J. eds. (1990). *Tribes and State Formation in the Middle East.* California: University of California Press

Krane, Jim (2009). *Dubai. The Story of the World's Fastest City.* New York.

Kroeber, A.L. & Kluckhohn, C. (1952). "Culture: A critical review of concepts and definitions". *In Papers of the Peabody Museum of American Archaeology and Ethnology,* Vol. 47. Cambridge, MA: Harvard University Press.

Kukemelk, Joel (2011). "Saudi Arabia Distributes $130 Billion", *LHV Persian Gulf Fund*

Kwek, D. (2003). "De-colonizing and Re-Presenting Culture's Consequences: A postcolonial critique of Cross-Cultural studies in Management". in A. Prasad (Ed.), *Postcolonial theory and Organizational analysis: A critical engagement.* New York: Palgrave MacMillan

Labour Market Regulatory Authority (2014), *Labour Market Indicators" Kingdom of Bahrain*, accessed 23 December 2014, http://blmi.lmra.bh/

Laurent, A. (1983). "The Cultural Diversity of Western Conceptions of Management", *International Studies of Management and Organisation*, Vol. 13, No. 1/2, p. 75 - 96.

Lindsey, G. (1991) .*Saudi Arabia.* New York: Hippocrene Books

Lippman, Thomas W. (2012). *Saudi Arabia on the Edge: The Uncertain Future of an American Ally.* Dulles VA: Potomac Books Inc.

Looney, Robert. (2004). "Saudization: A Useful Tool in the Kingdom's Battle against Unemployment?" *Journal of South Asian and Middle Eastern Studies*. 27(3): 13–33.

Luciani, Giacomo (1987). "Allocation vs. Production States: A Theoretical Framework", in Hazem Beblawi and Giacomo Luciani (eds), *The Rentier State*, Croom Helm, London.

Luciani, Giacomo (1990). "Allocation vs. Production States: A Theoretical Framework" in *The Arab State*, Luciani, Giacomo (ed.), University of California Press, Los Angeles

Luciani, Giacomo. (2005). "From Private Sector to National Bourgeoisie: Saudi Arabian Business". In Aarts, Paul. & Nonneman, Gerd. (eds.) *Saudi Arabia in the Balance: Political Economy*, Society Foreign Affairs. London: Hurst.

Luciani, Giacomo (2005). "The Resource Curse and the Gulf Development Challenge" in: Luciani, Giacomo (eds.) *Resource Blessed Diversification and the Gulf Development Model*,. Berlin: Gerlach Press.

Luhmann, Niklas (1990). *Essays on Self-Reference*. Columbia University Press.

Mack, John (1976). *A Prince of Our Disorder*, Boston: Little, Brown

Mahdavy, H. (1970). "The Patterns and Problems of Economic Development in Rentier States: the Case of Iran", in Michael Cook (ed), *Studies in the Economic History of the Middle East*, Oxford University Press, London.

Maleek, A. and Awadallah, B. (2011). "Economics of the Arab Spring". *Oxford Research Paper 79*. December. University of Oxford.

Malhotra, N.K. and Birks, D.F. (2003). *Marketing research: an applied approach*. (2nd edn) Harlow: Prentice-Hall

Maloney, W.F. (1998). "The Structure of Labor Markets in Developing Countries - Time Series Evidence on Competing Views". Working Paper No. 1940. *The World Bank* - Latin America and the Caribbean Region. Available online http://www-wds.worldbank.org/servlet/WDSContentServer/WDSP/IB/1998/06/01/000009265_3980901093456/Rendered/PDF/multi_page.pdf

Maududi, A.A. (1967). *Islamic Way of Life*. Kuwait: Al-Faisal printing

McKinsey (2013). *Education to Employment Report*.

McSweeney, B. (2002). "Hofstede's model of national cultural differences and their consequences: a triumph of faith- a failure of analysis", *Human Relations*, Vol. 55, No. 1, 89-118

Mead, R. and Andrews, T.G. (2009*). International Management: Culture and Beyond*, 4th edition. England: John Wiley & Sons

Migrant-rights.org (2012a). "Migrant workers under the kafala system in the GCC". [online] Available at: http://www.migrant-rights.org/2010/11/23/migrant-workers-under-the-%E2%80%9Ckafala%E2%80%9D-system-in-the-gcc/ [Accessed: 10 February 2012.

Migrant-rights.org (2012b*)*. "Workers - working conditions". [online] Available at: http://www.migrant-rights.org/category/workers/working-conditions/ [Accessed: 10 February 2012.

Ministry Of National Economy (2009). *Statistical Yearbook 2009*. Muscat: Ministry of National Economy.

Minkov, M. and Hofstede, G. (2011). "The Evolution of Hofstede's Doctrine". *Cross Cultural Management: An International Journal*. Vol. 18, No. 1.10-20.

Mirkin, B. (2010). "Population Levels, Trends and Policies in the Arab Region: Challenges and Opportunities". *Arab Human Development Report*, UNDP.

MoE (2012). "Educational Indicators for the academic year 2010/2011". Muscat: Ministry of Education.

Mohamed, A., Hamdy. H. (2008). "The Stigma of Wasta: The Effect of Wasta on Perceived"

Mohammed bin Rashid Al Maktoum Foundation and Price Waterhouse Coopers (PWC)

Mohammed, N.S. (2003). *Population and Development of the Arab Gulf States: The case of Bahrain, Oman and Kuwait*. Hampshire: Ashgate Publishing

MoMP (2012*)*. "Ministry of Manpower Annual Report 2012". Muscat: Ministry of Manpower.

Movius, L. (2010). "Cultural Globalisation and Challenges to Traditional Communication Theories". *PLATFORM: Journal of Media and Communication* Vol. 2, No.1 (January) 6-18

Muhammad, F. (2013). "Twitter usage in KSA grows '10 times the world average", *Saudi Gazette* [Online] 9th February. Available from: www.saudigazette.com.sa/index.cfm?method=home.regcon&contentid=20130106148256 [Accessed: 2nd February 2014.[

Mulholland, J. (1991). *The Language of Negotiation*. London: Routledge

Murphy, C. (2011). "Will the house of Saud adapt enough to survive ... again?", *The Star* [Online] 9th February. Available from: http://www.thestar.com/news/world/article/937967--will-the-house-of-saud-adapt enough-to-survive-again [Accessed: 14th February 2014.[

Murphy, C. (2013). *A Kingdom's Future: Saudi Arabia Through the Eyes of its Twentysomethings*, Washington, DC: Wilson Center.

Muscat Daily (2013). "Royal Orders to Standardize Grades, Salaries in Government Sector in Oman", 11 November, accessed 8 June 2014, http://www.muscatdaily.com/Archive/Oman/Royal-Orders-to-standardise-grades-salaries-in-govt-sector-in-Oman-2p4o.

Muysken, J. & S. Nour (2006). "Deficiencies in education and poor prospects for economic growth in the Gulf countries: The case of the UAE", *Journal of Development Studies.* 42(6). 957-980.

Nakaoka, Tetsuro (2004). *Nihon Kindai Gijutsu no Keisei.* Tokyo: Asahi Shinbun-sha.

Nakata, C. (2009). *Beyond Hofstede: Culture Frameworks for Global Marketing and Management.* Great Britain: Palgrave Macmillan

National Centre for Statistics and Information (NCSI) (2014a). *"Statistical Yearbook".*

National Centre for Statistics and Information (NCSI) (2014b). *"Monthly Statistics Bulletin",* August.

Nazir, S. and Tomppert, L. (2005). *Women's Rights in the Middle East and North Africa: Citizenship and Justice.* USA: Rowman and Littlefield Publishers

NBS (2013). Gross Domestic Product (2012). Published on 19 June, 2013. Available at http://www.uaestatistics.gov.ae/EnglishHome/ReportDetailsEnglish/tabid/121/Default.aspx?ItemId=2216&PTID=104&MenuId=1

NCSI (2012). *Statistical Yearbook 2012.* National Center for Information and Statistics. Available online: www.ncis.gov.om

NCSI (2013). *Informative Reports 2nd Issue, Women in Oman.* Muscat: National Center for Information and Statistics. Available online: www.ncis.gov.om

Neal, M. (2010). "When Arab-expatriate relations work well: Diversity and discourse in the Gulf Arab workplace". *Team Performance Management.* Vol. 16, No. 5/6. 242-266

Neal, M. (2012*). Heterogeneity of national culture and workplace values in the Arab region.* [Interview] Interview between Dr Mark Neal and the author, held at SOAS (Main Building), University of London, London. 10 February: 13:30hrs.

Neal, M. and Finlay, J.L (2008). "American Hegemony and Business Education in the Arab World." *Journal of Management Education*, Vol.32, No.1. February. 38-83.

Nehme, M. (2003). *Fear and Anxiety in the Arab World.* USA: University Press of Florida

Nevo, J. (1998). "Religion and National Identity in Saudi Arabia". *Middle Eastern Studies.*, Vol. 34, No. 3, 34-53.

Niblock, T. with Malik, M. (2007) *The Political Economy of Saudi Arabia*, Abingdon: Routledge.

Nietzsche, Friedrich, *Vom Nutzen und Nachteil der Historie für das Leben* (On the Use and Abuse of History for Life), originally published 1873

Noland, M. and Pack, H. (2007). *The Arab Economies in a Changing World.* USA: Peter G. Peterson Institute for International Economics

Noland. M. and Pack, H. (2004). "Islam, Globalization and Economic Performance in the Middle East?". *SAIS Review*, Vol. 24, No.2, 105-116.

Oman Economic Review (2014). "A stellar panel discusses and comes up with a range of solutions on the topic "in-country value Oman: identifying priorities" in session one of *Oman Debate 2014*', June, accessed 8 June 2014, http://www.oeronline.com/php/2014/June/coverstory.php.

Oman Ministry of Manpower (2014). *Omanisation Plan*, accessed 5 September 2014, http://www.manpower.gov.om/portal/en/OmanisationPlan.aspx.

Oman Observer (2013). *"More Omanis Leave Private Sector",* 10 November, accessed 8 June 2014, http://main.omanobserver.om/?p=28943.

Omanuna (Oman Government eServices) c. (2014). *Omanisation Policy,* accessed 5 September2014http://www.oman.om/wps/portal/!ut/p/c4/04_SB8K8xLLM9MSSzPy8xBz9CP0os3hjA3cDA39LT18Tp0AXAyMvI2_

TYEdjI4NgE_2CbEdFAJCSMWg!/?WCM_GLOBAL_CONTEXT=/wps/wcm/connect/EN/site/home/gov/gov2/gov22omanisationpolicy./

Ortmans, Jonathan (2010). *Entrepreneurship in the Arab World: A Report from Dubai,* posted on 8 March, 2010, at http://www.entrepreneurship.org/Blogs/Policy-Forum-Blog/2010/March/Entrepreneurship-in-the-Arab-World-A-Report-from-Dubai.aspx

Osella, Caroline & Osella, Filippo (2012). "Migration, Networks and Connectedness across the Indian Ocean," in: Kamrava, Mehran & Zahra, Babar (eds.), *Migrant Labor in the Persian Gulf,* Hurst & Company, London.

Owen, R. (1992). *State, Power and Politics in the making of The Modern Middle East.* London: Routledge

Owen, R. (2012). *Disparities and differences in the Arab region.* [Interview] *Interview between Professor Roger Owen and the autho*r, held at LSE (New Academic Building), University of London, London. 9 January: 20:00hrs.

Oxford Business Group (2014) . *Oman Working to Support SME Growth,* 13 May, accessed 3 June 2014, http://www.oxfordbusinessgroup.com/economic_updates/oman-working-support-sme-growth.

Pallant, J. (2007*). "SPSS survival manual* (3rd edn) England: McGraw-Hill Education

Palmer, Monte, Alghofaily, Ibrahim. & Alnimir, Saud (1984). "The Behavioral Correlates of Rentier Economies: A Case Study of Saudi Arabia" in Robert W. Stookey (ed.*) The Arabian Peninsula: Zone of Ferment.* Stanford: Hoover Institution Press: 17-36.

Pampanini, Andrea (1997). *Cities from the Arabian Desert: The Building of Jubail and Yanbu in Saudi Arabia.* London: Praeger.

Parker, Simon C. (2006). "Entrepreneurship, Self/Employment and the Labour Market", in *The Oxford Handbook of Entrepreneurship,* ed. Casson et al., 435-460. Oxford University Press, Oxford.

Partick, N. (2012). "Nationalism in the Gulf Arab states", in Held, D. and Ulrichsen, K. (2012*) The Transformation of the Gulf: Politics, economics and the global order.* Oxon: Routledge

Pathak, S. (2014). "Qatar Wants Private Sector to Create Jobs for 60,000", *Qatar Tribune,* 15 April, accessed 8 June 2014, http://www.qatar-tribune.com/viewnews.aspx?n=2FC669E9-DE76-4D8E-A12D-DF2DD98C72A2&d=20140415.

Pearce, C.L. and Osmond, C.P. (1999). "From Workplace Attitudes and Values to a Global pattern of Nations: An Application of Latent Class Modelling". *Journal of Management,* Vol. 25, No. 5, 759-778.

Pech, Robert (2009). "Emiratization: aligning education with future needs in the United Arab Emirates" *Education, Business and Society: Contemporary Middle Eastern Issues,* Vol. 2 No. 1, 57-65

Pei, Minxin (1994). "The Puzzle of East Asian Exceptionalism". *Journal of Democracy.* 5(4): 90–103.

Peninsula Times (2014). *"Saudi Electricity Consumption is Double that of World Average",* 5 June.

Peterson, J. E. (2012). "The GCC states: Participation, opposition, and the fraying of the social contract" Research Paper No.26, *Kuwait Programme on Development, Governance and Globalisation in the Gulf States,* London School of Economics and Political Science

Peterson, M.F. (2003). Review of the book *Culture's Consequences,* Administrative Science Quarterly, Vol. 48, No. 1, 127-31 (second edition by G. Hofstede.(

Piketty, T. (2013). *Capital in the Twenty-First Century.* Translated by Arthur Goldhammer. Belknap Press.

Piscatori, J. (1981). "The formation of the Saudi identity: A case study of the utility of transitionalism," in Stach, F. (ed), *Ethnic identities in a transitional world.* Westport: CT ; Islam in a World of nation states

Pistrui, D. and Fahed-Sreih, J. (2010). "Islam, entrepreneurship and business values in the Middle East" *International Journal of Entrepreneurship and Innovation Management.,* Vol. 12, No. 1, 107-118

Positive Psychology at Geelong Grammar School (2014). Retrieved on 22 May 2014 from http://www.ggs.vic.edu.au/School/Positive-Education/Research/Key-Considerations/KeyConsiderations

Possumah, Bayu Taufiq, Ismail, Abdul Ghafar, and Shahimi, Shahida (2013). "Bringing Work Back in Islamic Ethics." *Journal of Business Ethics.* January, Volume 112, Issue 2, 257-270. Pourmohammadi, E (2014a). "Shell Intilaaqah Motivating Youth Omani Entrepreneurs", *Times of Oman,* 30 April, accessed 3 June 2014, http://www.timesofoman.com/news/33190/Article-%E2%80%98Shell-Intilaaqah-motivating-young-Omani-entrepreneurs%E2%80%99.

Pourmohammadi, E. (2014b). "Why Private Sector Lags in Omanisation", Times of Oman, 6 April, accessed 18 September 2014, http://www.timesofoman.com/news/32071/Article-Why-private-sector-lags-in-Omanisation.

Prabhu, C. (2014). "SME Development Fund with Capital of RO 100 Million Launched", *Oman Daily Observer*, 10 May, accessed 3 June 2014, http://main.omanobserver.om/?p=79893.

Prahalad, C.K. (2010). *The Fortune at the Bottom of the Pyramid. Eradicating Poverty through Profits.* Upper Saddle River, New Jersey.

PwC (2013). *Enabling Job Creation in the Arab World – The Role for Regional Integration.*

Qatar General Secretariat for Development Planning (2011). *Qatar National Development Strategy 2011-2016.*

Qatar Leadership Program (2012). *"Future Leaders Excel at Qatar Leadership Centre Programs"*, 24 September, accessed 5 September 2014, http://qlc.org.qa/en/NewsRoomDetails_24_09_2012.html.

Qatar Ministry of Development, Planning and Statistics (2013). *2013 Labour Force Survey,* accessed 5 September 2014, http://www.qsa.gov.qa/eng/index.htm.

Qatar Science and Technology Park (QSTP) c. (2014). *Support Programs,* accessed 8 June 2014, http://qstp.org.qa/home/support-programs.

Qatar Statistics Authority (QSA) (2013). *Ministry of Development, Planning and Statistics Labour Force Survey,* accessed 5 September 2014, http://www.qsa.gov.qa/eng/index.htm.

Quinn, Ben (2012). "Ikea apologises over removal of women from Saudi Arabia catalogue." *The Guardian* [online]. 1 Oct 2012. Available from: http://www.theguardian.com/world/2012/oct/02/ikea-apologises-removing-women-saudi-arabia-catalogue. [Accessed 9 Nov 2014].

Quran. Trans. Sarwar, M. (1981). *Islamic Seminary*. Elmhurst: New York

Radcliffe, Damian (2014) . "In One Arab Country, 37% Surf on the Mobiles 6 Hours Per Day", *Your Middle East*, 4 March 2014

Rahahleh, Hazem (2012). "Discrepancies in Public and Private Sector Pay in Jordan, Qatar and the UAE" *Arab Centre for Research and Policy Studies*, Doha Qatar

Ramady, M. A. (2005). *The Saudi Arabian Economy: Policies, Achievements and Challenges*. Heidelberg, New York: Springer.

Ramady, M.A. (2010) *The Saudi Arabian Economy: Policies, Achievements, and Challenges,* Heidelberg, New York: Springer.

Ramady, M.A. (2014). *Political, Economic and Financial Country Risk: Analysis of the Gulf Cooperation Council*, Heidelberg, New York: Springer.

Ramady, M.A. (2013). "Gulf unemployment and government policies: prospects for the Saudi labour quota or Nitaqat system", *International Journal Economics and Business Research.* Vol. X. No. Y. 476–498.

Randeree, K. (2009). "Strategy, policy and practice in the nationalisation of human capital: Project Emiratisation?". *Research and Practice in Human Resource Management*. 17(1). 71-91.

Rehamn, Khalil Ur (2010). *The Concept of Labor in Islam*, Xlibris Corporation.

Rice, G. (1999). "Islamic Ethics and the Implications for Business", *Journal of Business Ethics*, Vol. 18, No. 4, 345-358

Ridge, N. (2014) ."*Education and the Reverse Gender Divide in the Gulf States: Embracing the Global, Ignoring the Local,"* New York: Teachers College Press.

Robertson, C., Al-Khatib, J., Al-Habib, M. and Lanoue, D. (2001). "Beliefs about Work in the Middle East and the Convergence Versus Divergence of Values". *Journal of World Business*, Vol. 36, No. 3, 223-244

Rocha, Vera (2012). *The Entrepreneur in Economic Theory: From an Invisible Man Toward a New Research Field.* FEP Working Paper, May 2012

Romaniuk, J. (2008). "Comparing methods of measuring brand personality traits". *Journal of Marketing Theory and Practice*. 16(2), 153-161.

Ronen, S. and Shenkar, O. (1985). "Clustering countries on attitudinal dimensions: A review and synthesis". *Academy of Management Review*, Vol. 10, No. 3, 435-454

Ross, M. (2001). "Does Oil Hinder Democracy?" *World Politics,* vol.53, April, 325-361.

Ross, M. (1999). "The Political Economy of the Resource Curse", *World Politics*, vol. 51, no. 2, January, 297-322.

Roudha Center for Entrepreneurship and Innovation c. (2014). "About Us", accessed 8 June 2014, http://www.roudha.org/about.php.

Roudi-Fahimi, F. & V. Moghadam (2003). "Empowering women, developing society: Female Education in the Middle East and North Africa". *MENA Policy Brief*. Washington: Population Reference Bureau.

Routledge Encyclopedia (2001). Search term: "Diversification", in R. J. B. Jones (ed.), *Routledge Encyclopedia of International Political Economy*. London: Routledge, Vol. 1, p. 360

Royal Embassy of Saudi Arabia. (2014). "The Basic Law of Governance." *Royal Embassy of Saudi Arabia* [online]. Available from: http://www.saudiembassy.net/about/country-information/laws/The_Basic_Law_Of_Governance.aspx. [Accessed 9 Nov 2014].

Reuters (2014). "Saudi Student Dies After Male Medics Not Allowed to Help Due to Gender Segregation." *RT.com* [online]. 10 Feb 2014. Available from: http://rt.com/news/saudi-arabia-segregation-women-110/. [Accessed 9 Nov 2014].

Rugh, A.B. (2007). *The Political Culture of Leadership in the United Arab Emirates*. New York: Palgrave MacMillan

Rugh, William (1973). "Emergence of a New Middle Class in Saudi Arabia". *Middle East Journal*. 27(1): 7–20.

Ruppert, E. (1999). "Managing Foreign Labor in Singapore and Malaysia - Are There Lessons for the GCC Countries". Working Paper No. 2053. *The World Bank - Middle East and North Africa Region*. Available online http://www-wds.worldbank.org/external/default/WDSContentServer/IW3P/IB/2000/02/24/000094946_99031911113873/additional/109509322_20041117144524.pdf

Rutledge, E., F. Al Shamsi, Y. Bassioni & H. Al Sheikh (2011). "Women, labour market nationalization policies and human resource development in the Arab Gulf states". *Human Resource Development International*. 14(2). 183-198.

Ryan, R. and Deci, E. (2000). "Intrinsic and Extrinsic Motivations: Classic Definitions and New Directions", *Contemporary Educational Psychology* (25) [Online] Available from: http://www.selfdeterminationtheory.org/SDT/documents/2000_RyanDeci_IntExtDefs.pdf [Accessed: 6th September 2014]

Sabri, Sharaf (2001) *The House of Saud in Commerce: A Study of Royal Entrepreneurship in Saudi Arabia*. New Delhi: I. S. Publications.

Sabry, Sara (2013). "Increase the number of Emiratis in the private sector is a main priority of ADTC" *Gulf News*, 2 October, 2013
http://gulfnews.com/news/gulf/uae/employment/increase-the-number-of-emiratis-in-the-private-sector-is-a-main-priority-of-adtc-1.1238490

Said, M. (2001). "Public sector employment and Labour markets in Arab countries: Recent developments and policy implications", in Salehi-Esfahani, D., eds, *Labor and Human capital in the Middle East*. Reading: Ithaca Press

Salama, Samir (2013). "Campaign lures Emiratis to jobs in private sector" *Gulf News*, 23 September, 2013, http://gulfnews.com/news/gulf/uae/employment/campaign-lures-emiratis-to-jobs-in-private-sector-1.1234526

Salama, Samir (2014). "UAE targets 15% Emiratisation in insurance by 2015, minister says" *Gulf News*, 24 June, 2014 http://gulfnews.com/news/gulf/uae/government/uae-targets-15-emiratisation-in-insurance-by-2015-minister-says-1.1351682

Salehi-Isfahani, D. (2011). "Population and human capital in the Persian Gulf", in *Center for International and Regional Studies. The Political Economy of the Gulf: Working Group Summary Report*, 13-14. Georgetown University, Qatar.

Salem, Fatma (2010). "Entrepreneur Connects Women with Pre-Owned Designer Bags," *Gulf News*, 11 December 2010.

Sarayrah, Y.K. (2004). "Servant Leadership in the Bedouin-Arab Culture". *Global Virtue Ethics Review*, Vol. 5, No. 3, 58-79.

Sarby, Sara; Zaman, Samihah (2013). "Emirati unemployment at 14%" *Gulf News*, 29 January, 2013 http://gulfnews.com/news/gulf/uae/employment/emirati-unemployment-at-14-1.1139425

Saudi Gazette (2014). "Panel to Boost Saudization" *Saudi Gazette* [online]. 10 April 2014. Availablefrom: http://www.saudigazette.com.sa/index.cfm?method=home.regcon&contentid=20140410201508. [Accessed 9 Nov 2014].

Saudi Hollandi Bank Report, (2012). "Labor And The Nitaqat Program: Effect On The Saudi Arabian Economy", June

SaudiBrit. (2011). "The Challenge of Change in Saudi Arabia: A Conversation with Thomas Lippman", *Saudi British Relations Information Service* [Online] Available from: www.saudibrit.com/2011/03/03/the-challenge-of-change-in-saudi-arabia-a-conversation-with-thomas-lippman/ [Accessed: 12th March 2014.

Schellen, Thomas, (2014). "Saudi Leads the Way in Regional Mega Projects", *Executive Magazine*, 4 April.

Schiliro, Daniele (2013). "Diversification and development of the UAE's economy" *MPRA Working Paper 47089* University Library of Munich, Germany, http://EconPapers.repec.org/RePEc:pra:mprapa:47089.

Schloderer, Florian & Mencias, Stephen J. (2013). "Azza al Qubaisi: the Artist Entrepreneur". INSEAD Case Study, Abu Dhabi.

Schroeder, Christopher M. (2013). *Startup Rising: The Entrepreneurial Revolution Remaking the Middle East.* New York: Palgrave Macmillan.

Schumpeter, Josef A. (1942/1975). *Capitalism, Socialism and Democracy.* New York.

Schumpeter, Josef A. (1949). "Economic Theory and Entrepreneurial History", in *Change and the Entrepreneur,* Harvard University Press, Boston.

Schwartz, S.H. (1994). "Beyond Individualism/collectivism: new cultural dimensions of values", in Triandis et al. (eds), *Individualism and Collectivism: Theory, Methods, and Applications.* CA: SAGE, 85-119

Schwedler, J. and Gerner, D.J. (2008). *Understanding the contemporary Middle East.* Colorado: Lynne Rienner Publishers

Seligman, M. E. P., Ernst, R. M., Gillham, J., Reivich, K., & Linkins, M. (2009). "Positive education: Positive psychology and classroom interventions". *Oxford Review of Education,* 35(3), 293-311.

Seligman, M. E. P., Steen, T. A., Park, N., & Peterson, C. (2005). "Positive psychology progress: Empirical validation of interventions". *American Psychologist*, 60, 410–421.

Seligman, M.E.P. (2002). *Authentic Happiness: Using the New Positive Psychology to Realize your Potential for Lasting Fulfillment.* New York, Free Press.

Sfakianakis, John, (2014). "Comprehensive Reform of the Labor Market in Saudi Arabia", *SUSTG,* 26 January

Sfakianaki, John (2014). "Why Technical and Vocational Training is an Urgent Need for Saudi Arabia's Future", *SUSTG*, 16 March 2014

Shah, N. (2004). "Gender and labour migration to the Gulf countries". *Feminist Review*, Vol. 77, 183-85.

Shah, N.M. (2008). "Restrictive Labour Immigration Policies in the Oil-Rich Gulf: Effectiveness and Implications for Sending Asian Countries". Publication no. *UN/POP/EGM/2006/03. United Nations Expert Group Meeting on International Migration and Development in the Arab Region.* Available on www.un.org/esa/population/migration/turin/Symposium_Turin_files/P03_Shah.pdf

Shah, N. (2009). "The management of irregular migration and its consequences for development: Gulf Cooperation Council". *Working Paper No. 19, Regional Office for Asia and the Pacific, ILO.*

Sharabi, H. (1988). *Neoptriarchy: A theory of distorted change in Arab society.* New York:

Sharakah, C. (2014). *Sharakah homepage*, accessed 3 June 2014, http://sharakah.om/index.php.

Shear, Michael D. (2013). "Obama Ends Overseas Trip With Award for Saudi." *The New York Times* [online]. 29 March 2014. Available from: http://www.nytimes.com/2014/03/30/world/middleeast/obama-saudi-arabia.html?_r=0. [Accessed 9 Nov 2014.]

Shediac, Richard and Samman, Hatem, (2010). *Meeting the Employment Challenge in the GCC: The Need for a Holistic Strategy,* Booz & Co., Inc, Dubai,

Shimbo, Hiroshi. & Saito, Osamu. (2004). "The Economy on the Eve of Industrialization", in Hayami, Akira, Shimbo, Hiroshi & Saito, Osamu (eds.) *The Economic History of Japan: 1600–1990, Volume 1: Emergence of Economic Society: 1600–1859*. Oxford: Oxford University Press.

Shobakky, Waleed (2008). "Petrodollar Science". *The New Atlantis*. [Online] Available at: http://www.thenewatlantis.com/publications/petrodollar-science [accessed 1 September 2014.[

Shoshani, A., & Ilanit Aviv, I. (2012). "The pillars of strength for first-grade adjustment – Parental and children's character strengths and the transition to elementary school". *Journal of Positive Psychology*, 7(4), 315-326.

Shoshani, A., & Slone, M. (2012). "Middle school transition from the strengths perspective: Young adolescents' character strengths, subjective well-being, and school adjustment". *Journal of Happiness Studies*.

Siew, I.N., Lee, J.A., and Soutar, G.N. (2007). "Are Hofstede's and Schwartz's value frameworks congruent?" *International marketing review*, Vol. 24 No. 2, 164-180.

Silatech.C. (2014*). Silatech in Qatar*, accessed 8 June 2014, http://www.silatech.com/home/silatech-in-qatar.

Singh, A., Jones, D.B., Hall, N. (2012). "Talent Management: A Research Based Case Study in the GCC Region", *International Journal of Business and Management*; Vol. 7, No. 24; 2012.

Sivakumar, K. and Nakata, C. (2001). "The stampede towards Hofstede's framework: avoiding the sample design pit in cross-cultural research". *Journal of International Business Studies*, Vol. 26, No. 4, 555-574.

Sleiman, Mirna (2013). "Just Falafel chain to IPO on Nasdaq as soon as October," *Reuters*, 17 September 2013.

Smith, Larry. & Abouammoh, Abdulrahman (eds.) (2013). *Higher Education in Saudi Arabia: Achievements, Challenges and Opportunities*. New York: Springer.

Smith, P.B, Dugan, S. and Trompenaars, F. (1996). "National culture and the values of organizational employees". *Journal of Cross-Cultural Psychology*, Vol. 27, No. 2, 231-264.

Smith, P.B. (2002). "Culture's consequences: something old and something new" [review article and response to McSweeney, 2002] *Human Relations*, Vol. 55, No. 1, 119-135.

Smith, P.B., Peterson, M.F. and Schwartz, S.H. (2002). "Cultural Values, sources of guidance, and their relevance to managerial behaviour: a 47 nation study", *Journal of Cross –cultural Psychology*, Vol. 33 No. 2, 188-208.

Smotherman, R., and Kooros, S. (2001). "Assessing Cultural Differences: Comparing Hofstede's and Trompenaars' Dimensions". *Journal of Business Disciplines*, Proc. Annual Meeting Academy of Business Disciplines: [online] Available at: http://edepot.wur.nl/44756. Accessed: 14th November 2011

State.gov (2011). *U.S. Department of state: Background note: United Arab Emirates*. [Online] Available from: http://www.state.gov/r/pa/ei/bgn/5444.htm [Accessed: 5th December 2011[

Sultan, N., Metcalfe, B.D., Weir, D. (2011) "Building the Foundation for a Post-Oil Era: The Case of the GCC Countries", in Sultan, N., Metcalfe, B.D., Weir, D. (eds.) *The New Post-Oil Arab Gulf: Managing People and Wealth*, London: Saqi Books.

Susris Webinar, (2014). "Saudi Labor in Transition" 18 May

Swan, Melanie (2013). "UAE unemployment: Women urged to join private sector internships" *The National*, 23 September, 2013 http://www.thenational.ae/uae/education/uae-unemployment-women-urged-to-join-private-sector-internships

Szyliowicz, Joseph. (1979). "The Prospects for Scientific and Technological Development in Saudi Arabia", *International Journal of Middle East Studies*. 10: 355–372.

Taher, Abdulhady. (2011). *Petroleum, Gas, and Development Strategies of Saudi Arabia*. London: Saqi.

Takahashi, Satoshi (2007) *Edo no Kyoiku-ryoku*. Tokyo: Chikuma Shobo.

Tamkeen (2010). *2010-2014 Strategy*.

Tamkeen, C.(2014)."Business Incubator Scheme", accessed 5 June 2014, http://www.lf.bh/en/pss/?p=Incubators#.U4_N7ZSSybI.

Tayeb, M. (2001). "Conducting research across cultures: Overcoming Drawbacks and Obstacles." *International Journal of Cross Cultural Management*. Vol.1, No.1, 91-108

Telegraph (2010). "Dubai: Strict morality laws behind western appearance". [online] 14 March. Available from: http://www.telegraph.co.uk/news/worldnews/middleeast/dubai/7443280/Dubai-strict-morality-laws-behind-Western-appearance.html [Accessed: 16 February 2012.

The Economist (2013). "Why is Youth Unemployment so High?" Retrieved from http://www.economist.com/blogs/economistexplains/2013/05/economist-explains-why-youth-unemployment-so-high, May 3

The National (2012). "Statistics Suggest Sorry State of Emiratisation in the Private Sector." Retrieved from http://www.thenational.ae/news/uae-news/statistics-suggest-sorry-state-of-emiratisation-in-private-sector

The Talent Enterprise. (2014). *Al Masar – Human Capital Imperatives Before, During and After Expo 2020.*

The Talent Enterprise. (2014). *MENA Labour Market Confidence Index.*

The World Bank. (2008). *The World Bank Indicator Database*. Available online: http://data.worldbank.org/indicator

Thompson, M. (2012). "Saudi Youth: Challenges for the Future", *Orient* (IV), 32–37.

Time Magazine (1953). *"Saudi Arabia: The First Strike"*, 2 November

Times News Service (2014). "Oman Expatriate Labour Ban: Two-Year Restrain on Expedite Local Hiring, Reduce Number of Expats", *Times of Oman*, 12 May, accessed 5 September 2014, http://www.timesofoman.com/news/33733/Article-Oman-expatriate-labour-ban-Two-year-restrain-on-expedite-local-hiring-reduce-number-of-expats.

Tong, Xinjia (2012). "An Analysis of Entrepreneurship across Five Major Nationality Groups in the United Arab Emirates", *Journal of Developmental Entrepreneurship*, Vol. 17, No. 2 (2012)

Toumi, H. (2011). "Public Sector in Qatar to Get 60 Percent Pay Rise", *Gulf News*, 7 September, accessed April 22, 2013, http://gulfnews.com/news/gulf/qatar/public-sector-in-qatar-to-get-60-per-cent-pay-rise-1.862595.

Trenwith, Courtney (2013) . "Saudi Princess Says Men Are Too Afraid to Allow Women's Rights." *Arabian Business.com* [online]. 26 May 2013.

Tripp, C. (2006). *Islam and the Moral Economy: The Challenge of Capitalism*. Cambridge University Press: United Kingdom

Trompenaars, F. (1993). *Riding the waves of culture*. London: Nicholas Brealey

UAE Cabinet (2010). *UAE Vision 2021: United in Ambition and Determination*. Abu Dhabi: Government of United Arab Emirates http://www.moca.gov.ae/?page_id=620&lang=en

UAE Interact (2009). "UAE cabinet approves record Dh43.6 billion federal budget for 2010",

UAE Interact (2013a). 'UAE real GDP exceeds Dh1trn for first time" *UAE Interact*, 15th October,2013,http://www.uaeinteract.com/docs/UAE_real_GDP_exceeds_Dh1trn_for_first_time/56470.htm

Ulrichsen, K. (2012) . "The Challenge of Transition: Gulf security in the twenty-first century", in Held, D. and Ulrichsen, K. (eds.) *The Transformation of the Gulf: Politics, economics and the global order,* Abingdon: Routledge.

Ulrichsen, Kristian Coates. (2012). "Knowledge Economies in the GCC States", in Kamrava, Mehran. (eds.) *The Political Economy of the Persian Gulf.* London: Hurst & Co.

UNDP (2003*). Arab Human Development Report: Building a Knowledge Society*. New York: United Nations.

UNDP (2010). *Population Levels, Trends and Policies in the Arab Region: Challenges and Opportunities.*

UNESCO (2014). "Education", *Institute of Statistic,* http://data.uis.unesco.org/#

United Nations(2013). *World Population Prospects: The 2012 Revision*, Department of Economic and Social Affairs, Population Division DVD Edition.

US Department of Education (2013). 'Digest of Education Statistics, 2012" in *National Center for Education Statistics*

US Embassy Manama (2008). "Bahrain"s Crown Prince Consolidating his Authority", *Wikileaks Cable* 08MANAMA89, 13 February, accessed 18 September 2014, http://www.telegraph.co.uk/news/wikileaks-files/bahrain-wikileaks-cables/8334484/BAHRAINS-CROWN-PRINCE-CONSOLIDATING-HIS-AUTHORITY.html.

US Embassy Muscat (2009). "Business Oligarchs and Government in Oman's Economy", *Wikileaks Cable* 09MUSCAT851, 16 August, accessed 17 August 2014, http://wikileaks.org/cable/2009/08/09MUSCAT851.html.

Valeri, Marc (2009*). Oman: Politics and Society in the Qaboos Stat*", Columbia University Press, New York

Vinken, H., Soeters., J. and Ester, P. (2004). *Comparing cultures: Dimensions of culture in a comparative perspective.* Boston, MA: Brill

Volkmann, Christine (2004). "Entrepreneurial Studies – An Ascending Academic Discipline in the 21st Century" in *Higher Education in Europe*, 29, No. 2, July 2004

Vom Bruck, G. (2012). *Differences in the Arab region: an anthropological perspective* [Interview*] Interview between Dr Gabriele vom Bruck and the author*, held at SOAS (Main Building), University of London, London. 6 February: 14:30hrs

Wagener, Andreas (2000). "Entrepreneurship and Social Security", in *FinanzArchiv / Public Finance Analysis,* 57, No. 3 (2000), 284-315

Wahab, Siraj, (2011). "Labor Ministry Outlines Details of Nitaqat Program", *Arab News*, 12 June

Wakamatsu, Yoshihito (2007). *Toyota-shiki Kaizen no Susume-kata.* Tokyo: PHP Institute.

Walker, L. (2014). "New Panel Established to Push Private Sector to Employ More Qataris", *Doha News*, 25 August, accessed 5 September 2014, http://dohanews.co/panel-push-private-sector-employ-qatari-nationals./

Warren, Elizabeth, and Tyagi, Amelia, (2004). *The Two-Income Trap: Why Middle-Class Parents are Going Broke*, New York: Basic Books

Weber, Max (1947). *The Theory of Social and Economic Organization.* (Translated by AM Henderson & Talcott Parsons). NY: The Free Press

Weber, M., & Ruch, W. (2012a) "The role of character strengths in adolescent romantic relationships: An initial study on partner selection and mates' life satisfaction". *Journal of Adolescence.*

Weber, Max, (1904, 1905). *Die Protestantische Ethik und der Geist des Kapitalismus,* originally published 1904, 1905

Welsh, D. and Raven, P. (2006). "Family business in the Middle East: an exploratory study of retail management in Kuwait and Lebanon". *Family Business Review*, Vol. 19, No. 1

Wenlin, T. (2011) "Tribal bonds, weak states threaten Middle East". *Global Times*, [online] 8 August. Available at: http://www.globaltimes.cn/NEWS/tabid/99/ID/669950/Tribal-bonds-weak-states-threaten-Middle-East.aspx [Accessed 2 December 2011.[

Wharton Global (2012). "Ikea's Women-Free Catalogue In Saudi Arabia Misses the Picture." *Wharton: The University of Pennsylvania* [online]. 16 Oct 2012. Available from: http://global.wharton.upenn.edu/post/ikeas-women-free-catalogue-in-saudi-arabia-misses-the-picture/. [Accessed 9 Nov 2014].

WikiLeaks Secret US Embassy Cables, (2006). "Ambassador Oberwetter to Secretary of State, A Possible Retreat On Saudization?", E.O.12958, Washington D.C., 6 July

Williams, Geoffrey & Zinkin, John (2010). "Islam and CSR: A Study of the Compatibility Between the Tenets of Islam and the UN Global Compact," *Journal of Business Ethics,* 91:519-533.

Williamson, D. (2002). "Forward from a critique of Hofstede's model of national culture", *Human Relations*, Vol. 55. No. 11, 1373-1395.

Woertz, Eckart, (2013). "Trouble in Oil Paradise: Domestic Challenges in Saudi Arabia and their Global Implications", *Norwegian Peacebuilding Resource Centre* (NOREF), November

World Bank (1999). *Education in the Middle East and North Africa: a strategy towards learning for development* World Bank, Human Development Sector, New York, NY

World Bank (2004.) *Unlocking the employment potential in the Middle East and North Africa: Toward a new social contract - MENA Development report.* New York: The World Bank

World Bank (2010). *World Bank Data* [Online] Available from: http://data.worldbank.org/country [Accessed: 28th November, 2011[

World Bank (2013). *Data- Population* http://data.worldbank.org/indicator/SP.POP.TOTL

World Bank (2013). *Doing Business 2014. Economy Profile: United Arab Emirates.* Washington, D.C.

World Bank (2014). *Doing Business: Starting a Business*, accessed 5 September 2014, http://www.doingbusiness.org/data/exploretopics/starting-a-business.

World Bank. (2004). *Middle East and North Africa, Annual Report."*

World Bank. (2012). *Bread, Freedom, and Dignity: Job Creation in the Middle East and North Africa,* World Bank.

World Economic Forum (2012). *Addressing the 100 Million Youth Challenge Perspectives on Youth Employment in the Arab World.*

World Economic Forum (2014). *Education and Skills, New Targets and Innovative Approaches.*

World Economic Forum. (2012). *Addressing the 100 Million Youth Challenge Perspectives on Youth Employment in the Arab World".*

Wyn, J. (2011). "Youth as a Social Category and as a Social Process", in Khalaf, S. and Khalaf, R. (eds.) *Arab Youth: Social Mobilization in Times of Risk*, London: Saqi Books.

Yamada, Makio (2011). "Gulf-Asia Relations as "Post-Rentier" Diversification?: The Case of the Petrochemical Industry in Saudi Arabia" *Journal of Arabian Studies.* 1(1): 99–116.

Yamada, Makio. (2015) "The China Model and the GCC Economies: Common Challenges in the Transition towards a Knowledge Economy", in Legrenzi, Matteo. (eds.) *The Gulf across East and West: Charting GCC and Iranian Inter-Asian Relations.* London: Ashgate.

Yamani, M. (2000). *Changed Identities: The Challenge of the New Generation in Saudi Arabia.* London: Royal Institute of International Affair

Yamani, M. (2011). "Saudi Youth: Initiative and Inertia", in Khalaf, S. and Khalaf, R. (eds.) *Arab Youth: Social Mobilization in Times of Risk*, London: Saqi Books.

Yates, D. (1996). *The Rentier State in Africa: Oil Rent, Dependency, and Neocolonialism in the Republic of Gabon, Africa*, World Press, Trenton.

Yousef, Tarik M. (2004). *Employment, Development and the Social Contract in the Middle East and North Africa.* The World Bank, Office of the Chief Economist, Middle East and North Africa Region

Zerovec, M. & M. Bontenbal (2011). "Labor nationalization policies in Oman: Implications for Omani and migrant women workers." *Asian Pacific Migration Journal.* 20(3-4). 365-387.

Zovighian, D. (2012). "Gulf women's participation in the labor market: Paid labor, care and social protection in patriarchal system", in Hertog S. (ed.). *National Employment, Migration and Education in the GCC. The Gulf Region: Economic Development and Diversification* 4. 183-230. Berlin: Gerlach.

Zulfiqar, Adnan A. (2013). "Religious Sanctification of Labor Law: Islamic Labor Principles and Model Provisions". *University of Pennsylvania Journal of Business Law, Vol. 9* Available at: http://scholarship.law.upenn.edu/jbl/vol9/iss2/6

About the Contributors

Marike Bontenbal is Assistant Professor at the German University of Technology in Oman. She has lived and worked in Oman since 2009. Bontenbal is an urban geographer with special interest in local and regional planning, urbanization, labor markets and demographic transition in the Arab Gulf region. She has recently completed a one-year research project on female labor participation in Oman funded by the Economic Research Forum. She has published in e.g. *Urban Studies*, *Journal of Arabian Studies*, *Asian Pacific Migration Journal*, and *Habitat International*. She obtained an MSc and PhD from Utrecht University, Department of Human Geography and Urban and Regional Planning.

Lorraine A. Charles is currently a researcher with Oxford Strategic Consultancy based between the UAE and the UK. She is also pursuing her PhD at the Institute of Arab and Islamic Studies at Exeter University, UK where her research examines the political economy of the UAE, specifically on Emiratization and economic diversification and the influence of social and cultural forces on these. Having lived in the GCC since 2004 her research focuses on the mainly in the region. She has published on issues such as energy security in the GCC, the role of women in economic development in the UAE and also on Syrian women in the context of the Arab Spring. She has conducted research projects for UNOCHA and ADEC. She holds an MA in International Policy and Diplomacy from Staffordshire University, UK.

David Cowan is a visiting scholar at the Boisi Center, USA, where he is researching diplomacy and communication regarding religion in American foreign policy, with a focus on Christianity and Islam. He is also a communications advisor with over twenty-five years' experience working for such organizations as the World Bank and the Institute of Islamic Banking & Insurance. He has lived and worked in North America, Europe and the Middle East. He is the author of Strategic Internal Communication (2014) and Economic Parables (2007), among other works. He contributed an essay on Religious Minorities & Biographical Entry on Aquinas to the International Encyclopedia of Political Science (CQ Press, Washington DC, 2010), and a major essay on Christianity and Economics in the Encyclopedia of Christian Civilization (Blackwells, Oxford, 2010). Cowan earned his Ph.D. at the University of St. Andrews, jointly undertaken in the School of Divinity and the School of International Relations, and holds a B.Th. and M.Th. from the University of Oxford, an M. Litt. from the University of St. Andrews.

Gauri Gupta is the Head of Analytics and Technology at The Talent Enterprise. With a strong background in quantitative research, including conducting large scale research and analytics. Gupta is an expert in working with big data and advanced statistical modeling, including techniques such as cluster analysis, factor analysis, structural equation modelling, discriminant, conjoint analysis etc. Gupta recently co-authored a paper on a 'Predictive Approach to Identify Leadership Strengths for the GCC', which was presented at the 2013 Joint Congress of IIAS-IASIA in Bahrain. She has written and presented papers on 'Employee Attrition Risk Assessment using Logistic Regression Analysis' and 'Clustering of Inflammatory Skin Disease Patients Using Latent Class Analysis' at an international data analytics conference organized by IIM Ahmedabad, India. Gupta holds a Master's degree in Business specializing in Market Research and Analytics from Mudra Institute of Communications, Ahmedabad (MICA), India. Gupta is a certified PMP

(Project Management Professional) from PMI and holds a Bachelor's degree in Economics from Delhi University, India.

Adel Hamaizia is a Doctoral Researcher at St Antony's College, University of Oxford, where he focuses on the Political Economy of the Maghreb. He is a Tutor at the Department of Politics and International Relations at the University of Oxford, where he teaches Middle East Politics. Hamaizia is also a Senior Teaching Fellow at the Department of Financial and Management Studies at SOAS, University of London, teaching on courses including International Human Resource Management, and Management/Economies in the Middle East and North Africa. His interests are MENA-oriented and include Political Economy, Rentierism, Labor Markets, and Human Capital Development. Hamaizia has lived and worked in the UAE, and has worked on various government and private sector projects throughout the GCC.

David Jones is the Founder and Managing Director of The Talent Enterprise, a human capital 'think' and 'do' tank. With a background in labor market economics, he is a senior advisor to policy-makers and organizational leaders. Jones is the co-author of the book titled 'Unlocking the Paradox of Plenty' by Motivate and has also published widely in academic journals as well as leading consulting reports such as the MENA Labor Market Confidence Index, Al Masar: Human Capital Imperatives for Expo 2020, The Qudurat report, The Aon Hewitt People Risk Index and so on. Jones has worked in the UAE for over 18 years and was previously the Chief Consulting Officer with Aon Hewitt MENA and also held senior leadership roles with Emirates Airlines, Dubai Civil Aviation & KPMG. Jones is a visiting lecturer at universities including the University of Cambridge, the European School of Management and Technology, Berlin and the University of Bradford. He is a regular columnist and spokesperson in the regional media.

Joachim Kolb studied in Islamic Studies and general linguistics at the universities of Hamburg, Alexandria, and Tübingen, and international management at SOAS, London, where he also obtained a doctorate in Financial and Management Studies. From 2010 to 2013, he was the representative of the German Academic Exchange Service (DAAD) in the UAE and the smaller GCC states. Since late 2013, he has been running J.K. Consulting FZE, a consultancy based at the RAK Free Trade Zone in Ras al Khayma. His research interests include regulatory systems in the Arab world, entrepreneurship, international business, as well as the literature of the GCC states. Dr. Kolb has taught at universities in Kyoto, London, and Abu Dhabi, and is currently an assistant professor at Trinity College Dublin.

Annika Kropf is a graduate of the Modern Middle Eastern studies program at the University of Erlangen-Nürnberg and obtained her PhD in 2012 from the University of Vienna. After fieldwork in Lebanon and Syria she has concentrated on the political economy of Arab Gulf states, testing the validity of common economic theories in this unique setting of resource abundance, labor migration and Islam. She has also specialized in qualitative and quantitative research methods. Apart from various positions at different universities, military academies and cultural institutions, her work as a consultant has given her insight into organizational structures in the Gulf as well as the challenges of working in multicultural teams. Kropf works as a lecturer at the University of Erlangen-Nürnberg and regularly provides further training for teachers of Islam in Austria. As a consultant for Faris Strategic Political Management, she regularly advises policymakers, companies and law firms on political and economic strategies regarding the Middle East. Her most recent publications include "The Gulf States as Multilateral Donors: the Case of the OPEC Fund for International Development (OFID)" (2014) and *Oil Export Economies: New Comparative Perspectives on the Arab Gulf States*, Gerlach Press 2015.

Cameron Mirza is head of projects and strategy for the Higher education council, Kingdom of Bahrain and has been in post since 2011. He is responsible for reform of the sector and is co-author of the nation's first national strategy for higher education. With 15 year's international reform experience across the public and private sector specializing in education reform at the highest level and working with two Prime Ministers, Mirza leads on transforming and improving performance of the higher education sector in Bahrain and to bring the sector closer to the needs of Industry and employers in a complex environment. Leading the drive to give students the skills, attributes and entrepreneurial mindset that are needed to create the SMART economy of the 21st Century in the MENA region, in additional to creating an ecosystem that supports research and innovation.

Jessie Moritz is a PhD candidate at the Centre for Arab and Islamic Studies (the Middle East and Central Asia) at the Australian National University. She is an advanced Arabic speaker and has travelled extensively in the region. In 2013 she was a Visiting Scholar at the Institute for Arab and Islamic Studies at the University of Exeter and from 2013-2014 she conducted over 120 interviews with Gulf citizens as a Graduate Fellow in the Gulf Studies Program at Qatar University. She was the co-editor of *The Contemporary Middle East: Revolution or Reform?* (Melbourne University Press, 2014), in which she also co-authored a chapter. Her current research focuses on the impact of rentier wealth on state-society relations in the Gulf during the post-2011 period. She obtained a Bachelor of Arts in International Relations and Politics (First Class Honours) from the Australian National University in 2011.

Tanya Cariina Newbury-Smith studied Islamic History at Oxford University, and Diplomacy in International Relations at the University of Buckingham, where she received her Masters Degree (Distinction) in "The Historiography of Arab Diplomacy". Her professional career focuses on political advisory and analysis on Middle Eastern policy for government officials, universities and academic institutes, specialising on current and historical Saudi Arabian foreign policy and intercultural relations. She is currently reading her PhD at the Institute for Arab and Islamic Studies at the University of Exeter. Tanya lived in Riyadh for many years, and continues to divide her time between Saudi Arabia and England.

Radhika Punshi is the Founder and Director of Innovation at The Talent Enterprise. As an HR professional and organizational psychologist, she has lived in the GCC for over 15 years. Her prime focus is on nationalization and local talent development, with an emphasis on gender and youth inclusion. Punshi is the co-author of a book titled 'Unlocking the Paradox of Plenty' by Motivate. Previously, Punshi was the Head of Applied Research for Aon Hewitt MENA where she conceptualized and led Qudurat, the largest workplace research project in the region, with over 25,000+ respondents from 150+ organizations. Punshi also worked with Campus Philly in the USA, focused on developing policy recommendations for student retention in Philadelphia. With an Ivy League education and two Masters Degrees in Organizational Behavior and Psychology, Punshi is the first person from the MENASA region to be awarded a degree in Positive Psychology. She served on founding Board of Directors of the prestigious International Positive Psychology Association.

Mohamed A. Ramady is currently a Visiting Associate Professor, Finance and Economics, at King Fahd University of Petroleum and Minerals, Dhahran, Saudi Arabia. He specializes on the geo-political risk assessment of the GCC economies, and energy. He has authored the following books published by Springer: *"The Saudi Arabian Economy: Policies, Achievements and Challenges"*, Second Edition, 2010, Editor of the "*GCC Economies: Stepping up to Future Challenges*", 2012, and *"Economic, Political and Financial Country Risk: An analysis of the GCC countries"* in 2014. Dr. Ramady has held senior executive positions in banking with Citibank, the Saudi American Bank, Chase Manhattan, First City Texas Bank, Qatar National Bank, and Qatar International Islamic Bank. He obtained his BA and PhD in Economics, at the University of Leicester, UK, a Postgraduate Master's Degree in Economic Development, University of Glasgow, UK. He is a Fellow of the UK's Chartered Institute of Bankers.

Mark C. Thompson is Assistant Professor of Middle East Studies at King Fahd University of Petroleum and Minerals, Dhahran, Saudi Arabia, where he has been teaching courses in International Relations and

Globalization since 2012. Thompson's principal research areas are Saudi socio-political development and societal transformation and he has published on topics such as Saudi youth issues and challenges facing Saudi women leaders. He published a book by I.B. Tauris: *"Saudi Arabia and the Path to Political Change: National Dialogue and Civil Society"*, 2014, and he is currently working on another book to be published by I.B. Tauris about societal issues and change from the perspective of young Saudi men. He obtained his MA in Middle East Policy Studies and PhD from the Institute of Arab & Islamic Studies, University of Exeter where he also taught a course on Political Reform in the Gulf.

Makio Yamada is a doctoral candidate in International Relations at St Antony's College at the University of Oxford. His research focuses on industrial diversification in the Gulf Cooperation Council (GCC) countries and the GCC countries' economic relations with Asian countries. He has authored the following journal article and book chapter: "Gulf–Asia Relations as 'Post-Rentier' Diversification?: The Case of the Petrochemical Industry in Saudi Arabia," *Journal of Arabian Studies*, 1 (1), 2011; and "The China Model and the GCC Economies: Common Challenges in the Transition towards a Knowledge Economy," in Matteo Legrenzi (ed.) *The Gulf Across East and West: Charting GCC and Iranian Inter-Asian Relations*. (London: Ashgate, 2015). He was a visiting fellow at the King Faisal Center for Research and Islamic Studies, Saudi Arabia, in 2013 and 2014.

Index